MODELING FOR GOVERNMENT AND BUSINESS

Modeling for Government and Business −

Essays in Honor of Prof. Dr. P. J. Verdoorn

edited by

C. A. VAN BOCHOVE

C. J. VAN EIJK

J. C. SIEBRAND

A. S. W. DE VRIES

A. VAN DER ZWAN

Martinus Nijhoff Social Sciences Division
Leiden 1977

ISBN 90 207 0732 9

Copyright © 1977 by H. E. Stenfert Kroese B.V., Leiden
No part of this book may by reproduced in any form by print, photoprint, microfilm or
any other means, without written permission from the publisher.

Printed in the Netherlands

Preface

This volume has been composed to commemorate the day, 25 years ago, that Dr. P. J. Verdoorn delivered his inaugural lecture after his appointment as professor of economics at the Netherlands School of Economics at Rotterdam. The prompt and enthusiastic reactions by several members of the profession on our request for a contribution illustrates the fact that Verdoorn is held in high esteem by those who worked with him and those who are acquainted with his work. We thank all the contributors for having helped us to realize our plan to honour Verdoorn with the publication of this 'liber amicorum'.

Verdoorn was appointed part time professor of business statistics, market research and marketing in 1952. He held this post until 1969. In that year he started lectures closer related to his work as deputy director of the Central Planning Bureau: general economic research. He became full professor of macro-economic policy in 1975. Verdoorn showed a great versatility in all the fields on which he worked. Without exaggeration he may be characterised as one of the most many-sided economists in the Netherlands. However much the subjects he studied may have varied, the methods he applied show persistent characteristics: theories are formulated to yield testable hypotheses which, when they can be maintained, are made operational for policy purposes. In all these phases of a research program Verdoorn showed a high level of inventivity. A combination of rigour and imagination enabled him to maintain a constant stream of high-quality publications.

The contributions in this volume are related to the various fields on which Verdoorn worked. The variety of the subjects the contributors dealt with illustrates the broadness of his interests. The book is organized roughly around the subjects: research methods, macro-economic models and policy analysis, international economics, and problems of market research and marketing.

The editors.

Contents

List of Contributors

C. A. VAN DEN BELD, Director Central Planning Bureau, The Hague, The Netherlands. Professor of Economics, Erasmus University Rotterdam, The Netherlands.

C. A. VAN BOCHOVE, Staff Member Institute for Economic Research, Erasmus University Rotterdam, The Netherlands.

C. J. VAN EIJK, Professor of Economics, Erasmus University Rotterdam, The Netherlands.

R. FERBER, Professor of Economics and Marketing, Director Survey Research Laboratory, University of Illinois, U.S.A.

Y. HAITOWSKY, Professor of Economics and Statistics, The Hebrew University of Jerusalem, Israel.

B. H. HASSELMAN, Staff Member Central Planning Bureau, The Hague, The Netherlands.

J. KOOYMAN, Head of Department, Central Planning Bureau, The Hague, The Netherlands.

LUCY CHAO LEE, Survey Research Laboratory, University of Illinois, U.S.A.

P. S. H. LEEFLANG, Associate professor of Business Administration and Management Sciences, University of Groningen, The Netherlands.

R. S. G. LENDERINK, Assistant professor of Macro-economics, Erasmus University Rotterdam, The Netherlands.

A. O'HAGAN, Lecturer of Statistics, University of Warwick, England.

K. S. PALDA, Professor of Marketing, Queen's University, Kingston, Canada.

J. J. POST, Staff Member Central Planning Bureau, The Hague, The Netherlands.

J. SANDEE, Scientific Adviser, Central Planning Bureau, The Hague, The Netherlands.

C. T. SAUNDERS, Professor at the Center for Contemporary European Studies, University of Sussex, England.

A. N. R. SCHWARTZ, Staff Member World Bank, Washington, U.S.A.

J. C. SIEBRAND, Associate professor of Macro-economics, Erasmus University Rotterdam, The Netherlands.

H. THEIL, Professor of Economics, Center for Mathematical Studies in Business and Economics, University of Chicago, U.S.A.

J. TINBERGEN, Emeritus professor of Economics, Erasmus University Rotterdam, The Netherlands.

J. VERHULP, Assistant professor of Marketing and Marketing Research, Erasmus University Rotterdam, The Netherlands.

A. S. W. DE VRIES, Staff Member, Institute for Economic Research, Erasmus University Rotterdam, The Netherlands.

T. M. WITHIN, Professor of Economics, Wesleyan University, Middletown, Connecticut, U.S.A.

A. VAN DER ZWAN, Professor of Marketing and Marketing Research, Erasmus University Rotterdam, The Netherlands.

Professor Dr. P. J. Verdoorn*

C. J. VAN EIJK*

P. J. Verdoorn, born on 21 March 1911 in Amsterdam, studied economics at the Municipal University of Amsterdam. He received a Ph. D. degree from the Netherlands School of Economics at Rotterdam in 1943, and his doctoral thesis was written under supervision of Professor J. Tinbergen.[1] After his doctoral examination (which is approximately the equivalent of a M.A. degree), he worked with the Dutch railways. In 1939 he joined the economics department of the Posts, Telegraphs and Telephones, the Dutch national communications organization. In these functions he was occupied with market research, which led him to apply econometric methods to market analytical problems. In 1939 he wrote, in co-operation with J. Tinbergen, an article on the demand for passenger-traffic by rail.[2] During this time he probably also collected part of the material for an important book on market analysis which was published in 1949.[3]

In 1945 he was appointed a staff member of the Central Planning Bureau of which Tinbergen was the first director. He became head of the section concerning 'Labour problems'. One of the issues he had to deal with was the low level of labour productivity in the Netherlands. Measures to improve it were suggested in an article in 'Economisch-Statistische Berichten' of 1946.[4]

An extensive analysis of the relationships between national welfare, productivity and working hours is given in his book 'Arbeidsduur en Welvaartspeil' published in 1947.[5] One of his conclusions was that a shortening

* The author would like to thank C. A. van Bochove and A. S. W. de Vries for their critical comments on an earlier version of this article.

1. P. J. Verdoorn. De Verstarring van de Produktiekosten. De Erven F. Bohn N.V. Haarlem, 1943.
2. J. Tinbergen en P. J. Verdoorn. De vraag naar personenvervoer per spoor. *De Nederlandsche Conjunctuur, C.B.S. 1939.*
3. P. J. Verdoorn. *Grondslagen en Techniek van de Marktanalyse.* Stenfert Kroese, Leiden, 1950.
4. P. J. Verdoorn. Het onbevredigende niveau onzer arbeidsproduktiviteit. Economisch Statistische Berichten, 7 augustus, 1946, page 503.
5. P. J. Verdoorn. *Arbeidsduur en Welvaartspeil.* Stenfert Kroese, Leiden, 1947.

of working hours might be necessary — notwithstanding the low level of national income — if other means proved insufficient to reduce unemployment.[6] In one of the appendices of the book, research is reported on the relationship between productivity, working hours, the volume of production and profits; it is cast in the form of an equation for employment.[7] This topic clearly had his interest. In 1949, in an article in *L'industria*, more statistical material for various countries and sectors of the manufacturing industry was presented.[8] [9] The same article also contained a simultaneous model from which the constancy of the elasticity between labour productivity and the volume of production could be derived. The empirical relation between these two variables came to be known as the 'Verdoorn Law',[10] and Verdoorn used it in different forms in several studies.

In 1950 Verdoorn became head of the division for structural problems of the Central Planning Bureau, which dealt with long-term planning and policy design. In this function he set up the first exploration of the long-term development of the Dutch economy. The aim was to find out whether full employment and equilibrium on the balance of payments could be restored and maintained in the ensuing twenty years. He developed a model of economic growth based on complementarity of the factors of production which contained four instruments of economic policy by means of which the government could help achieve these targets. As part of the production function, the model demonstrated the relation between labour productivity and the volume of production mentioned above, although in a form and theoretical setting somewhat different from that from which it was derived in the 1949 article. As far as I can see this was the first time that a problem of economic policy was analysed by means of an operational version of the Harrod-Domar growth model. It was published in *Econometrica* in 1956[11]

6. *op. cit.*, page 222.
7. *op. cit.*, page 227.
8. P. J. Verdoorn. Fattori che regolana lo sviluppo della produttività del lavoro. *L'Industria*, no. 1, 1949.
9. In 1948 and 1949 Verdoorn was a staff member of the Research and Planning Division of the E.C.E. at Geneva.
10. N. Kaldor. *Causes of the Slow Rate of Economic Growth of the United Kingdom*, an Inaugural Lecture, Cambridge University Press, Cambridge, 1966 page 10.
For recent discussions see: R. E. Rowthorn. What Remains of Kaldor's Law? *Economic Journal* 1975, page 10; H. W. Singer and Lyn Reynolds. Technological Backwardness and Productivity Growth. *Economic Journal* 1975, page 873; and N. Kaldor. Economic Growth and the Verdoorn Law – A Comment on Mr. Rowthorn's Article. *Economic Journal* 1975, page 891.
11. P. J. Verdoorn. Complementary and Long-range Projections. *Econometrica*, 1956, p. 429.

and the model was used by the Central Planning Bureau for several years. Research in this field continued; the scope was broadened. In 1958 the High Authority of the European Community for Coal and Steel set up a working group to study methods for long-term projections. Verdoorn was one of its members. A report published in 1960 gives an extensive survey of the methods which were available at the time.[12] It describes techniques for forecasting both productive capacity and the demand for final goods. It deals with production functions based on the hypothesis of complementarity as well as with those allowing for substitution between factors of production. It also reviews input-output analysis as a means for maintaining consistency between the disaggregated projections of production in various sectors of the economy. In 1959 Verdoorn had already developed a model of economic growth based on a Cobb-Douglas production function. It was presented in a colloquium in Brussels on the role of fixed capital in economic development.[13] In this paper he explicitly formulated the now-well-known theorem about the independence of the rate of growth on a steady state growth path and the propensity to save.[14]

In dealing with problems of economic policy for balanced economic growth in the early 1950's the issue of the establishment of a European Customs Union could not be ignored. In 1952 Verdoorn presented, for the annual meeting of the Dutch Economic Association (De Vereniging voor de Staathuishoudkunde), a systematic and quantitative analysis of the expected consequences of economic integration in Europe, in particular for the development of economic welfare in the Netherlands.[15] To estimate the expected changes in the flows of trade and the exchange rates he constructed a demand model for international trade. He specified demand equations in which the price elasticities of the imports from a certain country were written as a weighted average of the price elasticity of total imports and the elasticities of substitution between imports from different countries, the weights

12. Méthodes de prévision du développement économique à long terme. *Informations Statistiques*, 1960 no. 6, p. 525. Office Statistique des Communautés Européennes.
13. P. J. Verdoorn. The Role of Capital in long-term Projection Models. *Cahiers Economiques de Bruxelles*, no. 5, 1959, p. 49.
14. Verdoorn was one of the first authors – if not the first – to formulate this theorem explicitly. See: L. M. Koyck and Maria J. 't Hooft-Welvaars, Economic Growth, Marginal Productivity of Capital and the Rate of Interest, in: F. H. Hahn and F. P. R. Brechling (eds). *The Theory of Interest Rates*. Macmillan, London, 1966.
15. P. J. Verdoorn. Welke zijn de achtergronden en vooruitzichten van de economische integratie in Europa en welke gevolgen zou deze integratie hebben, met name voor de welvaart in Nederland. *Preadviezen* 1952 van de Vereniging voor de Staathuishoudkunde, Den Haag, 1952.

being the import shares. This decomposition, which also proved to be fruitful in later studies, is a formal analogy of that used by Allen and Hicks for the price elasticity of demand in their well-known article on the theory of value.[16] To give an impression of the possible effects of economic integration, Verdoorn presented ex ante estimates with the help of parameters obtained by Tinbergen and others. The results were fed into the explorations of the long-term development of the Dutch economy mentioned above to assess their significance for the long-term policy targets.[17]

In the following decades several studies were made to measure ex post the effects of economic integration. The first study to be mentioned here is that of the consequences of the Benelux affiliation.[18] It is in this study that both demand and supply equations were introduced in a model for international trade for the first time. By means of this model the expected effects of a hypothetical tariff reduction for alternative values of the coefficients were calculated. As a result of this, a rough impression was obtained of the possible impact of a customs union. Further, an effort was made to distinguish those changes in the flows of trade over the period 1938 to 1955 which might have been due to structural changes of a general character from those which might have been connected to the formation of the customs union. This was done by comparing the development of the Benelux intra-bloc trade with those in the trade pattern of the OECD countries. Finally the shift in the volume-substitution relation that might be attributed to the customs union was estimated by means of a regression equation relating the export shares to the price ratios and an indicator of economic activity. This study was published in 1957.

The study published in 1964 showed a further development in Verdoorn's ideas about the imputation of changes in trade patterns to tariff reductions and more general developments.[19] It deals with trade creation and trade diversion caused by the development of the European Economic Community. This time a weighted share index was used. It is defined as a weighted average of the indices of the import and export shares, the weighting coefficients being

16. R. G. D. Allen and J. R. Hicks. A Reconsideration of the Theory of Value. *Economica New Series I 1934*, p. 52 and p. 196.
Verdoorn uses this also in his theory of marketing. The demand elasticity for the product of a specific firm can be decomposed in a similar way. See: P. J. Verdoorn. *Het Commercieel Beleid bij Verkoop en Inkoop.* Stenfert Kroese, Leiden, 1964, page 281.
17. See the publication mentioned in note 15, §4.
18. P. J. Verdoorn. The intra-block trade of the Benelux, in: E. A. G. Robinson (ed.). *Economic Consequences of the Size of Nations.* Macmillan, London, 1960.
19. P. J. Verdoorn en F. J. M. Meyer zu Schlochtern. Trade Creation and Trade Diversion in the Common Market. *Intégration européenne et réalité économique.* 1964, p. 95.

the shares in the initial position, and it was designed to incorporate both demand and supply factors. This is one of the attractive aspects of the index. The index equals unity if the trade between two countries develops in a way that corresponds to the growth of their total trade. An index above unity may be interpreted as an indication of a trade development between the two countries that exceeds their performance in general. An index below unity gives rise to the suggestion of the reverse. In 1972 a new study was published on the effects of the E.E.C. and the E.F.T.A. The sample period was extended to 1959.[20] Some theoretical refinements were introduced. In addition an alternative estimate of the integration effects was presented. It is based on an analytical approach in which the traditional demand model is combined with the gravitational model earlier used by Waelbroeck for analysing this kind of problem. By means of regression analysis, the import price and substitution elasticities, the influence of the level of economic activity and that of integration variables were estimated. Further work in this field is still in progress.

In 1955 Verdoorn was appointed Deputy Director of the Central Planning Bureau. In that function his activities were extended and also comprised short-term planning. A few years earlier a research project was started on the econometric analysis of the Dutch economy. The supervisor was Professor H. Theil. When Theil left the Central Planning Bureau in 1954, Verdoorn took over in co-operation with Professor L. M. Koyck of the Netherlands School of Economics. The aim of the project was the construction of a new econometric model for short-term analysis of the Dutch economy. It was intended to describe the fluctuations in the Dutch economy and thus to provide a better instrument for short-term policy design than the existing one. Verdoorn made important contributions to this project, not least by the way in which he guided some of the staff members who were involved. A series of publications was initiated which presented subsequent versions of the new model and in which they were applied to both theoretical issues and economic policy problems.

A publication by the United Nations reveals most clearly the general character of the new models and gives evidence of the forecasting performance of one of them.[21] When compared with the models used by the Central

20. P. J. Verdoorn and A. N. R. Schwartz. Two Alternative estimates of the Effects of EEC and EFTA on the Pattern of Trade. *European Economic Review*, 1972, p. 291.
21. The Short term Model of the Central Planning Bureau and its forecasting performance (1953–1963) in: *Macro-Economic Models for Planning and policy-making*. U.N., Geneva, 1967.

Planning Bureau in the first half of the 1950's the new ones show a much more complicated dynamic structure. New also was the introduction of a capacity variable, curvilinearly derived from the level of unemployment. It reflects the fact that an economy may behave differently in a situation of near-full employment than it does when overcapacity exists. The variable contributes to the explanatory power of equations such as those for investment, imports, exports, some of the prices and the wage level. In their contribution to the Sixteenth Symposium of the Colston Research Society, Verdoorn and Post analysed the significance of the capacity variable for the multipliers of one of the new models.[22] The consequences of approaching the capacity limits were shown clearly.

The international sector of the models corresponds as far as possible with the new approaches towards the explanation of international trade mentioned above. In this respect the new macro-economic models benefitted greatly from the experience accumulated by the studies of the integration effects.

An example of an application to a problem of economic policy was given in a paper for a conference of the Social Science Research Council Committee on Economic Stability.[23] The problem to be analysed was whether or not the economic fluctuations in the post-war period differ from those in the inter-war period. It was shown that the former had a smaller amplitude and a shorter period. The 63^D-version of the new model revealed that the economic process after the war had become more sensitive for cyclical impulses, which probably is due to a greater dependence on the rest of the world and to a higher degree of capacity utilisation. This conclusion was also mentioned in the paper on the capacity variable.

Verdoorn also contributed to the Link-project, an international research project aimed at integrating national econometric models in order to improve the estimates of world trade.

Finally attention should be paid to a completely different field in economics for which Verdoorn broke new ground. His activities mentioned so far were connected to his position within the Central Planning Bureau. As part-time professor of economics at the Netherlands School of Economics he taught marketing, market analysis and business statistics. His book on

22. P. J. Verdoorn and J. J. Post. Capacity and Short-term Multipliers, in: *Econometric Analysis for National Economic Planning, Colston Papers*. No. 16, Butterworth, London, 1964.
23. P. J. Verdoorn and J. J. Post. Comparison of the Prewar and Postwar Business Cycles in The Netherlands, in: M. Bronfenbrenner, ed. *Is the Business Cycle Obsolete?* John Wiley & Sons, London, 1969.

market research has already been mentioned. Several of his contributions to the theory of marketing have established his name in this field. In his inaugural lecture of 1952 he suggested the applicability of Tinbergen's theory of economic policy to marketing theory.[24] This implies in the first place a clear distinction between instruments and targets which creates a logical ordering of the problems to be analysed. It also suggests the use of simultaneous models, comprising all aspects of a firm's policy, from which optimal decision rules can be derived. Verdoorn has also introduced the concept of the firm's functional position on the market, indicating the specific differences between the functions it performs and those performed by its immediate competitors. An analysis of its functional position helps the firm to discover its particular assets, an analysis of which may help in choosing the most efficient instruments it has at its disposal. In his textbook on marketing several applications of these ideas can be found.[25] Members of the profession find a fine specimen of his skill in this field in the way in which, by reformulating some of the relevant relations, he has improved in some respects the Dorfman-Steiner decision rules for determining the optimal volume of production and sales. Several of his ideas in this field have been recognized internationally.[26]

In addition to his pure scientific work, Verdoorn often took part in working groups and committees set up to analyse policy problems. For many years he was deputy member of the Dutch Social Economic Council. He was a member of the government commission for studying Dutch demographic developments and policy problems. He was chaiman of one of its working groups. Several times he acted as Senior Economic Advisor to the Economic Commission for Europe of the United Nations. The Dutch Government gave him the task of helping to prepare a long-term plan for the development of Surinam. For this purpose he visited this country in 1951 and 1954.

In 1953 he joined the marketing techniques team of the 'Contactgroep Opvoering Productiviteit' in a journey to the United States to study the changing pattern of marketing techniques as applied in the U.S.A. He made an important contribution to the report of the team.[27]

In 1961 Verdoorn was Visiting Professor of Economics at the University

24. P. J. Verdoorn. *De eigen markt der onderneming*. Stenfert Kroese, Leiden, 1952.
25. P. J. Verdoorn. *Het commercieel beleid bij Verkoop en Inkoop*. Stenfert Kroese, Leiden, 1964.
26. See: K. S. Palda. *Economic Analysis for Marketing Decision*. Prentice-Hall, Inc., Englewood Cliffs, New Yersey, 1969.
27. See: *Verkopen volgens plan*. Contactgroep Opvoering Productiviteit, Den Haag, 1954.

of California, Berkeley. In 1968–1969 he was Senior Fellow at the Centre for Advanced Studies, Wesleyan University. He is Fellow of the Econometric Society and Correspondent of the American Economic Review. From 1952 to 1969 he was a member of the Editorial Board of the well-known series *Contributions to Economic Analysis*.

In 1971 Verdoorn was awarded the Royal-Shell prize for his entire scientific work by the 'Hollandsche Maatschappij der Wetenschappen''. Verdoorn is 'Officier in de Orde van Oranje Nassau' and 'Ridder in de Orde van de Nederlandsche Leeuw', both Dutch Royal honours.

The Informational Analysis of Changes in Regional Distributions*

HENRI THEIL

INTRODUCTION

Today there are numerous data sets which describe some phenomenon according to two or more criteria, such as sales by product groups and regions or employees by industries and regions. An example of the latter type is shown in Table 1, which shows the number of employees in non-agricultural establishments in each of nine regions of the United States and for each of seven industry groups.[1] The data shown are in thousands of employees in 1973 and 1974. The analysis of such data is becoming more important because of increased 'regional feelings' in many countries. However, the systematic analysis of regional and industry changes from 1973 to 1974 is hampered by the fact that there are as many as $9 \times 7 = 63$ pairs of numbers to be compared, which increase to $63(T-1)$ when we extend the analysis to a time series of T successive tables. An informal model which reduces the dimensionality of the problem is desirable. The objective of this paper is to illustrate how this reduction can be performed elegantly by means of some elementary concepts from information theory.[2]

---

* Research supported in part by the National Science Foundation under Grant 41319X. I am indebted to Kenneth Laitinen for his able computational assistance.

1. Alaska and Hawaii as well as the mining category are deleted. The regions are as follows: *New England*: Maine, New Hampshire, Vermont, Massachusetts, Rhode Island and Connecticut; *Middle Atlantic*: New York, New Jersey and Pennsylvania; *East North Central*: Ohio, Indiana, Illinois, Michigan and Wisconsin; *West North Central*: Minnesota, Iowa, Missouri, North Dakota, South Dakota, Nebraska and Kansas; *South Atlantic*: Delaware, Maryland, District of Columbia, Virginia, West Virginia, North Carolina, South Carolina, Georgia and Florida; *East South Central*: Kentucky, Tennessee, Alabama and Mississippi; *West South Central*: Arkansas, Louisiana, Oklahoma and Texas; *Mountain*: Montana, Idaho, Wyoming, Colorado, New Mexico, Arizona, Utah and Nevada; *Pacific*: Washington, Oregon and California. The data used are the statistics on employees in the *Statistical Abstract of the United States*.
2. The adjustment procedure of equation (1.3) below is often called the RAS model and has been repeatedly applied in input-output analysis. It was shown by Bacharach [1, p. 84] and by Ireland and Kullback [2] that this model can be justified by means of the

TABLE 1

Employees by region and industry, 1973 and 1974

	Contract construction	Manufacturing	Transportation[a]	Trade	Finance[b]	Services[c]	Government	Total
	Numbers of employees (thousands) in 1973							
New England	230	1406	233	1010	268	901	707	4755
M. Atlantic	618	3935	921	2949	929	2630	2328	14310
E.N. Central	635	5192	845	3230	698	2362	2365	15327
W.N. Central	273	1308	389	1411	295	999	1132	5807
S. Atlantic	864	2887	714	2563	617	1916	2422	11983
E.S. Central	249	1371	231	879	180	618	806	4334
W.S. Central	434	1330	468	1614	364	1088	1285	6583
Mountain	243	424	204	750	156	607	727	3111
Pacific	426	2090	594	2169	549	1799	1941	9568
Total	3972	19943	4599	16575	4056	12920	13713	75778
	Numbers of employees (thousands) in 1974							
New England	220	1418	233	1024	275	933	726	4829
M. Atlantic	591	3870	908	2944	934	2691	2404	14342
E.N. Central	629	5135	862	3308	717	2478	2407	15536
W.N. Central	279	1336	398	1447	304	1042	1161	5967
S. Atlantic	876	2903	725	2623	651	2037	2542	12357
E.S. Central	258	1383	234	897	190	648	834	4444
W.S. Central	464	1375	489	1661	380	1152	1330	6851
Mountain	232	447	217	789	171	661	766	3283
Pacific	410	2137	602	2228	561	1886	2005	9829
Total	3959	20004	4668	16921	4183	13528	14175	77438

a. Including public utilities   b. Including insurance and real estate   c. Including miscellaneous

1. AN INFORMATIONAL APPROACH

The marginal totals of Table 1 show that the total number of employees in the U.S. for all industries increased from 75.778 millions in 1973 to 77.438 millions in 1974. Once we know this, all information on the numbers of employees is contained in proportions. We write p_{ij} for the number in the ith region and the jth industry in 1973, measured as a fraction of the total of 75.778 millions of that year, and indicate by q_{ij} the analogous proportion of 1974. These two sets of proportions are shown in Table 2 in percentage form. We write the marginal proportions of $[q_{ij}]$ as

$$q_{i.} = \sum_j q_{ij} \quad \text{and} \quad q_{.j} = \sum_i q_{ij},$$

where the summations are over $j=1,\dots,n$ and $i=1,\dots,m$, with $m=9$ and $n=7$ in the case of Table 2.

To analyze the change that took place from 1973 to 1974, we approximate $[q_{ij}]$ by an array $[\hat{q}_{ij}]$ which is as close as possible to the earlier array $[p_{ij}]$ but subject to the constraint that $[\hat{q}_{ij}]$ satisfies the marginal proportions of $[q_{ij}]$. As the criterion of closeness we use a minimum value of

$$I(\hat{q} : p) = \sum_{i=1}^m \sum_{j=1}^n \hat{q}_{ij} \log \frac{\hat{q}_{ij}}{p_{ij}} \tag{1.1}$$

which is, in the language of information theory, the expected information of the message which transforms the p_{ij}'s as 'prior probabilities' into the $\hat{q}_{ij}$'s as 'posterior probabilities' [3, Chapter 2; 4, Chapter 2].

The conditional minimum problem is solved by means of the Lagrangean function,

$$\sum_{i=1}^m \sum_{j=1}^n \hat{q}_{ij} \log \frac{\hat{q}_{ij}}{p_{ij}} - \sum_{i=1}^m \lambda_i \left(\sum_{j=1}^n \hat{q}_{ij} - q_{i.} \right) - \sum_{j=1}^n \mu_j \left(\sum_{i=1}^m \hat{q}_{ij} - q_{.j} \right)$$

which has the following derivative with respect to $\hat{q}_{ij}$[3]

$$1 + \log \hat{q}_{ij} - \log p_{ij} - \lambda_i - \mu_j \tag{1.2}$$

We equate this to zero to find that $\log(\hat{q}_{ij}/p_{ij})$ equals $\lambda_i + \mu_j - 1$, which is an

criterion function (1.1). The latter authors also proved (2.1); the results of Sections 3 and 4 are original as far as I am aware. I am indebted to Professor Stephen E. Fienberg of the University of Minnesota for mentioning Ireland's and Kullback's article to me.
3. All logarithms in this paper are natural logarithms. Equating the derivative (1.2) to zero corresponds to the first-order minimum condition; see footnote 4 for the second-order condition.

TABLE 2

Percentage employment distributions, 1973 and 1974

	Contract con-struction	Manu-facturing	Trans-portation	Trade	Finance	Services	Govern-ment	Total
	Observed percentage distribution in 1973 (100p$_{ij}$)							
New England	.30	1.86	.31	1.33	.35	1.19	.93	6.27
M. Atlantic	.82	5.19	1.22	3.89	1.23	3.47	3.07	18.88
E.N. Central	.84	6.85	1.12	4.26	.92	3.12	3.12	20.23
W.N. Central	.36	1.73	.51	1.86	.39	1.32	1.49	7.66
S. Atlantic	1.14	3.81	.94	3.38	.81	2.53	3.20	15.81
E.S. Central	.33	1.81	.30	1.16	.24	.82	1.06	5.72
W.S. Central	.57	1.76	.62	2.13	.48	1.44	1.70	8.69
Mountain	.32	.56	.27	.99	.21	.80	.96	4.11
Pacific	.56	2.76	.78	2.86	.72	2.37	2.56	12.63
Total	5.24	26.32	6.07	21.87	5.35	17.05	18.10	100

Observed percentage distribution in 1974 ($100q_{ij}$)

								Total
New England	.28	1.83	.30	1.32	.36	1.20	.94	6.24
M. Atlantic	.76	5.00	1.17	3.80	1.21	3.48	3.10	18.52
E.N. Central	.81	6.63	1.11	4.27	.93	3.20	3.11	20.06
W.N. Central	.36	1.73	.51	1.87	.39	1.35	1.50	7.71
S. Atlantic	1.13	3.75	.94	3.39	.84	2.63	3.28	15.96
E.S. Central	.33	1.79	.30	1.16	.25	.84	1.08	5.74
W.S. Central	.60	1.78	.63	2.14	.49	1.49	1.72	8.85
Mountain	.30	.58	.28	1.02	.22	.85	.99	4.24
Pacific	.53	2.76	.78	2.88	.72	2.44	2.59	12.69
Total	5.11	25.83	6.03	21.85	5.40	17.47	18.30	100

Adjusted percentage distribution for 1974 ($100\hat{q}_{ij}$)

								Total
New England	.29	1.81	.30	1.32	.36	1.21	.94	6.24
M. Atlantic	.78	5.01	1.18	3.81	1.21	3.49	3.04	18.52
E.N. Central	.81	6.69	1.10	4.23	.92	3.17	3.13	20.06
W.N. Central	.35	1.71	.51	1.87	.40	1.36	1.52	7.71
S. Atlantic	1.12	3.78	.94	3.41	.83	2.62	3.26	15.96
E.S. Central	.32	1.79	.30	1.16	.24	.84	1.08	5.74
W.S. Central	.57	1.76	.62	2.16	.49	1.50	1.74	8.85
Mountain	.32	.57	.28	1.02	.21	.85	1.00	4.24
Pacific	.55	2.72	.78	2.87	.73	2.44	2.60	12.69
Total	5.11	25.83	6.03	21.85	5.40	17.47	18.30	100

additive function of i and j. Taking antilogs, we obtain the familiar multiplicative result

$$\hat{q}_{ij} = r_i s_j p_{ij} \qquad \begin{array}{l} i = 1, ..., m \\ j = 1, ..., n \end{array} \tag{1.3}$$

To derive r_i and s_j, we write the marginal constraints

$$\sum_j \hat{q}_{ij} = q_{i.} \quad \text{and} \quad \sum_i \hat{q}_{ij} = q_{.j}$$

in the form

$$r_i \sum_{j=1}^{n} s_j p_{ij} = q_{i.} \qquad i = 1, ..., m \tag{1.4}$$

$$s_j \sum_{i=1}^{m} r_i p_{ij} = q_{.j} \qquad j = 1, ..., n \tag{1.5}$$

We solve this system of $m+n$ equations by putting $s_1 = ... = s_n = 1$ in (1.4), which yields a first solution of r_i equal to

$$q_{i.}/p_{i.}, \quad \text{where} \quad p_{i.} = \sum_j p_{ij}.$$

These solutions for all r_i's are substituted in (1.5) and then solved for s_j, after which these solutions for all s_j's are substituted in (1.4), and so on. The converged values of the r_i's and s_j's are all positive (no zero or negative r_i's and s_j's emerge in any step of the iteration), so that (1.3) also yields a positive $\hat{q}_{ij}$ when p_{ij} is positive.[4]

The adjustment coefficients r_i and s_j for Table 2 are shown in the 1973–74 rows of Tables 3 and 4,[5] and the associated $\hat{q}_{ij}$'s in the bottom part of Table 2. These $\hat{q}_{ij}$'s are the closest approximations (in the information-theoretical sense) to the 1973 proportions which satisfy the 1974 marginal constraints.

4. The first-order derivative of the Lagrangean function with respect to $\hat{q}_{ij}$ is given in (1.2); the corresponding second-order derivative is $1/\hat{q}_{ij}$ and all second-order cross-derivatives vanish. The positive sign of $\hat{q}_{ij}$ thus guarantees that the solution is a minimum.
5. The convergence is very rapid. For all cases analyzed in this paper, checks are accurate in more than 10 digits after at most 10 iterations.

TABLE 3

Adjustment coefficients for regions

	New England	Middle Atlantic	East North Central	West North Central	South Atlantic	East South Central	West South Central	Mountain	Pacific
1953–54	1.0014	.9996	.9882	1.0070	1.0091	1.0096	.9995	1.0005	1.0089
1954–55	.9874	.9835	1.0104	.9880	1.0076	1.0026	1.0065	1.0267	1.0098
1955–56	.9975	.9886	.9842	.9809	1.0206	1.0002	1.0134	1.0244	1.0341
1956–57	.9855	1.0072	.9946	.9886	.9933	.9980	1.0099	1.0189	1.0110
1957–58	.9988	.9979	.9651	1.0108	1.0286	1.0104	1.0122	1.0308	1.0158
1958–59	1.0001	.9813	1.0082	1.0044	1.0073	1.0045	.9886	1.0288	1.0117
1959–60	.9982	.9937	.9905	.9938	1.0106	1.0089	.9904	1.0258	1.0201
1960–61	1.0081	.9940	.9903	1.0038	1.0096	.9993	1.0022	1.0204	1.0059
1961–62	.9876	.9876	.9966	.9915	1.0076	1.0131	1.0109	1.0167	1.0160
1962–63	.9859	.9835	.9983	.9987	1.0158	1.0139	1.0056	1.0106	1.0115
1963–64	.9853	.9921	1.0016	.9928	1.0093	1.0143	1.0113	.9918	1.0027
1964–65	.9972	.9896	1.0071	.9960	1.0093	1.0102	1.0053	.9861	.9954
1965–66	.9887	.9843	1.0034	1.0027	1.0048	1.0089	1.0129	1.0010	1.0082
1966–67	.9937	.9893	.9945	1.0067	1.0100	.9962	1.0176	.9944	1.0080
1967–68	.9983	.9892	.9994	.9942	1.0088	.9994	1.0046	1.0039	1.0096
1968–69	.9858	.9952	.9970	.9918	1.0113	1.0038	1.0087	1.0089	1.0027
1969–70	1.0015	.9955	.9902	.9943	1.0146	1.0126	.9999	1.0241	.9988
1970–71	.9980	.9856	.9959	.9962	1.0188	1.0199	1.0083	1.0371	.9873
1971–72	.9803	.9764	.9847	1.0051	1.0152	1.0250	1.0211	1.0538	1.0091
1972–73	.9883	.9722	.9951	1.0044	1.0254	1.0115	1.0116	1.0137	1.0055
1973–74	.9940	.9805	.9936	1.0047	1.0093	1.0051	1.0178	1.0301	1.0036
					Logarithmic summary measures				
Mean	−.0066	−.0112	−.0053	−.0021	.0117	.0079	.0075	.0163	.0083
St. dev.	.0071	.0080	.0097	.0076	.0072	.0072	.0080	.0159	.0090
V. Neumann	2.23	1.29	2.63	1.56	3.00	1.09	1.32	.81	1.52

TABLE 4

Adjustment coefficients for industries

	Contract construction	Manu-facturing	Trans-portation	Trade	Finance	Services	Government
1953–54	1.0114	.9542	.9797	1.0240	1.0556	1.0412	1.0362
1954–55	1.0200	1.0023	.9765	.9959	1.0215	1.0070	.9953
1955–56	1.0149	.9876	.9918	1.0080	1.0184	1.0171	.9966
1956–57	.9816	.9785	.9881	1.0093	1.0171	1.0319	1.0178
1957–58	.9869	.9534	.9728	1.0148	1.0431	1.0408	1.0523
1958–59	1.0003	1.0417	.9718	.9349	.9849	.9993	1.0309
1959–60	.9708	.9818	.9727	.9971	1.0354	1.0662	1.0005
1960–61	.9713	.9707	.9725	.9968	1.0365	1.0462	1.0338
1961–62	.9852	1.0083	.9701	.9893	1.0003	1.0143	1.0041
1962–63	1.0037	.9905	.9798	.9972	1.0008	1.0207	1.0107
1963–64	1.0147	.9889	.9824	1.0033	1.0028	1.0167	1.0033
1964–65	.9984	1.0005	.9813	.9990	.9844	1.0082	1.0060
1965–66	.9788	1.0114	.9747	.9915	.9706	.9997	1.0159
1966–67	.9447	.9823	.9950	.9964	1.0008	1.0296	1.0280
1967–68	1.0026	.9854	.9828	1.0012	1.0173	1.0181	1.0084
1968–69	1.0073	.9870	.9922	1.0034	1.0167	1.0178	.9980
1969–70	.9707	.9571	1.0039	1.0153	1.0263	1.0312	1.0223
1970–71	.9983	.9563	.9896	1.0144	1.0256	1.0207	1.0270
1971–72	1.0374	.9914	.9781	1.0075	1.0038	1.0151	.9872
1972–73	1.0422	1.0050	.9797	1.0024	1.0026	1.0117	.9741
1973–74	.9730	.9832	.9929	.9984	1.0099	1.0248	1.0101
			Logarithmic summary measures				
Mean	−.0044	−.0138	−.0179	−.0001	.0128	.0224	.0121
St. dev.	.0234	.0212	.0091	.0172	.0198	.0153	.0177
V. Neumann	1.54	2.30	1.21	2.08	1.42	2.20	1.74

2. DISCUSSION OF THE ADJUSTMENT COEFFICIENTS

Substitution of the solution (1.3) in (1.1) gives

$$\sum_{i=1}^{m} \sum_{j=1}^{n} \hat{q}_{ij} \log \frac{r_i s_j p_{ij}}{p_{ij}} = \sum_{i=1}^{m} \sum_{j=1}^{n} \hat{q}_{ij} (\log r_i + \log s_j)$$

$$= \sum_{i=1}^{m} q_{i.} \log r_i + \sum_{j=1}^{n} q_{.j} \log s_j$$

where the second step is based on the marginal constraints which are imposed on the $\hat{q}_{ij}$'s. Therefore, when $\bar{I}(\hat{q}:p)$ stands for the minimum value of the criterion function (1.1), we have

$$\bar{I}(\hat{q}:p) = \sum_{i=1}^{m} q_{i.} \log r_i + \sum_{j=1}^{n} q_{.j} \log s_j \tag{2.1}$$

This result can be used to normalize the adjustment coefficients. Since these coefficients have one multiplicative degree of freedom,[6] we can obtain unique values by making the two expressions in the right-hand side of (2.1) equal

$$\sum_{i=1}^{m} q_{i.} \log r_i = \sum_{j=1}^{n} q_{.j} \log s_j = \tfrac{1}{2} \bar{I}(\hat{q}:p) \tag{2.2}$$

This means that both $r_1, ..., r_m$ and $s_1, ..., s_n$ have a weighted geometric mean, with weights equal to the corresponding marginal proportions, whose logarithm equals one-half of the minimum value of the criterion function (1.1).

The adjustment coefficients $r_1, ..., r_m$ are shown in Table 3 for each pair of successive years from 1953 to 1974, and the corresponding s_j's are given in Table 4; the normalization used is (2.2). If $r_1 > r_2$ for some pairs of successive years, the implication is that the first region has grown relative to the second in these years – at least, according to the adjustment [see (1.3)]. Similarly, $s_1 > s_2$ implies that the first industry has grown relative to the second.

When we have a time series of adjustment coefficients, as in Tables 3 and 4, it is convenient to provide a statistical summary. We write r_{it} and s_{jt} for the adjustment coefficients corresponding to the pair of years $(t-1, t)$ and ρ_{it} and σ_{jt} for the logarithms of r_{it} and s_{jt}, respectively. For our 21 pairs of successive years, the means are

$$\bar{\rho}_i = \frac{1}{21} \sum_{t=1}^{21} \rho_{it} \quad \text{and} \quad \bar{\sigma}_j = \frac{1}{21} \sum_{t=1}^{21} \sigma_{jt} \tag{2.3}$$

---

6. Multiply r_i by $c > 0$ for each i and s_j by $1/c$ for each j. This has no effect on the right-hand side of (1.3).

and their standard deviations are

$$\sqrt{\frac{1}{21} \sum_{t=1}^{21} (\rho_{it} - \bar{\rho}_i)^2} \quad \text{and} \quad \sqrt{\frac{1}{21} \sum_{t=1}^{21} (\sigma_{jt} - \bar{\sigma}_j)^2} \qquad (2.4)$$

and their Von Neumann ratios are defined as

$$\frac{21}{20} \times \frac{\sum_{t=2}^{21} (\rho_{it} - \rho_{i,t-1})^2}{\sum_{t=1}^{21} (\rho_{it} - \bar{\rho}_i)^2} \quad \text{and} \quad \frac{21}{20} \times \frac{\sum_{t=2}^{21} (\sigma_{jt} - \sigma_{j,t-1})^2}{\sum_{t=1}^{21} (\sigma_{jt} - \bar{\sigma}_j)^2} \qquad (2.5)$$

The values of these three sets of statistics are shown in the last three rows of Tables 3 and 4. The Von Neumann ratios suggest some positive autocorrelation on the average, but the evidence is not very strong.[7] Positive means ($\bar{\rho}_i$ or $\bar{\sigma}_j$) indicate which regions or industries have grown relative to others during the period 1953–1974, and negative means indicate those which declined relative to the others. The most striking difference is that between the standard deviations of the ρ_i's and those of the σ_j's. The former standard deviations are between .007 and .009 with only one exception, whereas the latter tend to be much larger: between .015 and .024, also with one exception. This means that, over the course of time, the relative growth or decline of a region is much more steady than that of an industry.

3. HOW ACCURATE IS THE ADJUSTMENT PROCEDURE?

In the opening paragraph of this paper we described a reduction of dimensionality as a desirable goal. Since the r_i's and s_j's in each of the first 21 rows of Tables 3 and 4 have only one subscript, we have reached that goal. It is clear, however, that the extent to which the adjustment (1.3) is satisfactory depends on the degree to which the adjusted $\hat{q}_{ij}$'s approximate the observed q_{ij}'s. The issue of the quality of this approximation, both in absolute form and relative to no-change extrapolation, is the main subject of the remainder of this paper.

One way of verifying the quality of the $\hat{q}_{ij}$'s as approximations of the true

7. For 21 observations the 1 percent significance limit of the Von Neumann ratio in the test against positive autocorrelation is 1.11, and that against negative autocorrelation is 3.09. (These limits are based on the assumption of normality.) The median of the Von Neumann ratios is 1.52 in Table 3 and 1.74 in Table 4, which suggests a slightly stronger positive autocorrelation on the average for the ρ's than for the σ's.

q_{ij}'s is by means of a pairwise comparison of the q_{ij}'s in the middle part of Table 2 with the corresponding $\hat{q}_{ij}$'s in the lower part. But this is very tedious. In fact, it is not necessary, since a straightforward comparison can be made in terms of informational concepts. The criterion function (1.1) measures the extent to which the p_{ij}'s differ from the $\hat{q}_{ij}$'s. Hence the degree to which the $\hat{q}_{ij}$'s differ from the true q_{ij}'s is measured by

$$I(q : \hat{q}) = \sum_{i=1}^{m} \sum_{j=1}^{n} q_{ij} \log \frac{q_{ij}}{\hat{q}_{ij}} \tag{3.1}$$

It will be interesting to compare this with

$$I(q : p) = \sum_{i=1}^{m} \sum_{j=1}^{n} q_{ij} \log \frac{q_{ij}}{p_{ij}} \tag{3.2}$$

which measures the extent to which the p_{ij}'s differ from the same q_{ij}'s. In the case of Table 2, (3.2) describes the degree to which the 1973 proportions fail to describe the 1974 proportions; it gives the inaccuracy of no-change extrapolation. We should expect that (3.2) will not be smaller than (3.1) since the $\hat{q}_{ij}$'s do and the p_{ij}'s do not satisfy the marginal constraints of $[q_{ij}]$.

We use (1.3) to write the right-hand side of (3.1) as

$$\sum_{i=1}^{m} \sum_{j=1}^{n} q_{ij} \log \frac{q_{ij}}{r_i s_j p_{ij}} = \sum_{i=1}^{m} \sum_{j=1}^{n} q_{ij} \log \frac{q_{ij}}{p_{ij}} - \sum_{i=1}^{m} \sum_{j=1}^{n} q_{ij} \log (r_i s_j)$$

$$= I(q : p) - \sum_{i=1}^{m} q_{i.} \log r_i - \sum_{j=1}^{n} q_{.j} \log s_j$$

where the second step is based on (3.2). So, using (2.1) also, we have

$$I(q : \hat{q}) = I(q : p) - \bar{I}(\hat{q} : p) \tag{3.3}$$

or, equivalently,

$$I(q : p) = I(q : \hat{q}) + \bar{I}(\hat{q} : p) \tag{3.4}$$

Since $\bar{I}(\hat{q}:p)$ is nonnegative, (3.3) confirms that no-change extrapolation cannot be more accurate than the adjustment procedure (1.3). The equivalent result (3.4) implies that, given the inaccuracy of no-change extrapolation, the adjusted $\hat{q}_{ij}$'s are more accurate approximations of the true q_{ij}'s when the minimum value of the criterion function $I(\hat{q}:p)$ is larger, i.e., when the marginal constraints imposed on the $\hat{q}_{ij}$'s force these proportions to differ more from the p_{ij}'s.

The values of the successive I's in (3.4) are shown in the first three columns of Table 5. The results indicate that the inaccuracy $I(q:p)$ of no-change extrapolation exceeds the inaccuracy $I(q:\hat{q})$ of the adjustment procedure by a substantial margin. In fact, $I(q:\hat{q})$ is below $\bar{I}(\hat{q}:p)$ in all cases except for 1964–65, and the ratio of the means is less than 1 to 3 (see the last row of the

TABLE 5

Summary of informational measures

	$I(q:p)$	$I(q:\hat{q})$	$\bar{I}(\hat{q}:p)$	$I_1(q:p)$	$I_2(q:p)$
1953–54	.996	.231	.764	.079	.735
1954–55	.251	.125	.126	.074	.050
1955–56	.335	.093	.242	.176	.082
1956–57	.335	.094	.241	.053	.200
1957–58	1.286	.203	1.083	.342	.855
1958–59	1.149	.200	.949	.084	.871
1959–60	.568	.094	.474	.069	.412
1960–61	.602	.101	.501	.053	.469
1961–62	.192	.061	.131	.054	.073
1962–63	.184	.038	.146	.077	.076
1963–64	.167	.073	.094	.037	.059
1964–65	.139	.079	.060	.033	.027
1965–66	.209	.059	.149	.046	.103
1966–67	.398	.087	.312	.052	.270
1967–68	.154	.044	.110	.030	.084
1968–69	.150	.059	.091	.030	.064
1969–70	.607	.094	.513	.064	.469
1970–71	.585	.059	.525	.120	.427
1971–72	.381	.071	.310	.211	.106
1972–73	.352	.075	.277	.142	.131
1973–74	.273	.062	.210	.089	.128
Arithmetic mean	.443	.095	.348	.091	.271

Note: All entries are to be divided by 1000.

table). We conclude that, for the data as a whole, the inaccuracy of the adjustment procedure which remains after the marginal proportions (the q_i.'s and $q_{.j}$'s) have been used is between 20 and 25 percent. Equivalently, the adjustment coefficients which are derived from these marginal proportions [see (1.4) and (1.5)] account, on the average, for between 75 and 80 percent of the observed changes in the bivariate proportions from one year to the next. This is the justification of the adjustment procedure (1.3).

4. REGIONS AND INDUSTRIES CONSIDERED SEPARATELY

The ratios $q_{i1}/q_{i.}, ..., q_{in}/q_{i.}$ describe the distribution of employees of the ith region over the n industries. The corresponding adjusted and no-change extrapolation ratios are of the form $\hat{q}_{ij}/q_{i.}$ and $p_{ij}/p_{i.}$, respectively. Hence, for the ith region the inaccuracy of the adjusted values is

$$I_{i.}(q:\hat{q}) = \sum_{j=1}^{n} \frac{q_{ij}}{q_{i.}} \log \frac{q_{ij}/q_{i.}}{\hat{q}_{ij}/q_{i.}} \tag{4.1}$$

and that of the no-change extrapolations is

$$I_{i.}(q:p) = \sum_{j=1}^{n} \frac{q_{ij}}{q_{i.}} \log \frac{q_{ij}/q_{i.}}{p_{ij}/p_{i.}} \tag{4.2}$$

and the inaccuracy of the no-change extrapolations with respect to the adjusted values is

$$I_{i.}(\hat{q}:p) = \sum_{j=1}^{n} \frac{\hat{q}_{ij}}{q_{i.}} \log \frac{\hat{q}_{ij}/q_{i.}}{p_{ij}/p_{i.}} \tag{4.3}$$

Three obvious questions arise. First, do these regional inaccuracies satisfy a rule similar to (3.3) for the bivariate inaccuracies? Second, if we weight the regional inaccuracies by multiplying them by $q_{i.}$ and summing over i, what is the nature of such average inaccuracies? Third, what is the relation between these average inaccuracies and those of the individual regions? We shall consider the second question first.

4.1. *Weighted Means of Regional Inaccuracies*
Note that the two $q_{i.}$'s on the far right in (4.1) cancel each other out. So, when we multiply (4.1) by $q_{i.}$ and sum over i, we obtain the double sum of $q_{ij} \log (q_{ij}/\hat{q}_{ij})$, which equals $I(q:\hat{q})$ in view of (3.1). Therefore

$$\sum_{i=1}^{m} q_{i.}I_{i.}(q:\hat{q}) = I(q:\hat{q}) \tag{4.4}$$

We proceed similarly for (4.2)

$$\sum_{i=1}^{m} q_{i.} I_{i.}(q:p) = \sum_{i=1}^{m} \sum_{j=1}^{n} q_{ij} \left(\log \frac{q_{ij}}{p_{ij}} - \log \frac{q_{i.}}{p_{i.}} \right)$$

$$= \sum_{i=1}^{m} \sum_{j=1}^{n} q_{ij} \log \frac{q_{ij}}{p_{ij}} - \sum_{i=1}^{m} q_{i.} \log \frac{q_{i.}}{p_{i.}}$$

It follows from (3.2) that this can be written as

$$\sum_{i=1}^{m} q_{i.} I_{i.}(q:p) = I(q:p) - I_1(q:p) \tag{4.5}$$

where

$$I_1(q:p) = \sum_{i=1}^{m} q_{i.} \log \frac{q_{i.}}{p_{i.}} \tag{4.6}$$

In the same way, we multiply (4.3) by $q_{i.}$ and sum over i,

$$\sum_{i=1}^{m} q_{i.} I_{i.}(\hat{q}:p) = \sum_{i=1}^{m} \sum_{j=1}^{n} \hat{q}_{ij} \left(\log \frac{\hat{q}_{ij}}{p_{ij}} - \log \frac{q_{i.}}{p_{i.}} \right)$$

$$= \sum_{i=1}^{m} \sum_{j=1}^{n} \hat{q}_{ij} \log \frac{\hat{q}_{ij}}{p_{ij}} - \sum_{i=1}^{m} q_{i.} \log \frac{q_{i.}}{p_{i.}}$$

which can be written as

$$\sum_{i=1}^{m} q_{i.} I_{i.}(\hat{q}:p) = \bar{I}(\hat{q}:p) - I_1(q:p) \tag{4.7}$$

We conclude from (4.4) that the weighted mean of the regional inaccuracies of the adjusted values is simply the inaccuracy of these adjusted values in the bivariate array. In the two other cases, (4.5) and (4.7), we subtract $I_1(q:p)$ on the right. It follows from (4.6) that $I_1(q:p)$ can be viewed as the inaccuracy of the no-change extrapolation of the marginal proportions of the regions or, equivalently, as the amount of information revealed by the $q_{i.}$'s, given the $p_{i.}$'s of the previous year.

4.2. Weighted Means of Industry Inaccuracies
When we consider the jth industry rather than the ith region, the inaccuracies (4.1) to (4.3) are replaced by

$$I_{.j}(q:\hat{q}) = \sum_{i=1}^{m} \frac{q_{ij}}{q_{.j}} \log \frac{q_{ij}/q_{.j}}{\hat{q}_{ij}/q_{.j}} \tag{4.8}$$

$$I_{.j}(q:p) = \sum_{i=1}^{m} \frac{q_{ij}}{q_{.j}} \log \frac{q_{ij}/q_{.j}}{p_{ij}/p_{.j}} \qquad (4.9)$$

$$I_{.j}(\hat{q}:p) = \sum_{i=1}^{m} \frac{\hat{q}_{ij}}{q_{.j}} \log \frac{\hat{q}_{ij}/q_{.j}}{p_{ij}/p_{.j}} \qquad (4.10)$$

It is a matter of straightforward algebra to verify that the weighted means of these industry inaccuracies are

$$\sum_{j=1}^{n} q_{.j}I_{.j}(q:\hat{q}) = I(q:\hat{q}) \qquad (4.11)$$

$$\sum_{j=1}^{n} q_{.j}I_{.j}(q:p) = I(q:p) - I_{2}(q:p) \qquad (4.12)$$

$$\sum_{j=1}^{n} q_{.j}I_{.j}(\hat{q}:p) = \bar{I}(\hat{q}:p) - I_{2}(q:p) \qquad (4.13)$$

where

$$I_{2}(q:p) = \sum_{j=1}^{n} q_{.j} \log \frac{q_{.j}}{p_{.j}} \qquad (4.14)$$

which measures the amount of information received by the marginal proportions of the industries, given the $p_{.j}$'s of the previous year.

The last two columns of Table 5 contain $I_{1}(q:p)$ and $I_{2}(q:p)$ for each pair of successive years. The results clearly show that $I_{2}(q:p)$ is on the average substantially larger than $I_{1}(q:p)$. The means of the right-hand sides of (4.4), (4.5) and (4.7), computed from the last row of Table 5, are shown in the first row of Table 6; the second row contains the analogous figures for (4.11) to (4.13). The figures indicate that, on the average, last year's proportions are less accurate with respect to this year's proportions (both observed and adjusted) for regions than for industries.

TABLE 6

Average inaccuracies for regions and industries,
averaged over 1953–74

	$q:p$	$q:\hat{q}$	$\hat{q}:p$
Regions	.352	.095	.257
Industries	.172	.095	.077

Note: All entries are to be divided by 1000.

Recall that we concluded at the end of Section 2 that regional changes are much more steady than industry changes. The larger values of $I_2(q:p)$ relative to those of $I_1(q:p)$ imply that the marginal proportions of the industries tend to be subject to larger changes than those of the regions. Therefore, industry changes are not only less steady but also of larger size.

4.3. *Individual Region and Industry Inaccuracies Compared with Their Means*
We now turn to the third question raised in the opening paragraph of this section: What is the relationship between the inaccuracies (4.1) to (4.3) of an individual region and the corresponding weighted means? A convenient way of analyzing this problem is by means of the ratio of an individual inaccuracy to the corresponding weighted mean. It follows from (4.5) that, in the case of (4.2), the logarithm of this ratio is

$$\log \frac{I_{i.}(q:p)}{I(q:p) - I_1(q:p)} \qquad (4.15)$$

The analogous expressions for (4.1) and (4.3) are

$$\log \frac{I_{i.}(q:\hat{q})}{I(q:\hat{q})} \qquad \log \frac{I_{i.}(\hat{q}:p)}{\bar{I}(\hat{q}:p) - I_1(q:p)} \qquad (4.16)$$

We can compute (4.15) for each i and each pair of successive years, which yields $21m = 189$ numbers. The distribution of these numbers is shown in the first column of Table 7, and those of the two logarithms of (4.16) in the second and third columns; the lower part of the table provides the corresponding distributions for industries, obtained by interchanging subscripts in (4.15) and (4.16) in accordance with (4.8) to (4.14). The results show that the distributions in the third column, referring to the second logarithm of (4.16) and its industry counterpart, are very tight around zero. The distributions in the first and second columns do not have this property. We conclude that $I_{i.}(\hat{q}:p)$ for $i = 1, \ldots, m$ are close to their weighted mean (4.7) and similarly, that $I_{.j}(\hat{q}:p)$ for $j = 1, \ldots, n$ are close to the weighted mean (4.13). This means that, *as a first approximation, last year's distribution is equally accurate with respect to this year's adjusted distribution for all regions, and also for all industries.*

What is the cause of this striking phenomenon? Why does it apply only to the third column of Table 7, and not to the first and second? The answer to the latter question is basically that $I_{i.}(\hat{q}:p)$ and $I_{.j}(\hat{q}:p)$ are the only $I_{i.}$'s and $I_{.j}$'s which do not involve the q_{ij}'s [see (4.1) to (4.3) and (4.8) to (4.10)].

Regarding the former, we prove in Appendix A that

$$I_{i.}(\hat{q}:p) \approx \tfrac{1}{2}V_i \tag{4.17}$$

where V_i is a weighted variance of $s_1, ..., s_n$

$$V_i = \sum_{j=1}^{n} \frac{p_{ij}}{p_{i.}}\left(s_j - \sum_{k=1}^{n}\frac{p_{ik}}{p_{i.}}s_k\right)^2 \tag{4.18}$$

TABLE 7

Distributions of certain logarithmic ratios

	$q:p$	$q:\hat{q}$	$\hat{q}:p$	(4.19)	(4.21)
			Regions		
Smaller than —1	18	40	0	0	0
Between —1 and —.5	48	25	0	0	0
Between —.5 and —.1	43	29	22	0	22
Between —.1 and —.05	5	5	25	0	26
Between —.05 and —.01	4	6	42	11	41
Between —.01 and .01	3	3	19	165	21
Between .01 and .05	3	5	37	13	36
Between .05 and .1	4	8	30	0	30
Between .1 and .5	27	17	14	0	13
Between .5 and 1	25	33	0	0	0
Larger than 1	9	18	0	0	0
Total	189	189	189	189	189
			Industries		
Smaller than —1	30	35	0	0	0
Between —1 and —.5	31	29	0	0	0
Between —.5 and —.1	29	19	8	0	8
Between —.1 and —.05	2	6	9	0	9
Between —.05 and —.01	2	2	27	0	26
Between —.01 and .01	1	3	19	147	19
Between .01 and .05	1	7	51	0	52
Between .05 and .1	3	2	28	0	28
Between .1 and .5	17	14	5	0	5
Between .5 and 1	15	12	0	0	0
Larger than 1	16	18	0	0	0
Total	147	147	147	147	147

The approximation (4.17) is verified in the fourth column of Table 7, which contains the distributions of the logarithmic ratio of the two sides of the equation and of the analogous logarithmic ratio for the industries,

$$\log \frac{\frac{1}{2}V_i}{I_{i.}(\hat{q}:p)} \qquad \log \frac{\frac{1}{2}W_j}{I_{.j}(\hat{q}:p)} \tag{4.19}$$

where

$$W_j = \sum_{i=1}^{m} \frac{p_{ij}}{p_{.j}}\left(r_i - \sum_{h=1}^{m} \frac{p_{hj}}{p_{.j}} r_h\right)^2 \tag{4.20}$$

The distributions in the fourth column of Table 7 are even tighter around zero than those in the third, thus confirming that (4.17) provides a close approximation.

Finally, it is frequently the case that weighted variances are rather insensitive to changes in the weights. If this applies to (4.18) in the sense that V_i is in first approximation independent of i, we have proved what we wanted to prove. For this purpose we consider

$$\log \frac{V_i}{V} \qquad \log \frac{W_j}{W} \tag{4.21}$$

where

$$\overline{V} = \sum_{i=1}^{m} p_{i.}V_i \qquad \overline{W} = \sum_{j=1}^{n} p_{.j}W_j \tag{4.22}$$

The distributions of the logarithmic ratios (4.21) in the last column of Table 7 confirm our conjecture, since they are virtually identical to the corresponding distributions in the third column.

4.4. *Relations Among the Individual Region and Industry Inaccuracies*
Finally, we turn to the first question raised in the opening paragraph of this section: Do the regional inaccuracies (4.1) to (4.3) satisfy a rule similar to (3.3)? The answer is no, and the reason is simple. If (3.3) applied to each region

$$I_{i.}(q:\hat{q}) = I_{i.}(q:p) - I_{i.}(\hat{q}:p)$$

the implication would be that the adjustment procedure always yields approximations of $q_{ij}/q_{i.}$ that are at least as close as no-change extrapolations in the information-theoretical sense. There is no reason why this should be so. The adjustment procedure is designed to handle all *mn* bivariate proportions simultaneously; it cannot claim merits for any row in particular, nor for any column. The relation among the regional inaccuracies (4.1) to (4.3) is

$$I_{i.}(q:\hat{q}) = I_{i.}(q:p) - I_{i.}(\hat{q}:p) + \hat{\sigma}(i) - \sigma(i) \tag{4.23}$$

where

$$\hat{\sigma}(i) = \sum_{j=1}^{n} \frac{\hat{q}_{ij}}{q_{i.}} \log s_j \qquad \sigma(i) = \sum_{j=1}^{n} \frac{q_{ij}}{q_{i.}} \log s_j \tag{4.24}$$

The result (4.23) is derived in Appendix B.

5. EXTENSIONS

The above approach can be extended straightforwardly to arrays of three and more dimensions. For example, if $[p_{ijk}]$ is the previous array and $[q_{ijk}]$ is to be approximated, the criterion function (1.1) becomes a triple sum and yields adjusted proportions of the form $\hat{q}_{ijk} = r_i s_j t_k p_{ijk}$ when the univariate marginal proportions of $[q_{ijk}]$ are known. If we know the univariate marginal proportions $[q_{i..}]$ and the bivariate marginal proportions $[q_{.jk}]$, the adjusted proportions take the form $\hat{q}_{ijk} = r_i s_{jk} p_{ijk}$.

An extension of a different type is that in which the marginal proportions $q_{i.}$ and $q_{.j}$ are not known but are estimated. The adjustment procedure (1.3) can then be derived from (1.4) and (1.5) with $q_{i.}$ and $q_{.j}$ replaced by their estimates. However, using such estimates makes (3.3) invalid. The correct result, which resembles (4.23), is derived in Appendix C.

APPENDIX A

Derivations for Table 7
Consider any set of n positive pairs $(x_1, y_1), \ldots, (x_n, y_n)$ satisfying

$$\sum_i x_i = \sum_i y_i = 1.$$

By definition

$$I(y:x) = \sum_{i=1}^{n} y_i \log \frac{y_i}{x_i} \qquad I(x:y) = \sum_{i=1}^{n} x_i \log \frac{x_i}{y_i} \tag{A.1}$$

We use the lemma

$$\log c = c - 1 - \tfrac{1}{2}(c-1)^2 + O_3 \quad \text{if} \quad c-1 = O_1 \tag{A.2}$$

where O_1 and O_3 stand for terms of the first and the third order of smallness, respectively. Therefore, under the condition

$$\frac{x_i}{y_i} - 1 = O_1 \qquad i = 1, ..., n \tag{A.3}$$

we have

$$I(y:x) = -\sum_{i=1}^{n} y_i \log\frac{x_i}{y_i}$$

$$= -\sum_{i=1}^{n} y_i\left[\frac{x_i}{y_i} - 1 - \tfrac{1}{2}\left(\frac{x_i}{y_i} - 1\right)^2 + O_3\right]$$

$$= \tfrac{1}{2}\sum_{i=1}^{n} y_i\left(\frac{x_i}{y_i} - 1\right)^2 + O_3$$

which can be written as

$$I(y:x) = \tfrac{1}{2}\sum_{i=1}^{n} \frac{(x_i - y_i)^2}{y_i} + O_3 \tag{A.4}$$

Similarly, since (A.3) implies $y_i/x_i - 1 = O_1$,

$$I(x:y) = \tfrac{1}{2}\sum_{i=1}^{n} \frac{(x_i - y_i)^2}{x_i} + O_3$$

A comparison with (A.4) shows that

$$I(y:x) = I(x:y) + O_3 \tag{A.5}$$

which follows from

$$\sum_{i=1}^{n} \frac{(x_i - y_i)^2}{y_i} - \sum_{i=1}^{n} \frac{(x_i - y_i)^2}{x_i} = \sum_{i=1}^{n} \frac{y_i^2}{x_i}\left(\frac{x_i}{y_i} - 1\right)^3 = O_3$$

We assume

$$\frac{q_{i.}}{p_{i.}} - 1 = O_1 \qquad \frac{q_{.j}}{p_{.j}} - 1 = O_1 \tag{A.6}$$

for each i and each j, respectively. It follows from (1.4) and (1.5) that $r_i - 1 = O_1$ and $s_j - 1 = O_1$, so that $\hat{q}_{ij}/p_{ij} - 1 = O_1$ [see (1.3)] and hence

$$\frac{\hat{q}_{ij}/q_{i.}}{p_{ij}/p_{i.}} - 1 = O_1$$

Application of (A.5) gives

$$I_{i.}(\hat{q} : p) = I_{i.}(p : \hat{q}) + O_3 \tag{A.7}$$

where

$$I_{i.}(p : \hat{q}) = \sum_{j=1}^{n} \frac{p_{ij}}{p_{i.}} \log \frac{p_{ij}/p_{i.}}{r_i s_j p_{ij}/q_{i.}} \tag{A.8}$$

$$= \log \frac{q_{i.}}{r_i p_{i.}} - \sum_{j=1}^{n} \frac{p_{ij}}{p_{i.}} \log s_j$$

Given that $s_j - 1 = O_1$, application of (A.2) gives

$$\sum_{j=1}^{n} \frac{p_{ij}}{p_{i.}} \log s_j = \sum_{j=1}^{n} \frac{p_{ij}}{p_{i.}} \left[s_j - 1 - \tfrac{1}{2}(s_j - 1)^2 + O_3 \right] \tag{A.9}$$

$$= \frac{q_{i.}}{r_i p_{i.}} - 1 - \tfrac{1}{2} \sum_{j=1}^{n} \frac{p_{ij}}{p_{i.}} (s_j - 1)^2 + O_3$$

where the second step is based on

$$\sum_{j=1}^{n} \frac{p_{ij} s_j}{p_{i.}} = \frac{q_{i.}}{r_i p_{i.}} \tag{A.10}$$

which follows from (1.4).

We substitute (A.9) in (A.8) and apply (A.7) also

$$I_{i.}(\hat{q} : p) = \log \frac{q_{i.}}{r_i p_{i.}} - \frac{q_{i.}}{r_i p_{i.}} + 1 + \tfrac{1}{2} \sum_{j=1}^{n} \frac{p_{ij}}{p_{i.}} (s_j - 1)^2 + O_3 \tag{A.11}$$

Since each s_j and hence also the left-hand side of (A.10) differ from 1 to the order O_1, this must hold for the right-hand side of (A.10) also. It thus follows from (A.2) that the sum of the first three terms on the right in (A.11) equals

$$- \tfrac{1}{2} \left(\frac{q_{i.}}{r_i p_{i.}} - 1 \right)^2 + O_3 = - \tfrac{1}{2} \left(\sum_{j=1}^{n} \frac{p_{ij}}{p_{i.}} s_j - 1 \right)^2 + O_3$$

where the equal sign is based on (A.10). Substitution in (A.11) gives

$$I_{i.}(\hat{q} : p) = - \tfrac{1}{2} \left(\sum_{j=1}^{n} \frac{p_{ij}}{p_{i.}} s_j - 1 \right)^2 + \tfrac{1}{2} \sum_{j=1}^{n} \frac{p_{ij}}{p_{i.}} (s_j - 1)^2 + O_3$$

The sum of the first two terms on the right is, apart from the factor 1/2, a second moment of the s_j's around 1 minus the square of the corresponding first moment, and hence equal to the variance. Therefore,

$$I_{i.}(\hat{q}:p) = \tfrac{1}{2} \sum_{j=1}^{n} \frac{p_{ij}}{p_{i.}} \left(s_j - \sum_{k=1}^{n} \frac{p_{ik}}{p_{i.}} s_k \right)^2 + O_3 \tag{A.12}$$

which confirms (4.17) and specifies that the approximation error is of the third order of smallness.

APPENDIX B

Relations Among Individual Inaccuracies
We substitute (1.3) in (4.3),

$$I_{i.}(\hat{q}:p) = \sum_{j=1}^{n} \frac{\hat{q}_{ij}}{q_{i.}} \log \frac{r_i s_j p_{ij}/q_{i.}}{p_{ij}/p_{i.}}$$

$$= - \log \frac{q_{i.}}{r_i p_{i.}} + \sum_{j=1}^{n} \frac{\hat{q}_{ij}}{q_{i.}} \log s_j$$

It follows from (4.24) that this can be written as

$$I_{i.}(\hat{q}:p) = - \log \frac{q_{i.}}{r_i p_{i.}} + \hat{\sigma}(i) \tag{B.1}$$

Next we write (4.1) as

$$I_{i.}(q:\hat{q}) = \sum_{j=1}^{n} \frac{q_{ij}}{q_{i.}} \log \frac{q_{ij}/q_{i.}}{r_i s_j p_{ij}/q_{i.}}$$

$$= \sum_{j=1}^{n} \frac{q_{ij}}{q_{i.}} \left(\log \frac{q_{ij}/q_{i.}}{p_{ij}/p_{i.}} + \log \frac{q_{i.}}{r_i s_j p_{i.}} \right)$$

$$= I_{i.}(q:p) + \log \frac{q_{i.}}{r_i p_{i.}} - \sum_{j=1}^{n} \frac{q_{ij}}{q_{i.}} \log s_j$$

where the last step is based on (4.2). Using (4.24) also, we obtain

$$I_{i.}(q:\hat{q}) = I_{i.}(q:p) + \log \frac{q_{i.}}{r_i p_{i.}} - \sigma(i) \tag{B.2}$$

The proof of (4.23) is completed by adding (B.1) and (B.2).
It can similarly be shown that

$$I_{.j}(q:\hat{q}) = I_{.j}(q:p) - I_{.j}(\hat{q}:p) + \hat{p}(j) - p(j) \tag{B.3}$$

where

$$\hat{\rho}(j) = \sum_{i=1}^{m} \frac{\hat{q}_{ij}}{q._j} \log r_i \qquad \rho(j) = \sum_{i=1}^{m} \frac{q_{ij}}{q._j} \log r_i \qquad \text{(B.4)}$$

Note that the differences $\hat{\rho}(j) - \rho(j)$ and $\hat{\sigma}(i) - \sigma(i)$ are not necessarily small.

The Adjustment Based on Estimates of Marginal Proportions
Let $\hat{q}_{i.}$ and $\hat{q}._j$ be estimates of $q_{i.}$ and $q._j$, respectively. Minimization of (1.1) subject to the constraint that the $\hat{q}_{ij}$'s satisfy the estimated marginal proportions yields (1.3), but r_i and s_j are now obtained from

$$r_i \sum_{j=1}^{n} s_j p_{ij} = \hat{q}_{i.} \qquad s_j \sum_{i=1}^{m} r_i p_{ij} = \hat{q}._j \qquad \text{(C.1)}$$

which is (1.4) and (1.5) with the right-hand $q_{i.}$'s and $q._j$'s replaced by their estimates.

For the minimum value of the criterion function we proceed as in the discussion preceding (2.1). This yields

$$\bar{I}(\hat{q} : p) = \sum_{i=1}^{m} \sum_{j=1}^{n} \hat{q}_{ij} (\log r_i + \log s_j) \qquad \text{(C.2)}$$

$$= \sum_{i=1}^{m} \hat{q}_{i.} \log r_i + \sum_{j=1}^{n} \hat{q}._j \log s_j$$

which is identical to (2.1) except that the $q_{i.}$'s and $q._j$'s are replaced by estimates.

Next we write (3.1) as

$$I(q : \hat{q}) = \sum_{i=1}^{m} \sum_{j=1}^{n} q_{ij} \log \frac{q_{ij}}{r_i s_j p_{ij}} \qquad \text{(C.3)}$$

$$= \sum_{i=1}^{m} \sum_{j=1}^{n} q_{ij} \log \frac{q_{ij}}{p_{ij}} - \sum_{i=1}^{m} \sum_{j=1}^{n} q_{ij} (\log r_i + \log s_j)$$

$$= I(q : p) - \sum_{i=1}^{m} q_{i.} \log r_i - \sum_{j=1}^{n} q._j \log s_j$$

where the last step is based on (3.2). We define, similarly to (B.4) and (4.24),

$$\hat{\rho} = \sum_{i=1}^{m} \hat{q}_{i.} \log r_i \qquad \rho = \sum_{i=1}^{m} q_{i.} \log r_i \tag{C.4}$$

$$\hat{\sigma} = \sum_{j=1}^{n} \hat{q}_{.j} \log s_j \qquad \sigma = \sum_{j=1}^{n} q_{.j} \log s_j \tag{C.5}$$

so that (C.2) and (C.3) become $\bar{I}(\hat{q}:p) = \hat{\rho} + \hat{\sigma}$ and $I(q:\hat{q}) = I(q:p) - \rho - \sigma$, respectively. Therefore,

$$I(q : \hat{q}) = I(q : p) - \bar{I}(\hat{q} : p) + (\hat{\rho} - \rho) + (\hat{\sigma} - \sigma) \tag{C.6}$$

which should be compared with (B.3) and (4.23). The inaccuracy of the adjustment procedure on the left in (C.6) may exceed $I(q:p)$ on the right.

REFERENCES

[1] Bacharach, M. (1970). *Biproportional Matrices and Input-Output Change.* Cambridge University Press.

[2] Ireland, C. T., and S. Kullback. (1968). Contingency Tables with Given Marginals. *Biometrika*, 55, pp. 179–188.

[3] Theil, H. (1967). *Economics and Information Theory.* New York: Elsevier/North-Holland, Inc., and Amsterdam: North-Holland Publishing Company.

[4] Theil, H. (1972). *Statistical Decomposition Analysis with Applications in the Social and Administrative Sciences.* New York: Elsevier/North-Holland, Inc., and Amsterdam: North-Holland Publishing Company.

A Bayesian Simultaneous Equation Theorie Applied to an Underidentified Econometric Model

YOEL HAITOVSKY and A. O'HAGAN*

1. INTRODUCTION

It has been recognized by econometricians for some time that underidentified models can be estimated by the Bayesian approach [see Drèze (1962) and Fisher (1966)]. Although the sample data alone are inadequate for performing this estimation, they are supplemented in Bayesian theory by a prior distribution, which reflects the information the researcher has on the model parameters before observing his sample data. Once the data have been observed, inferences about the parameters of the model are made using the posterior distribution. The otherwise unidentified parameters can be estimated only if the posterior distribution contains information about them which comes from the prior distribution. As a matter of fact the classical identification problem does not arise at all in the Bayesian framework as long as proper prior distributions are postulated on all the parameters in the model, including the error covariance matrix, since the posterior distribution is then also proper and hence inferences are possible. However, we shall see here that this condition is too strong and some degree of impropriety can be allowed. We shall only assume here that the prior distribution is sufficiently strong for posterior estimation to be possible.

The use of a prior distribution to provide identifying information may be criticized, but we believe it to be justified on at least two counts. First, on a general count, namely, that to a fully committed Bayesian the existence and appropriateness of a prior distribution are beyond question, having been proved by fundamental arguments. The second justification is more specific to the problem of simultaneous equations and arises from the fact that the alternative is to force upon the model deterministic restrictions rather than

* The research reported here was supported by the Science Research Council and was carried out at University College, London. We are indebted to Dennis V. Lindley for his assistance. We also benefitted from suggestions made by J. F. Richard on an earlier version presented at the European Meeting of the Econometric Society at Oslo, August, 1973.

probabilistic specifications, as required by the Bayesian approach. We can best quote here Drèze (1962):

'A common feature of [the traditional approach] is that the *a priori* restrictions are imposed in *exact* form, through equations or inequalities with known, non-stochastic coefficients. Typically, however, the *a priori* information provided by economic theory, past observation (casual or systematic), etc., is not of such an exact nature and would be better reflected in probabilistic statements. The weakness of the traditional approach is thus two-fold... (i) restrictions are imposed in exact form, whereas they should rather take a stochastic form, reflecting the imprecise nature of the prior information; (ii) certain parameters are left completely unrestricted, about which some prior information is available... the traditional approach lacks flexibility in that it relies upon *too few a priori* restrictions that are, however, *too strict*. A more realistic formulation would call for submitting more – eventually all – parameters to be estimated to stochastic *a priori* restrictions.'

Bayesian methods have been successfully applied to regression models containing errors in the regressor variables [see Lindley and El-Sayyad (1968), Florens et al (1974) and Zellner (1970)], but to the best of our knowledge they have only once been applied to an apparently underidentified simultaneous equations model, in Drèze (1971). Drèze's approach differs from ours in that he replaces deterministic zero constraints by prior distributions highly concentrated about zero. His analysis is then restricted to the coefficients which were identified in the conventional application. In this respect his formulation was only slightly weaker than the traditional one.

We find it surprising that so little of Bayesian methods have been applied in the estimation of econometric models in practice, while the exercise of judgement in the process of estimation is common among practitioners. Judgement is commonly used not only in the imposition of *a priori* restrictions, but also in the selection process in the search for the preferred specification among alternative estimated models (or equations), and in the application made with estimated econometric models. Probably the most important application of econometric models to date is in forecasting. In this respect, it will serve our purpose best to quote Verdoorn (1970) who has been engaged for a very long time in very intensive practical use of econometric models as a tool in policy making.

'In practice, model forecasts are but seldom uniquely based on a straightforward solution of the system. Usually the straightforward or 'provisional' output is used as the input for the formation of expert opinion. Feed-back of this opinion, together with other relevant independent information into the model results, after a process of interaction, in a new set of values for the predictions. This new set, then, is at the same time compatible with the existing expert opinion on future developments, and consistent with the restrictions and observed behavior pattern of the social and economic system as reflected by the structural equations. Apart from being a mere mathematical forecasting tool, an econometric model, therefore, serves too as a vehicle for the consistent allocation and processing of such available information as was not originally contained in the model.'

The natural way to combine sample information with 'expert opinion' is via Bayesian method, and it is high time that practitioners took notice of it, especially, in view of the fact that in other professions, including those in which sample data are more easily accessible relative to *a priori* information than in economics, Bayesian methods are much more prevalent.

In Section 2 we define a general linear simultaneous equation model and construct a formal Bayesian theory for its analysis.

In Section 3 this theory is applied to a simple aggregate demand model, where consumer expenditures and business savings (the induced part of investment) are simultaneously determined by disposable income and by gross investment plus consumption respectively. This model was originally set up and estimated by Haavelmo (1947) using 'classical' maximum likelihood methods. Chetty (1968) later employed a Bayesian approach to estimate the marginal propensity to consume, and to investigate whether investment is autonomously determined, or whether at least part of it is induced. In the present paper we apply the Bayesian technique to a class of problems that cannot be analyzed by the 'classical' maximum likelihood method. This is the problem of whether variables responsive to, say, disposable income are equally responsive to its various components. Here specifically we generalize the model so as to be able to answer the question whether consumption and business savings, respectively, are equally responsive to the 'gross disposable income' and 'gross business investment' components of disposable income. In order to answer these questions it was necessary to add more parameters (variables) to the originally just identified model, causing underidentification.

We wish to emphasize, though, that our analysis of the Haavelmo model should be viewed as merely expository aiming at exemplifying the Bayesian technique, at exhibiting the potential application of Bayesian methods to a class of questions that cannot be analyzed, within the context of the present model, by classical methods, and at showing some informal Bayesian ways of examining data. The Haavelmo model is surely too oversimplified to be of real value, but a more realistic situation in which Bayesian methods become useful arises in the construction of medium sized models, where the econometrician occasionally faces a problem of competing constraints. That is, he feels there may be a justification for the inclusion of various variables in a particular equation (and in letting the data help in deciding whether or not they should be there), but these variables cannot all be included without causing underidentification. In such situations the Bayesian method allows one to include them all and the prior distribution would reflect the feeling that whereas their associated coefficients are likely to be zero there is a chance that some may not be.

Very little applied Bayesian analysis of any kind has been published to date, and we hope that our study will be useful in this field.

2.   THE GENERAL STATISTICAL MODEL AND ITS ANALYSIS

2.1. *Model and Likelihood*

Consider the linear simultaneous equations model comprising s stochastic equations and m identities

$$BY + \Gamma X = \begin{bmatrix} E \\ 0 \end{bmatrix} \tag{1}$$

where B and Γ are respectively $(s+m) \times (s+m)$ and $(s+m) \times t$ matrices with $|B| \neq 0$, Y and X are $(s+m) \times n$ and $t \times n$ matrices of n observations on each of the $(s+m)$ endogenous and t predetermined variables respectively, E is an $s \times n$ matrix of structural random disturbances and 0 is an $m \times n$ matrix of zeros.

Partition B and Γ so as to write the stochastic and identity parts of (1) separately as

$$B_1 Y + \Gamma_1 X = E$$

$$B_2 Y + \Gamma_2 X = 0$$

so that B_1, B_2, Γ_1 and Γ_2 are $s \times (s+m)$, $m \times (s+m)$, $s \times t$ and $m \times t$, respectively. The last equation represents the identities in the system and as such need not be estimated, i.e., the elements of B_2 and Γ_2 are all known. We also define $\varDelta = (B_1, \varGamma_1)$ and $Z' = (Y', X')$, with dimensions $s \times r$ and $n \times r$ respectively, where $r = s + m + t$, in order to write the stochastic equations simply as $\varDelta Z = E$.

It is assumed that each column of E is jointly normally distributed identically and independently for all $i = 1, \ldots, n$ with zero means, and covariance matrix $\varSigma$, that is

$$E \sim N(0, I \otimes \varSigma).$$

The parameters to be estimated in this model consist of $\varDelta$ and $\varSigma$, although one may wish to place restrictions on certain of their elements. It is convenient in the subsequent development to work with $\varPhi = \varSigma^{-1}$ rather than with $\varSigma$ itself. The likelihood function of $\varDelta$ and $\varSigma$ may be found by substituting the m identities into the s stochastic equations which, provided the identities contain no inconsistencies or redundancies, may be done in such a way as to leave a system of s stochastic simultaneous equations. Whichever of the possible substitutions one chooses, the transformation from E to the s endogenous variables of this system has Jacobian proportional to $\|B\|^n$, the absolute value of $|B|^n$, and we arrive eventually at the likelihood function

$$L(\varDelta, \varPhi \mid Z) \propto \|B\|^n \, |\varPhi|^{n/2} \, \exp\left\{ -\tfrac{1}{2} \operatorname{tr} \varPhi \varDelta Z Z' \varDelta' \right\}. \tag{2}$$

To obtain equation (2), however, we require the assumption that any random exogenous elements of X are distributed independently of $\varDelta$ and $\varPhi$, so that they contribute no information by themselves. This includes the usual assumption that the exogenous variables are independent of the error variables.

2.2. *Prior Distributions*

Bayesian methods now require us to express the prior knowledge we have concerning $\varDelta$ and $\varPhi$ in the form of a distribution. Since this knowledge will vary from one application to another so will the distribution, and it is usual in developing a Bayesian theory for a particular model to describe posterior inferences for a class of prior distributions, from which class a single member is chosen which most closely represents the researcher's prior beliefs in a particular case. The class should therefore be large enough to contain members representing most kinds of practical prior knowledge. Rothenberg (1963) has shown that a 'natural conjugate' class does not meet this requirement for the simultaneous equations model. Thus, a more complicated family is necessary. We shall use the family of which a typical member has density

$$p(\varDelta, \varPhi) \propto |\varPhi|^{c/2} \exp\{-\tfrac{1}{2}\operatorname{tr}\varPhi Q\} \tag{3}$$

$$q_{ij} = p_{ij} + (\varDelta_i - D_i)' V_{ij}(\varDelta_j - D_j) \qquad i, j = 1, ..., s$$

where q_{ij} is the (i, j)-th element of the $s \times s$ symmetric matrix Q, and $\varDelta_i$ is the i-th column of $\varDelta'$. The entire family is generated from (3) by varying the 'hyperparameters', which are

    c, a scalar;

    P, an $s \times s$ positive definite symmetric matrix;

    D, an $s \times r$ matrix;

    V, an $sr \times sr$ positive definite symmetric matrix.

In (3) p_{ij} is the (i, j)-th element of P, D_i is the i-th column of D', and V_{ij} is the (i, j)-th block when V is partitioned into s^2 blocks each $r \times r$.

Combining (2) and (3) by Bayes Theorem gives the posterior density

$$p(\varDelta, \varPhi \mid Z) \propto L(\varDelta, \varPhi \mid Z)\, p(\varDelta, \varPhi) \propto \|B\|^n\, |\varPhi|^{c^*/2} \exp\{-\tfrac{1}{2}\operatorname{tr}\varPhi Q^*\} \tag{4}$$

where

$$c^* = c + n \quad \text{and} \quad q_{ij}^* = q_{ij} + \varDelta_i' ZZ'\, \varDelta_j.$$

2.3. *Parameter Constraints*

Suppose that there are some exact constraints on elements of $\varDelta$ or $\varPhi$. Although such restrictions are not necessary in the Bayesian analysis to provide identification, they may be felt desirable for other reasons, e.g. normalisation. The simplest way to incorporate these into the Bayesian framework is to consider the prior and posterior distributions for the whole of $\varDelta$ and $\varPhi$, equations (3) and (4), conditional on the constraints. Thus the hyperparameters of the prior density are chosen to fit the conditional prior distribution to prior beliefs and the conditional posterior distribution is used to provide inferences. These conditional distributions have the same forms as (3) and (4) but are confined to the appropriate subset of the parameter space.

    Within such a subset it will generally be possible to reduce computation by simplifying Q and Q^*. Consider constraints of the form

$$\delta_i^0 = f_i, \tag{5}$$

where δ_i^0 is a vector comprising a subset of the elements of $\varDelta_i$ and f_i is a known fixed vector. We will suppose that constraints of this form exist in all equations, i.e. for all i, but results corresponding to (7) and (8) below can be inferred for other cases by letting f_i be a zero-length vector for some i.

For each i we choose an $r \times r$ permutation matrix K_i which rearranges Δ_i such that

$$K_i \Delta_i = \begin{bmatrix} \delta_i \\ \delta_i^0 \end{bmatrix} \quad \text{and} \quad K_i' K_i = I,$$

where δ_i is a vector, of length r_i say, comprising all the unconstrained elements of Δ_i, i.e., the unknown coefficients in the i-th equation of the model. The conditional prior and posterior densities are confined to the subset of the space of the Δ_i's in which the constraints hold. By substituting the constraints into the densities we eliminate the constrained parameters altogether, and the required subset is the whole space of the δ_i's. By virtue of (5)

$$K_i \Delta_i = \begin{bmatrix} \delta_i \\ f_i \end{bmatrix}.$$

Let also

$$K_j V_{ji} D_i = \begin{bmatrix} d_{i(j)} \\ d_{i(j)}^0 \end{bmatrix},$$

$$K_i V_{ij} K_j' = \begin{bmatrix} W_{ij} & U_{ij} \\ U_{ji}' & V_{ij}^0 \end{bmatrix}, \tag{6}$$

$$K_i (V_{ij} + ZZ') K_j' = \begin{bmatrix} W_{ij}^* & U_{ij}^* \\ U_{ji}^{*\prime} & V_{ij}^* \end{bmatrix},$$

where $d_{i(j)}$ is an r_j-vector and W_{ij}, W_{ij}^* are $r_i \times r_j$. Then we may rewrite q_{ij} and q_{ij}^* as

$$q_{ij} = \delta_i' W_{ij} \delta_j - \delta_i' g_{j(i)} - g_{i(j)}' \delta_j + h_{ij} \tag{7}$$

$$q_{ij}^* = \delta_i' W_{ij}^* \delta_j - \delta_i' g_{j(i)}^* - g_{i(j)}^{*\prime} \delta_j + h_{ij}^* \tag{8}$$

where

$$g_{i(j)} = d_{i(j)} - U_{ji} f_i, \; g_{i(j)}^* = d_{i(j)} - U_{ji}^* f_i,$$

$$h_{ij} = p_{ij} + f_i' V_{ij}^0 f_j - f_i' d_{j(i)}^0 - d_{i(j)}^{0\prime} f_j + D_i' V_{ij} D_j$$

$$h_{ij}^* = p_{ij} + f_i' V_{ij}^* f_j - f_i' d_{j(i)}^0 - d_{i(j)}^{0\prime} f_j + D_i' V_{ij} D_j$$

$$= h_{ij} + f_i' (V_{ij}^* - V_{ij}^0) f_j.$$

Equations (4) and (5) together define a set of conditional posterior distributions which is equivalent to the 'extended natural conjugate' family of Morales (1971, section 2) and is a subset of the family described by Richard (1973, section II.3) for the case $s = 2$. [See also Drèze and Morales (1976)].

2.4. *Choice of Prior Hyperparameters*

We wish to find that member of the family (3) which is closest in some sense to representing our true prior beliefs on the parameters Δ and Σ. This is usually done by requiring the prior distribution to have specific values for its low-order moments, although other characteristics could be used. Enough moments are specified to define a unique member of the prior family. Relevant prior information in our case is more likely to involve moments of Σ than of Φ and therefore we shall suppose that we are attempting to find a member of the family (3) with specified values of (a) the means of Σ and the unconstrained elements of Δ, (b) the variances and covariances of the unconstrained elements of Δ, (c) the variances of diagonal elements of Σ. These will be referred to as the 'required' values.

To choose the matrices D and V we first notice that in equation (3)

$$\text{tr}(\Phi Q) = \text{tr}(\Phi P) + \sum_{i,j} (\Delta_i - D_i)' \, \phi_{ij} \, V_{ij} (\Delta_j - D_j),$$

so that in the absence of constraints the conditional distribution of Δ given Φ is seen to be normal with mean D and with a precision matrix, i.e., inverse of the covariance matrix of Δ 'stacked' into a vector, composed of the submatrices $\Phi_{ij} V_{ij}$. By choosing the U_{ij} (which consist of elements of V_{ij}) in (6) to be zero matrices for all i and j we can make the δ_i independent of all the δ_i^0, given Φ, so that implementing the constraints (5) by further conditioning on the δ_i^0 does not alter the means and covariances of the δ_i. Thus we may choose the elements of D corresponding to the δ_i equal to their required prior means. We shall suppose that the remaining elements of D are set equal to the corresponding elements of the f_i, so that zeros are introduced into $(\Delta - D)$ under the constraints (5). The covariance matrix of $(\delta_1, \delta_2, ..., \delta_s)$ given Φ (and the constraints) is found to be

$$\begin{bmatrix} \phi_{11} W_{11} \cdots \phi_{1s} W_{1s} \\ \cdots\cdots\cdots\cdots\cdots\cdots \\ \phi_{s1} W_{s1} \cdots \phi_{ss} W_{ss} \end{bmatrix}^{-1} \tag{9}$$

and since their mean is independent of Φ, their unconditional covariance matrix is the expectation of (9) with respect to Φ. Since (9) is a very complicated function of Φ, we cannot easily choose the W_{ij} to obtain the required covariances. It is therefore suggested that as an approximation the ϕ_{ij} in (9) are set equal to their required prior means, and that the W_{ij} are then obtained by equating the result to the required covariance matrix of the δ_i.

We shall find that the choice of the remaining elements of V, the V_{ij}^0 is quite arbitrary.

The elements of P and c are chosen to suit the required prior moments of Σ. Looking at (3) we see that the conditional distribution of Φ given Δ is Wishart with $(c+s+1)$ degrees of freedom and mean $(c+s+1)Q^{-1}$. A theorem of Siskind (1972) shows that therefore

$$E(\Sigma|\Delta) = c^{-1} Q$$

provided c is positive. The mean of Σ is therefore c^{-1} times the expectation of Q, i.e. from (3)

$$E(\sigma_{ij}) = c^{-1} E(q_{ij}) = c^{-1} \{p_{ij} + \text{tr}(W_{ij} T_{ij})\}, \tag{10}$$

where $T_{ij} = E\{(\delta_j - d_j)(\delta_i - d_i)'\}$, an $r_i \times r_j$ matrix, and d_i is the subvector of D_i corresponding to δ_i, and we have used the fact that the remaining elements of D_i have been set equal to the corresponding elements of f_i and the constraints (5) apply.

Therefore if we set T_{ij} to the appropriate matrix of required covariances of the δ_i we may solve (10) for any given c and W_{ij} to obtain P, giving the required mean for Σ. The result is only approximate because the actual T_{ij} resulting from our choice of the W_{ij} are only approximately equal to the required covariances of the δ_i.

Siskind (1972) also gives second-order moments of the inverse of a Wishart variable, so that we may express the variances and covariances of the elements of Σ in terms of fourth-order moments of Δ. In particular we find that provided $c > 2$,

$$\text{Var}(\sigma_{ii}) = 2(c-2)^{-1}\{E(\sigma_{ii})\}^2 + \{c(c-2)\}^{-1}\text{Var}(q_{ii})$$
$$> 2(c-2)^{-1}\{E(\sigma_{ii})\}^2.$$

Thus for required values of $E(\sigma_{ii})$ and $\text{Var}(\sigma_{ii})$, $i = 1, 2, \ldots, s$, we can choose

$$c = 2\left[1 + \min_i \frac{\{E(\sigma_{ii})\}^2}{\text{Var}(\sigma_{ii})}\right],$$

and this is a conservative value of c, i.e. leads to larger actual variances for the σ_{ii} than the required values.

Therefore we may choose the hyperparameters as above to at least approximately obtain the required moments. A simplification which is exploited in the example of Section III is to let $W_{ij} = 0$ when $i \neq j$. The result of this is to give zero prior correlations between all pairs of elements from different rows of Δ. In this case the marginal distribution of Φ depends only on P and c.

2.5 Posterior Analysis

With the aid of the posterior density we may make inferences about the structural parameters. Point estimates of parameters may be obtained from modes, medians or means of the posterior distribution (4), modified by (8). A wide variety of modal estimates is possible since joint modes are not usually identical with marginal modes, whereas means of joint distributions are the same as marginal means. Medians are only defined in marginal distributions. Two different sets of modal estimates may be obtained quite simply with the aid of the following theorem,

Theorem:

(a) The modes of the joint distribution of $\{\delta_i; i=1, ..., s\}$ are the solutions $\{\hat{\delta}_i; i=1, ..., s\}$ of the equations

$$
\begin{bmatrix} \hat{\delta}_1 \\ \vdots \\ \hat{\delta}_s \end{bmatrix} = \begin{bmatrix} \psi_{11} W_{11}^* \dots \psi_{1s} W_{1s}^* \\ \dots\dots\dots\dots\dots\dots \\ \psi_{s1} W_{s1}^* \dots \psi_{ss} W_{ss}^* \end{bmatrix}^{-1} \begin{bmatrix} \sum_{j=1}^{s} \psi_{1j} g_{j(1)}^* + \eta_1 \\ \vdots \\ \sum_{j=1}^{s} \psi_{sj} g_{j(s)}^* + \eta_s \end{bmatrix}
\tag{11}
$$

and

$$
\begin{bmatrix} \psi_{11} \dots \psi_{1s} \\ \dots\dots\dots \\ \psi_{s1} \dots \psi_{ss} \end{bmatrix} = Q^{*-1}
\tag{12}
$$

where

$$
n_i = \frac{n}{c^* + s + 1} \frac{\partial \log \|B\|}{\partial \delta_i}
$$

and where both Q^* and the n's are evaluated at $\delta_i = \hat{\delta}_i$, for all i.

(b) The modes of the joint distribution of Φ and $\{\delta_i; i=1, ..., s\}$ are the solutions $\hat{\Phi}$ and $\{\hat{\delta}_i; i=1, ..., s\}$ of the equations (11) and

$$
\begin{bmatrix} \psi_{11} \dots \psi_{1s} \\ \dots\dots\dots\dots \\ \psi_{s1} \dots \psi_{ss} \end{bmatrix} = c^{*-1} \hat{\Phi} = Q^{*-1}, \qquad n_i = \frac{c}{c^*} \frac{\partial \log \|B\|}{\partial \delta_i}
\tag{13}
$$

(c) In equations (12) and (13) both Q^* and the n_i are to be evaluated at $\delta_i = \hat{\delta}_i$ for all i.

Proof:

(a) follows directly by differentiation of the posterior density; and

(b) is obtained by applying Theorem 1 of O'Hagan (1976).

In practice the above equations are solved by iteration, alternately obtaining $\hat{\delta}$'s from equations (11), then ψ's and η's from equations (12) or (13), until the $\hat{\delta}$'s converge. If required, $\hat{\phi}$ is calculated when convergence is complete. In the example described in Section III, this method was implemented on a computer using prior means as starting values for the δ's. The iteration always converged rapidly. Notice however that there will nearly always exist multiple solutions to the equations, some of which may be saddle-points rather than modes. Starting at prior modes would tend to ensure that the solution obtained is the highest mode, but other starting points could be used as a check.

It is considerably more difficult to obtain marginal densities, and thence means, of individual parameters. We can however find the densities of the following parameter groups analytically:

(i) Φ and β, where β consists of the unconstrained elements of B_1;

(ii) if $s = 2$ and we write $\Phi = \begin{bmatrix} \phi_{11} & \phi_{12} \\ \phi_{12} & \phi_{22} \end{bmatrix}$, $\phi_{12} (\phi_{11} \phi_{22})^{-1/2}$ and β;

(iii) $\{\delta_i; i = 1, ..., s\}$;

(iv) $\{\delta_i; i = 1, 2, ..., s, i \neq j\}$ for any particular j.

The resulting densities may be complicated to evaluate. When $s > 2$ there will generally remain too many parameters for numerical integration to be feasible, but for $s = 2$ programs exist to evaluate marginal densities and moments in a reasonable amount of computer time.

The presence of constraints which are not of the form (5) may make analysis more difficult. Linear constraints on Δ are not difficult to handle, but cross-equation constraints, nonlinear constraints or constraints on Φ will generally make it impossible to obtain some of the above densities analytically.

3. THE ANALYSIS OF EXTENDED HAAVELMO'S MODEL

The Bayesian estimation theory developed in the last section will now be applied to an extension of Haavelmo's model.

Consider the three equation model:

$$c = \beta 1 + \alpha y + u \qquad \text{(aggregate consumption equation)}$$
$$r = v1 + \mu(c + x) + v \qquad \text{(gross business saving equation)}$$
$$y = c + x - r \qquad \text{(disposable income identity)}$$

where Greek letters designate unknown parameters, 1 is an n-component unit vector, and Roman letters designate n-component vectors defined as:

$c \equiv$ consumer's expenditures
$y \equiv$ disposable income   } endogenous variables
$r \equiv$ gross business saving
$x \equiv$ gross investment   exogenous variable

and u and v are the structural disturbances whose components are assumed to be identically independently (bivariate) normally distributed, independent of x, with means zero, variances σ_{uu}, σ_{vv}, and covariance σ_{uv}. All variables represent annual per capita figures measured in constant dollars for the years 1929–41. For more detailed definitions see Haavelmo (1947).

Haavelmo's Model I is obtained by assuming $\sigma_{uv} = \mu = 0$, causing the gross business saving equation to drop from the model and r to become independent of the system and hence exogenous. The result is a two equations model. If either $\sigma_{uv} \neq 0 \neq \mu$ we obtain Haavelmo's Model II.

It serves our purpose better to rewrite Model II in an extended form

$$c = \beta 1 + \alpha y + \gamma r + u$$
$$r = v1 + \mu(c + x) + \lambda x + v$$
$$y = c + x - r.$$

Model II is obtained by setting $\gamma = \lambda = 0$, while the departure of these two parameters from zero measures the extent to which the MPC ($\equiv \partial c / \partial x$) differs for the $z \equiv c + x$ and r components of disposable income and MPI ($\equiv \partial r / \partial z$) differs for the c and x components of what Haavelmo calls 'gross disposable income', z. This can be best seen by rewriting the new consumption equation as

$$c = \beta 1 + \alpha(c + x) + (\gamma - \alpha)r + u.$$

A $\gamma \neq 0$ indeed measures the alleged differences. A similar argument applies to the second equation.

The extended model is unidentified for unrestricted γ and λ and we have to use Bayesian methods for making inferences about these two values and for estimating the remaining parameters.

The next step is to form opinions about the model parameters, B, Γ and Φ (or Σ) and their second moments.

It seems reasonable to assume a priori that α should lie between 0.6 and 0.8 and μ somewhere between 0 and 0.6. We furthermore postulate that β may vary between 40 and 200, but we leave the prior information on ν vague. The mid-range values of these priors with 3 standard deviation on each side yield $E(\alpha)=.7$, $\sigma_\alpha=.033$; $E(\mu)=.3$, $\sigma_\mu=.1$; $E(\beta)=120.0$, $\sigma_\beta=25.0$; and $\sigma_\nu=\infty$. We still need to form prior opinions on σ_{ij} $(i,j=u,v)$ and on the covariances between the model coefficients. We found it difficult to provide prior information directly on σ_{uu} and σ_{vv}, but easier to do so on the corresponding coefficients of determination R^2 and to derive the former from it. Judging from numerous aggregate demand and retained earnings studies in the U.S. and other Western countries, it seems that $R^2=.975$, for the consumption equation and .50 for the business saving equation are reasonable choices. The corresponding σ_{uu} and σ_{vv} values are approximately 60 and 100 respectively. As for σ_{uv}, it seems reasonable to expect it to be a positive value, because of the following argument. It is reasonable to assume that gross business savings are positively correlated with total sales or with profits, which are in turn positively correlated with consumer's expenditure. We believe that a correlation coefficient between the two equations error terms u and v of slightly over 1/2 is a reasonable one. It corresponds to $\sigma_{uv}=40$. It is interesting to note that the stated value for σ_{uv} is also obtained by assuming a priori that the covariance between the model reduced form disturbances is low, but positive, and the model coefficients are assigned their a priori mean values.

Similar reasons led us to postulate a low positive prior correlation between α and μ, say of 0.25, all the other prior covariances between the coefficients were assumed zero. However, we found that the posterior distribution of the model parameters hardly changed when the above prior was replaced by a zero covariance, while there are important analytical and computational advantages to the latter, arising from the fact that zero covariances between all the coefficients result in $V_{ij}=0(i\neq j)$ and a diagonal V_{ii} in equation (3). We also set c in equation (3) arbitrarily equal to six, reflecting a low precision associated with the prior information on $\sigma_{ij}(i,j=u,v)$.

Finally we set both prior means γ and λ equal to zero, reflecting a 'null hypothesis' that Haavelmo's Model II is the correct specification (or, alternatively, that the marginal propensities within each equation do not differ from each other). The corresponding standard deviations were arbitrarily set initially equal to 60 percent of the prior standard deviations of

α and μ respectively, yielding $\sigma_\gamma = .02$, and $\sigma_\lambda = .06$. We then let these standard deviations grow gradually.

Given all this prior information, we found after a little experimentation that the following density fits quite well:

$$p(\varDelta, \Phi) \propto |\Phi|^3 \exp\left\{-\tfrac{1}{2} \operatorname{tr} \Phi \begin{bmatrix} 42\,t_{11} & 240 \\ 240 & 70\,t_{22} \end{bmatrix}\right\}$$

where

$$t_{11} = 6 + (\beta - 120.0)^2/724 + (\alpha - 0.7)^2/.00147 + \gamma^2/.00046$$

$$t_{22} = 6 + (\mu - .3)^2/.0123 + \lambda^2/.0046.$$

As was stated, the divisors of γ^2 and λ^2 were increased in subsequent runs.

The marginal posterior distributions of α, μ, β, ν, γ, and λ are plotted in Figures 1–6. Their prior and posterior means and standard deviations, and their joint modes are listed in Table 1, together with the joint modes of the posterior distribution of Φ. These values can be compared with the estimates of Haavelmo (1947), who used the maximum likelihood method, and Chetty (1968), who used vague priors, but restricted μ and α to between 0 and unity.

Figure 1. Posterior Density of α with $\sigma(\gamma) \doteq .02$, $\sigma(\lambda) = .06$

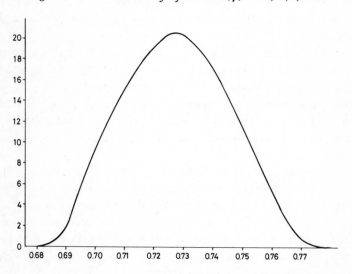

TABLE 1

Estimates of the Model Parameters and the Assumed Prior Parameters

Parameters	β	α	γ	ν	μ	λ	ϕ_{uu} [a]	ϕ_{vv}	ϕ_{uv}
Prior mean	120.0	0.7	0	—	.3	0	.0227	.0136	−.0091
std. deviation	(25.0)	(.033)	(.02)[b]	(∞)	(.1)	(.06)[b]			
Haavelmo's estimates (maximum likelihood)	95.05	0.712	—	−34.30	.158	—	.0251	.0313	−.0257
Chetty's estimates ($\sigma_{uv}\neq0$)	n.r.	n.r.	—	n.r.	n.r.	—	n.r.	n.r.	n.r.
$0<\mu,\ \alpha<1$	n.r.	.7123		n.r.	.1564				
		(.036)			(.022)				
The Extended Model									
$\sigma(\gamma)=.02$, $\sigma(\lambda)=.06$ — Posterior joint mode	88.78	.7280	.00238	−54.25	.2006	−.01651	.0293	.0303	−.0101
Posterior mean	88.96	.7274	.00218	−53.53	.1993	−.01851			
std. deviation	(7.8)	(.017)	(.02)	(6.0)	(.015)	(.048)			
$\sigma(\gamma)=32$, $\sigma(\lambda)=.06$ — Posterior joint mode	90.54	.7024	.2153	−55.48	.2021	−.01142	.0340	.0297	−.0096
Posterior mean	90.53	.7018	.2131	−55.07	.2012	−.01315			
std. deviation	(6.7)	(.016)	(.14)	(6.0)	(.015)	(.049)			
$\sigma(\gamma)=.02$, $\sigma(\lambda)=32$ — Posterior joint mode	88.50	.7287	.00150	−75.73	.2840	−.2655	.0282	.0282	−.0079
Posterior mean	88.68	.7281	.00117	−72.72	.2715	−.2412			
std. deviation	(7.8)	(.018)	(.02)	(9.8)	(.014)	(.105)			
$\sigma(\gamma)=32$, $\sigma(\lambda)=32$ — Posterior joint mode	89.87	.7100	.1548	−72.83	.2701	−.2164	.0319	.0284	−.0076
Posterior mean	89.89	.7077	.1581	−69.69	.2575	−.1915			
std. deviation	(5.5)	(.016)	(.15)	(7.8)	(.014)	(.106)			

a. $\phi_{uu}=.0227$, $\phi_{vv}=.0136$ and $\phi_{uv}=-.0091$ correspond to $\sigma_{uu}=60$, $\sigma_{vv}=100$, and $\sigma_{uv}=40$.

b. ≡ Initial prior.

n.r. ≡ not reported by authors.

Figure 2. Posterior Density of μ with σ(γ)=.02, σ(λ)=.06

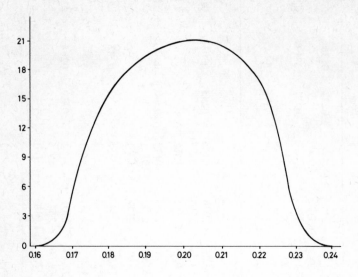

Figure 3. Posterior Density of β with σ(γ)=.02, σ(λ)=.06

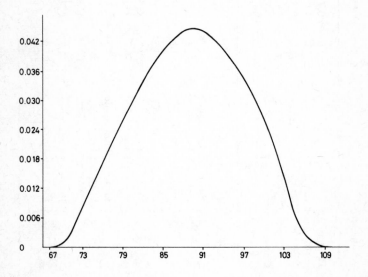

The first thing to note is that the coefficient estimates i.e. their posterior means are within one prior standard deviation from the prior means. (The only exception is β, lying about one and a quarter prior standard deviation from its prior mean). This is expected since we happened to choose priors close enough to the maximum likelihood estimates (MLE). Indeed the departures from the prior means were more pronounced for β and μ (for small σ_λ), for which the prior means are less in agreement with the MLE's.

Secondly, comparing now the estimates for $\sigma_\gamma = .02$ and $\sigma_\lambda = .06$ with Chetty's and Haavelmo's, we should expect close agreement, because the prior distributions of γ and λ are closely confined near zero. In fact this is true of β and α (and γ and λ), but not for μ and v, when measured in terms of the corresponding posterior standard deviations. Although some departure is expected in view of the choice of the prior mean for μ and the vagueness of v, its extent is surprising.

Thirdly, considering now the results for $\sigma_\lambda = .06$ and $\sigma_\gamma = 32$, which effectively corresponds to a vague prior distribution for γ, we first notice that the only large change is in the estimate of γ from zero to 0.2. The prior restraint on γ has been removed, and it is free to take the values suggested by the sample data. However, the unrestricted value does not seem to be 'significantly' different from zero. This can be even better appreciated by looking at Figure 5: when σ_γ is allowed to grow the posterior distribution becomes very flat and its range easily contains the zero value. Furthermore,

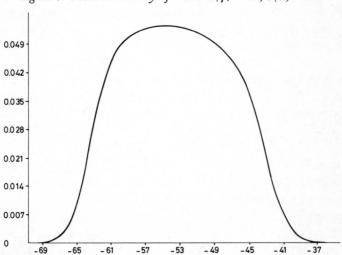

Figure 4. Posterior Density of v with $\sigma(\gamma) = .02$, $\sigma(\lambda) = .06$

Figure 5. Posterior Densities of γ with $\sigma(\lambda) = .06$.

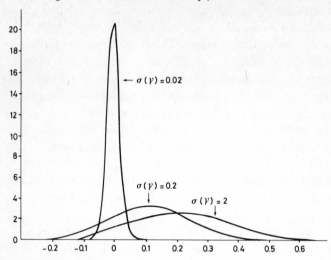

the fact that the estimates for α and β change only very slightly indicates that these estimates are consistent with quite a wide choice of γ. We therefore infer that, although there is some evidence that γ is close to zero, the sample we have is not really capable of distinguishing between Haavelmo's $\gamma = 0$ and our more general specification, even with the aid of prior information on the other parameters.

On the other hand, when we let σ_λ grow, eventually corresponding to a vague prior distribution for λ, but maintain σ_γ at its initial level, the estimates of v, μ, and λ have all changed noticeably from their initial estimates with $\sigma_\gamma = .02$, whereas the estimates of β, α, and γ remain unchanged. The estimate of λ is 'significantly' different from zero (cf. also Figure 6) and it is interesting that its modal estimate is almost exactly the negative of the estimate of μ. We infer that although again the data do not provide enough information on λ, they suggest that a better identified specification of the second equation is

$$r = v1 + \mu c + v^*$$

rather than Haavelmo's.

The estimates with $\sigma_\gamma = \sigma_\lambda = 32$ merely confirm the previous conclusions by combining the changes produced by the separate relaxation of σ_γ and σ_λ, respectively.

In fact results for some intermediate prior variances of γ and λ were also tried (not shown in Table 1). These show that the change in parameter estimates as the variances increased occurred in a monotonic 'smooth' fashion, reaching effectively the results shown for variances of 32 with variances as low as 3. A number of results using a variety of specifications of the hyper-parameters c and P, defining different prior distributions of ϕ, are also omitted. These demonstrate a remarkable robustness of the estimates of α, μ, β, ν, γ, and λ to such changes.

In view of the third point, namely that the sample data only suggest the specifications of the two equations and do not provide more conclusive evidence, it would have been advisable to increase the sample size. We have attempted it, but unfortunately could not obtain data compatible enough with Haavelmo's.

An important feature of the results is the fact that the posterior modes are always very close to the corresponding means. Since the theorem of section 2.5 makes the computation of modes very quick and easy it is suggested that the effort required in computing means is unnecessary if simple point estimates are all that is required.

Figure 6. Posterior Densities of λ with $\sigma(\gamma) = .02$

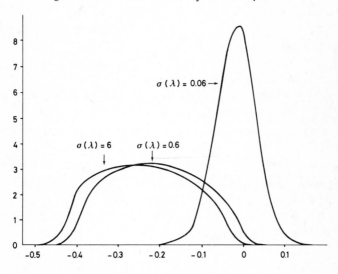

REFERENCES

Chetty, V. K. (1968). Bayesian analysis of Haavelmo's models. *Econometrica*, 36, pp. 582–602.

Dreze, J. H. (1962). *The Bayesian approach to simultaneous equations estimation*. ONR Research Memorandum 67, The Technological Institute, Northwestern University, p. 2.

Dreze, J. H. (1971). *Bayesian limited information analysis of the simultaneous equations model*. Louvain: CORE Discussion Paper, No. 7111.

Dreze, J. H. and Morales, J. A. (1976). Bayesian full information analysis of simultaneous equations. *J. Am. Statist. Ass.* 71, pp. 919–23.

Fisher, Franklin M. (1966). *The Identification Problem in Econometrics*, New York: McGraw-Hill, pp. 183–4.

Florens, J.-P., Mouchart, M. and Richard, J.-F. (1974). Bayesian inference in error-in-variables models. *J. Multivar. Anal.* 4, pp. 419–52.

Haavelmo, T. (1947). Methods of measuring the marginal propensity to consume. *J. Amer. Statist. Assoc.*, 42, pp. 105–2.

Lindley, D. V. and El-Sayyad, G. M. (1968). The Bayesian estimation of a linear functional relationship. *J. Roy. Statist. Soc. B.*, pp. 190–202.

Morales, J. A. (1971). *Bayesian Full Information Structural Analysis*. Berlin: Springer-Verlag.

O'Hagan, A. (1976). On posterior joint and marginal modes. *Biometrika*, 63, pp. 329–33.

Richard, J.-F. (1973). *Posterior and Predictive Densities for Simultaneous Equation Models*. Berlin: Springer-Verlag.

Rothenberg, T. (1963). *A Bayesian analysis of simultaneous equations systems*. Rotterdam: Econometric Institute, Report No. 6315.

Siskind, V. (1972). Second moments of the inverse Wishart-matrix elements. *Biometrika*, 59, pp. 690–1.

Verdoorn, P. J. (1970) 'The Feasibility of Long-Term Multi-Sector Forecasts of Manpower Requirements by Econometric Models' in O.E.C.D. Conference on Forecasting Manpower Requirements, mimeographed.

Zellner, A. (1970). Estimation of regression relationships containing unobservable independent variables. *Int. Econ. Rev.*, 11, pp. 441–4.

Welfare and the GNP

C. T. SAUNDERS*

1. INTRODUCTION

1.1. *Criticisms of GNP as a measure of welfare*

For several years, the concept of gross national product (or gross domestic product, or national income), as measured by existing national and international conventions, has come under attack (indeed it has never been free from criticism). In a somewhat melodramatic form, the current attack has been described as 'dethroning the GNP'. The concept of material product used in the Soviet Union and other 'centrally planned' countries is open to the same – even stronger – criticisms. The essential reason for these criticisms is that the conventional concepts fail to measure the 'welfare' of the population concerned – or changes in it. The conventional measurements ignore many activities which can be said to be 'welfare-producing' and include many activities which produce no welfare, or even detract from welfare. The criticisms come from many sources: from the development economists who find the comparisons of GNP per head between rich and poor countries misleading indicators of relative 'welfare' – and growth rates of GNP as either overstating or understating real economic and social progress; from those who feel that the emphasis on macro-economic aggregates distracts attention from the problems of distribution of income and wealth; from the social philosophers who dislike the materialistic connotations of GNP; from critics who feel that the GNP ignores the disamenities involved in much economic activity....

The easy answer may be that the GNP was never intended to be a *comprehensive* measure of the elusive concept of 'welfare'; nevertheless, it serves a variety of useful purposes – and, incidentally, measures some not unim-

* This paper draws in part, with permission, on one written by the author, as a consultant to the Statistical Commission of the United Nations, on *The feasibility of welfare-oriented measures to complement the national accounts and balances* (UN reference E/CN.3/477 of 17 February 1976).

portant, if materialistic, elements in the welfare of a people. Whether this answer is adequate is the subject of this paper.

The reader will perceive, from the way the question is phrased, and from the length of the paper which follows, that I do not believe this answer to be adequate. It is, in my view, the manifold actual and potential uses of the current national accounting system as a whole which give it value – not the fact that the system yields an impressive aggregate called GNP (of which the value, taken by itself, is quite limited).

In the long history of the measurement in monetary terms of the size and progress of national economies, a history now spanning nearly three centuries, an evolution can be traced. The originators, from Gregory King and others, were concerned in part with international comparison, in part with State administration, in part with taxable and military resources, in part with a quantitative analysis of economic history. As the late Paul Studenski has shown[1], many of the contemporary arguments about what should be included in any such more or less comprehensive account of the wealth of nations have been continuously debated. In the early days, the interest lay in describing and comparing economic structures. It was only in the 1920's that the centre of interest in the industrial West shifted, to become focussed on *short period* or cyclical analysis – and, later, with the development of Keynesian theory – on the use of national income and expenditure statistics as an essential instrument for the control of economic fluctuations and the allocation of resources through the State budget. In this development, Pieter Verdoorn, with the distinguished teams at the Netherlands Central Planning Bureau, has played a leading part; it began with his pioneer work on the formulation of a systematic national accounting framework for the post-war reconstruction of the Netherlands. Verdoorn's pioneer work continued in the bold and sophisticated elaboration of econometric analysis for short-term forecasting and particularly for the control of demand. For this purpose, the national accounting structure as we know it has proved indispensable – even if the signals given have been misread or ignored by policy-makers, and even if errors or tardiness of the data, or misinterpretations of the dynamics of the system, may have borne some responsibility for faulty policies.

At the same time, national accounting has developed another function: a frame for the elaboration of *long-term* plans or projections and for close analysis of long-term, or structural, trends. Probably the first operational

1. Studenski, Paul, *The Income of Nations*, New York University Press, 1961.

use of macro-economic data (in the form of the material product) was in connection with the ex-ante balancing processes for the first Soviet experiments in planning in the 1920s. Most countries, East and West, developed and developing, are now accustomed to presenting their long-term plans or projections in the national accounting form. The point to be made is that the formal statistical, or accounting, framework is generally the same whether the compilers are looking ahead to a 3-month, or 12-month or 5 year or 20 year horizon (or, for that matter, however far the analyst or historian is looking backward).

Whether the formal structure of the accounts is equally appropriate to the short and the long term is one relevant issue. Certainly, a common accounting structure makes for convenience of presentation, especially when all the problems arise of integrating short-term policies with long-term aims of development. But it must also be said that the substantial issues of policy can be very different: the problems of control in the short-term are essentially concerned with the management of demand. In the long-term, especially if some kind of planning is involved, the primary policy decisions are bound to be concerned chiefly with supply – i.e. with long-term trends in production and resources.

1.2. *A response to the criticisms*

I believe that there is a challenge to be met by those responsible for the design and compilation of national accounts. As one who has played some part – although 20 years ago – in the production of the British accounts, and as a fairly frequent user of national accounts of various countries for economic analysis, I would like to put forward the following propositions for consideration.

1. The existing SNA, if fully implemented, and allowing for minor national peculiarities, is by and large an adequate instrument for its major purpose in developed Western countries – the analysis, forecasting and policy control of short-term fluctuations in the national economy. If intelligence for macro-economic policy-making is often enough lacking, that is due not to the conceptual weaknesses of the statistical system, but to difficulties or delays in obtaining important information. Several countries have not solved the problems of getting adequate and timely information on corporate profits and, partly for this reason, on important financial flows; up-to-date records of fixed investment are often insufficient, and other similar shortcomings could be listed. Sometimes, too, statisticians may exhibit an excessive

perfectionism, so that advance and partial indicators of major variables are not fully exploited.

2. Moreover, an extensive superstructure of research, analysis and forecasting has been built upon the existing series – not least in the Netherlands Central Planning Bureau. Major revisions of the content and definition of the variables, requiring new formulations of important relationships, would be unlikely for a very long time to improve our understanding of the short-term dynamics of economic systems.

3. But when we come to the causes and consequences of long-term growth, the arguments for a broader approach than a record of market transactions (plus the few elements of imputation included in SNA), seem very strong. The changes to be considered could include both measurement (generally by imputation) of various non-market services (the classical problem of unpaid housewives' services being one case), and a new kind of treatment of activities included in GNP some of which many would regard as intermediate, or instrumental, activities – as inputs rather than final products – and some of which can be regarded as deleterious to any usual concept of 'welfare'. Again, the usual, and for many purposes necessary, division of national accounting aggregates between sectors and types of transaction conceals distinctions of considerable importance: one example is the contribution of public expenditure, on income transfers or on provision of services in kind, to household consumption. The activities coming under these heads are fairly familiar; some of them will be discussed below.

4. One answer to the problem raised is to formulate an alternative aggregate which, on the one hand, includes a variety of non-market activities and, on the other, excludes many activities which are not properly described as final output. Enterprising and most instructive approaches on these lines have been made , and are in progress, in the United States and Japan. Nordhaus and Tobin have constructed a 'measure of economic welfare' (MEW, with three variants) for the United States; their estimates are described as a 'primitive and experimental measure' …. attempting to 'allow for the more obvious discrepancies between GNP and economic welfare'[2]. To indicate the extent of the 'discrepancy', their estimate of the MEW for 1965 (on their preferred variant) was about twice as great as the official GNP, and increased

2. Nordhaus, William and Tobin, James. Is Growth Obsolete? in Moss, Milton (ed.). *The Measurement of Economic and Social Performance*. National Bureau of Economic Research, New York 1973.

between 1929 and 1965, at constant prices, by 2.3 times against 3 times for GNP. Much more intensive studies of the measurement of the relevant items are in progress in the National Bureau of Economic Research's large-scale research project on 'The Measurement of Economic and Social Performance'[3]. While not aiming at an aggregate to be described as a measure of 'welfare', the project leads to a figure of 'extended gross national product' incorporating by imputation a number of welfare-related additions to GNP and the exclusion of certain other activities. The Japanese estimates are frankly described as a measure of 'Net National Welfare' (NNW); they were established by the NNW Measurement Committee set up by the Economic Council of Japan[4]. The methodology follows in many but by no means all respects the principles proposed by Nordhaus and Tobin. The results are not intended as a substitute for the GNP but as an alternative: the policy maker and analyst can use the two measures like a 'fencer with two swords'. It is interesting to observe that, in strong contrast with the Nordhaus/Tobin estimates for the United States, the Japanese estimate of NNW comes out at about the same figure as the official estimate of net national product (although, as in the US, the rate of growth of the new measure is much less than that of official GNP). The difference between the results for the two countries, despite the similarity in principle of the approach, might indeed indicate real differences of considerable interest; the Japanese make a much smaller proportional addition for non-market services but a much bigger deduction for pollution effects. But it is impossible without very detailed comparison of empirical methods – for example in the measurement of pollution costs – to say how far the differences derive from the method of measurement, how far from a genuine difference in the size of the problem. Far more research is clearly required before these broader concepts reach a stage where international comparisons become useful. (There are still enough problems in international comparisons of the conventional GNP!)

5. The biggest objection to the formulation of a new kind of aggregate of 'welfare' is the uncertainty about what is being measured. It is not 'welfare', since that would include the whole range of human activity; national accounting methods are certainly a multipurpose instrument, but they are not an all-purpose instrument. The examples of alternative aggregates quoted are in effect the conventional GNP plus or minus a necessarily rather

3. Moss, (ed.) *op. cit.*
4. Net National Welfare Measurement Committee, *Measuring Net National Welfare in Japan.* Economic Council of Japan, Tokio 1973.

arbitrary selection of welfare-related variables (or 'ill-fare' related variables) to which monetary values are, in various ingenious ways, attached. The significance of the aggregate remains in doubt. (True, the significance of the conventional GNP aggregate, however carefully defined, is also not wholly unambiguous: it includes not only some arbitrary imputations but also a good many statistics based on conventions – notably conventions established by commercial accountants for distinguishing capital from current expenditures, for valuing inventories, etc.).

6. Moreover, if we are interested in international comparability, the situation is likely to be even further confused by setting up new aggregates. It is just possible (although quite difficult) to imagine that after long and fascinating debate international experts might reach some kind of agreement of what should be included and what omitted in a new aggregate of welfare-related variables measurable in money. But one cannot imagine that statistical offices would be in a position to convert the concepts into actual statistics within any reasonable length of time. Many statistical offices would, with good reason, resist any such diversion of resources. Others might include some of the suggested variables but not all. Others, again, might substitute the new aggregate for the old one – finding the fencer, in the Japanese image, unable to wield two swords simultaneously. Taking account also of the wide range of possible empirical applications of any suggested new principles, there is a serious risk that the progress already made towards international comparability of conventional national accounts would be seriously impaired.

7. These criticisms of any new *aggregate* – whether or not described as a measure of 'welfare' – are not intended to contradict the need for new approaches to long-term analysis in monetary terms. I suggest, however, that at present the reasonable approach is, rather, to promote:

a. the presentation in national accounts not only of the GNP and its components, but also, as separated, 'below the line' items, of valuations of a number of variables which may be supposed to contribute to, or detract from, 'welfare'. The presentation would thus be open-ended. It would be for the user, if he wished, to make his own adjustments to the conventional GNP; he could choose à la carte if the table d'hôte menu failed to meet his particular appetite.

b. research into, and discussion of, alternative methods of valuation.

This approach would serve two purposes. First, it would do something to deflect attention from the too common use of GNP (or material product) as the *exclusive* indicator of overall, long-term economic performance. Secondly, it would promote the presentation of information about individual items, either ignored in the national accounts (e.g. unpaid domestic activities), or hidden away in sub-totals because they have not hitherto been regarded as deserving separate specification (e.g. public expenditures supplementing household consumption).

8. Two final points must be made:

a. The matters dealt with in this paper are looked at mainly from the point of view of nation-wide estimates. But in considering matters related to comparisons of welfare, it is obvious that the *distribution* of income and expenditure – between income groups, social and professional groups, racial groups, different types of household, geographical region – is of primary importance. It is gradually being recognized that the development of macro-economic measurement in recent years, and of macro-economic policies, has tended to overstress national aggregates and to ignore, for example, the distributional effects of policy actions. Distribution of GNP has been seen in terms of distribution between institutional sectors, or between factors of production – important enough, but not touching all the social implications of distribution of the fruits of growth. However, that is not the subject of the present essay, although the development of distributional aspects of national accounts may well be regarded as more important than many of the subjects which are discussed.

b. The recent development of interest in the more systematic collection and presentation of social and demographic statistics bears very closely on the need for broader approaches to the measurement of social and economic progress[5]. It will, indeed, be seen that the possibility of applying monetary valuations depends upon a full corpus of social and demographic statistics and other information in non-monetary terms. For most policy purposes, indeed, the non-monetary statistics – e.g. about the state of pollution or housing conditions – are the important ones. The purpose of 'monetising' some of them is to add a dimension which may quite often help the determination of priorities and the analysis of relationships.

5. See, for example: United Nations, *Towards a System of Social and Demographic Statistics*. UN, New York 1975 (UN Sales No. E.74.XVII, 8).

We may now turn to a number of specific issues which have arisen in earlier discussions of the appropriate content of national income or GNP, or which arise from current criticisms.

We will consider first some important human activities which are normally excluded from the agreed conventions. By the 'agreed conventions' I mean the broad outlines of the accounting system as set out in the United Nations *System of National Accounts* (SNA), and applied, at least grosso modo, by official statisticians in the market economies – whether developed or developing. Most of the issues concern equally the Material Product System (MPS) used in the centrally planned economies. I will not, however, discuss here the major difference between SNA and MPS – the restriction in the MPS of the boundary of production to material product and directly associated services – except to suggest that for a number of analytical purposes, not necessarily for all, the addition of 'non-material services' to material product would have its value.

In each case to be discussed, the first criterion to be applied is, in a sense, the theoretical criterion; but this can be taken to mean for what purposes – analytical or policy-oriented – would the inclusion of a given activity be helpful? The second criterion is whether data can be found, or estimates made, which are accurate enough for the purposes in view.

2. IMPUTATIONS AND THE BOUNDARY OF PRODUCTION

The current conventions about the extent to which values should be imputed to non-market activities represent a compromise. Thus there is general agreement to include a limited number of imputations for activities which are very directly competitive with market activities. The first is *agricultural production for own use* – a measure of what is rather misleadingly described as the 'subsistence economy'. The practical reasons for including it, especially in the accounts for developing countries, are obvious enough. The shift from own account production to production for the market would otherwise give a much exaggerated view of economic growth and grossly exaggerate intercountry differences in economic level. A recent OECD study has collated the data for 70 developing countries, from which it appears that the relative importance of own account production varies immensely – from 30 per cent or more of measured GNP in a few African countries heavily dependent on agriculture down to less than 10 per cent in a few semi-industrial or mining economies such as Iraq or Mexico; the median proportion is about 15 per cent[6]. It is equally clear that the quality of the data used is very uneven; that methods of imputation can be very different (although the old controversy between producers' prices and retail market prices seems to have been resolved in practice by the general use of producers' prices, as recommended by the SNA); and finally that the range of activities covered is diverse (practically all countries include crop and livestock production; most include forestry, fishing and own account dwelling construction; a few cover also hunting, handicrafts and various other kinds of construction).

The second generally recognized imputation is the net rental value of *owner-occupied dwellings* – of more interest to developed countries than own account agricultural production. The reasons for including it are much the same but the amount is naturally very small (3 per cent of household income in the United Kingdom).

By contrast, it has for long been the almost universal practice to exclude from GNP any imputation for other non-market, non-paid household activities and, in particular, for the unpaid domestic activities of housewives about which there was considerable argument in the past. One can understand the practical reasons for this exclusion: the GNP would otherwise be swollen by a very large volume of 'mythical' transactions. But as a matter of logical consistency, why should the growing on own account of an important proportion of food be included, while the preparation of the same food for the table in the same family is excluded? It is undeniable that changing participation rates of women in paid employment, or differences in participation rates between countries, can contribute significantly to the explanation of some part of long-term growth rates and to international differences of measured GNP levels – being in this respect no different from the consequences of the shift from own account food production to production for the market.

2.1. *Unpaid housewives' services*

This ancient issue (and others like it) are worth reviving in view of the increasing interest in wider approaches to the measurement of economic activity and welfare. It may even be worthwhile to repeat the old text-book conundrum: if a man marries his paid housekeeper, is it correct that, ceteris paribus, the national income should decline? The reply is a test of the respondent's concept of the purpose of GNP statistics. If he aims simply at a

6. Blades, Derek W., *Non-monetary (Subsistence) Activities in the National Accounts of Developing Countries*. OECD Development Centre Paris 1975.

record of market transactions for conjunctural analysis, control and fore-casting, he can reasonably answer Yes. But if he takes a broader view of the purpose of the measurement, the answer may very well be No. So long as the lady continues to perform domestic services, the flow of goods and services continues as before – and 'welfare', one may hope, does at least not diminish. The question is not just trivial if *long-term* trends are being analysed. The large-scale inflow of women into paid employment increases GNP and the output of certain kinds of goods and services – but also has consequences for domestic welfare (whether positive or negative consequences is a matter for the sociologist). It also has consequences for the pattern of production (it may be, for example, a reason for the development of domestic appliances). The question has even entered into the controversies over women's rights: the national accountants are accused of subscribing to 'male chauvinism' by excluding from GNP a major contribution of women to social life.

In the past, when the concepts of national income were less rigorously defined, it was not uncommon to include the unpaid services of housewives. Paul Studenski quotes unofficial estimates made in the 1930s for Hungary, Italy and Sweden[7]; and Simon Kuznets, although after due consideration omitting housewives' services from his early estimates of United States national income, provided an imputed estimate of their importance[8]. The amounts involved are naturally very large. A compilation by Oli Hawrylshyn of estimates made at various times for the United States, the United Kingdom and Sweden, adjusted for comparability, suggests that inclusion of housewives' services could add between 30 and 40 per cent to GNP[9]. The amount would of course vary greatly both with the method of imputation adopted and with the big international differences in women's participation rates (e.g. among industrial countries, from 60 per cent and over of women of working age in the socialist countries down to 30 per cent in the Nether-lands).

There is, of course, a variety of methods of imputation for the value of housewives' services. But in principle they seem to be reducible to three, all of which have been applied at various times:

a. The first is the 'opportunity cost' – what the woman might have earned if she had chosen to take up, or continue, a paid employment appropriate

---

7. Studenski, Paul, *op. cit.* part 2 page 17.
8. Kuznets, Simon, *National Income and its Composition 1919–1938*. National Bureau of Economic Research, New York 1941, Vol. II pp. 431–433.
9. Hawrylshyn, Oli, *The Value of Household Services: a Survey of Empirical Estimates*.

to her qualifications. This would imply valuing the housework of a qualified doctor or teacher at a higher rate than that of a wife who had left school at 16 – irrespective of their domestic accomplishments; the necessary data may or may not be available from censuses.

b. If only an aggregate is required, somewhere near the same 'unit value' could be reached by the simple method of applying the average pay of employed women (thus if relative women's pay increases, e.g. as a result of equal pay legislation, the corresponding valuation of housewives' services would also increase – a perfectly logical result since women's measured relative contribution to market activities would also increase).

c. The third method is a weighted average of the market rates of pay for the mix of activities which a housewife performs – cooking, child care, housecleaning, etc. This seems a reasonable enough method – provided that a sensible analysis can be made of how housewives distribute their time.

The difference between the methods is substantial. An American estimate gives (for 1972) $ 7000 a year as the average pay of women in full-time employment (method b) – and presumably method a) would lead to a similar result – but only $ 4700 for the mix of jobs assumed to be done (mostly fairly low-paid jobs in the labour market)[10]. These are figures of pay before tax but, as Hawrylshyn points out, pay after income tax would be a better measure, and incidentally would narrow the differences between the various methods.

Naturally, there should be no discrimination between the sexes. An estimate should also be made for the similar activities of men. And there should also be an estimate for the household services performed by men and women who are in paid employment.

This raises the question of how much *time* is spent in non-market activities. It is worth calling attention to the fairly novel expansion of the system of *'time budgets'* – analogous to the surveys of household expenditure budgets – in which a sample of people report the amount of time spent in various activities. Some readers will be familiar with the enterprising international project organized by the European Coordination Centre for Research and Documentation in the Social Sciences[11]. Time budgets on a uniform classi-

10. Economic Value of a Housewife, *Research and Statistics*, Social Security Administration Note No. 9, 1975. The estimates were made with a view to calculating the 'economic costs' of disease and were based on specially collected time-budgets for 45,000 married couples.
11. Szalai, Alexander, (ed.) *The Use of Time.* Mouton for the European Co-ordination Centre for Research and Documentation in the Social Sciences, 1972.

fication were collected in 12 countries. A finding relevant to our present purpose is that full-time housewives report, on average, about the same amout of hours devoted to household functions as those reported as spent at work (plus travel to and from work) by full-time employed men. This might raise some suspicion of respondent bias: but if the sceptic might be inclined to wonder how many minutes reported as household duties are devoted to gossip outside the supermarket, let him be reminded that only a proportion of factory or office workers are continuously engaged in their 'economic' activity from opening to closing time. (Of course, time budgets serve a variety of more practical purposes than imputation in national accounts. They have been used quite extensively in the United States and Eastern Europe for transport planning, for urban planning generally, and for the planning of leisure-time facilities. And market researchers have used them e.g. for planning radio and television programmes).

2.2. *Other unpaid domestic activities*

Similar considerations apply to a variety of other unpaid activities within the household. Thus the increasing facilities for selfservice or 'do-it-yourself' activities, associated with the increasing relative cost of marketed labour-intensive services, is a not unimportant trend in living habits influencing the structure of market production, expenditure and employment. In principle, such activities could be measured in money terms, with the aid of time budgets and imputed valuations, in the same way as housewives' services. Perhaps the most important quantitatively – indeed one of the most signi-ficant social trends – is the long-term shift from public to private transport. Its importance is very inadequately measured in present systems of national accounting, where the use of private transport, and particularly of motor cars, is represented only by the purchase of vehicles plus their running costs. Comparisons between countries, or over time, of the cost of *marketed* trans-port activity alone completely fail to indicate differences in the importance of transport as a form of human activity. This is an area where imputed valuations of the opportunity cost of time spent in driving one's own vehicle are quite common (even if the methods of imputation are controversial) for cost/benefit analysis of transport projects.

The unpaid household, or self-service, activities so far mentioned are all, in a certain sense, competitive with analogous activities in 'the market'. In this, as has been noticed, they resemble food production for own use. The arguments for making some sort of computation of their value in monetary terms are quite strong, since such a computation could assist a quantitative explanation of long-term trends in an economy. Once again, I would stress that I would not myself attach importance to their being included in some new aggregate of 'national welfare'. Their purpose, it seems to me, would be adequately served by putting the resulting figures 'below the line' – and even this would be helpful only if the methods of imputation are made quite explicit. In this kind of question, where so much depends on methods of imputation which are necessarily arbitrary and unfamiliar, nothing is more useless – and potentially misleading – than a precise statistic without explanation.

This leads to the problem of data. I would emphasise that the important data are *not* the monetary estimates but the demographic statistics, in particular of women's participation rates, supplemented by estimates of allocation of time. For the latter, time budgets appear to be a promising statistical tool worth developing for a variety of reasons of social policy and understanding; but it is also relevant to observe that the ordinary statistics of working time are in many developed countries unnecessarily inadequate (they are often restricted to manual workers, or to industrial sectors, and do not provide full information about holidays, absences for sickness, etc.).

The problems of imputation of appropriate values are philosophical rather than due to lack of data in any country with a reasonable array of statistics of pay by occupation. The philosophers may continue to argue over the 'correctness' of the various methods. The main point is that a consistent method should be used and it would be good if some uniform method could be agreed internationally; for the most important case – housewives' services – I would favour some mix of analogous paid activities but could have no serious quarrel with the simpler formula of average pay of all women in full-time employment.

2.3. *The valuation of leisure time*

Some more adventurous analysts have attempted to extend their comprehensive estimates to include estimates and value imputations for leisure time. The argument is that leisure – like domestic work – is an alternative use of time to production for pay. Decisions about the use of time can be regarded (as in Becker's theoretical work) as an allocation of resources and subjected to economic analysis and to rational processes of optimizing in the same way as decisions about the use of money or of factors of production. Survey data about the use of time have an obvious value for forecasting expenditure patterns, etc.. And some part of the differences in GNP per head between nations, or over time, can be 'explained' by what may be regarded as a changing social preference for leisure as against paid, or unpaid, work.

However, the idea that individuals can choose between leisure and work by a rational process comparable with the consumer's choice between jam and cheese, seems to stretch the use of the process rather far – especially since, for most of us, the principal uses of each 24 hours, work and sleep, are determined either institutionally or physiologically within fairly narrow limits. There are also more severe practical objections to an empirical application than in the case of unpaid household activities. First, it seems somewhat unrealistic to value all leisure time at the same price as paid work; there may be, for some, a possibility of rational choice at the margin but can it be extended to a macro-economic concept in any useful sense?[12] And how should the enforced leisure, especially of the unemployed, be valued? Secondly, there are even greater problems of defining 'leisure' even if time-budget data are available. For example, the Nordhaus/Tobin estimates, apparently based more or less on the old adage of 8 hours for work, 8 for sleep and 8 for leisure, leisure hours being valued at average hourly earnings, necessarily yields a valuation of aggregate leisure hours not very different from the value of the conventional GNP. On the other hand, the Japanese 'net national welfare' includes an imputed valuation of leisure time – also based on average earnings, but differentiated by age and sex – yielding an aggregate equal to less than 10 per cent of conventional GNP. The difference is due not so much to the more austere habits of the Japanese as to a much more restrictive definition of leisure (perhaps significantly, the Japanese exclude 'social intercourse', as well as eating, from leisure time).

I would take the view that to impute a monetary value to aggregate leisure time is an interesting statistical curiosity but not one likely to add much to social or economic analysis that cannot be derived from adequate statistics of hours of work, of holidays, of necessary travel, etc..

3. 'INSTRUMENTAL' EXPENDITURES

We turn now from possible 'welfare-producing' additions to the GNP to examine activities which are normally included in GNP but which, many would hold, are better regarded as detracting from welfare; such activities are sometimes described as 'regrettable necessities' (although in some cases their 'necessity' might be questioned).

12. The Japanese imputation is in fact based on a survey in which respondents were asked how much extra pay they would require to do an extra hour of work.

National accounting aims at an aggregation of 'final' products and activities, as distinct from 'instrumental', or 'intermediate' or 'defensive' products and activities – the latter being those which are produced or carried out as a means to some other end. It has always been recognized that the distinction is necessarily an arbitrary one; no clear philosophical and statistically applicable dividing line can be hoped for. It has been remarked by George Jaszi that 'food expenditures defend against hunger....clothing and housing expenditures defend against cold and rain....religious outlays against the fires of hell'.[13] However, there are certain goods and services which seem more obviously means to an end than others – even if the differences are matters of degree rather than of kind. Some food is consumed because eating is found not only necessary to maintain energy but agreeable – although the statistician is not likely to find out how much is spent on each of these two worthy objectives.

In past discussions of national accounting concepts, the problem of an appropriate dividing line has been most discussed in connection with governmental expenditures.[14] Thus it has been argued that expenditure on defence, on police and justice, on tax collection, general administration, etc. are essentially the necessary costs of a complex society and should be treated as inputs rather than as final products or added values. If it is argued that these inputs in fact result in a final product, or an element of welfare – national security, safety of life and property – it can be replied that the relationship between the expenditure and the final product is, to say the least, uncertain and controversial (what is the relationship between the amount of crime and expenditure on police forces?) Such relationships cannot be compared with that between the input of fuel and the output of a power plant. These arguments may be reinforced by the additional difficulty of expressing in a meaningful way the *output* of many public authority activities – but that is a separate, although related issue.

The convention adopted by the SNA and by most Western statistical offices is to cut the philosophical knot by treating all government expenditure on goods and services as final product. But the problem cannot be looked at simply in terms of a new division of *government* expenditures. Current convention is often criticised because it leads to an apparent 'anomaly'. For example, expenditure by public health authorities on the disposal of sewage and other wastes is a final product and appears in GNP as such. But expendi-

---

13. George Jaszi, quoted by Peskin, Henry M., National Accounting and the Environment. *Artikler fra Statistisk Sentralbyra* No. 50, Oslo 1972.
14. See Studenski, Paul, *op. cit.* Part 2.

ture by an enterprise on disposing of its own waste products is an intermediate cost to the enterprise and appears in GNP only as part of the value of whatever final product (e.g. paper) the firm in question produces. This example illustrates two issues which should be kept distinct.

a. If it is felt that waste disposal should be excluded, as a purely 'instrumental' activity or regrettable necessity, from a welfare-oriented aggregate of final product, then it should be identified and excluded whether the activity is performed by an enterprise or by the government.
b. If it is desired to know, for purposes of analysis or policy, how much is spent on waste disposal, then both public and enterprise expenditure must be identified.

In either case, the first necessity is not so much a new definition of GNP but an improved classification of both public and enterprise expenditures. An improved classification means more information – not only for a better measurement of welfare-related activities but for handling specific policy problems. And the example of waste disposal is just one of a number of such problems embraced by contemporary concern about the effects of economic activity on the maintenance of the natural environment. The conceptual debate on the treatment in national accounts of activities which pollute the environment, and of activities directed to lessen this pollution, is rightly giving way to more practical discussion about what it is useful to measure, and how it should be measured.

3.1. *The functional analysis of public expenditure*
We may consider first the need for more information about government activities – in relation not only to environmental protection but also to other activities which can be regarded as on the borderline, from the point of view of welfare, between instrumental and final activities. Just because of these uncertainties, the statistical objective should surely be a much more detailed analysis of public expenditures, classified by function or purpose, within the national accounting framework, than most countries – even statistically well-equipped countries – seem able to provide at present.[15] It appears, indeed, paradoxical that the official national accounts for so many countries give so little detailed information about public expenditure. Even the rather aggregative classification recommended in the SNA – nine functio-

15. The UN Statistical Office has indeed put forward for consideration a much more detailed purpose classification of public expenditure than that in the revised SNA (UN paper E/CN.3/479).

nal categories of expenditure – is not completed by a considerable number of countries, as the UN *Yearbook of National Accounts Statistics* shows. Some reasons for these failings are well known: the difficulties of getting detailed information about the expenditure of public authorities below the level of central government (e.g. there are nearly 80,000 local government units in the United States); the problems of fitting the categories of expenditure used in State budgets – generally based on administrative organizations – into any functional or economic classification. The whole analysis of public expenditure into useful categories is in many countries in an underdeveloped state and needs active promotion – for many reasons in addition to those with which this paper is concerned. (I am glad to say that these problems were, for the most part, solved fairly satisfactorily for the United Kingdom national accounts many years ago; but it involved a big effort to achieve the necessary cooperation between the Central Statistical Office and the spending Ministries and local authorities). Gradually, the national accounting presentation of public expenditure has come to take precedence over the traditional presentation based on administrative units[16]. This form of analysis if fully developed allows for quite a good à la carte selection, from which the user may choose those items which he would like to regard as 'instrumental' rather than final products. The statistical office can then be absolved from the disagreeable responsibility of determining whether the police force is an instrument for preserving the property of the capitalist class or a contribution to the welfare of society as a whole.

Such a functional analysis would also permit a clear separation of public services which might be regarded as additions to household consumption, or as alternatives to spending out of disposable household income. The usefulness of this is discussed below under 'A wider concept of "consumption"'.

3.2. *Instrumental household expenditure*
Efforts have been made, similarly, to distinguish certain elements of household expenditure as 'instrumental' to the achieving of other ends. A high level of consumption in an industrial and, generally, urban society imposes all sorts of inconveniences and disamenities and consequent expenditures; these, it is suggested, should be treated as costs of the high level of con-

---

16. See annual issues of the UK Central Statistical Office's *National Income and Expenditure*, especially Table 10.2 (in the 1976 edition), 'Analysis of Public Expenditure'. The expenditure of the Central government and local authorities is consolidated and divided into 29 functional categories, each sub-divided between current expenditure on goods and services, fixed capital formation, subsidies, transfers and loans to other sectors, etc.

sumption rather than part of consumption. Once again, no agreement is likely on what items of consumption should be regarded as truly 'final'.

An example is the cost of travel to and from work. It can plausibly be asserted that few people would endure, and pay for, the daily journey at the rush hour – whether by overcrowded and germ-laden public transport or by frustrating private car – if it were not a necessity for acquiring an income. It could also be argued that if employers generally adopted the practice of paying the travel costs of their workers, then – other things being equal – the GNP (at constant prices of final products) would be fallaciously reduced, without any change in 'real' activities. Thus both Tobin and Nordhaus, and the Japanese, in their welfare estimates quoted above, subtract from household consumption some very rough calculations of commuting costs. The Japanese add to this an imputed valuation of the time lost in this kind of travel. Such estimates can be of considerable importance to traffic and transport planners, to urban planners, to the authorities concerned with location of new industry; and if policy makers in these areas are to make rational decisions, the data are very necessary. Thus it would be helpful if transport statistics could be designed to specify separately those categories of traffic which approximate to 'commuting'. If that were done, travel for purposes of work could well be distinguished from other categories of travel in the national accounting presentation of consumption; the user could, if he wished, deduct them. However, the conceptual argument would not be settled. It can be argued, for example, that the costs of commuting are offset by an increase in 'welfare' (and, in some places, lower housing costs) of living in desirable and supposedly healthy suburbs. Against that, it may be suggested that suburban life reduces 'welfare' by depriving people of the social and cultural amenities of the big city. So the argument can continue, rather fruitlessly....

Other rather clear regrettable necessities to be deducted from household consumption have been proposed: various kinds of personal business expenditures (legal and insurance costs associated with ownership of property? costs of expert advice in minimizing tax liabilities?). The arguments are much the same. The deduction for work-travel and personal business expenditure – singled out by both the Nordhaus/Tobin and Japanese estimates as 'non-welfare' items – come to as much as 7 or 8 per cent of household consumption for the USA and about 4 per cent of GNP for Japan[17].

17. An intriguing item of 'personal business expenses' in the Japanese welfare estimates is that of 'ceremonial expenses' amounting to 1–2 per cent of GNP (entertaining business superiors? subscriptions to golf-clubs? – the content is not elaborated).

The analysis of household consumption raises other much-discussed issues which need only be mentioned. One is the treatment of private expenditure on health and education. In part, at least, these expenditures might be regarded as 'inputs' – or, rather, as 'investments' – instead of final consumption. Again, the main point is that such expenditures should be separately stated in sample surveys of household expenditure or by other means. At present, presumably because the amounts concerned are often small since public expenditure predominates, they are frequently ignored; among other things, this can lead to misleading international comparisons of the resources devoted to these services.

Then there is the vexed question of the treatment of consumer durables: should the purchase of cars, household appliances – even clothing or jewellery – be regarded as 'consumption' at the time of purchase, or (as with dwellings) should 'consumption' be the (necessarily imputed) services derived from them? Which is the best estimate of the 'welfare' derived from such possessions? There is a conjunctural argument and a welfare argument. As regards the former, it is generally recognized that the understanding and forecasting of household consumption and saving requires a separation of at least the major durables – since purchasing decisions to some extent resemble investment behaviour. Thus conjunctural analysis could be assisted (apart from the disturbance to statistical continuity) if the big fluctuations in purchases of durables were transferred from household consumption to a consumers' capital account.

On the welfare side, there is certainly much to be said for current use (or 'imputed rental values') rather than purchases as the main measure. The statistical data problem is not so much the method of imputation – which must anyway be arbitrary – as the absence of adequate information on the existing stock. Once more, it can be suggested that data on consumers' stocks of durables, expressed in money terms in much the same way as the capital stock of enterprises, would have many analytical uses in its own right. An imputation of the services derived could be a useful 'pro memoria' addition to the household accounts, not very difficult to calculate once the stock is known. In fact, the estimates of Nordhaus and Tobin for USA and the 'net national welfare' estimates for Japan both include such imputations and it happens that the amounts shown, for recent years, are of the same order of magnitude as the expenditure on net purchases included as household consumption[18].

18. However this similarity would obviously not apply in a phase of fast growth. Thus the ratio of imputed services to actual expenditure increases in Japan from 54 per cent in 1960 to 88 per cent in 1970.

3.3. *Accounting for pollution*

One of the main attacks mounted against the GNP concept comes from critics rightly concerned with the pollution of air, water and soil, and with environmental damage generally, associated with economic development. Thus an increase in GNP due, for example, to increased production in the polluting pulp and paper industry is accorded the same value as a corresponding increase in the production of the relatively harmless (from this point of view) precision engineering industry. And an enterprise which decides to add to 'welfare' (or, rather, to reduce ill-fare) by diverting resources from its final product to expensive cleaning-up of its pollutant wastes will – other things being equal – reduce the real GNP. And if a household is obliged to forego a planned holiday in order to pay for hospital treatment (or to pay taxes for a public health service) on account of bronchial disease brought about by life in an air-polluted environment, the national accountant blithely ignores the difference between the expenditures in adding up his GNP. Of course, these are not necessarily paradoxes in the context of the 'boundary of production' as defined in the SNA. But there are, nonetheless, qualitative distinctions between different kinds of expenditure included in GNP and these distinctions – even if they need have no influence on conjunctural macro-economic decision-making – are important from many points of view.

How can the national accountant – and the problem is one not only for national accounting specialists but for economic statisticians generally – meet this particular challenge?

It is very clear that policies for coping with pollution, and with environmental damage generally, stand sadly in need of a far more substantial body of quantitative information that is at present available. In part, this is a problem for the physical and medical scientists. The ways of measuring physical concentrations of polluting agents; the danger thresholds; the amounts of disease and contamination of human, animal, bird, marine and plant life attributable to specific kinds of pollution – all these problems contain large areas of dispute and sheer ignorance. The first requirement is clearly *physical* information. This is, indeed, extensively being developed. Statisticians can play an important part not only in formulating methodologies of measurement but also in linking the results of various disciplines concerned (in particular there seems to be a real need for a closer link between medical research on mortality and morbidity from causes attributable to pollution and the geographical and socio-economic characteristics of the victims). The development of international standards for statistical measurement of environmental damage is indeed being pursued by the international statistical organizations[19].

A full and refined development of national accounting – or economic statistics generally – in this area must probably wait upon much improved physical measurements. But a number of useful experiments in measurement are going forward. In a sense, the economic measurements, in financial terms, are directed towards some form of cost-benefit analysis – it being recognized, that as usual, costs are more easily measurable than benefits. The conceptual problem from the point of view of national accounting, together with proposals for, and examples of, statistical application, have been much discussed[20].

For public expenditures, the need for an adequate functional analysis has been discussed above and it should clearly include a separate specification of expenditures concerned with preventing or counteracting pollution and environmental damage. But the amount of *enterprise* expenditure for these purposes is rarely known. The most complete data are probably those recently found in the United States. Data on current and capital costs of pollution abatement and control are now collected from all non-farm businesses. It has thus been possible to build up for the United States an overall estimate (some elements being admittedly insecure) of total 'national expenditure on pollution abatement and control'. The figure for 1972 amounted to $ 19 billion, equal to 1 1/2 per cent of GNP – of which business organizations accounted for about half[21]. Obviously this measure of actual costs of *counteracting* pollution is no measure of the total damage; but it is an essential element of information to set against the more hypothetical estimates which are sometimes made either of the total damage, or of the estimated costs of bringing environmental standards up to given levels. An estimate of the latter kind is made in the Japanese report *Measuring net national welfare in Japan* referred to above. The method is to estimate, very tentatively, the increase in emissions of major polluting substances since a base year (generally 1955, when pollution is imagined not to have been harmful) and then to estimate the costs of treatment. The costs for 1970 so arrived

19. Meetings of experts from the international organizations have been organized by the UN Statistical Commission in conjunction with the Conference of European Statisticians (See, for example, *Conclusions of the Seminar on Environmental Statistics*, Warsaw 1973, in UN/ECE: CES/SEM.6/11). Work is also going on in the OECD on these problems (OECD, *Environmental Damage Costs 1974*).
20. See, for example, Peskin, Henry M. (reference 13 above).
21. For methods and results, see US Dept of Commerce, *Survey of Current Business* February 1975.

at, add up to the remarkably large amount of 9 per cent of GNP – and the whole of this sum is deducted from the official GNP to yield the estimate of 'net national welfare'.

The whole subject is obviously an important area for fact-finding – both physical and financial facts. The estimates so far made cannot be used – and certainly not compared between countries – without full study of the methods used and of the purposes of the measurement. The fact-finding – whether the adequate monitoring of physical and medical phenomena, or the collection of special financial statistics in the administrations and in enterprises – is bound to be extremely expensive. Whether the policy benefits are likely to exceed the fact-finding costs has to be determined and, no doubt, priority areas decided. However, the effort is going ahead, and can be greatly assisted, and probably cheapened, by international comparisons and exchange of experience. The national accountants and economic statisticians can give considerable assistance – more effectively, at the present stage, in devising methods of measurement and in ensuring an adequate presentation of results than in conceptual controversy.

4. A WIDER CONCEPT OF 'CONSUMPTION'

I turn now to a rather different aspect of the wider approach to national accounting, but one which brings in some of the matters already discussed. International comparisons of household consumption, and comparisons over time equally, can suffer because of the somewhat restrictive 'sectoral' framework of most national accounts. I have particularly in mind the concept of consumption. The private consumption expenditure of the household sector is often presented in great detail. It includes, of course, expenditure financed not only by income (after tax) from work and property but also by monetary transfers from public authorities. On the other hand, public provision in kind of many similar goods and services is to be found (if it is to be found at all) in a different sectoral account – that for general Government. Consequently, it can be very misleading to compare the recorded household consumption between two countries in one of which consumers pay for, in particular, health and education largely out of their own pockets while in the other such services are largely provided 'free' (i.e. out of taxation).

The solution seems to lie in applying the concept of 'total consumption of the population' which brings together goods and services of a consumption-type provided both by households themselves and by public authorities (plus some provided by enterprises – see below). This concept has long been a major accounting aggregate in the Material Product System of the socialist countries (although restricted to goods and material services). It is now recommended for use as a complement to the SNA by the UN Statistical Commission[22].

The usefulness of the concept of total consumption, irrespective of method of financing, is demonstrated in the most valuable study of international comparisons contained in the UN *International Comparison Project* (ICP)[23]. Comparisons of real consumption per head, based on international prices, are made for a number of countries. To the usual estimates of private household consumption are added such 'government components' as rent subsidies, medical supplies, the services of medical staff, hospitals, entertainment and recreation, and education. (The authors note, significantly, that for a number of countries these important data are not available in published sources and had to be obtained by special inquiries). The differences in any assessment of relative consumption levels between the limited SNA figures of consumption per head and the more comprehensive estimates of total consumption, emerge from the following summary figures[24]:

| | Per capita consumption 1970 | | |
| | ICP binary comparisons US=100 | | |
	(1) ICP total consumption	(2) SNA consumers' expenditure	(3) (1) as % of (2)
France	68.1	67.2	101
Japan	47.4	45.5	104
F.R. Germany	61.5	57.8	106
Italy	48.1	45.0	107
Un. Kingdom	63.6	55.7	114
Hungary	38.3	31.1	123

22. See UN *Draft System of Statistics of the Distribution of Income, Consumption and Accumulation* (E/CN 3/425 para 153) and UN *Towards a System of Social and Demographic Statistics* (UN Sales No. E.74.XVII 8, New York 1975) Chapter XIII.
23. The first results are published in Kravis, Irving B. *et al.*, *A System of International Comparisons of Gross Product and Purchasing Power*. Johns Hopkins University Press 1975.
24. Kravis. *op. cit.* Tables 13.1 to 13.9.

Such data are obviously relevant to 'welfare' comparisons.

The basic needs for such an analysis are:

a. A satisfactory specification of public expenditures on goods and services, by function, as was stressed above for a variety of purposes.
b. A classification of private expenditure, e.g. from sample household expenditure surveys, which shows separately expenditures on services, such as health and education, which are also provided by, or subsidised by, government.

As a further example, the following table draws on the published United Kingdom national accounting statistics to show some main elements (not all are available) of a more comprehensive account of total household consumption (the items of public expenditure cover rather more than the ICP estimates quoted above). Some items may be questioned. But the general picture is clear. By direct expenditure on consumption-type goods and services, and by subsidies to reduce the market prices of such goods and services, public authorities added about 14 per cent to the national accounting figure of household consumption in 1965 and by 1975 this addition had increased to 25 per cent. Put in another way, over these 10 years private household consumption as recorded in the national accounts increased 2.8 times but 'total consumption of the population' increased 3.0 times. These figures are all at current market prices. At 1970 prices, private consumption increased only by 23 per cent; even the UK Central Statistical Office has not attempted to deflate all these individual items of public expenditure, but their estimates show that public expenditure at constant prices on the two major items, health and education, increased by 50 per cent from 1965 to 1975.

This type of presentation, rarely used by commentators tied to the formal categories of the national accounts, although easily put together from the published data, can add much to any analysis of the development of living standards.

One other refinement of national accounting for a comprehensive statement of consumption should be mentioned. This is the 'subsidies' to particular items of private consumption paid by enterprises (and presumably incorporated in the prices of other goods and services). Thus enterprises finance newspapers, radio and TV services etc. – even football matches – below cost by taking advertisements from other enterprises producing quite different commodities. Public transport can in a way be financed similarly by advertising. The buyer of soap is involuntarily buying a bit of 'soap opera'. Also, the employees of some enterprises benefit from their employers' ex-

United Kingdom: private and public household consumption
£ million at current market prices

	1965	1975
1. *Total private consumers' expenditure*	*22,845*	*63,373*
(national accounts concept) of which,		
Education	NA	NA
Health	NA[a]	NA[a]
2. Public current expenditure[b]		
on certain consumption-related goods and services –		
Public health service	30	130
Parks, pleasure grounds, etc.	55	328
Libraries, museums and arts	44	226
Education	1061	5163
National health service	1176	4864
Personal social services	83	958
School meals, etc.	127	397
Social security benefits[c]	109	491
3. Public subsidies to consumption-type services		
Transport and communications[d]	77	420
Other industry and trade[d]	3	315
Agriculture and food	237	1378
Housing	169	1051
Total of public expenditure (2+3)	3171	15721
Total private plus public expenditure (1+2+3)	26016	79094
Public as % of total expenditure	12.2	19.9
Total consumption as % of private consumption	113.9	124.8

a. Expenditure on 'Chemists' goods' is the nearest, and inadequate, approximation
b. The source gives capital expenditure also
c. Excluding transfer payments
d. Half of total subsidies are attributed here to household consumption

Source: U.K. Central Statistical Office *National Income and Expenditure* 1965–75, HMSO 1976 Table 4.9 for private expenditure and Table 10.2 for public expenditure (comprising Central and local government)

penditure on medical, educational, recreational, etc. facilities and various forms of income in kind; again, the cost – if known – might be regarded as a kind of involuntary subsidy to the consumption of some members of the community financed by expenditure on the goods produced by the benefi-cent enterprises. However, this seems to be a matter of allocation of ex-penditure between the various categories of goods and services rather than calling for any adjustment of aggregates.

* * *

5. CONCLUDING NOTE

This paper, it will be seen, is conservative in approach. No fundamental recasting of the SNA or redefining of the main aggregates is proposed; much progress would indeed be made if more countries could fill with actual figures some important gaps in the present system.

But I have tried to stress that the new arguments – or, rather the revival of old arguments – about the content and purposes of national accounts now call for an effort to meet a wider range of statistical needs for policy and analysis, especially for *long-term* policy and analysis; and that these needs should be met in a manner which conforms with and complements the national accounting framework. It is not the function of official statistical offices to prescribe any one definition of the nebulous concept of 'welfare'; but they can reasonably be asked to provide for general use, so far as this is practicable and useful for many social purposes, more details of the building blocks from which the national accounts are constructed, and the blocks of information from which experimental alternative constructions can be built by the serious user.

The Fix-Point Estimation Method and a Revision
of the 69-C Annual Model

B. H. HASSELMAN, J. J. POST AND C. A. VAN DEN BELD[*]

1. INTRODUCTION

For nearly two decades P. J. Verdoorn has worked on the construction of annual models for the Dutch economy (the models 61, 63-D and 69-C), which were intended to be used for both forecasting and policy evaluation purposes.[1] These models are simultaneous and, as is well known, Ordinary Least Squares (OLS) is not an appropriate estimation method for simultaneous systems. For the final versions of the models, therefore, use was made of simultaneous estimation methods, such as Limited Information Maximum Likelihood and Two Stage Least Squares (TSLS). Recently, however, Van der Giessen [5] applied the (Recursive) Fix-Point estimation method to the 69-C model. His results suggest that the annual model might benefit from the application of this method.

The present paper reports on an experiment with Fix-Point estimation with respect to a revised version of the 69-C model. The revised model is fully based on recent ideas of Verdoorn, which implies that its specification resembles that of its predecessor. The estimation methods used are Ordinary Least Squares and Recursive Fix-Point. The plan of this paper is as follows. In Section 2 a brief introduction to the Recursive Fix-Point estimation method is given. Section 3 describes the model and examines the estimation results. Section 4 considers the predictive power of the model in a dynamic context and the economic characteristics of the model by means of an impulse analysis. In Section 5 some conclusions are formulated.

2. THE FIX-POINT ESTIMATION METHOD

Large econometric models present a well-known problem for the model-builder as far as the application of simultaneous estimation methods is

* We would like to thank R. J. A. den Haan for his assistance in the computational work and H. den Hartog for his comments on earlier versions of this paper.
1. A description of these models can be found in [2], [11] and [12].

concerned. The sample period is often small and the number of observations is often, if not always, insufficient either for estimating the unrestricted reduced form (necessary for the first stage of Two Stage Least Squares) or for calculating the variance-covariance matrix of the residuals, which has to be non-singular (necessary for Full Information Maximum Likelihood). The second problem, of singularity of the variance-covariance matrix, is unsolvable. A solution to the first problem, proposed by Kloek and Mennes [7], is the use of principal components, where a subset of principal components of the entire set of predetermined and exogenous variables is used as an approximation to the unrestricted reduced form. The selection of the subset of principal components, however, is quite arbitrary and different model-builders could easily obtain quite different estimates of the coefficients of the model. Wold has suggested a way out of this problem with his Fix-Point estimation method. The method will be illustrated with an overidentified two equation-model (Summers-model)

$$y_1 = \alpha_1 y_2 + \beta_1 x_1 + \beta_2 x_2 + v_1 \tag{2.1}$$

$$y_2 = \alpha_2 y_1 + \beta_3 x_3 + \beta_4 x_4 + v_2 \tag{2.2}$$

where

y_1, y_2 : endogenous variables
x_1, x_2, x_3, x_4 : exogenous variables
v_1, v_2 : residuals.

The reduced form of this system is

$$y_1 = \frac{\beta_1 x_1 + \beta_2 x_2}{1 - \alpha_1 \alpha_2} + \frac{\alpha_1 \beta_3 x_3 + \alpha_1 \beta_4 x_4}{1 - \alpha_1 \alpha_2} + \frac{v_1 + \alpha_1 v_2}{1 - \alpha_1 \alpha_2} \tag{2.3}$$

$$y_2 = \frac{\alpha_2 \beta_1 x_1 + \alpha_2 \beta_2 x_2}{1 - \alpha_1 \alpha_2} + \frac{\beta_3 x_3 + \beta_4 x_4}{1 - \alpha_1 \alpha_2} + \frac{\alpha_2 v_1 + v_2}{1 - \alpha_1 \alpha_2} \tag{2.4}$$

A rigorous discussion of the Fix-Point estimation method is beyond the scope of this paper. An intuitive justification of Fix-Point is, however, available, when it is seen as a modification of the TSLS method. The TSLS-procedure can be described as follows:

– regress y_1 and y_2 on x_1, x_2, x_3 and x_4; the resulting residuals are denoted by w_1 and w_2
– regress y_1 on $(y_2 - w_2)$, x_1 and x_2
– regress y_2 on $(y_1 - w_2)$, x_3 and x_4

The reduced form residuals, w_1 and w_2, are called unrestricted as they are estimated without taking into account restrictions imposed on the coefficients of x_1, x_2, x_3 and x_4 in eqs. (2.3) and (2.4) by the structure of the model as given by eqs. (2.1) and (2.2).

The Fix-Point method does not use the unrestricted reduced form residuals w_1 and w_2 but the residuals of the restricted reduced form (call these u_1 and u_2), and then regresses y_1 on (y_2-u_2), x_1 and x_2 and y_2 on (y_1-u_1), x_3 and x_4. The obvious difficulty associated with this method is how to obtain estimates of u_1 and u_2. Straightforward computation is not possible; some iterative method has to be used. The procedure that has been used in estimating the revised 69-C model is the Recursive Fix-Point method (RFP) developed by Bodin [1]. In terms of the model given by equations (2.1) and (2.2) this procedure can be illustrated as follows, where the superscript's' refers to the iteration:

- regress y_1 on $y_2-u_2^{(s-1)}$, x_1 and x_2; the residual is $u_1^{(s)}$.
- regress y_2 on $y_1-u_1^{(s)}$, x_3 and x_4; the residual is $u_2^{(s)}$.
- repeat these two regressions in the given order until the estimated parameters differ less than a specified amount in two consecutive iterations.

In iteration 1 $u_2^{(s-1)}$ is not available; the simplest solution of this problem is to set $u_2^{(s-1)}$ equal to zero, implying that in the first iteration the first equation is estimated with OLS. Once the procedure has converged the residuals u_1 and u_2 are the reduced form residuals. This can be shown, when the estimated model is written as follows

$$y_1 = \alpha_1(y_2 - u_2) + \beta_1 x_1 + \beta_2 x_2 + u_1 \tag{2.5}$$

$$y_2 = \alpha_2(y_1 - u_1) + \beta_3 x_3 + \beta_4 x_4 + u_2 \tag{2.6}$$

The reduced form equations of this system are

$$y_1 = \frac{\beta_1 x_1 + \beta_2 x_2}{1 - \alpha_1 \alpha_2} + \frac{\alpha_1 \beta_3 x_3 + \alpha_1 \beta_4 x_4}{1 - \alpha_1 \alpha_2} + u_1 \tag{2.7}$$

$$y_1 = \frac{\alpha_2 \beta_1 x_1 + \alpha_2 \beta_2 x_2}{1 - \alpha_1 \alpha_2} + \frac{\beta_3 x_3 + \beta_4 x_4}{1 - \alpha_1 \alpha_2} + u_2 \tag{2.8}$$

which proves the proposition. For non-linear systems the same holds (see EDGERTON [3]). For an excellent survey of the Fix-Point estimation method, an extensive list of references and a discussion of the statistical properties of the Fix-Point method, the reader is referred to Lyttkens [9].

The method, outlined above, is equivalent to solving a system of non-linear equations by the non-linear Gauss-Seidel method and applying Ordinary Least Squares to the stochastic equations, using as regressors the calculated values for the endogenous variables.[2] In order to apply Gauss-Seidel an ordering of the equations is needed (a sequence of solution); for a large model a gigantic number of orderings is possible and there is no guarantee that an arbitrarily chosen one will provide convergence. Van der Giessen has proposed a method for obtaining an ordering, which in our experience always provided convergence (the algorithm will not be discussed here: see Van der Giessen [4] and Bodin [1]). In order to calculate the RFP-estimates for the model to be discussed in the next sections, 15 to 20 iterations were needed to obtain an accuracy of 10^{-3} in the coefficients. The procedure implies that the usual statistics (t-ratio's, R^2 and the Von Neumann-ratio) for the RFP-estimates are based on the reduced form residuals and therefore cannot be compared to their OLS counterparts. This should be kept in mind when examining the results of Section 3.

3. THE STRUCTURE OF THE MODEL AND THE ESTIMATION RESULTS

3.1. *Introduction*

This section has two aims. The first one is to provide a bird's eye view of the general structure of the model and a brief summary of the main elements in the structural equations; this will be done in Subsection 3.2. Differences between the present model and its predecessor will be pointed out in the course of the discussion, whenever necessary. The second aim is to examine the consequences of using Ordinary Least Squares and Recursive Fix-Point in the estimation of the model; in Subsection 3.3 the estimation procedure will be examined and in Subsection 3.4 the estimation results are assessed.

The equations of the complete model and a list of symbols are given in the Appendix to this paper; the estimation results appear in Table 1. The sample period covers the years 1925–1938 and 1953–1972; the subperiods are referred to as the pre-war and post-war (sample) periods respectively.[3]

3.2. *The Structure of the Model*

The model contains both demand and supply elements. The demand side consists of two markets, one for goods and services and one for labour. Final demand for goods and services consists of six components: private

2. For an extensive discussion of the non-linear Gauss-Seidel and related methods, see Ortega and Rheinboldt [10].
3. For the 69-C model the corresponding periods were 1923–1938 and 1949–1966.

consumption, gross business investment (excluding housing, ships and aeroplanes), exports of goods, autonomous expenditure (comprising investment in housing, ships and aeroplanes, government material consumption and -investment), stockbuilding and net exports of invisibles. Autonomous expenditures and net exports of invisibles are exogenous in the model. On the demand side of the labour market employment in enterprises (wage earners) is endogenous whereas government employment is exogenous.

Total final demand can be met from two sources: domestic productive capacity and imports. The former is determined by available capital, when capital is relatively scarce and by labour supply, when labour is relatively scarce; the latter is related to the components of final demand. Labour supply depends mainly on demographic factors, while changes in available capital are seen to be generated by net business investment. An equation for the wage rate in enterprises and four price equations (for private consumption, gross business investment, exports of goods and autonomous expenditures) complete the supply side of the model. Finally the model has a simple monetary sector, consisting of an equation for the mass of liquidities.

The main differences between the present model and its predecessor are the replacement of the equation for unemployment by an equation for labour supply, the explicit introduction of the concept of surplus capacity, and the use of real wage costs as one of the explanatory variables in the labour demand equation. Minor differences are involved in the definition of business investment and labour productivity.[4]

Thus, one of the new elements in the model is the introduction of the concept of surplus capacity. Its basic idea is that surplus capacity is seen as being determined by available plant and machinery when labour is abundant, and by labour supply when capital is abundant. In the first case surplus capacity is determined as follows

$$\tilde{q}_k = 100 \left(\beta \frac{\tilde{h}_c^{.75} \tilde{k}_{-1}}{\tilde{y}} - 1 \right) \tag{3.2.1}$$

where

$\tilde{q}_k$ = relative surplus capacity when labour is relatively abundant
$\tilde{h}_c$ = index of contractual working hours

---

4. In the present model business investment includes investment of government enterprises, which in the 69-c model was included in autonomous expenditures. Labour productivity is now defined as gross business value added divided by employment in enterprises. Pre-war labour productivity in the consumption-price equation is defined in the 69-c way, i.e. as the ratio of adjusted total sales (v') to employment in enterprises.

$\tilde{k}_{-1}$ = capital stock, beginning of period
$\tilde{y}$ = production of enterprises
β = a parameter

The elasticity of .75 for contractual working hours is based on the existence of multiple shift industries where shortening of working hours may have no effect on production. The parameter β has been chosen in such a way that for the post-war sample period (1953–1972) the ratio of $\tilde{q}_k$ to $\tilde{q}_a$ (see eq. (3.2.2)) equals 1, which implies that β is a normalized output capital ratio.

In the second case, of labour scarcity, surplus capacity is determined by a transformation of the rate of unemployment

$$\tilde{q}_a = 100(1.01 + .02\tilde{w}')^2 - 100 \tag{3.2.2}$$

where

$\tilde{q}_a$ = relative surplus capacity when labour is relatively scarce
$\tilde{w}'$ = $(\tilde{W}/\bar{a})\,100$
$\tilde{W}$ = number of unemployed
$\bar{a}$ = employment in enterprises (wage-earners)

Eq. (3.2.2) implies that:

– 1% more labour input leads to 2% more production, given sufficient capital.
– total unemployment, the sum of registered and non-registered unemployment, is assumed to be twice as large as registered unemployment; additionally, it is assumed that labour hoarding by enterprises amounts to 1% of existing employment.

The effective rate of surplus capacity is the minimum of $\tilde{q}_a$ and $\tilde{q}_k$. However, as the model is simultaneous a continuous weighting of $\tilde{q}_a$ and $\tilde{q}_k$ is chosen in order to prevent difficulties arising from the iterative solution of the model. The method used in the weighting is analogous to the Constant Elasticity of Substitution function

$$\tilde{q} = [.5\tilde{q}_k^{-\rho} + .5\tilde{q}_a^{-\rho}]^{-1/\rho} \tag{3.2.3}$$

where

$\tilde{q}$ = rate of surplus capacity
ρ = a positive parameter

If the parameter ρ is very large, eq. (3.2.3) tends to its limit

$$\tilde{q} = \min(\tilde{q}_a, \tilde{q}_k) \tag{3.2.4}$$

In the model ρ was given the value 8; a modification of the procedure was necessary for the pre-war period as no data on pre-war capital stock were available: $\tilde{q}_k$ was simply assumed to equal $\tilde{q}_a$, which had to be defined differently in order to prevent $\tilde{q}_a$ becoming too large, due to high unemployment rates (see Appendix eq. 40).

The procedure outlined above is merely a technical matter and should not be interpreted as implying substitutability of capital and labour. From the discussion of the determination of surplus capacity it can be seen that capital and labour have been assumed to be complementary production factors in the short run.

This completes the description of the major new elements in the model. The remaining (structural) equations will now be discussed in their order of occurrence in the Appendix and Table 1.

Private consumption is determined mainly by disposable wage- and transfer income and disposable non-wage income, both with a constant marginal propensity to consume. Price changes occurring between deciding to spend income and actual spending are assumed not to effect the volume of consumption. This implies some dissaving in the short run, when prices rise. The labour market situation has some influence too on private consumption. The main difference with the 69-C consumption equation is the assumption of constant marginal propensities to consume instead of constant elasticities for the income variables. Statistically, the two assumptions are equivalent; from a theoretical point of view, however, the first assumption is easier to interpret than the second, which is the reason for preferring the former to the latter.

Business investment depends on demand factors such as the lagged growth rate of production and unlagged surplus capacity; and on financial factors: gross disposable profits and liquidities available at the beginning of the year. Some influence of autonomous changes in fiscal investment and depreciation allowances and of a price accelerator was also found. New in comparison to the investment equation of the 69-C model are the lagged growth rate of production and the autonomous changes in investment and depreciation allowances. Exports are determined by the same factors as in the 69-C model: world trade, relative export prices, profit margins and finally, surplus capacity as a proxy for 'home pressure of demand'. The stock formation equation has been derived from a flexible accelerator adjustment model and its specification is identical to the equation in the 69-C model.

The main factors determining imports are sales excluding stock formation and net invisibles, together with stock formation as a separate variable; the margin between the price of imports and domestic sales and trade policy measures also have some effect on imports[5]. The present import equation is a simplified version of the 69-c equation; only the main influences determining imports have been retained. No statistically significant influence of pressure of demand could be found.

Employment in enterprises is related to an indicator of output of enterprises and real wage costs. For the pre-war period total sales, reweighted according to the labour intensity of final demand components, was chosen as output variable, while real wage costs were assumed constant. For the post-war period gross value added (production) appeared to be the best output indicator. In the case of (reweighted) sales the margin between the price of imports and domestic sales was added as explanatory factor in order to compensate for import substitution. For the post-war period lagged real wage costs and the change in contractual working hours were included as additional determinants of employment growth.

Registered labour supply depends on population growth, the real wage rate, the lagged participation rate, supposed to represent a lower reserve of labour at a higher level of participation, and finally on lagged unemployment. Some dummy variables had to be added for the pre-war period.

The wage rate in enterprises simply depends on the price of consumption, labour productivity and unemployment. All four prices, for private consumption, business investment, exports and autonomous expenditures depend mainly on labour costs and import prices. Influence of pressure of demand could only be found in the case of the price of investment.

Finally, liquidities are determined by demand factors such as the value of domestic sales, inventory formation and supply factors such as the balance of payments, trade credit and inflationary government financing.

All structural equations have now been accounted for; in the next subsection the estimation procedure will be discussed.

3.3. *The Estimation Procedure*
Before examining the estimation results, the procedure by which the specification of the current model was arrived at needs some elaboration. For each structural equation an extensive screening with Ordinary Least Squares was carried out. Particular attention was paid to possible differences between

---

5. The price of domestic sales was used instead of the price of total sales as the import share of exports of goods consists mainly of imported raw materials, assumed to be (almost) complementary to output.

pre- and post-war coefficients of the behavioural equations.[6] These differences appeared to be of some importance in all equations, except in the equations for private consumption, stockbuilding and the price of autonomous expenditures (see Table 1). Whether they are due to actual structural changes in the behaviour of the economy, mis-specification of the relevant equations or poor quality of the pre-war relative to the post-war time-series, is difficult, if not impossible, to judge.

The results of the OLS-screening procedure were subsequently used as a starting point for a preliminary Recursive Fix-Point estimation of the model; the outcomes indicated that some of the stochastic equations were not correctly specified. Next, alternative specifications, satisfactory from both a statistical and an economic point of view, were tested, largely on a trial and error basis. These tests will not be discussed in this paper. It is, however, possible to formulate some general conclusions. First, high goodness of fit of an OLS-estimated equation hardly guarantees succesful Fix-Point estimation. The second conclusion that may be drawn from the experiments is that the Fix-Point estimation method tends to leave the modelbuilder with only the bare essentials of each equation. An indication of this phenomenon is the number of estimated coefficients in the present model (58) which is much smaller that the corresponding number in the 69-C model (91). A possible disadvantage associated with this tendency is that theoretically important variables may vanish, in the sense that the coefficients of these variables become quantitatively negligible or have the wrong sign. As Fix-Point is a full information method in that it utilizes all the information contained in the restrictions imposed on the reduced form by the structure of the model, this may be caused by misspecification of either the relevant equation or some other equation(s)[7]. As far as the authors know, no foolproof methods, applicable to Fix-Point estimation, exist for tracing cases of misspecification. Consequently, the researcher only has recourse to a careful consideration of the specification of each equation within the framework of the whole model, in any case a prerequisite for model construction, but of particular importance in full-information simultaneous estimation.

Summarizing, the specification of the present model is the result of screening with OLS and subsequently with RFP. The final version was re-estimated with OLS. These OLS-results should therefore be interpreted as

---

6. In his investigation of the 63-D model Kooyman [8] found this to be important.
7. In contrast to Full Information Maximum Likelihood (FIML) Fix-Point is not a full information method in the sense that it utilizes the variance-covariance matrix of the residuals of the stochastic equations.

TABLE 1.

The results of OLS and RFP estimation (sample period 1925–1938 and 1953–1972).

1. Private consumption (C)

RFP

$$C = C_{aut} + 1.057 \left(\frac{\tilde{L}^D}{\tilde{C}}\right)_{-1} L^D_{-\frac{1}{4}} + .187 \left(\frac{\tilde{Z}^D}{\tilde{C}}\right)_{-1} Z^{D'}_{-\frac{1}{4}} + .342\Delta p_c - 1.898\Delta\tilde{w}_{l-\frac{1}{4}} - .308$$

$$(18.9) \qquad\qquad (1.9) \qquad\qquad (3.6) \qquad (3.0) \qquad (1.0)$$

$$R^2 = .947 \quad \text{VNR} = 2.14$$

OLS

$$C = C_{aut} + 1.009 \left(\frac{\tilde{L}^D}{\tilde{C}}\right)_{-1} L^D_{-\frac{1}{4}} + .254 \left(\frac{\tilde{Z}^D}{\tilde{C}}\right)_{-1} Z^{D'}_{-\frac{1}{4}} + .362\Delta p_c - 1.298\Delta\tilde{w}_{l-\frac{1}{4}} - .305$$

$$(28.7) \qquad\qquad (4.1) \qquad\qquad (5.8) \qquad (3.1) \qquad (1.3)$$

$$R^2 = .979 \quad \text{VNR} = 1.96$$

2. Gross business investment (excl. housing, ships and aeroplanes) (I)

RFP

$$I = I_{aut} + .160 \{(\tilde{y}/\tilde{i})_{-1} y\}_{-1^{1}/_3} + .843 ZNG_{-1\frac{1}{2}} + .533(1 + 1.664d_1)\Delta p_i - 10.451(1 + .866d_1) \Delta\tilde{Q} +$$

$$(3.3) \qquad\qquad (1.6) \qquad\qquad (5.0) \qquad\qquad (2.7)$$

$$+ .625 G_{-1} + 15.157 VAY - 1.469$$

$$(3.4) \qquad (2.3) \qquad (.8)$$

$$R^2 = .843 \quad \text{VNR} = 1.80$$

OLS

$$I = I_{aut} + .101 \{(\tilde{y}/\tilde{i})_{-1} y\}_{-1^{1}/_3} + .882 ZNG_{-1\frac{1}{2}} + .403(1 + 1.664d_1) \Delta p_i - 19.917(1 + .866d_1) \Delta\tilde{Q} +$$

$$(3.4) \qquad\qquad (2.8) \qquad\qquad (6.6) \qquad\qquad (8.3)$$

$$+ .515 G_{-1} + 14.642 VAY + 1.687$$

$$(4.8) \qquad (3.8) \qquad (.4)$$

$$R^2 = .946 \quad \text{VNR} = 1.97$$

3. Exports of goods (b)

RFP

$$b = b_{aut} + .993 m_{Tw} - 2.330 \left\{\frac{1}{3}\sum_0^2 (p_b - p'_b)_{-i}\right\} - .412(k_n - p_b)_{-\frac{1}{4}} + 10.006 d_2 \Delta\tilde{Q}_{-\frac{1}{4}} + .595$$

$$(10.0) \qquad (3.2) \qquad\qquad\qquad\qquad (1.5) \qquad\qquad\qquad (2.6)$$

$$R^2 = .858 \quad \text{VNR} = 1.84$$

OLS

$$b = b_{aut} + .991 m_{rw} - 2.397 \left\{ \frac{1}{3} \sum_0^2 P_b - p_b)_{-i} \right\} - 487(k_n - p_b)_{-\frac{1}{4}} + 10.015 d_2 \Delta \tilde{Q}_{-\frac{1}{4}} + .698$$
$$(11.0) \quad (3.6) \quad\quad (1.8) \quad\quad (2.5) \quad\quad (.8)$$
$$R^2 = .866 \quad \text{VNR} = 2.00$$

4. Stock formation (N)

RFP

$$N = .231 v'_{-1/3} - .768 N_{-1} - .976(100 \check{N}_{-2}/\bar{V}'_{-1}) + .144 p_m + .257 i^* - .108$$
$$(3.1) \quad (6.3) \quad (7.4) \quad\quad (5.7) \quad (3.9) \quad (.8)$$
$$R^2 = .742 \quad \text{VNR} = 2.12$$

OLS

$$N = .284 v'_{-1/3} - .792 N_{-1} - 1.039(100 \check{N}_{-2}/\bar{V}'_{-1}) + .135 p_m + .280 t^* - .347$$
$$(3.7) \quad (6.9) \quad (8.0) \quad\quad (5.5) \quad (4.4) \quad (.8)$$
$$R^2 = .769 \quad \text{VNR} = 2.10$$

5. Imports of goods (m)

RFP

$$m = .976 v' + 2.110 N - .650(.1 d_1 p_{m-vd} + d_2 p_{m-vd-1}) + .364 \widetilde{TP} + .826$$
$$(5.1) \quad (6.4) \quad (3.0) \quad\quad\quad (4.7) \quad (.8)$$
$$R^2 = .889 \quad \text{VNR} = 1.85$$

OLS

$$m = 1.296 v' + 1.823 N - .389(.1 d_1 p_{m-vd} + d_2 p_{m-vd-1}) + .231 \widetilde{TP} - .405$$
$$(9.6) \quad (9.5) \quad (2.5) \quad\quad\quad (4.3) \quad (.5)$$
$$R^2 = .945 \quad \text{VNR} = 2.94$$

6. Employment in enterprises (a)

RFP

$$a = .630 d_1 v_a + .102 d_1 p_{m-vd} + .287 d_2 y_{-1/3} - .399 h_{c-1} - .915 d_2 PLY - 3.930 d_1 + 3.841$$
$$(7.3) \quad (3.1) \quad\quad (2.6) \quad\quad (1.1) \quad (2.9) \quad (2.6)$$
$$R^2 = .790 \quad \text{VNR} = 1.89$$

OLS

$$a = .612 d_1 v_a + .079 d_1 p_{m-vd} + .362 d_2 y_{-1/3} - .475 h_{c-1} - .843 d_2 PLY - 3.252 d_1 + 3.062$$
$$(12.3) \quad (3.6) \quad\quad (4.0) \quad\quad (2.1) \quad (3.9) \quad (2.9) \quad (2.8)$$
$$R^2 = .904 \quad \text{VNR} = 1.99$$

TABLE 1 (continued)

7. Dependent working population (a_a)

RFP

$$a_a = a_x + .125(l - p_c)_{532} - .531 \Delta \tilde{w}_{-\frac{1}{2}} - .336(100\bar{a}_a/\bar{a}_x)_{-1} + 3.188 d_{29} + 2.239\, d_{3233} - 1.320 d_1 + 19.179$$
$$\quad\quad\quad\;\; (1.4)\quad\quad\quad (7.7)\quad\quad\quad (4.7)\quad\quad\quad\quad\quad (7.1)\quad\quad (7.0)\quad\quad (2.8)\quad\quad (4.0)$$

$$R^2 = .850 \quad \text{VNR} = 2.10$$

OLS

$$a_a = a_x + .102(l - p_c)_{532} - .507 \Delta \tilde{w}_{-\frac{1}{2}} - .371(100\tilde{a}_a/\tilde{a}_x)_{-1} + 2.448 d_{29} + 1.827 d_{3233} - 1.365 d_1 + 18.471$$
$$\quad\quad\quad\;\; (1.2)\quad\quad\quad (7.2)\quad\quad\quad (4.3)\quad\quad\quad\quad\quad (5.1)\quad\quad (5.5)\quad\quad (2.7)\quad\quad (4.4)$$

$$R^2 = .850 \quad \text{VNR} = 1.87$$

8. Wage rate in enterprises (l)

RFP

$$l = .953\{(.85 - .4d_1)\, p_c + (.15 + .11 d_1)\, p_{c-1}\} + .713\, d_2(y - a)_{-\frac{1}{2}} - .863\{d_1 \tilde{w}_{l-1} + .5\, d_2 \tilde{w}_l + .25\, d_2 \tilde{w}_{l-1}\} - 7.024$$
$$(10.3)\quad\quad\quad\quad\quad\quad\quad\quad\quad\quad\quad\quad\quad (4.4)\quad\quad\quad\quad (4.4)\quad\quad\quad\quad\quad\quad\quad\quad (4.8)$$

$$R^2 = .946 \quad \text{VNR} = 2.07$$

OLS

$$l = 1.033\{(.85 - .4d_1)\, p_c + (.15 + .11 d_1)\, p_{c-1}\} + .705\, d_2(y - a)_{-\frac{1}{2}} - .705\{d_1 \tilde{w}_{l-1} + .5\, d_2 \tilde{w}_l + .25\, d_2 \tilde{w}_{l-1}\} - 6.118$$
$$(10.3)\quad\quad\quad\quad\quad\quad\quad\quad\quad\quad\quad\quad\quad (3.9)\quad\quad\quad\quad (4.2)\quad\quad\quad\quad\quad\quad\quad\quad (4.9)$$

$$R^2 = .961 \quad \text{VNR} = 1.53$$

9. Price of private consumption (p_c)

RFP

$$p_c = p_{cau} + .446\, k_c - .459\, Z^*_{c-1} + 2.002\, d_1 \Delta \bar{r}_{k-2/3} + .594$$
$$\quad\quad\quad\quad (7.6)\quad\quad (3.0)\quad\quad\quad (2.8)\quad\quad\quad (2.0)$$

$$R^2 = .850 \quad \text{VNR} = 1.43$$

OLS

$$p_c = p_{cau} + .464\, k_c - .526\, Z^*_{c-1} + 1.910\, d_1 \Delta \bar{r}_{k-2/3} + .594$$
$$\quad\quad\quad\quad (10.6)\quad\quad (4.5)\quad\quad\quad (3.4)\quad\quad\quad (2.5)$$

$$R^2 = .909 \quad \text{VNR} = 1.26$$

10. Price of exports (p_b)

RFP

$$p_b = .681\,k_n + .536\,p'_{b-\frac{1}{4}} + .151\,\Delta m_{Tw} + 2.824\,d_1 - 1.745 \qquad R^2 = .972 \ \text{VNR} = 2.22$$
$$(6.6)\qquad(5.5)\qquad\quad(4.5)\qquad\qquad(5.4)\qquad\quad(4.9)$$

OLS

$$p_b = .604\,k_n + .599\,p'_{b-\frac{1}{4}} + .156\,\Delta m_{Tw} + 2.606\,d_1 - 1.568 \qquad R^2 = .969 \ \text{VNR} = 2.37$$
$$(5.9)\qquad(6.1)\qquad\quad(4.3)\qquad\qquad(4.7)\qquad\quad(4.2)$$

11. Price of business investment (p_i)

RFP

$$p_i = .322\,H_{-\frac{1}{4}} + .248\,p_{mi-1/6} + .322\,p_{mr-1/3} - 4.890\,d_2\,\Delta\tilde{Q}_{-\frac{1}{4}} + .924 \qquad R^2 = .935 \ \text{VNR} = 2.77$$
$$(5.3)\qquad\quad(4.0)\qquad\qquad(6.5)\qquad\qquad(3.1)\qquad\qquad(3.0)$$

OLS

$$p_i = .341\,H_{-\frac{1}{4}} + .236\,p_{mi-1/6} + .329\,p_{mr-1/3} - 2.884\,d_2\,\Delta\tilde{Q}_{-\frac{1}{4}} + .892 \qquad R^2 = .949 \ \text{VNR} = 2.85$$
$$(6.8)\qquad\quad(4.2)\qquad\qquad(7.5)\qquad\qquad(2.0)\qquad\qquad(3.3)$$

12. Price of autonomous expenditure (p_x)

RFP

$$p_x = .620\,l - .207\,(y - a) + .430\,p_{m-1/4} - .181 \qquad R^2 = .854 \ \text{VNR} = 1.53$$
$$(6.6)\quad(1.2)\qquad\qquad(7.1)\qquad\quad(.3)$$

OLS

$$p_x = .676\,l - .384\,(y - a) + .407\,p_{m-1/4} - .056 \qquad R^2 = .908 \ \text{VNR} = 1.68$$
$$(9.9)\quad(3.1)\qquad\qquad(8.5)\qquad\quad(.1)$$

TABLE 1 (continued)

13. Liquidities (G)

RFP

$$G = .848\,V'_{D-1/3} + .598\,(1 + 3.119\,d_1)\,N + 1.882\,\bar{E}_D + 4.018\,\{100\bar{H}_{K-5/12}/\bar{V}'_{D-1}\} + 2.058\,\{100\bar{S}_{c-1/3}/\bar{V}'_{D-1}\} +$$

$$(7.9) \qquad (5.7) \qquad\qquad (6.3) \qquad (2.9) \qquad\qquad (4.7)$$

$$+ 3.866\,\{\Delta\tilde{r}_{L-1/6} - .76\,(1 + .605\,d_1)\,\Delta\tilde{r}_K\} - 2.537$$

$$(4.8) \qquad\qquad\qquad (2.5)$$

$$R^2 = .805 \quad \text{VNR} = 2.00$$

OLS

$$G = .716\,V'_{D-1/3} + .524\,(1 + 3.119\,d_1)\,N + 1.092\,\bar{E}_D + 4.195\,\{100\bar{H}_{K-5/12}/\bar{V}'_{D-1}\} + 2.162\,\{100\bar{S}_{c-1/3}/\bar{V}'_{D-1}\} +$$

$$(8.4) \qquad (6.7) \qquad\qquad (7.0) \qquad (3.4) \qquad\qquad (5.6)$$

$$+ 4.456\,\{\Delta\tilde{r}_{L-1/6} - .76\,(1 + .605\,d_1)\,\Delta\tilde{r}_K\} - 1.885$$

$$(5.9) \qquad\qquad\qquad (2.2)$$

$$R^2 = .850 \quad \text{VNR} = 1.60$$

OLS: Ordinary Least Squares; RFP: Recursive Fix-Point.

Below each coefficient a t-ratio is given between parentheses.

R^2 = coefficient of multiple determination.

VNR = Von Neumann ratio.

d_1 = 1 in the period 1925–1938

    = 0 in the period 1953–1972

$d_2 = 1 - d_1$

The symbols are explained in the Appendix; a complete version of the model including definition equations is also given in the Appendix.

single equation estimates of a specification obtained by means of a simultaneous estimation technique. Table 1 gives both the OLS and the RFP estimation results.

3.4. *Estimation Results*

The two methods used in estimating the model will be compared to one another in two ways. First, the parameter estimates are discussed. Then, the performance of both versions of the model within the sample period is evaluated.

Examination of the estimation results, given in Table 1, shows some remarkable differences between the OLS and RFP estimates. In the business investment equation (equation 2, Table 1) the coefficient of the growth of production variable as estimated by RFP is more than 50% higher than the corresponding OLS estimate. The opposite (in absolute value) holds for the coefficient of effective surplus capacity. Several explanations for this phenomenon can be thought of. The first one is misspecification of the investment equation. Secondly, the simultaneous equation bias associated with OLS, in this case at least, is rather large. Thirdly, misspecification somewhere else in the model may cause the difference, a possibility mentioned in the previous subsection. The second explanation seems most likely, especially since in the 69-C model a similar tendency occurred in the Limited Information Maximum Likelihood estimation of the investment equation. The third possibility cannot, however, be rejected off-hand. Another example of a large difference between OLS and RFP estimates concerns the import equation (equation 5, Table 1); the coefficient of the relative price variable changes from $-.389$ (OLS) to $-.650$ (RFP) .The latter estimate, as compared to the former, seems more reasonable, in view of the high proportion of price sensitive components in imports.

In most cases, however, the difference between the OLS and RFP estimates cause no undue alarm. One might conjecture that the specific OLS-estimation procedure is the main explanation. A comparison of the distribution of the differences between the OLS and RFP estimates for the present model and its predecessor, the 69-C model, the main structure of which was not the result of RFP-estimation, confirms this to some extent (see Table 2).

Especially worth mentioning is that the proportion of differences greater than 50% (Column 3, Table 2) for the present model is about half as large as the corresponding proportion in the 69-C model.

We now turn to the evaluation of the performance of both versions of the

TABLE 2.

Distribution of the differences between the OLS- and RFP-estimates for the present model and the 69-C model[a].

	1	2	3
69–C[b]	.341	.472	.187
present model	.500	.414	.086

a. The differences have been calculated as $|(C_{RFP}-C_{OLS})/C_{OLS}|$ where C_j denotes the parameter estimate for estimation method j.
The number of differences is given as a proportion of the total number of parameters of the corresponding model. Columns 1–3 refer to differences less than 10%, between 10 and 50% and larger than 50% respectively.
b. Calculated from the results obtained by Van der Giessen [4].

model within the sample period. If one compares the R^2's of each stochastic equation, as given in Table 1 for the OLS and the RFP estimations, it would be tempting to conclude that in most cases OLS scores better than RFP. However, the R^2's for RFP are based on the reduced form residuals, as was explained in Section 2; for OLS this is not the case. The only comparison possible must be based on the reduced form residuals of both versions of the model, which requires the calculation of such residuals for the OLS-case too. Then, the statistic used for the comparison is the root mean square error (RMSE) defined as

$$\left(\sum_{t=1}^{T} u_t^2 / T \right)^{\frac{1}{2}}$$

where u_t represents the reduced form residual for period t of the sample period.

For the stochastic equations and a limited number of important variables, such as for instance the level of unemployment, these are tabulated in Table 3 for the sample period as a whole and for three sub-periods, viz. the pre- and post-war sample periods as well as the period covering the last ten years of the sample period.

Comparison of the RMSE's for the sample period as a whole shows that RFP scores better than OLS in nearly all cases. Reductions of more than 10% in RMSE's occur in three cases: business investment (I), imports (m) and employment in enterprises (a). Considering the differences in the coefficients estimates of the first two mentioned equations, the better performance of

TABLE 3.

Root mean square errors of the reduced form residuals[a]

	Model estimated with							
	OLS[b]				RFP			
	25-38	53-72	total	63-72	25-38	53-72	total	63-72
C	1.532	1.398	1.455	1.203	1.408	1.249	1.316	1.121
c	1.932	1.512	1.698	1.678	1.918	1.654	1.768	1.840
I	9.356	4.593	6.961	5.925	6.842	4.560	5.613	4.703
i	8.787	4.697	6.691	5.733	6.638	4.565	5.514	4.324
b	3.710	2.476	3.045	2.262	3.735	2.431	3.037	2.221
N	1.399	.734	1.059	.616	1.323	.720	1.013	.588
m	4.329	2.271	3.279	2.254	3.664	1.983	2.800	2.069
y	2.348	1.595	1.941	1.602	2.239	1.674	1.927	1.667
a	1.988	.732	1.393	.770	1.557	.682	1.128	.746
a_a	.532	.306	.414	.331	.440	.322	.375	.344
$\tilde{W}$	.031	.020	.025	.023	.028	.017	.022	.021
$\tilde{E}_D$	1.969	1.309	1.614	1.422	1.637	1.180	1.386	1.239
p_c	1.719	1.423	1.552	1.398	1.696	1.397	1.527	1.498
p_b	1.447	1.138	1.274	1.116	1.480	1.087	1.264	1.110
p_i	1.604	1.180	1.370	.982	1.580	1.093	1.316	.992
p_x	2.010	2.433	2.269	1.702	2.192	2.319	2.267	1.653
l	1.200	1.603	1.450	1.628	1.161	1.475	1.355	1.533
G	3.295	3.139	3.204	3.326	3.282	2.584	2.892	2.555
$\tilde{q}$	3.284	2.238	2.718	2.363	2.974	2.014	2.455	2.169

a. The symbols are explained in the Appendix.
b. On the basis of RFP-specification (cf. text).

RFP versus OLS is hardly surprising. The case of employment is related to the investment equation, the influence of which asserts itself by means of the (reweighted) sales variable for the pre-war period. For the sub-periods of the total sample largely similar conclusions can be drawn.

In conclusion it may be stated that the estimation of the model with Recursive Fix-Point has yielded satisfactory results and that the performance of the RFP-estimated model on the whole is better than its OLS-rival. The fact remains, however, that neither the OLS- nor the RFP-estimated model can fully explain actual developments. This is already evident from the RMSE's in Table 3. It is illustrated in Figure 1, where for a selected group of

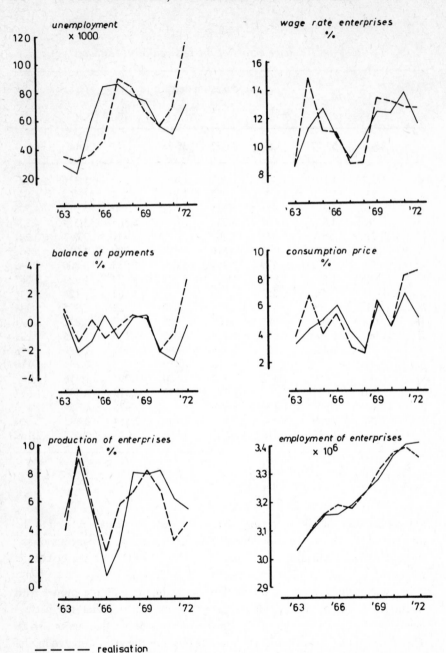

- - - - - realisation
———— prediction RFP

Figure 1. Year-to-year simulation results

variables actual developments are compared with year-to-year predictions of the RFP-estimated model.

4. DYNAMICS OF THE MODEL

4.1. *Introduction*
The model discussed in the previous section contains many lagged endogenous variables. In the estimation of the model as well as in the year-to-year simulation in Figure 1, these variables were set equal to their actual values, i.e. they were regarded as being predetermined. However, when the model is used for predicting a time path of more than one year, lagged endogenous variables cannot be regarded as predetermined, which implies an inconsistency between the assumptions underlying prediction and estimation.

In this paper no attempt will be made to re-estimate the model in a manner consistent with prediction of a time path.[8] The model will only be simulated over a number of years (1963–1967 and 1963–1972) in order to obtain an impression as to its medium- and long-term prediction properties. This is done in Subsection 4.2. In Subsection 4.3 some multipliers are computed; these give an indication of the economic properties of the system.

4.2. *Dynamic Simulation of the Model*
The computations involved in preparing a dynamic simulation proceed as follows. For the first period of the time path all lagged endogenous variables are set equal to their actual values; then the model is solved. For the second period all one period lagged endogenous variables are set equal to the values predicted by the model for the corresponding variables in the previous period. For the third and consecutive periods the procedure is analogous.

For the present model such a dynamic simulation has been carried out for the last ten years of the sample period (1963–1972) as well as for the medium-term 1963–67. The resulting root mean square errors (RMSE's) for the same set of variables as in Table 3, can be found in Table 4. These results do not point to a clear superiority of RFP to OLS. For the ten year simulation RFP scores better than OLS in 5 cases out of a total of 13; for the five year simulation the corresponding number is 8. For the level variable unemployment ($\tilde{W}$), the balance of payments as a percentage of domestic sales ($\tilde{E}_D$) and the rate of effective surplus capacity ($\tilde{q}$), RFP scores better than OLS.

---

8. For an interesting attempt to do this, see [6].

TABLE 4.

Root mean square errors for the dynamic simulation[a]
(1963–1967 and 1963–1972)

| | Model estimated with | | | |
| | OLS[b] | | RFP | |
	63-72	63-67	63-72	63-67
C	1.788	1.924	1.814	1.637
c	2.452	2.136	2.811	2.062
I	5.899	5.380	4.465	3.032
i	5.637	4.912	4.310	2.204
b	2.811	2.446	2.369	2.163
N	.633	.531	.603	.591
m	1.842	1.786	1.892	1.838
y	1.309	1.613	1.734	1.682
a	1.030	.613	1.048	.491
a_a	.399	.334	.467	.359
$\widetilde{W}$	.037	.027	.031	.024
$\widetilde{E}_D$	1.743	1.428	1.435	1.080
p_c	1.457	1.257	1.712	1.255
p_b	1.062	1.161	1.080	1.159
p_i	1.005	.759	1.024	.797
p_x	1.844	.972	1.915	.999
l	1.800	1.862	1.654	1.601
G	3.088	3.083	2.499	2.104
$\tilde{q}$	3.339	3.579	3.092	2.693

a. The symbols are explained in the Appendix.
b. On the basis of RFP-specification.

In Figure 2 the simulation results for a number of variables are shown. The variables chosen are: the level of unemployment, the level of employment in enterprises and the balance of payments surplus as a percentage of domestic sales; furthermore the percentage rates of change of the wage rate in enterprises, the price of private consumption and the volume of production of enterprises. The main reason for paying attention to levels instead of changes in the first three variables mentioned is that medium to long-term economic policy is more concerned with levels than changes with respect to these variables. Therefore the performance of the model in predicting levels is more important than in predicting changes. Figure 2 shows that the model is quite

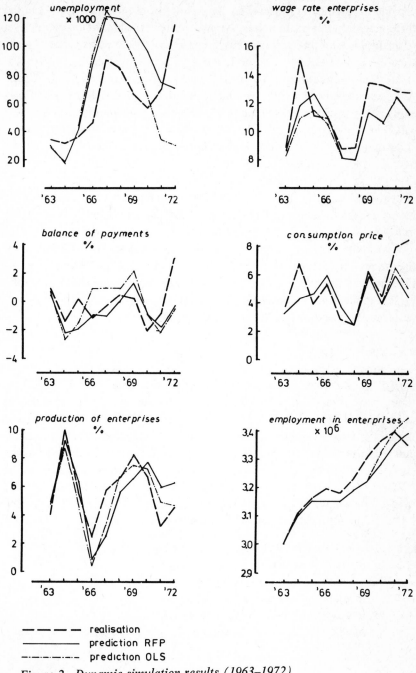

Figure 2. Dynamic simulation results (1963–1972)

capable of predicting the level of the balance of payments surplus and the three rates of change, but error systematically in the prediction of the level of unemployment and employment; from 1965–1970 these are continuously over- and underestimated respectively. The main cause is the, admittedly small, underestimation of the rate of change of production of enterprises. As could be expected in a dynamic simulation, cumulation of errors may easily occur: apparently both the employment and unemployment predictions suffer badly from this phenomenon. In general, however, Figures 1 and 2 show that the dynamic simulations compare rather well with the predictions one year ahead, with the exception of the level of employment and unemployment; these are predicted more accurately in the one year predictions. The extreme residuals for 1971 and 1972 should not be taken too seriously as there is reason to believe that employment and also unemployment, probably to a somewhat lesser extent, are subject to some measurement error.

The results of the dynamic simulations suggest that the performance of the OLS and RFP estimated versions of the model is more or less equal. Considering that a dynamic simulation is a very severe test and that neither the present model nor its predecessors were constructed for medium- and long-term prediction purposes, the results are satisfactory.

4.3. *Impulse Analysis*

This subsection analyses the model by introducing shocks in an exogenous variable or a stochastic equation. First a dynamic simulation for a specific time-period is made along the lines of the previous subsection; next an impulse is given to the system (in the first year of the dynamic simulation) and the model is again solved dynamically. The differences between the latter and the former simulation represent the effects of the impulse at issue, given an initial situation; they are the so-called impact multipliers, which can be used to evaluate certain policy measures or the dynamic stability of the model. The simulations were carried out for a period of three years, starting in 1970. The following shocks were given to the system:

- a 1% increase in world trade
- a 1% increase in autonomous expenditure
- a 10% increase in business investment
- a 1% increase in the price of consumption
- a 1% increase in the wage rate in enterprises
- a 1% increase in the price of competing exports and all import prices.

For the following variables multipliers have been calculated for both the OLS and RFP estimated versions of the model:

- the volume of private consumption
- the volume of exports
- the volume of business investment
- the volume of production of enterprises
- the balance of payments surplus as a percentage of sales, excluding inventory formation and net invisibles
- the rate of unemployment
- the wage rate in enterprises
- the price of private consumption
- the rate of surplus capacity.

The results are presented in tables 5 to 10.

An idea of how the model works can be obtained from two of the simulations, one for a demand shock, e.g. in world trade and the other for a price impulse, e.g. in the wage rate or the price of consumption. An increase in world trade (see Table 5) stimulates exports, not to the full extent however, due to slightly rising export prices and increasing pressure of demand, continuing into the second and third year. The increase in exports stimulates business investment, private consumption and production. Employment also rises causing a rise in the wage rate and a (slight) decline in the price of consumption. This decline is due to increasing labour productivity and is caused partly by the non-inclusion of a demand pressure effect in the consumption price equation. It is also a possible indication of the tendency mentioned in Subsection 3.3, of Fix-Point to leave only a bare minimum of explanatory variables in each equation. In the first and second year unemployment decreases, but this effect is partially offset by an increase in the third year.

An increase in the wage-rate in enterprises (see Table 9) sets in motion the wage-price spiral. Private consumption increases in the first year due to increasing real disposable wage income; in the second and third year rising unemployment causes consumption expenditure to decline, both directly and indirectly. Exports appear to be particularly sensitive to increases in the wage rate due to the high elasticity of relative export prices. In the second year all components of demand decline; employment therefore also decreases; this decrease is reinforced by rising real wage costs. A rather sharp rise in the unemployment rate in the second and third year is the result. The dependent working population amounts to approximately 4 million man-years, implying that 1% increase in the nominal wage rate generates approximately ten thousand additional unemployed two years later — a considerable number.

TABLE 5

Impact multipliers for a 1% increase in world trade.

variable	present model OLS				present model RFP			
	years				years			
	1	2	3	1+2+3	1	2	3	1+2+3
c	.15	.24	.05	.44	.17	.28	.09	.54
b	.84	—.04	—.02	.78	.83	—.11	—.05	.67
i	.39	.43	—.06	.76	.22	.65	.26	1.13
y	.32	.13	—.01	.44	.35	.18	.05	.58
$\tilde{E}_D$	.11	—.06	—.03	—.03	.15	—.03	—.04	—.04
$\Delta\tilde{w}$	—.05	—.03	.02	—.06	—.04	—.02	.02	—.04
l	.03	.13	.06	.22	.06	.17	.10	.33
p_c	—.07	.01	.01	—.05	—.07	—	—	—.07
$\tilde{q}$	—.33	—.40	—.32	—.32	—.37	—.52	—.48	—.48

TABLE 6

Impact multipliers for a 1% increase in autonomous expenditure.

variable	present model OLS				present model RFP			
	years				years			
	1	2	3	1+2+3	1	2	3	1+2+3
c	.06	.08	.01	.15	.08	.10	.01	.19
b	—.02	—.02	.03	—.01	—.03	—.05	.01	—.07
i	.17	—.04	—.15	—.02	.10	.07	—.05	.12
y	.14	.02	—.02	.14	.16	.04	—.01	.19
$\tilde{E}_D$	—.13	—.14	—.10	—.10	—.10	—.13	—.11	—.11
$\Delta\tilde{w}$	—.02	—	.01	—.01	.02	—	—.01	.01
l	.01	.05	.01	.07	.03	.07	.02	.12
p_c	—.03	.01	—	—.02	—.03	.01	—	—.02
$\tilde{q}$	—.15	—.13	—.09	—.09	—.16	—.19	—.16	—.16

It is along such lines that we can obtain indications of the economic properties of the system. Apart from these properties, we may conclude from the impulse analysis and from the dynamic simulations undertaken in Section 4.2 that the model shows no tendency to explode.

TABLE 7

Impact multipliers for a 10% increase in business investment.

variable	present model OLS				present model RFP			
	years				years			
	1	2	3	1+2+3	1	2	3	1+2+3
c	.60	.69	—.03	1.26	.69	.89	.22	1.80
b	—.20	—.15	.39	.04	—.23	.02	.80	.59
i	10.93	—.63	—1.60	8.70	10.17	—.07	—.77	9.33
y	1.31	.09	—.22	1.18	1.42	.37	.16	1.95
$\tilde{E}_D$	—1.15	—1.16	—.74	—.74	—.94	—1.01	—.70	—.70
$\Delta\tilde{w}$	—.20	—.03	.09	—.14	—.15	—.03	.06	—.12
l	.11	.46	.09	.66	.25	.63	.24	1.12
p_c	—.29	.10	.05	—.14	—.28	.07	—.02	—.23
$\tilde{q}$	—1.33	—1.02	—.58	—.58	-1.46	—.75	.02	.02

TABLE 8

Impact multipliers for a 1% increase in consumption price.

variable	present model OLS				present model RFP			
	years				years			
	1	2	3	1+2+3	1	2	3	1+2+3
c	—.30	—.24	—.30	—.84	—.39	—.32	—.39	-1.10
b	—.25	—.36	—.33	—.94	—.22	—.24	—.18	—.64
i	—.53	.15	—.05	—.43	—.34	.17	—.17	—.34
y	—.25	—.26	—.33	—.84	—.29	—.35	—.44	-1.08
$\tilde{E}_D$	.26	—.20	.10	.10	.24	.14	.03	.03
$\Delta\tilde{w}$	.03	.05	.06	.14	.02	.03	.04	.09
l	1.21	.29	.03	1.53	1.04	.16	—.11	1.09
p_c	1.45	.24	.20	1.89	1.40	.22	.18	1.80
$\tilde{q}$	.25	.41	.71	.71	.30	.61	1.06	1.06

TABLE 9

Impact multipliers for a 1% increase in the wage rate in enterprises.

variable	present model OLS				present model RFP			
	years				years			
	1	2	3	1+2+3	1	2	3	1+2+3
c	.49	—.04	—.36	.09	.50	—.05	—.47	—.02
b	—.33	—.23	.01	—.55	—.34	—.33	—.10	—.77
i	—.16	—.83	—.56	—1.55	—.13	—.09	—.45	—.67
y	.11	—.21	—.26	—.36	.12	—.20	—.39	—.47
$\widetilde{E}_D$	—.06	—.03	.08	.08	—.04	—.13	—.07	—.07
$\Delta\widetilde{w}$	.02	.10	.10	.22	.03	.10	.10	.23
l	1.39	.15	—.03	1.51	1.33	.10	—.12	1.31
p_c	.43	.16	.12	.71	.39	.13	.11	.63
$\widetilde{q}$	—.09	.46	.92	.92	—.12	.09	.49	.49

TABLE 10

Impact multipliers for a 1% increase in import prices and competing export prices.

variable	present model OLS				present model RFP			
	years				years			
	1	2	3	1+2+3	1	2	3	1+2+3
c	—.06	.01	.11	.06	—.08	.06	.16	.14
b	.11	—	—.05	.06	.11	—.04	—.12	—.05
i	—.33	—.28	.29	—.32	—.30	—.23	.47	—.06
y	.05	.06	.01	.12	.02	.18	.02	.22
$\widetilde{E}_D$	—.13	.18	.08	.08	—.15	.22	.07	.07
$\Delta\widetilde{w}$	—.01	—.01	—	—.02	—.01	—.02	—	—.03
l	.36	.17	.12	.65	.31	.16	.15	.62
p_c	.40	.09	.09	.58	.38	.05	.09	.52
$\widetilde{q}$	—.05	—.09	—.11	—.11	—.02	—.24	—.32	—.32

5. CONCLUDING REMARKS

In the preceding sections an application of the Fix-Point estimation method to the revised 69-c model has been considered. The method is easy to use and its application to the present model presented no problems such as excessive use of computer time or convergence difficulties. In estimating the stochastic equations of the model, it utilizes all the information contained in the restrictions imposed on the reduced form by the specification of the model. It is not surprising therefore that the estimation results appear to be sensitive to the specification of the model. It was found that Fix-Point tends to leave the researcher with merely the bare essentials of each structural equation. Considering these two points, there is a distinct possibility of leaving out important explanatory factors in some of the stochastic equations. The modelbuilder will have to excercise his prior theoretical judgement since to the knowledge of the authors no test exists for detecting these occurrences within the framework of the Fix-Point estimation method. It was also found that high goodness of fit with OLS, as measured by R^2, provides no guarantee whatsoever for satisfactory Fix-Point estimation results. If the researcher wishes to use Fix-Point in estimating his model, a large amount of time spent in testing alternative specifications by means of Ordinary Least Squares is to some extent a waste of energy.

As far as the model presented in this paper is concerned, a comparison of the estimation results based on RFP and OLS estimation leads us to conclude that the Fix-Point method scores better than OLS with respect to predictions one period ahead; the superiority of the Fix-Point estimated model is, however, less marked in medium- to long-term predictions.

Finally, the gain in short-term predictive performance, even if it is small, seems to have justified the application of Fix-Point in the construction of the present model; however, additional experiments with other models are needed before final appraisal of the Fix-Point method is possible.

APPENDIX. THE EQUATIONS OF THE MODEL.

Behavioural Equations (RFP-coefficients)

1. $C = C_{aut} + 1.057 (\check{L}^D/\check{C})_{-1} L^D_{-\frac{1}{4}} + .187 (\check{Z}^D/\check{C})_{-1} Z^{D'}_{-\frac{1}{4}} + .342 \Delta p_c - 1.898 \Delta \check{w}_{l-1/2} - .308$

2. $I = I_{aut} + .160 \{(\check{v}/\check{\imath})_{-1} \cdot y\}_{-1^{1}/_3} + .843 ZNG_{-1\frac{1}{2}} + .533 (1 + 1.664 d_1) \Delta p_i - 10.451 (1 + .866 d_1) \Delta \check{Q} +$
   $+ .625 G_{-1} + 15.157 VAY - 1.469$

3. $b = b_{aut} + .993 m_{TW} - 2.330 \left\{ \frac{1}{3} \sum_{i=0}^{2} (p_b - p'_b)_{-i} \right\} - .412 (k_n - p_b)_{-\frac{3}{4}} + 10.006 d_2 \Delta \check{Q}_{-\frac{1}{4}} + .595$

4. $N = .231 v'_{-1/3} - .768 N_{-1} - .976 \{100 (\check{N}_{-2}/\check{V}'_{-1})\} + .144 p_m + .257 t^* - .108$

5. $m = .976 v' + 2.110 N - .650 \{.1 d_1 p_{m-vd} + d_2 p_{m-vd-1}\} + .364 \widetilde{TP} + .826$

6. $a = .630 d_1 v_a + .102 d_1 p_{m-vd} + .287 d_2 y_{-1/3} - .399 h_{c-1} - .915 d_2 PLY' - 3.930 d_1 + 3.841$

7. $a_a = 1.00 a_x + .125 \{l - p_c\}_{532} - .531 \Delta \check{w}_{-\frac{1}{4}} - .336 \{(100 \check{a}_a/\check{a}_x)_{-1}\} + 3.188 d_{29} + 2.239 d_{3233} - 1.320 d_1 + 19.179$

8. $l = .953 \{(.85 - .4 d_1) p_c + (.15 + .11 d_1) p_{c-1}\} + .713 d_2 (y - a)_{-\frac{1}{4}} - .863 \{d_1 \check{w}_{l-1} + .5 d_2 \check{w}_l + .25 d_2 \check{w}_{l-1}\} + 7.024$

9. $p_c = p_{cau} + .446 k_c - .459 Z^*_{c-1} + 2.002 d_1 \Delta \tilde{r}_{k-2/3} + .594$

10. $p_b = .681 k_n + .536 p'_{b-1/4} + .151 \Delta m_{TW} + 2.824 d_1 - 1.745$

11. $p_i = .322 H_{-\frac{1}{4}} + .248 p_{mi-1/6} + .322 p_{mr-1/3} - 4.890 d_2 \Delta \check{Q}_{-\frac{1}{4}} + .924$

12. $p_x = .620 l - .207 (y - a) + .430 p_{m-1/4} - .181$

13. $G = .848 V'_{D-1/3} + .598 (1 + 3.119 d_1) N + 1.882 \check{E}_D + 4.018 \{100 \check{H}_{K-5/12}/V'_{D-1}\} + 2.058 \{100 \check{S}_{c-1/3}/ V'_{D-1}\} +$
   $+ 3.866 \{\Delta \tilde{r}_{L-1/6} - .76 (1 + .605 d_1) \Delta \tilde{r}_k\} - 2.537$

Definitions

1. $\quad c \quad = (C - p_c)/(1 + .01p_c)$

2. $\quad B \quad = b + p_b + .01bp_b$

3. $\quad i \quad = (I - p_i)/(1 + .01p_i)$

4. $\quad X \quad = x + p_x + .01xp_x$

5. $\quad M \quad = m + p_m + .01mp_m$

6. $\quad I_{-wo} = (\tilde{I}_{-1} \cdot I + 100 \Delta \tilde{I}_{sv})/\tilde{I}_{-wo-1}$

7. $\quad i_{-wo} = (\tilde{i}_{-1} \cdot i + 100 \Delta \tilde{i}_{sv})/\tilde{i}_{-wo-1}$

8. $\quad V'_D \quad = (\tilde{C}_{-1} \cdot C + \tilde{I}_{-wo-1} \cdot I_{-wo} + \tilde{X}_{-1} \cdot X)/\tilde{V}'_{D-1}$

9. $\quad v'_D \quad = (\tilde{c}_{-1} \cdot c + \tilde{i}_{-wo-1} \cdot i_{-wo} + \tilde{x}_{-1} \cdot x)/\tilde{v}'_{D-1}$

10. $\quad p_{vd} \quad = (V'_D - v'_D)/(1 + .01v'_D)$

11. $\quad v' \quad = (\tilde{c}_{-1} \cdot c + \tilde{i}_{-wo-1} \cdot i_{-wo} + \tilde{x}_{-1} \cdot x + \tilde{b}_{-1} \cdot b)/\tilde{v}'_{-1}$

12. $\quad p_{v'} \quad = (V' - v')/(1 + .01v')$

13. $\quad V \quad = [\tilde{V}'_{-1} \cdot (V' + N) + \tilde{D}_{-1} \cdot D]/\tilde{V}_{-1}$

14. $\quad v \quad = [\tilde{v}'_{-1} \cdot (v' + N) + \tilde{d}_{-1} \cdot d]/\tilde{v}_{-1}$

15. $\quad Y \quad = (\tilde{V}_{-1} \cdot V - \tilde{M}_{-1} \cdot M)/\tilde{Y}_{-1}$

16. $\quad y \quad = (\tilde{v}_{-1} \cdot v - \tilde{m}_{-1} \cdot m)/\tilde{y}_{-1}$

17. $\quad p_y \quad = (Y - y)/(1 + .01y)$

18. $\quad T_K \quad = T'_K + V' + .01T'_K V'$

19. $\quad Z \quad = (\tilde{Y}_{-1} \cdot Y - \tilde{L}_{-1} \cdot L - \tilde{F}_{-1} \cdot F - T_{K-1} \cdot T_K)/\tilde{Z}_{-1}$

20. $\quad L \quad = l + a + .01a \cdot l$

21. $\quad L^D \quad = \tilde{L}_{-1}(L + O'_L)/\tilde{L}^D_{-1}$

22. $\quad Z^D \quad = \tilde{Z}_{-1}(Z + O'_z)/\tilde{Z}^D_{-1}$

23. $\quad a_d \quad = (\tilde{a}_{-1} \cdot a + 100\Delta \tilde{a}_g)/\tilde{a}_{d-1}$

24. $\quad \tilde{a}_a \quad = (1 + .01 a_a)\, \tilde{a}_{a-1}$

25. $\quad \tilde{a}_d \quad = (1 + .01 a_d)\, \tilde{a}_{d-1}$

26. $\quad \tilde{W} \quad = \tilde{a}_a - \tilde{a}_d$

27. $\quad \Delta \widetilde{BPC} = .01\tilde{B}_{-1} \cdot B - .01\tilde{M}_{-1} \cdot M + .01\tilde{D}'_{-1} \cdot D'$

28. $\quad \widetilde{BPC} = \widetilde{BPC}_{-1} + \Delta \widetilde{BPC}$

29. $\quad \tilde{E}_D \quad = (\widetilde{BPC}/\tilde{V}'_{D-1})\, 100$

30. $\quad \tilde{w} \quad = (\tilde{W}/\tilde{P}a_{a_B})\, 100$

31. $\quad \tilde{w}_l \quad = 4.34\, ln(\tilde{w} + 2) - .2\tilde{w}$

32. $\quad H \quad = l - (y - a)$

33. $\quad k_n \quad = .44H + .56p_{mr}$

34. $\quad H_c \quad = l - d_1(v' - a) - d_2(y - a)$

35. $\quad k_c \quad = .7H_c + .3p_m + 1.0 OB$

36. $\quad \tilde{a} \quad = (1 + .01a)\, \tilde{a}_{-1}$

37. $\quad \tilde{w}' \quad = (\tilde{W}/\tilde{a})\, 100$

38. $\quad \tilde{q}_{a_1} \quad = [(1.00 + .01\tilde{w}')^2 - 1]\, 100$

39. $\quad \tilde{q}_{a_2} \quad = [(1.01 + .02\tilde{w}')^2 - 1]\, 100$

40. $\quad \tilde{q}_a \quad = .819d_1\tilde{q}_{a_1} + 1.000d_2\tilde{q}_{a_2}$

41. $\quad \tilde{q}_{k_2} \quad = \left(.825\, \dfrac{\tilde{h}_c^{.75}\, \tilde{k}_{-1}}{\tilde{y}} - 1\right) 100$

42. $\quad \tilde{q}_k \quad = d_1\tilde{q}_a + d_2\tilde{q}_{k_2}$

43. $\quad \tilde{q} \quad = (.5\tilde{q}_a^{-8} + .5\tilde{q}_k^{-8})^{-1/8}$

44. $\quad \Delta\tilde{q} \quad = \tilde{q} - \tilde{q}_{-1}$

45. $\quad \Delta\tilde{Q} \quad = \Delta\tilde{q}/(6 + \tilde{q}_{-1})$

46. $\quad \tilde{k} \quad = \tilde{k}_{-1} + \tilde{i}_{-wo} - \tilde{f}_{-wo}$

47. $\quad v_a \quad = .46c + .18b + .36\, \dfrac{(\tilde{i}_{-wo-1} \cdot i_{-wo} + \tilde{x}_{-1} \cdot x)}{\tilde{i}_{-wo-1} + \tilde{x}_{-1}}$

48. $\quad p_{m-vd} = p_m - p_{vd-1/2} + .06T'_{K-1/3}$

49. $\quad Z_c \quad = p_c - k_c - p_{c_{au}}$

50. $\quad Z_c^* \quad = .326Z_c + .372Z_{c-1} + .302Z_{c-2}$

51. $\quad Z^{D'} = Z^D - (\tilde{V}' \cdot N / \tilde{Z}^D_{-1})$

52. $\quad ZNG = (\tilde{Z}^D_{-1} \cdot Z^D + \tilde{F}_{-1} \cdot F - \tilde{V}'_{-1} \cdot N)/\tilde{Y}_{-1}$

53. $\quad PLY = .85PLY_{-1} + .15(l - p_y)_{-1}$

54. $(l - p_c)_{532} = .5(l - p_c) + .3(l - p_c)_{-1} + .2(l - p_c)_{-2}$

55. $\quad VAY = 100\Delta\widehat{VAIA}_{-1^7/_{10}} / \tilde{Y}_{-1}$

LIST OF SYMBOLS

The model runs in terms of relative changes (unless otherwise indicated). Upper case symbols generally refer to relative changes in values, lower case symbols to relative changes in volumes or prices. Relative changes have no special indication. Levels are indicated by a swung dash ($\sim$). Exogenous variables are underlined. Lags are indicated by a subscript ($X_{-\alpha} = (1-\alpha) X + \alpha X_{-1}$ for $0 \leqslant \alpha \leqslant 1$). First differences are indicated by the difference operator $\Delta (\Delta X = X - X_{-1})$.

a	employment in enterprises
a_a	dependent working population
a_d	total employment
a_g	employment by government
a_x	working population (14–64 years of age) adjusted for school-going youth (14–16 age bracket) and self-employed
$B \quad b$	exports of goods
b_{aut}	effect of natural gas exports on exports of goods
BPC	balance of payment on current account
$C \quad c$	private consumption
C_{aut}	effects of anticipatory purchases on private consumption
d_1	pre-war constant (1 for 1923–1938, 0 for 1953–1972)
d_2	post-war constant (0 for 1923–1938, 1 for 1953–1972)
d_{29}	1 in 1929, 0 elsewhere
d_{3233}	1 in 1932, -1 in 1933, 0 elsewhere
$D \quad d$	balance of invisible trade (excluding net incomes from abroad)
D'	balance of invisible trade (including net incomes from abroad)
$\tilde{E}_D$	balance of payments on current account as a percentage of domestic sales (excluding inventory formation).
F	depreciation in enterprises

f_{-wo}	depreciation in enterprises (excluding dwellings)
G	primary and secondary liquidities (end of period)
$\tilde{h}_c$	contractual working hours in enterprises (index 1959 = 1)
$\tilde{H}_k$	short-term trade credit
H	wage-costs per unit of output
H_c	wage-costs per unit of consumption goods
$I \quad i$	gross business investment (excluding residential construction and ships and aeroplanes)
I_{aut}	effect of natural gas exploitation (1964) and dummy variable 1969/1970
$I_{sv} \quad i_{sv}$	investment in ships and aeroplanes
$I_{-wo} \quad i_{-wo}$	business investment (excluding residential construction)
k	capital stock
k_c	$.7H_c + .3p_m + OB$
k_n	$.44H + .56p_{mr}$
l	wage rate in enterprises
L	wage bill in enterprises
L^D	disposable wage income
M	imports of commodities
m_{Tw}	world imports (reweighted by the geographical distribution of Dutch exports)
N	change in stock formation as a percentage of lagged total sales (excluding stock formation and invisible trade)
$\tilde{N}$	stock formation
OB	effect of indirect taxes on price level of private consumption (prior to 1969)
O'_L	government wage-bill, including income transfers and direct taxes on wage- and transfer-income (% of wage income)
O'_z	do., for non-wage income
p_b	price of exports of commodities
p'_b	price of foreign competitors
p_c	price of private consumption
p_{cau}	autonomous effects on the price of private consumption[9]
p_i	price of gross business investment
p_m	price of imports of commodities
p_{mi}	price of imports of investment goods

---

9. Rents, value added tax from 1969 onwards, Kennedy-round, EEC measures, price effect of imported consumption goods.

p_{mr}	price of raw materials imports
p_{m-vd}	the margin between the price of imports and domestic sales, adjusted for the incidence of indirect taxes
$p_v{}'$	price of total expenditure (v')
p_x	price of autonomous expenditures
p_y	price of domestic production
$\tilde{q}_{a_1}, \tilde{q}_{a_2}, \tilde{q}_a$	excess capacity based on labour
$\tilde{q}_{k_1}, \tilde{q}_{k_2}, \tilde{q}_k$	excess capacity based on capital
$\tilde{q}$	effective excess capacity
$\tilde{r}_k$	short-term rate of interest (official discount rate)
$\tilde{r}_l$	long-term rate of interest (interest on long-term government bonds)
$\tilde{S}_c$	inflationary government financing
t^*	decreasing trend (pre-war)
$\widetilde{TP}$	effect of trade policy measures on imports (import restrictions 1932–1936; trade liberalisation 1949–1953)
T_K	indirect taxes minus subsidies
$T_K{}'$	incidence of indirect taxes minus subsidies $((\tilde{T}_K / \tilde{V}')100)$
v_a	total expenditure, reweighted according to labour-intensity of final demand components
$V'\quad v'$	total expenditure (excl. stock formation and net invisible trade)
$V\quad v$	total expenditure
$V'_D\ v'_D$	total domestic expenditure (excl. stock formation)
$\widetilde{VAIA}$	autonomous changes in fiscal depreciation and investment allowances
$\tilde{W}$	level of unemployment (man-years)
$\tilde{w}$	rate of unemployment $((\tilde{W}/\tilde{a}_a)100)$
$\tilde{w}_l$	curvilinear function of unemployment $(4.34ln(\tilde{w}+2)-.2\tilde{w})$
$X\quad \underline{x}$	autonomous expenditure
$Y\quad y$	production of enterprises
Z	non-wage income
Z_c	$p_c-k_c-p_{cau}$
Z_c^*	$.326Z_c+.372Z_{c-1}+.302Z_{c-2}$
Z^D	disposable non-wage income
$Z^{D'}$	do., adjusted for stock formation

REFERENCES

[1] Bodin, L. (1974). *Recursive Fix Point Estimation, theory and applications.* Selected Publications, Vol. 32. University of Uppsala. Sweden.

[2] Central Planning Bureau (1961). Commentary on the equation system for 1961. pp. 113–127 Annex I, *Central Economic Plan 1961.* The Hague.

[3] Edgerton, D. L. (1973). *Nonlinear Interdependent Systems.* F.D. Thesis. University of Uppsala, Sweden.

[4] Giessen, A. A. van der (1970). Solving non-linear systems by computer; a new method. *Statistica Neerlandica,* vol. 24 no. 1.

[5] Giessen, A. A. van der (1974). Evaluation of the recursive fix point method for the Dutch 69-C econometric annual model. *Occasional Paper no. 10,* Central Planning Bureau. The Hague.

[6] Johnston, H. N., L. R. Klein and K. Shinjo, (1974). Estimation and prediction in dynamic econometric models, in *Econometrics and Economic Theory, Essays in honor of Jan Tinbergen* (ed. Willy Sellekaerts). Macmillan. London.

[7] Kloek, T. and L. B. M. Mennes, (1960). Simultaneous equation estimation based on principal components of predetermined variables. *Econometrica,* 28, January.

[8] Kooyman, M. A. (1971). *Onechte variabelen in de ekonometrie.* Assen.

[9] Lyttkens, E. (1973). The fix point method for estimating interdependent systems with the underlying model specification. *Journal of the Royal Statistical Society (Series A),* vol. 135, part. 3.

[10] Ortega, J. M. and W. C. Rheinboldt, (1970). *Iterative solution of non-linear equations in several variables.* Academic Press, New York.

[11] Verdoorn, P. J. (1967). The short term model of the Central Planning Bureau and its forecasting performance (1953–1963), in *Macro-Economic Models for Planning and Policy-making.* United Nations publication, Geneva.

[12] Verdoorn, P. J., J. J. Post and S. S. Goslinga, (1971). *Het jaarmodel 1969,* The Hague.

Employment and Production in the Dutch Empirical Tradition

R. S. G. LENDERINK AND J. C. SIEBRAND

1. INTRODUCTION

Macro-economic model building in the Netherlands – like anywhere else – has suffered from the deficient micro-economic foundation of macro-economics in the post 'General Theory' era. Much work seems to be based on the notion that in the long run 'classical' relations – often labeled 'structural' – are relevant, whereas 'Keynesian' types of relations dominate the scene in the short run. But the way in which both types of analysis could be integrated was not yet clear in the absence of theories about quantity and price adjustment over time in a setting where the agent's possibilities to carry out his anticipations are constrained both by his earlier decisions and the anticipations of his trading partners.[1]

The theoretical disintegration explains a tendency to separate empirical short-run and long-run analysis. The drawbacks of this separation induced attempts to reintegrate the analysis of short- and medium-term development in a later stage. In fact, a spectrum of approaches was developed during the course of time, often without obvious interconnections. The purpose of this paper is to show that much of the empirical work with regard to the relations between employment and production becomes more or less interpretable if vintage production models are combined with disequilibrium theory. Most of our examples are linked in one way or another to the work of the Dutch Central Planning Bureau.

Our ex post exegesis – which sometimes strongly deviates from the original interpretations – starts with a discussion on the instruments for the integration. In Section 2 we will present the assumptions of the clay-clay production model together with some of their basic consequences.

Section 3 contains a brief treatment of the determination of transactions in disequilibrium and the interactions between product, labour and money markets ('spill-over effects').

1. Cf. Clower [6], Iwai [12], Benassy [3].

In Section 4 we demonstrate that Verdoorn's law is consistent with the production model in equilibrium if economic obsolescence is of a particularly regular form.

The coefficients of the linear relationship between labour productivity development and production growth turn out to be interpretable in terms of either the age of the eldest vintage in use combined with the labour income share and the rate of technical deterioration or – alternatively – the latter rate and the average age of the capital stock and its mean square age.

Out of equilibrium, the relation between employment and production is 'tilted' by a number of disequilibrium effects. In Section 5 we study their impact on short-run employment and compare the results with the specification of the employment relation in the short-run model −69-C, which offers some striking similarities.

The mutual relations between production, capacity and employment in the combined medium-term – short-term 'c.s.'-model are investigated in Section 6. Here again we specify certain assumptions which bring these relations roughly in line with the consequences of the combination of clay-clay models with modern disequilibrium theory.

Section 7 comments briefly on recent developments such as the VINTAF-model, the disequilibrium approach of the present authors and Sandee's contributions.

2. THE CLAY-CLAY PRODUCTION MODEL*

This section contains a brief discussion on assumptions underlying a clay-clay production function. Next we arrive at some basic equations with regard to production capacity and corresponding capacity labour demand as well as the macro-economic income distribution.

2.1. *The Assumptions*
A brief summary of the assumptions usually made with regard to a clay-clay production function may suffice[2]:

a. A single homogeneous commodity is produced with the aid of two factors of production, labour and capital.

---

* All symbols used in the following sections are explained in an appendix.
2. See R. S. G. Lenderink and J. C. Siebrand [14], where the reader may find an extensive list of references concerning clay-clay production models.

b. Labour consists of homogeneous units[3], called man-years. Capital is disaggregated into units, labeled machines, of different types. Assuming technical change to be of the embodied labour saving type, machines will be distinguished by their period of construction (τ), called vintages.

c. For any vintage τ, labour and capital are complementary factors of production.

In order to produce one unit of output under normal operating conditions α_τ man-years and κ_τ machines are used.

The capital output ratio is equal for all vintages and does not change over time.

Labour productivity, $\phi_\tau = 1/\alpha_\tau$, remains constant during the course of time on any vintage and on vintage τ exceeds that on vintage $\tau-1$ by $\eta\%$. These differences are caused by a greater efficiency of machines, constructed in period τ, relative to those constructed in an earlier period. The rate of technical change is considered to be constant and is therefore a datum in our model[4]. The following relation between α_τ and $\alpha_{\tau-1}$ may be stated

$$\phi_\tau = \phi_{\tau-1}(1 + \eta')$$

or

$$\frac{1}{\alpha_\tau} = \frac{1}{\alpha_{\tau-1}}(1 + \eta') \tag{2.1.1.}$$

where

$$\eta' = \eta/100$$

d. Due to technical factors $\rho\%$ of each vintage becomes obsolete each year, starting in the second year of use. This assumption is made for mathematical convenience[5].

e. The gestation period of machines is assumed to be one year.

f. In the production process, assuming cost minimizing behaviour on the part of entrepreneurs, priority will be given to the newest machines; the next candidates are the one year older machines and so forth. The age of

3. This assumption could (and should) be modified; for a theoretical and empirical analysis see J. Kooyman and A. H. Q. M. Merkies [13].
4. This assumption could be modified by assuming a putty-clay instead of a clay-clay world. Compare [17].
5. We could have assumed specific survival rates for machinery of a certain age, as was done in the VINTAF-model; see H. den Hartog, Th. C. M. J. van de Klundert & H. S. Tjan [10].

the eldest vintage in operation is determined by the (scrapping) rule that product revenue at least equals variable (i.e. labour-) costs on the eldest vintage, given the wage rate and the price level. The so-called material (economic) production capacity is calculated as the sum of production on all vintages eligible for operation, assuming the existence of some idle machinery, i.e. 'machinery stored in mothballs'[6].

g. Machines of different construction periods will be represented by the volume of gross investment by enterprises in equipment. (The whole analysis is applied to industries).

h. The operating time of each vintage in any period is the same for all vintages and equals labour time. In this stage we exclude the possibility of changes in the yearly machine operating and labour working time.[7]

So far some basic assumptions featured in a clay-clay world. These assumptions enable us to draw some conclusions to be dealt with in the next section.

2.2. *Some Consequences*

In this section we will arrive at a number of consequences of the assumptions and properties sketched above.

We will pay attention especially to the relationships between production capacity and corresponding capacity employment on one side and the macro-economic income distribution on the other.

For $i_{\tau,\,t}$, the number of machines still available of any vintage τ in year t can be stated

$$i_{\tau,t} = i_\tau (1 - \rho')^{t-1-\tau}, \ \tau = t - 1, t - 2, ..., t - m. \qquad (2.2.1).$$

where:

i_τ : volume of investment in equipment constructed in year τ

ρ': rate of technical deterioration of machinery $(=\rho/100)$

This number of machines, approximated to by investment in equipment, can be translated into production capacity (production volume at normal operating rates) and capacity employment in the following way

$$y^*_{\tau,t} = \frac{(1 - \rho')^{t-1-\tau} i_\tau}{\kappa} = \phi_\tau a^*_{\tau,t}, \ \tau = t - 1, t - 2, ..., t - m. \qquad (2.2.2.)$$

---

6. See R. G. D. Allen [1].
7. Later we allow for implicit short-term fluctuations within a disequilibrium framework.

where:

$y_{\tau,t}^*$: production capacity on vintage τ in year t
$a_{\tau,t}^*$ capacity employment on vintage τ in year t.

Symbolizing the age of the eldest vintage in use by m and summing over vintages yields formulas for total production capacity and total capacity employment in year t

$$y_t^* = \frac{1}{\kappa} \sum_{\tau=t-1}^{t-m_t} [1 - \rho']^{t-1-\tau} \, i_\tau = \frac{k_t}{\kappa} \qquad (2.2.3.)$$

and

$$a_t^* = \frac{1}{\kappa} \sum_{\tau=t-1}^{t-m_t} \frac{[1 - \rho']^{t-1-\tau} \, i_\tau}{\phi_\tau} \qquad (2.2.4.)$$

where:

y_t^*: total production capacity in year t
a_t^*: total capacity employment in year t
k_t: capital stock in year t

Labour supply is implicitly assumed to exceed or at least to be equal to capacity employment. Otherwise labour supply would be the determinant of production capacity. We do abstract from this complication here, but will take up this matter below.

Next the functional income distribution will be treated. A vintage will remain in operation as long as its variable costs, i.e. labour costs, are lower than or equal to its product revenue. Given the existence of some machines stored in mothballs[8] and assuming free competition on both the product and the labour markets, the wage rate equals the product of labour productivity on the eldest vintage in use and the product price. Every vintage will show the same real labour remuneration due to the labour homogeneity assumption, implying that capitalists receive a quasi-rent on all vintages in use except the eldest one[9].
In symbols

$$\frac{l_t}{p_{y_t}} = \phi_{t-m_t} \qquad (2.2.5.)$$

8. Compare R. G. D. Allen [1].
9. Symbolizing the quasi-rent on vintage τ in year t by $r_{\tau,t}$ we can state

$$r_{\tau,t} = p_{y_t} y_{\tau,t}^* - l_t a_{\tau,t}^*, \quad \tau = t-1, t-2, ..., t-m_t \qquad (2.2.5.A)$$

The quasi-rent varies inversely with the age of the vintage under consideration.

where

l_t/p_{y_t}: real wage rate per worker.

Substituting eq. (2.1.1.) into eq. (2.2.5.) yields[10]

$$\frac{l_t}{p_{y_t}} = \frac{1}{\alpha_{t-m_t}} = \frac{1}{\alpha_t [1 + \eta']^{m_t}}$$

(2.2.6.)

After this exposition of the consequences of the vintage model, we will study the impact of disequilibrium.

3. THE CONSEQUENCES OF DISEQUILIBRIUM

The observation of actual economic development yields abundant information that might be interpreted as indicative of the existence of disequilibria. Unemployment and excess capacity data suggest that actual employment differs generally from (potential) labour supply and that production is not equal to production capacity as a rule. Credit rationing and changing liquidity ratios may indicate similar situations in the monetary sector. As Eckstein and Fromm [7] put it: 'Indeed, the continuous clearing case, where production equals supply and supply equals demand, is probably an exception. Disequilibrium is the more common situation'.

Modern disequilibrium theory suggests that both prices and quantities are subject to dynamic adjustment processes, which contain both the decision making of economic agents based on incomplete information and the confrontation of inconsistent plans of different agents on 'markets'. Ex ante, agents can adjust to perceived constraints; ex post, they tend to be forced to 'adjust' to realized constraints. Generally, the adjustment to constraints on one market will tend to condition both the plans for and the operations on other markets. A general explanation of at first sight widely differing phenomena like income – constrained consumption[11], output –

---

10. From eq. (2.2.6.) it follows

$$\Delta m_t = m_t - m_{t-1} = 1 - \frac{\overset{\circ}{l}_t - \overset{\circ}{p}_{y_t}}{\eta}$$

(2.2.6.A)

A real wage increase exceeding the rate of technical progress causes a reduction in the age of the eldest vintage in use. Hence eq. (2.2.6.A) describes economic obsolescence.
11. Cf. Benassy [3].

conditioned investment[12] and unemployment – conditioned wage changes,[13] appears possible along these lines.

Explicit empirical implementation of this recent theoretical development has hardly emerged yet, but, of course, 'ad hoc' empirical macro-economics 'anticipated' these theories.

In this paper we will follow some of Siebrand's suggestions for the empirical implementation of explicit disequilibrium analysis, in which the basic assumptions are – globally –:

1. Potential demand (supply) is defined as that ex ante, planned value of demand (supply) that could and would be realized in the absence of any tension on the market(s),
2. The tension on the market is defined as the ratio between potential demand and potential supply,
3. Actual transactions are a weighted average of potential demand and potential supply rather than equal to the minimum of these quantities.

The potential values as described above come close to Clower's concept of notional values. Of course, ex ante variables may be defined in several stages, depending on the information and the constraints taken into account. For empirical implementation it seems important to note that the closer the stages to which the variables refer approach to the 'initial' stage of the plan, the more the relevant theory tends to come in line with '(neo-)classical' and 'long-run' theorizing.

Therefore, long-run elements, in which presumably time consuming substitution processes play a dominant role, may constitute the core of the approximation to potential values of demand and supply. Actually, these potential values are not necessarily confronted on markets, as agents may (ex ante) adapt their plans to perceived constraints on the market under consideration, or possibly to realized constraints on other markets (the so-called spill-over effects). Therefore Clower [6] uses the concept effective demand (supply) to describe orders (offers) made on the market. It seems reasonable to assume, that, as a rule, the relationship between effective demand (supply) and potential demand (supply) will be dominated by inconsistencies between ex ante demand and ex ante supply[14]. Reactions

---

12. Cf. Grossman [8].
13. Cf. Phillips [15].
14. This theorizing on the relationship between transactions and potential variables is taken from and elaborated in J. C. Siebrand [19]. For an earlier application, see R. S. G. Lenderink and J. C. Siebrand [14].

to perceived constraints may reveal themselves as (akin to) compromising.

In our view also the ultimate confrontation of plans on markets may induce reactions, the results of which are similar to compromising. The general argument at a micro level is that some adjustment to the plans of the trading partners may tighten trade relations over time and therefore decrease information costs in an uncertain world. Moreover, conflicting plans on one market may cause reactions on other markets that do not show up in a partial analysis and therefore may seem to imply compromising. At a macro level, the fiction of homogeneity of markets should, of course, not close our eyes to the fact that excess demand or excess supply is a grey rather than a black or white phenomenon.

As compromises, or formally equivalent situations, may result in any stage of decision making and implementation we will describe transactions directly as resulting from the confrontation of potential demand and potential supply. The CES-function seems particularly suitable to express this relationship[15]. It contains both the conventional minimum case and equal weights for both demand and supply in the determination of transactions as special cases.

$$x_t^f = \left[\zeta (x_{s_t, T}^p)^{-\varepsilon} + (1 - \zeta) (x_{d_t, T}^p)^{-\varepsilon} \right]^{-1/\varepsilon} \tag{3.1.}$$

where:

$x_{s_t, T}^p$: volume of potential supply anticipated in period T for period t
$x_{d_t, T}^p$: idem demand
x_t^f : volume of actual transactions in period t

In this formulation actual transactions are a weighted average of demand and supply. A proper variation of ζ and ε may yield demand weights that are relatively low in the case of abundant excess supply and inversely. For $0 < \zeta < 1$ and $\varepsilon \to \infty$ the actual transactions, x_t^f, approach to min. $(x_{s_t, T}^p, x_{d_t, T}^p)$, the conventional assumption, based on the 'principle of voluntary exchange'.

It is worth while to note that differentiation of eq. (3.1.) with respect to time yields in relative first differences:

$$\overset{\circ}{x}_t^f = u \overset{\circ}{x}_{s_t, T}^p + [1 - u] \overset{\circ}{x}_{d_t, T}^p \tag{3.2.A}$$

---

15. In [14] we use a transformation of the hyperbolic tangent for this purpose. Sandee brought the advantages of the CES-function to our attention. A similar device is used in the revision of the model 69-C, presented elsewhere in this volume.

where:

$$u = \left[1 + \frac{1 - \zeta}{\zeta} \left(\frac{x_{s_t, T}}{x_{d_t, T}} \right)^{\varepsilon} \right]^{-1} \tag{3.2.B}$$

Now, we apply eq. (3.2.A) to the determination of production and employment, being the volume of actual transactions on product and labour market respectively; this yields

$$\mathring{y}^f = [1 - u_1] \, \mathring{y}_d^p + u_1 \, \mathring{y}_s^p \tag{3.3.}$$

$$\mathring{a}^f = [1 - u_2] \, \mathring{a}_d^p + u_2 \, \mathring{a}_s^p \tag{3.4.}$$

where y refers to product and a to labour, while the time suffixes are deleted for simplicity reasons. The weights u_1 and u_2 can be determined by using eq. (3.2.B).

As we argue in [14], also the determination of actual labour supply – in contrast to potential labour supply – may follow a pattern comparable to that of actual labour demand as a consequence of the so called 'discouraged worker effect'. This assumption amounts to

$$\mathring{a}_s^f = [1 - u_3] \, \mathring{a}_d^p + u_3 \, \mathring{a}_s^p \tag{3.5.}$$

where $\mathring{a}_s^f$ stands for the actual labour supply.

So far we neglected any possible impact of ex ante inconsistencies in other markets for the determination of transactions on one specific market.

Several examples are conceivable. Here we will specify some possible spill-overs that seem of particular interest for the relation between employment and production.

Potential product supply may not only be dependent on the material production capacity but also on the availability of both labour for its employment and liquid assets to finance the production process.

This may be formulated by

$$\mathring{y}_s^p = \mathring{y}^* + \alpha [\mathring{a}_s^p - \mathring{a}_d^p] + \gamma [l\mathring{q}_s^p - l\mathring{q}_d^p] \tag{3.6.}$$

where $\mathring{y}^*$ stands for the production capacity and $l\mathring{q}_s^p$ and $l\mathring{q}_d^p$ symbolize potential supply of and demand for liquid assets respectively[16]. For simpli-

---

16. An alternative for the second term on the right-hand side of eq. (3.6.) would be

$$\alpha' [\mathring{a}_s^p - \mathring{a}^*],$$

where a^* stands for capacity employment (at a normal utilization rate of capital).

city reasons time suffixes are suppressed and the elasticities α and γ are assumed to be constant.

We may assume a similar form of the impact of tension on product and financial markets on the actual demand for labour. This yields:

$$\mathring{a}_d^p = \mathring{a}^* + \beta\,[\mathring{y}_d^p - \mathring{y}^*] + \delta\,[l\mathring{q}_s^p - l\mathring{q}_d^p] \tag{3.7.}$$

where $\mathring{a}^*$ stands for capacity employment (at a normal utilization rate of capital).

If $0 < \beta < 1$, underutilization of capital leads to a less than proportional underemployment.

4. EMPLOYMENT AND PRODUCTION IN EQUILIBRIUM: THE LONG-RUN RELATIONSHIP BETWEEN EMPLOYMENT AND PRODUCTION EMBODIED IN VERDOORN'S LAW

In terms of relative first differences Verdoorn's law relates labour productivity development to production growth in the following way[17]

$$\mathring{y} - \mathring{a} = \alpha_1\mathring{y} + \beta_1 \tag{4.1.}$$

where α_1 and β_1 are constant.

This relationship is assumed to have a 'structural' character, which implies that it is associated with long-term economic development and that it does not contain the consequences of short-term cyclical fluctuations. The basic assumption seems to be that the labour market is in equilibrium.

To derive a relationship between labour productivity growth and production growth under this assumption in a clay-clay world we start with a reformulation of eqs. (2.2.3.) and (2.2.4.) in relative first differences.

For eq. (2.2.3.) this yields[18]

$$\mathring{k}_t = 100\,\frac{k_t - k_{t-1}}{k_{t-1}} = 100\,\frac{i_{t-1}}{k_{t-1}} - \rho - 100\,\frac{\Delta k_t^e}{k_{t-1}} \tag{4.2.}$$

The right-hand side of eq. (4.2.) is composed as follows:

1. Newly installed machinery,
2. Loss in machinery due to technical deterioration,

---

17. In Anglo-Saxon countries this law is also associated with N. Kaldor. Compare [16]. We base ourselves on Verdoorn's writings [22] and [23].
18. Compare R. S. G. Lenderink and J. C. Siebrand [14] ch. 4.

3. Loss in machinery due to economic obsolescence, where:

$$100 \frac{\Delta k_t^e}{k_{t-1}} = \frac{100}{k_{t-1}} \sum_{\tau=t-1-m_t}^{t-1-m_{t-1}} (1 - \rho')^{t-\tau} i_\tau$$

Rewriting eqs. (2.2.3.) and (2.2.4.) in a similar way yields

$$\mathring{y}_t^* = 100 \frac{y_t^* - y_{t-1}^*}{y_{t-1}^*} = \frac{100}{\kappa} \frac{i_{t-1}}{y_{t-1}^*} - \rho - 100 \frac{\Delta y^{*e}}{y_{t-1}^*} \tag{4.3.}$$

and

$$\mathring{a}_t^* = 100 \frac{a_t^* - a_{t-1}^*}{a_{t-1}^*} = \frac{100}{\kappa} \cdot \frac{[1 + \eta']^{-m_{t-1}}}{\lambda_{t-1}} \cdot \frac{i_{t-1}}{y_{t-1}^*} - \rho - 100 \frac{\Delta a^{*e}}{a_{t-1}^*} \tag{4.4.}$$

where

$$\Delta y_t^{*e} = \frac{\Delta k_t^e}{\kappa}, \quad \lambda_{t-1} = \frac{a_{t-1}^*}{y_{t-1}^*} \cdot \frac{l_{t-1}}{p_{y_{t-1}}} \quad {}^{19}$$

and

$$100 \frac{\Delta a^{*e}}{a_{t-1}^*} = \frac{100}{a_{t-1}^*} \sum_{\tau=t-1-m_t}^{t-1-m_{t-1}} \frac{[1 - \rho']^{t-\tau}}{\phi_\tau} i_\tau$$

The right-hand side of the eqs. (4.3.) and (4.4.) can be verbally described as:

1. Production capacity and capacity employment respectively, on newly installed machinery,
2. Loss in production capacity and loss in capacity employment respectively, caused by technical deterioration of machinery,
3. Loss in production capacity and loss in capacity employment respectively, due to economic obsolescence of machinery.

Economic obsolescence of machinery causes losses in production capacity and capacity employment, as pointed out above. The following relationship between both losses can be stated in an approximate way

$$\Delta y_t^{*e} \approx \Delta a_t^{*e} \frac{l_{t-1}}{p_{y_{t-1}}} \tag{4.5.}$$

19. The term λ_{t-1} comes to the same thing as labour's share in total production if, as it is assumed here, an economy's production and employment is completely 'vintage-structured'.
Some amendements are necessary in different cases, see [10] and [11].

Eq. (4.5.) has a simple economic interpretation. It holds exactly in such cases in which every year just one vintage becomes economically obsolete – it holds approximately presupposing a moderate movement in m. Eq. (4.5.) can be rewritten in the following way

$$100 \frac{\Delta y_t^{*e}}{y_{t-1}^*} \approx \lambda_{t-1} \, 100 \frac{\Delta a_t^{*e}}{a_{t-1}^*} \quad ^{20} \tag{4.6.}$$

From eqs. (4.3.), (4.4.) and (4.6.) a relation can be derived, expressing the relative change in labour productivity:

$$\overset{\circ}{y}_t^* - \overset{\circ}{a}_t^* = \frac{100}{\kappa} \cdot \frac{i_{t-1}}{y_{t-1}^*} \left\{ 1 - \frac{[1 + \eta']^{-m_{t-1}}}{\lambda_{t-1}} \right\} + 100 \frac{1 - \lambda_{t-1}}{\lambda_{t-1}} \cdot \frac{\Delta y_t^{*e}}{y_{t-1}^*} \tag{4.7.}$$

Substituting eq. (4.3.) into eq. (4.7.) yields an approximation to Verdoorn's law in a clay-clay world:

$$\overset{\circ}{y}_t^* - \overset{\circ}{a}_t^* = \left\{ 1 - \frac{[1 + \eta']^{-m_{t-1}}}{\lambda_{t-1}} \right\} \{ \overset{\circ}{y}_i^* + \rho \} +$$

$$+ \left\{ -\frac{[1 + \eta']^{-m_{t-1}}}{\lambda_{t-1}} \right\} 100 \frac{\Delta y_t^{*e}}{y_{t-1}^*} \tag{4.8.}$$

This expression can be written in the form of eq. (4.1.) in the following way

$$\overset{\circ}{y}_t^* - \overset{\circ}{a}_t^* = \alpha_2 \overset{\circ}{y}_t^* + \beta_2 \tag{4.9.}$$

where

$$\alpha_2 = 1 - \xi_{t-1}$$

$$\beta_2 = [1 - \xi_{t-1}] \rho + 100 \, [\lambda_{t-1}^{-1} - \xi_{t-1}] \frac{\Delta y^{*e}}{y_{t-1}^*}$$

$$\xi_{t-1} = \frac{[1 + \eta']^{-m_{t-1}}}{\lambda_{t-1}}$$

Evidently, the validity of Verdoorn's law depends on the constancy of α_2 and β_2. Now, α_2 is constant if η', m and λ are constant. For constancy of β_2

20. One may recognize in this scrapping equation a partial negative tendency towards Verdoorn's law.

also ρ and $\Delta y^{*e}/y_{t-1}^{*}$ should be constant[21]. Some of the entities just mentioned are constant by assumption: the rate of technical progress η' and the rate of technical deterioration of machinery ρ; of the others m refers to the capital stock and λ to the income distribution. As proved in [11] we are able to express the latter variable in terms of demographic characteristics of the capital stock as well:

$$\lambda_t \approx [1 + \eta']^{-m_t-1} [1 + \eta' g_t + 0.5 (\eta')^2 s_t] \qquad (4.10.)$$

where g_t and s_t represents the average age and the mean square age of the capital stock respectively, defined as:

$$g_t = \frac{1}{k_t} \sum_{\tau=t-1}^{t-m_t} (t - \tau) i_\tau$$

$$s_t = \frac{1}{k_t} \sum_{\tau=t-1}^{t-m_t} (t - \tau)^2 i_\tau$$

Therefore, the requirements of Verdoorn's law may be described as a constant age composition of the capital stock, combined with a constant rate of economic obsolescence. This can be met when steady-state growth occurs[22].

We may conclude that Verdoorn's law may be valid in a clay-clay world, but only if rather strong requirements regarding the shape of the capital age composition and the regularity of economic scrapping are met.

21. In the absence of economic obsolescence the following expression for the growth rate of labour productivity can be derived from (19):

$$\mathring{y}_t^* - \mathring{a}_t^* \approx [g_{t-1} \eta'] \mathring{y}_t^* + [g_{t-1} \eta'] \rho \qquad (4.9.A)$$

It is interesting to note that in this case the background of α_1 and β_1 solely and merely is to be found in the rate of technical progress, the average age of the capital stock and the rate of technical deterioration of machinery.
22. Because λ and m are fixed during steady-state growth it follows that real wages increase by $\eta\%$ per annum. According to

$$\lambda_t = \frac{a_t^*}{y_t^*} \cdot \frac{l_t}{p_{y_t}}$$

one can arrive at

$$\mathring{y}_t^* - \mathring{a}_t^* = \eta.$$

5. EMPLOYMENT AND PRODUCTION OUT OF EQUILIBRIUM:
THE DETERMINATION OF EMPLOYMENT IN THE SHORT-TERM MODEL 69-C

The employment equation in model 69-c runs as follows [23]

$$\mathring{a}^f = [0,24\,\mathring{v}_a + 0,09\,\{\mathring{p}_{m'} - \mathring{p}_{v'-1/2} + 0,06\,\mathring{T}_{k'-1/3}\}] - 0,25\,i'_{-1}/v'_{-2}$$
$$+ 0.05\,\mathring{c}^r_{pr} + 0.30\,[\mathring{p}_{v'} - 0.27\,\mathring{l} - 0.30\,\mathring{p}_{m'} - 0.06\,\mathring{T}_{k'-1/3}]$$
$$- 1.47\,\Delta w_{l-1} + 2.77 \tag{5.1.}$$

We can come in the neighbourhood of this specification by combining the vintage equations (4.3.), (4.4.) and (4.6.) with the disequilibrium equations (3.4.), (3.5.) and (3.7.).[24] This yields

$$\mathring{a}^f = \beta\mathring{y}^p_d + \varepsilon_1\frac{i_{t-1}}{y^*_{t-1}} + \delta\,[\mathring{lq}_s - \mathring{lq}_d] - \varepsilon_2\frac{\Delta y^{*e}}{y^*_{t-1}} + \varepsilon_3\,[\mathring{a}^f_s - \mathring{a}^f] + \varepsilon_4 \tag{5.2.}$$

where

$$\varepsilon_1 = \frac{100}{\kappa}[\lambda^{-1}_{t-1}(1+\eta')^{-m_{t-1}} - \beta]$$

$$\varepsilon_2 = 100\,[\lambda^{-1}_{t-1} - \beta]$$

$$\varepsilon_3 = \frac{u_2}{u_3 - u_2}$$

$$\varepsilon_4 = -\rho\,[1-\beta]$$

Now many of the elements seem more or less in line with those of eq. (5.1.). The first term on the right-hand side of eq. (5.1.) stands for the first term of eq. (5.2.) if we assume a substitution relationship [25] according to

$$\mathring{m}'^p_d - \mathring{y}^p_d = \varepsilon_5\,[\mathring{p}_{m'} - \mathring{p}_y] \quad \varepsilon_5 < 0 \tag{5.3.}$$

combined with two definitions of the types:

$$\mathring{p}_{v'} = \gamma_{m'}\mathring{p}_{m'} + [1 - \gamma_{m'}]\,\mathring{p}_y \tag{5.4.}$$

and

$$\mathring{v}'^p_d = \gamma_{m'}\mathring{m}'^p_d + [1 - \gamma_{m'}]\,\mathring{y}^p_d \tag{5.5.}$$

23. Compare [24] and [5].
24. The weights u are assumed constant in all derivations; the tension between demand and supply occurring in eq. (3.2.B) is approximated to by its initial level.
25. Compare e.g. J. C. Siebrand [18] for similar assumptions.

From the last three equations we may derive:

$$\overset{\circ}{y}{}^p_d = \overset{\circ}{v}{}'^p_d - \varepsilon_5 \frac{\gamma_{m'}}{1 - \gamma_{m'}} [\overset{\circ}{p}_{m'} - \overset{\circ}{p}_{v'}] \qquad (5.6.)$$

from which the similarity with the term between square brackets in eq. (5.1.) is clear.

Also the other terms of eqs. (5.1.) and (5.2.) are more or less akin. The investment ratio's differ only in the denominator, the monetary terms are interpretable along the same lines, while both fifth terms imply a transformation of the change in the unemployment ratio.

A break-down of $p_{v'}$ in the fourth term (gross profits per unit of output) of eq. (5.1.) according to eq. (5.4.) yields a partial effect of $[\overset{\circ}{p}_y - l]$ in this term which seems part of the explanation of economic obsolescence specified in the fourth term of eq. (5.2.).[26] But in spite of all this similarity the 'explanation' fails as the signs of ε_1, ε_3, and ε_4 seem the opposite of their counterparts in eq. (5.1.).[27]

Therefore we will investigate an alternative to eq. (5.2.). Using the entire system of eqs. (3.3. – 3.7.) together with the eqs. (4.3.), (4.4.) and (4.6.) we can derive[28]

$$\overset{\circ}{a}{}^f = \beta \overset{\circ}{y}{}^p_d - \varepsilon_5 \frac{i_{t-1}}{y^*_{t-1}} + \varepsilon_6 [l\overset{\circ}{q}{}^p_s - l\overset{\circ}{q}_d] - \varepsilon_7 [\overset{\circ}{a}{}^p_s - \overset{\circ}{a}{}^p_d] + \varepsilon_8 \qquad (5.7.)$$

where

$$\varepsilon_5 = \frac{100}{\kappa} \left[\frac{1}{\lambda_{t-1}} - \frac{(1 + \eta')^{-m_{t-1}}}{\lambda_{t-1}} \right]$$

$$\varepsilon_6 = \delta - \gamma \left[\frac{1}{\lambda_{t-1}} - \beta \right]$$

$$\varepsilon_7 = \alpha \left[\frac{1}{\lambda_{t-1}} - \beta \right] - u_2$$

$$\varepsilon_8 = \left[\frac{1}{\lambda_{t-1}} - 1 \right] \rho + \left[\frac{1}{\lambda_{t-1}} - \beta \right] \overset{\circ}{y}{}^p_s$$

26. Compare eq. (2.2.6.A).
27. It seems rather difficult if not impossible to find values for λ, η' and m which make
$$\lambda^{-1}_{t-1} [1 + \eta']^{-m_{t-1}} < \beta = 0,24 \text{ and consequently } \varepsilon_1 < 0.$$
28. This derivation procedure will appear as a discussion paper of the Institute for Economic Research, Erasmus University Rotterdam.

The use of eq. (5.6.) for $\overset{\circ}{y}{}_d^p$ in eq. (5.7.) makes the first term on the right-hand side of eq. (5.1.) plausible. The second term on the right-hand side of eq. (5.7.) has a negative sign as the corresponding term in eq. (5.1.). The monetary terms in both equations have equal signs as well, providing $\varepsilon_6 > 0$. The same holds, apart from a one year lag, with regard to $[\overset{\circ}{a}{}_s^p - \overset{\circ}{a}{}_d^p]$ which is transformed into $\varDelta w_{l-1}$ in the 69-c model. Possibly we may assume $\varepsilon_7 > 0$.

Next we turn to the constant term in eq. (5.1.) Maybe this constant should be read as an approximation to ε_8. The gross-profit margin featured in eq. (5.1.) is lacking in eq. (5.7.). Perhaps this term stands for an impact of profitability in the transformation of expected short-term product demand into intended short-term product supply, absent from eq. (3.7.). We leave the relevant interpretation of this term to the reader.

6. THE INTEGRATION OF SHORT-TERM AND MEDIUM-TERM ANALYSIS: THE RE-
   LATIONSHIPS BETWEEN PRODUCTION CAPACITY, PRODUCTION AND EM-
   PLOYMENT IN THE C.S.-MODEL.

The c.s.-model was constructed by van den Beld [2] in the mid-sixties to integrate short-term and medium-term macro-economic analysis. Its main new feature relevant in this context is the separate treatment of production and production capacity. The first was conceived of as determined by demand for products, while the latter was related to the available amounts of factors of production, as follows:

$$\overset{\circ}{y}{}_t^* = \lambda_{t-1}\, \overset{\circ}{a}{}_{s_t}^{tr} + 0.275\, \frac{i_{t-1}}{y_{t-1}^*} + \overset{\circ}{y}{}_{au_t}^* \qquad (6.1.)$$

where $\overset{\circ}{a}{}_s^{tr}$ symbolizes labour supply's trend value and $\overset{\circ}{y}{}_{au}$ stands for autonomous changes in production capacity, such as those caused by weather conditions and labour time shortening.

For a similar equation we may substitute an expression for

$$100\, \frac{\varDelta y^{*e}}{y_{t-1}^*}$$

solved from eq. (4.3.) into (4.7.); this yields

$$\overset{\circ}{y}{}_t^* = \lambda_{t-1}\, \overset{\circ}{a}{}_t^* + \frac{100}{\kappa}\, [1 - (1 + \eta')^{-m_{t-1}}]\, \frac{i_{t-1}}{y_{t-1}^*} - (1 - \lambda_{t-1})\, \rho \qquad (6.2.)$$

The identification of capacity employment ($\mathring{a}_t^*$) with the trend value of labour supply ($\mathring{a}_s^{tr}$) may be interpreted as resting on the assumption that labour demand equals labour supply over the cycle.

The constancy of the coefficient of the investment ratio in eq. (6.1.) implies that the C.S.-model abstracts from any change in m (the age of the eldest vintage in use) and consequently from changes in the age composition of capital [29]. Apparently, the technical deterioration represented in the last term of the right-hand side of eq. (6.2.) was either neglected or considered as a constant fraction of investment.

The equilibrium character of the production capacity relation in the C.S.-model might be associated with medium- or long-term development. In the C.S.-employment equation however disequilibrium elements play an additional role. This equation runs as follows

$$\mathring{a}_t^f = \mathring{y}_t^* - 0.40[\mathring{y}_t^* - \mathring{y}_t] - 0.03 \sum_{t}^{t-6} [\mathring{I} - \mathring{p}_i']_{t-1} - 3.3 \qquad (6.3.)$$

Again, our basic system allows for a similar expression after a number of simplifications. From eqs. (3.4.) and (3.7.) we derive (neglecting the monetary impact by putting $\delta = 0$)

$$\mathring{a}_t^f = [1 - u_2]\,\mathring{a}_t^* + \beta[1 - u_2]\,[\mathring{y}_{d_t}^p - \mathring{y}_t^*] + u_2\,\mathring{a}_{s_t}^p \qquad (6.4.)$$

If we identify potential labour supply ($\mathring{a}_s^p$) with trendwise labour supply ($\mathring{a}_s^{tr}$) and the latter as before with capacity employment ($\mathring{a}_t^*$) eq. (6.4.) may be transformed into

$$\mathring{a}_t^f = \beta[1 - u_2]\,[\mathring{y}_{d_t}^p - \mathring{y}_t^*] + \mathring{a}_t^* \qquad (6.5.)$$

Next we neglect the monetary impact in eq. (3.6.) by assuming $\gamma = 0$ and also abstract from the impact of labour availability on potential product supply ($\alpha = 0$).

Then potential product supply ($\mathring{y}_s^p$) equals production capacity ($\mathring{y}^*$) and by combination of eq. (6.5.) with eqs. (3.3.) and (4.9.), eq. (6.5.) may be transformed into

$$\mathring{a}_t^f = \xi_{t-1}\,\mathring{y}_t^* - \beta\frac{(1 - u_2)}{(1 - u_1)}[\mathring{y}_t^* - \mathring{y}_t] - 100[\lambda_{t-1}^{-1} - \xi_{t-1}]\frac{\Delta y_t^{*e}}{y_{t-1}^*}$$

$$- (1 - \xi_{t-1})\rho \qquad (6.6.)$$

Obviously, the terms $[\mathring{y}_t^* - \mathring{y}_t]$ in eqs. (6.3.) and (6.6.) are comparable while

29. W. C. Verbaan and P. B. de Ridder explicitly took changes in m into account, see [21].

the relative factor costs term in eq. (6.3.) may stand for economic obsolescence represented in eq. (6.6.) by its third term on the right-hand side. The
other corresponding terms in both equations reveal similarities as well, but
apart from possible variations in the parameters during the course of time
there seems to be an important deviation in the coefficient of $\overset{\circ}{\hat{y}}_t^*$.[30]

7. SOME RECENT DEVELOPMENTS

After 1970, a changing economic scene, in which growth and nearly full
employment no longer seem warranted, induced an increased attention
to product supply in Dutch macro-economic model building.

Den Hartog and Tjan [9] were first in specifying a production sector
explicitly based on clay-clay assumptions. Later they merged this analysis in
a more complete macro-economic framework [10]. This work became the
centre of a vivid discussion on the relevance of real wages for the Dutch
employment situation.

At the same time the present authors applied a very similar production
model to a disequilibrium analysis of the Dutch labour market [14]. This
partial analysis discerns ex ante and ex post labour demand and supply. A
specially developed but rather general iterative estimation procedure serves
to approximate to the potential entities on the basis of ex post data and
assumptions specified in the sections 3 and 4 of the present paper. Our
implied interpretation of the Dutch employment development during the
sixties confirms that of Den Hartog and Tjan.

Sandee's tentative studies [17] and [17A] on the relevance of a putty-clay
model for the description of output and employment in the Netherlands and
Den Butter's suggestions [4] to relax the assumption on perfect competition
mark the recent discussions as well.

If we may extrapolate recent theoretical and empirical trends we can
expect an explicit integration of vintage models and modern disequilibrium
theory in a rather broad setting in the near future.

---

30. Presumably Van den Beld based his production capacity and employment relation on
a Cobb-Douglas production function combined with integral technical progress. In this
case one might expect in eq. (6.3.) a coefficient of 1,0 for $\overset{\circ}{\hat{y}}_t^*$. Furthermore the third term
on the right-hand side of eq. (6.3.) can then be read as a substitution impact, inspired by
the development between labour and capital costs.

LIST OF SYMBOLS

I. General:

1. Lower-case letters stand for quantities in terms of constant prices or price variables; capital symbols refer to values in current prices.
2. Greek letters indicate coefficients.
3. Letters with a dot denote (annual) percentage changes; letters without a dot denote levels of variables.
4. Variables for the current year do not have a numerical suffix. They may or may not have the suffix t.
   A lag of 1, 2, ..., n years is indicated by -1, -2, ..., $-n$ or by $t-1$, $t-2$, ..., $t-n$.
5. Actual variables – in contrast to potential variables – are indicated by the upper index f.
6. Potential variables are denoted by an upper index p and a lower index d(emand) or s(upply).
7. Capacity variables are denoted by an asterisk (*).

II. Main variables:

a	employment
a_s	labour supply
Δa^{*e}	change in capacity employment due to economic obsolescence of machinery
a_s^{tr}	trend value of labour supply
a^*	capacity employment
c_{pr}^r	deposits
g	average age of the capital stock
i'	gross investments (excluding residential construction)
i	gross investments in equipment
k	capital stock
Δk^e	change in capital stock due to economic obsolescence of machinery
l	wage rate
lq	liquidities
m	age of the eldest vintage in use
m'	imports
$p_{m'}$	import price
p_y	product price deflator
$p_{i'}$	price gross investment (excluding residential construction)
$p_{v'}$	price of total expenditure (less inventory changes and net invisibles)

s mean square age of the capital stock
$T_{k'}$ incidence of indirect taxes minus subsidies
v' total expenditure less inventory changes and net invisibles
v_a idem (components reweighted by intensity of labour demand)
Δw_l curvilinear function of unemployment
y production
y^* production capacity
y^*_{au} autonomous factors in production capacity
Δy^{*e} change in production capacity due to economic obsolescence of machinery.

REFERENCES

[1] Allen, R. G. D. *Macro-Economic Theory*. London 1967.

[2] Beld, C. A., van den. *A Macro Model for the Dutch Economy*. C.E.I.R. Model Building Symposia, New York 1968.

[3] Benassy, J.-P., Neo-Keynesian Disequilibrium Theory in a Monetary Economy. *Review of Economic Studies*, October 1975.

[4] Butter, F. A. G., den. De optimale economische levensduur van kapitaalgoederen in een jaargangenmodel met een vaste kapitaalcoëfficiënt. *Maandschrift Economie*, april 1976.

[5] *Centraal Economisch Plan*. 1971.

[6] Clower, R. C. The Keynesian Counterrevolution: A Theoretical Appraisal, in: F. H. Hahn and F. Brechling (eds.). *The Theory of Interest Rates*. London 1965.

[7] Eckstein, O., and G. Fromm. The Price Equation. *American Economic Review*, Vol. 58, No. 5 part 1 (1968), p. 1159–1183.

[8] Grossman, H. I. A Choice-Theoretic Model of an Income Investment Accelerator. *American Economic Review*, September 1972.

[9] Hartog, H., den en H. S. Tjan. *Investeringen, lonen, prijzen en arbeidsplaatsen (Een jaargangenmodel met vaste coëfficiënten voor Nederland)*. Central Planning Bureau, The Hague, August 1974.

[10] Hartog, H., den, Th. C. M. J. van der Klundert en H. S. Tjan. De structurele ontwikkeling van de werkgelegenheid in macro-economisch perspectief. *Preadvies Vereniging voor de Staathuishoudkunde*. 's-Gravenhage 1975.

[11] Hasselman, B. H., and R. S. G. Lenderink. *An Approximation to Capacity Output, The Dutch Case*. Institute for Economic Research, Erasmus University Rotterdam, Discussion Paper Series, 7604/G, Rotterdam 1976.

[12] Iwai, Katsuhito. The Firm in Uncertain Markets and its Price, Wage and Employment Adjustments. *Review of Economic Studies*, April 1974.

[13] Kooyman, J., and A. H. Q. M. Merkies. *Possible Growth in the Netherlands up to 1985*. Occasional Paper no. 1/72, Central Planning Bureau, The Hague 1972.

[14] Lenderink, R. S. G., and J. C. Siebrand. *A Disequilibrium Analysis of the Labour Market*. Rotterdam University Press, Rotterdam 1976.

[15] Phillips, A. W. The Relation between Unemployment and the Rate of Change of Money Wage Rates in the United Kingdom, 1861–1957. *Economica*, 26, November 1958.

[16] Rowthorn, R. E. What remains of Kaldor's Law? *The Economic Journal*, no. 337, Vol. 85, March 1975.

[17] Sandee, J. *A Putty-Clay Model for the Netherlands*. Central Planning Bureau, The Hague 1976.

[17A] Idem. *Revised Edition*.

[18] Siebrand, J. C. Potential Demand and External Trade. *De Economist*, 120, Vol. 3, 1972.

[19] Siebrand, J. C. *Recursieve onevenwichtigheidsmodellen voor goederenmarkt en arbeidsmarkt*. Institute for Economic Research, Erasmus University Rotterdam, Discussion Paper Series, 7608/G, Rotterdam 1976.

[20] Siebrand, J. C. *Some Operational Disequilibrium Macro-Economics*. Forthcoming.

[21] Verbaan, W. C., en P. B. de Ridder. Uniforme modelstructuur voor meerdere Landen. *De Economist*, 121, 1973.

[22] Verdoorn, P. J. Fattori che Regolano lo Sviluppo della Produttivita del Lavoro. *L'Industria*, 1949.

[23] Verdoorn, P. J. *Preadvies Vereniging voor de Staathuishoudkunde 1952*. Martinus Nijhoff, 's-Gravenhage 1952.

[24] Verdoorn, P. J., J. J. Post and S. S. Goslinga. *The 1969 Re-estimation of the Annual Model (69ᶜ)*. Memorandum of the Central Planning Bureau, The Hague, January 1970.

Planned Shortages and Price Theory

T. M. WHITIN

1. INTRODUCTION

In economic literature it is frequently the case that one or more of the assumptions of a model are not stated explicitly. Sometimes this neglect is not serious, but it can be of the utmost importance. One such assumption is that the quantity demanded and the quantity supplied are the same. In the following it is shown that it can be profitable for a monopolist to intentionally supply less than is demanded. Thus the conventional monopolist of economic theory who produces and sells that output for which marginal cost and marginal revenue are equal can be shown to be failing to maximize profits. Furthermore, the cost function and the demand function are interdependent in a manner which prevents the usual separation of these functions. Indeed it is this interrelationship which makes shortages profitable for appropriate cost and revenue parameter values.

First, a monopoly model is constructed which explicitly includes inventory-associated costs such as the cost of placing orders and the costs of carrying goods in inventory. Although it could be argued that the inclusion of these costs is itself an extension of conventional monopoly theory, a generous interpretation of the latter could be that these costs are implicitly included in the cost curves. Other typically unstated assumptions such as that the model is stationary over time and that only one price can be charged will also be considered part of the conventional apparatus.[1] A 'conventional monopoly solution' for the model is then provided. However, it is possible for the monopolist to obtain profits in excess of those consistent with the conventional analysis. These higher profits are shown to result from intentionally choosing to run out of stock. Although such policies obviously reduce the total revenue received, the concomitant reduction in total cost more than

---

1. It has been shown by the author that setup costs, *no matter how small*, result in intertemporal price variations. See Output Dimensions and Their Implications for Cost and Price Analysis, *The Journal of Business*, Vol. 45, 1972, pp. 305–15.

compensates for the lost revenue. Much of the analysis is carried out in terms of a specific model in pointing out a basic failure in conventional monopoly analysis. One can no longer assume that the marginal cost equals marginal revenue solution is, in general, optimal.

2. THE CONVENTIONAL MODEL

The monopoly analysis of this section differs from the usual only in making explicit the inventory cost components. It is assumed that an ordering cost, A, is increased each time an order is placed. Also, the cost of carrying inventories is assumed to be I per unit of inventory per year. If batch orders are placed for Q units per batch the addition to annual costs caused by the inventory terms when annual demand is X units is

$$\frac{X}{Q} A + \frac{Q}{2} I \tag{1}$$

Here $Q/2$ is the average level of the inventory which varies from Q to 0. The term $(X/Q)A$ is merely the number of orders multiplied by the cost per order. It is well known that for any given X, the optimum value of Q is $Q^* = \sqrt{\frac{2XA}{I}}$, as can be verified by setting the derivative of (1) with respect to Q equal to zero. Substituting Q^* in (1) and simplifying gives $\sqrt{2XAI}$.

Let $R(X)$ represent total revenue per year and $T(X)$ represent total costs per year exclusive of inventory costs. Then the monopolist's annual profit, $\Pi(X)$, is

$$\Pi(X) = R(X) - T(X) - \sqrt{2XAI} \tag{2}$$

The conventional monopolist then sets the derivative of (2) with respect to X equal to zero, obtaining

$$R'(X) = T'(X) + \sqrt{\frac{AI}{2X}} \tag{3}$$

where $R'(X)$ and $T'(X)$ are marginal revenue and marginal cost (exclusive of inventory costs) respectively. The right-hand side of (3) is, then, marginal cost including a term for inventory costs and order costs.

3. A REVISED FORMULATION

The above model implicitly assumed that X represented both the annual rate of production and the annual rate of demand. In the revised formulation of this section, X will represent the annual rate of production and actual sales. The rate of demand is designated by X_d. The new problem, then, is to select optimal values for X and X_d since it is no longer assumed that the two are the same. The optimal value of X_d will determine the optimal price. For any X_d the corresponding price will be designated by $p(X_d)$. Total revenue is then $p(X_d)X$. The cost of carrying inventories, when X is less than or equal to X_d, is $(X/X_d)(QI/2)$ representing the new situation where stock is on hand for fraction X/X_d of the year and is at zero level the remaining fraction of time. Figure 1 portrays the behavior of stocks over time when $X < X_d$. The average stock level is a weighted average of $Q/2$ for time Q/X_d and zero for time $(Q/X - Q/X_d)$, i.e.,

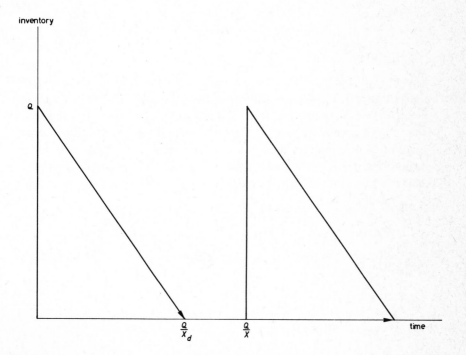

Figure 1

$$\frac{\dfrac{Q}{2}\dfrac{Q}{X_d} + 0\left(\dfrac{Q}{X} - \dfrac{Q}{X_d}\right)}{\dfrac{Q}{X}} = \frac{Q}{2}\frac{X}{X_d}$$

The number of orders per year when X is the total amount supplied per year is X/Q. The revised expression for profits, Π_2, can be written

$$\Pi_2(X, X_d) = p(X_d)X - T(X) - \frac{X}{Q}A - \frac{X}{X_d}\frac{Q}{2}I \qquad (4)$$

From the last two terms the optimal batch size $Q^* = \sqrt{2X_dA/I}$ can be found by equating their derivative with respect to Q to zero. Substituting Q^* into (4) and simplifying gives

$$\Pi_2(X, X_d) = p(X_d)X - T(X) - X\sqrt{\frac{2AI}{X_d}} \qquad (5)$$

$\Pi_2(X, X_d)$ can be maximized by setting $\partial\Pi_2/\partial X_d$ and $\partial\Pi_2/\partial X$ equal to zero

$$\frac{\partial \Pi_2}{\partial X_d} = p'(X_d)X + X\sqrt{\frac{AI}{2X_d^3}} = 0, \qquad (6)$$

$$\frac{\partial \Pi_2}{\partial X} = p(X_d) - T'(X) - \sqrt{\frac{2AI}{X_d}} = 0 \qquad (7)$$

Equation (6) can be solved for the optimal value of X_d, X_d^*, and thus the optimal price $p(X_d^*)$.[2] These values can be substituted in (7) which can then be solved for the optimal level of sales and output, X^*. This solution of (6) and (7) only applies when $X^* < X_d^*$. In the event that $X^* = X_d^*$, the 'revised' solution is the same as the conventional monopoly solution, as can be demonstrated simply by showing that when $X^* = X_d^*$, the satisfaction of (6) and (7) implies that the conventional monopolist's marginal revenue is equal to marginal cost (3).

$$R'(X) = p(X) + Xp'(X)$$

$$= T'(X) + \sqrt{\frac{2AI}{X}} - X\sqrt{\frac{AI}{2X^3}} \qquad (8)$$

$$= T'(X) + \sqrt{\frac{AI}{2X}}$$

$$= MC(X)$$

2. Note that the optimal value of X_d, and hence the optimal price $p(X_d^*)$ are determined from (6) without use of $T(X)$, certainly at considerable variance with 'cost-plus' theories.

Thus the conventional monopoly solution results as the special case of the revised model where $X^* = X_d^*$. It also follows that when $X^* = X_m^*$ (the monopoly optimum), X^* is equal to X_d^* and no shortages occur. From the optimality of X^*, it follows from (6) and (7) that

$$p(X)_d + X^*p'(X_d) = T'(X^*) + \sqrt{\frac{2AI}{X_d^*}} - X^*\sqrt{\frac{AI}{2X_d^{*3}}} \qquad (9)$$

The optimality of X_m^* implies that

$$p(X^*) + X^*p'(X^*) = T'(X^*) + \sqrt{\frac{AI}{2X^*}} \qquad (10)$$

which is consistent with (9) only for $X_d^* = X^*$.

Equations (3) and (7) enable one to specify when $X^* < X_m^*$ for conditions when conventional marginal cost $T'(X)$ is increasing. Restating (3) and (7), one obtains

$$T'(X) = R'(X) - \sqrt{\frac{AI}{2X}} \qquad (11)$$

and

$$T'(X) = p(X_d) - \sqrt{\frac{2AI}{X_d}} \qquad (12)$$

If the right-hand side of (12) is less than the right-hand side of (11) when evaluated at the conventional monopoly solution, it follows that the optimal value of X in the revised formulation is less than X_m^*. That is, $X^* < X_m^*$ if

$$p(X_m^*) - \sqrt{\frac{2AI}{X_m^*}} < R'(X_m^*) - \sqrt{\frac{AI}{2X_m^*}} \qquad (13)$$

This can be simplified to

$$|\eta| > p(X^*)\sqrt{\frac{2X_m^*}{AI}} \qquad (14)$$

where η is the elasticity of demand.

In the event that the demand curve is linear, say $p(X) = a - bX$, then it follows that $X^* < X_m^*$ for all values of

$$X_m^* < \left(\frac{AI}{2b^2}\right)^{1/3}.$$

Also, a linear demand function used in (6) yields

$$X_d^* = \left(\frac{AI}{2b^2}\right)^{1/3}.$$

4. EXAMPLE

The following numerical example assumes a simple conventional marginal cost function $T(X) = CX + \alpha X^2$ where $C = 12$ and $\alpha = .9$. Values of the other parameters are: $A = 4; I = 4; p(X) = a = bX; a = 22; b = .1$. For the conventional monopolist, profits are

$$\Pi(X) = (a - bX)X - CX - \alpha X^2 - \sqrt{2XAI}$$

$$= (22 - .1X)X - 12X - .9x^2 - 4\sqrt{2X} \qquad (15)$$

The conventional $MC = MR$ solution[3] results in an optimal monopoly output, $X_m^* = 4.32$, and an optimal price, $p_m^* = 21.57$. These quantities result in a total revenue of $\$93.18$, a total cost of $\$80.40$, and a profit of $\$12.78$. This result, it is here contended, is consistent with a generous interpretation of conventional monopoly theory.

It remains to show numerically that it is possible for the monopolist to generate additional profits by intentionally running out of stock. Equation (5) for the parameter values specified is

$$\Pi_2(X, X_d) = (22 - .1X_d) X - 12X - .9X^2 - 4X \sqrt{\frac{2}{X_d}}$$

Equation (6) yields

$$X_d^* = \left(\frac{8}{(.1)^2}\right)^{1/3} \cong 9.28$$

Therefore, $p^*(X_d^*) \cong 21.07$.
Equation (7) can next be solved for X^*

$$21.07 = 12 + 1.8X - \sqrt{\frac{32}{9.28}}$$

$$X^* \cong 4$$

---

3. Here the $MR = MC$ condition results in the equation $2X + 2\sqrt{2/X} = 10$ which results in $X^* = 4.32$.

The resulting total revenue is $84.44, total cost[4] is $69.98, and profits are $14.45.

Note that using (7) in equation (2) gives the following profit evaluation

$$\Pi_2(X, X_d) = XT'(X) - T(X)$$

which for the numerical example here simplifies to αX^2.

Consider next, as another example, the effect of increasing C to $15 and proportionately increasing I to $5. The conventional monopoly solution is $X_m^* = 2.5$; $p_m^* = 21.75; total revenue = $54.375; total cost = $53.125; and profits = $1.25.

The revised formulation results in $X_d^* = 10$; $p^*(X_d^*) = 21; $X^* = 2.22; total revenue = $46.66; total cost = $42.22 and profits = $4.44. Thus the effect of raising the marginal cost curve has been to lower the optimal price. This can be seen immediately from the equation $X_d^* = (AI/2b^2)^{1/3}$. Thus, in the linear demand case, raising inventory carrying charge I by increases in C always leads to an increase in X_d^* and hence a decrease in price. The results are in the relevant range until $X^* = 0$. In the present example, if I is kept at the constant one-third fraction of C, the upper limit of X_d^* is 10.77 for $C = 18.76, with the resulting optimal output and profits approximately 0. The highest C at which the conventional monopoly solution results in positive profits is $15.47. Here the optimal value of X_m is 2.18, the monopoly price is $21.78. Total costs are $47.45 compared with total revenue of $47.48, leaving about $.03 profit. At this value of C, the revised model solution is given by: $X_d^* = 10.1$; $p^* = 20.99$; $X^* = 1.944$. These values result in a total revenue of $40.80, a total cost of $37.40, and a resulting profit of $3.40.

5. ADJUSTMENT TO CHANGES IN DEMAND

The adjustment mechanism of the planned shortage monopoly model provides an interesting number of variations. It is possible that an increase in demand brings about an increase or a decrease in the optimal 'rate of demand'. To facilitate the presentation of these somewhat bizarre findings, a graphical approach to the model is presented here. Equation (6) above can be written as an equation with the marginal benefits of increasing X_d on the

---

4. Of the total, $7.44 constitutes the inventory-related costs, equally divided between order costs and inventory carrying charges.

left-hand side and the concomitant marginal losses (through lower price) on the right-hand side

$$\sqrt{\frac{AI}{2X_d^3}} = -p'(X_d) \tag{16}$$

The intersection of the two curves in Figure 2 (at point F) illustrates the level of X_d which equates these marginal benefits and losses for the case of a linear demand function.

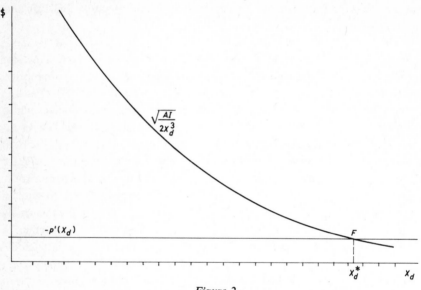

Figure 2

When the optimal level of X_d, i.e., X_d^*, is inserted in the demand equation the optimal price level (p^*) is determined. This price and marginal cost, inclusive of inventory-associated cost, determine the optimal rate of supply, X^*. Figure 3 illustrates the manner in which X^* is determined in the case of linear demand and marginal cost functions. Before turning to more complicated functions, the effects of a horizontal shift (right) in the linear demand curve will be examined. First of all, observe that Figure 2 is completely unchanged by a parallel shift in demand. Therefore X_d^* is the same. Because the new demand curve is higher, the new optimal price is higher. From Figure 3 it is obvious that the new X^* value will be higher at the higher price. However, there is a limit to the demand shifts for which the above remarks apply. This limit occurs when the demand curve goes through point

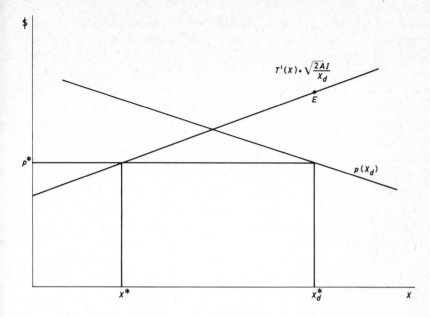

Figure 3

E (directly above X_d^*) of Figure 3. For this demand curve $X^* = X_d^*$, as can be seen from Figure 3. Also, as pointed out above (see Equation (8), the optimal conventional monopoly solution has the same value as X^* and X_d^*. Further increases in demand continue to yield the conventional monopoly solution.

Next, assume that the demand curve becomes flatter as X_d increases, i.e., that it is convex to the origin. What happens if the demand curve shifts horizontally? The horizontal shift in demand implies an equal horizontal shift in $p'(X_d)$, which causes the intersection (F) to move to the left, reducing X_d^* and hence increasing p^*. However, it has not yet been shown that X^*, as determined by the intersection of the price line at p^* with marginal cost, inclusive of inventory-associated costs, has increased. The increase in X^* is lessened by an upward shift in the marginal cost curve caused by the reduced value of X_d^*. Whether the net result of these opposing forces is to increase or decrease X^* depends on the shape of the total cost function (exclusive of inventory costs) $T(X)$. It was shown above that profits under optimal policy may be written:

$$\Pi_2(X^*, X_d^*) = X^*T'(X^*) - T(X^*)$$

This profit expression increases with X if $T''(X) > 0$, i.e., if the traditional marginal cost curve is upward sloping. The result is that increases in demand must increase X^*, as the following argument demonstrates. One possible response to the demand increase would be to leave price and (actual) sales quantity unchanged by increasing the proportion of planned shortage time. The result would be an increase in profits due to lower inventory costs at the higher demand rate. An optimal response to the demand increase must be at least as profitable as the above passive response, thus always increasing profits. Since optimal profits only increase when X^* increases, it immediately follows that X^* must have increased, as long as $T''(X^*) > 0$.

Next, consider the case where the demand function is concave to the origin resulting in an upward sloping curve for minus $p'(X_d)$. A horizontal increase in demand moves the $p'(X_d)$ curve to the right, increasing X_d^*. Intersection F occurs lower on the graph, however, indicating a flatter slope of the demand curve under optimal policy. For the concave demand curves under consideration here, this means an increase in p^*. In this case the reduction in marginal cost due to an increased X_d^* and the higher p^* reinforce each other in increasing X^*.

It is also possible for a non-parallel demand increase to result in an increase in X_d^*, accompanied by a decrease in p^*. Here the price change partially offsets the increase in X^* due to a downward shift in the marginal cost curve. Again the availability of increased profit implies an increase in X^*. An example of the type of demand increase that would yield a decrease in p^* is a shift to the right of the previous X_d^* value accompanied by a decrease in steepness. The slope change leads to a higher X_d^* which in turn can reduce p^*.

6. RELEVANCE TO COMPETITIVE MODELS

The above discussion was limited to monopoly to avoid controversial assumptions concerning the demand curve. Classical models of perfect competition are based on the unrealistic assumption of a horizontal demand curve which allows the firm to (instantly) sell its entire output at the prevailing market price. If this assumption is true, competitive firms would not need to inventory their final products at all. The competitive firm can be considered to be a price taker *and* a *quantity taker*. It cannot in general control the 'X' variable on the horizontal axis. It can control X only when the actual sales rate, X_d, exceeds the X it wishes to sell. If $T(X) = CX + \alpha X^2$ represents the total cost function exclusive of inventory-associated costs, profits are

$$\Pi(X) = pX - CX - \alpha X^2 - X\sqrt{\frac{2AI}{X_d}} \tag{17}$$

Equating the derivative of profits with respect to X to zero yields, for $X \le X_d$,

$$X^* = \frac{p - C - \sqrt{\frac{2AI}{X_d}}}{2\alpha} \tag{18}$$

In the absence of stockouts it follows from (2) above that marginal cost, including inventory carrying charges and costs of ordering, is

$$C + 2\alpha X + \sqrt{\frac{AI}{2X}} \tag{19}$$

Equating this expression to price yields the classical $MC = p$ solution. In fact, there is no reason to suppose that the actual quantity demanded is the quantity corresponding to the intersection of the marginal cost curve with the horizontal demand curve. However, to avoid controversy on this point, assume that the demand rate at the given market price is the rate consistent with the $MC = $ price intersection. Specifically, this results in

$$X_d = \frac{p - C - \sqrt{\frac{AI}{2X_d}}}{2\alpha} \tag{20}$$

or

$$p = 2\alpha X_d + C + \sqrt{\frac{AI}{2X_d}} \tag{21}$$

Also, $\Pi(X_d)$ can be simplified, substituting (21) in (17)

$$\Pi(X_d) = pX_d - CX_d - \alpha X_d^2 - \sqrt{2AIX_d}$$

$$= \alpha X_d^2 - \sqrt{\frac{AIX_d}{2}} \tag{22}$$

From (17) and (18) it can easily be shown that

$$\Pi(X^*) = \alpha(X^*)^2 \tag{23}$$

Profits resulting from (23) are higher than from (22)

$$\Pi(X^*) - \Pi(X_d) = \alpha(X^*)^2 - \alpha X_d^2 + \sqrt{\frac{AIX_d}{2}}$$

$$= \alpha(X^* + X_d)(X^* - X_d) + \sqrt{\frac{AIX_d}{2}} \tag{24}$$

Using (18) and (20) one readily obtains

$$\alpha(X^* + X_d) = p - C - \frac{3}{2}\sqrt{\frac{AI}{2X_d}} \tag{25}$$

and

$$X^* - X_d = -\frac{1}{2\alpha}\sqrt{\frac{AI}{2X_d}} \tag{26}$$

Substituting (25) and (26) in (24) and simplifying, results in

$$\Pi(X^*) - \Pi(X_d) = \frac{AI}{8\alpha X_d}$$

The right-hand term provides a simple expression for the additional profits attributable to shortages. From (23) and (24) it can be shown that

$$X^* = X_d - \frac{1}{2\alpha}\sqrt{\frac{AI}{2X_d}} \tag{27}$$

The conclusions that $\Pi(X^*) > \Pi(X_d)$ and that $X^* < X_d$, where X_d represents the demand rate at which the marginal cost expression (19) equals price, are valid under more general cost conditions. The effect of incurring stockouts is to raise the marginal cost of output X_d by $\sqrt{AI/2X_d}$. Therefore, the new marginal cost curve intersects the price line at a lower output. The shaded area in Figure 4 shows the increase in profit due to reducing output from X_d to X^*. Total costs corresponding to the highest MC curve are less than for the middle curve for all $X < X_d$. The marginal cost curves intersect at $X_d/4$.

It is of interest to note that here, as well as in the monopoly model, the marginal cost curve of the revised model is a function of the demand rate; i.e., the higher the demand, the lower the marginal cost. Thus it is not possible to separate the forces operating on demand from those influencing supply in the traditional manner.

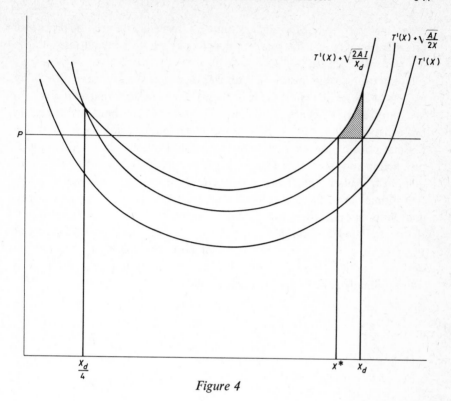

Figure 4

7. CONCLUSION

The revised model has shown cases where a monopolist can increase his profits by intentionally incurring shortages or stockouts. Indeed, in the case of a linear demand function, whenever the classical monopoly solution results in an 'optimal' output of less than the specified critical value of $(AI/2b^2)^{1/3}$, shortages can increase monopoly profits. More generally, shortages will increase profits whenever the demand elasticity exceeds $p\sqrt{2X_m^*/AI}$ where X_m^* is the conventional monopoly output. The conventional or textook models of monopoly are therefore not, in general, true, even if one assumes that they include inventory costs and ordering costs. The conventional models have implicitly assumed that the supply and demand rate are the same, i.e., that the monopolist meets all demands at the price he sets. The revised model shows that one must distinguish between the optimal demand rate and the optimal sales (and production) rate. The revised model also incroporates another quantity dimension, namely the batch size or order quantity which typically differs from both the demand rate and the optimal sales rate.

In addition to the basic result above, there are several other interesting aspects of the revised model. One of these is the possibility that an increase in inventory carrying charges or in unit cost can bring about a *decrease* in optimal price. Another is that setting a maximum price level below the optimal price of conventional monopoly results in lower rather than higher production and sales levels. For the particular cost function $T(X) = CX + \alpha X^2$ and linear demand function it was true that the optimal price was less than the optimal price for the conventional monopolist whenever the optimal conventional output was less than $k = (AI/2b^2)^{1/3}$, since the optimal X_d for the revised model in this case is equal to k. Finally, an important aspect of the revised model is that its marginal cost function is a function of demand, making it impossible to separate the supply and demand functions as traditionally done in the literature.

Optimum Policy Alternatives

J. SANDEE

1. INTRODUCTION

Sometimes, advisers provide policy makers with a prediction of the likely consequences of a single, given policy. More often, however, policy makers wish to be informed about the effects of a number of alternative policies. Supposing the economy behaves almost linearly in the area between these alternatives, policy makers can then without further information reach the compromise within that area that suits them best.

The selection of the alternatives to be submitted to policy makers in such a case is a constrained optimization problem to be solved by advisers. In the present study we have simplified this problem so much that a numerical example could be solved on the computer.

In the first part of the study we discuss this simplification; the second part shows the numerical example.

PART I GENERAL DISCUSSION

2. CONSTRAINTS ON ALTERNATIVES

2.1. *Dimension*

Policy makers rarely consider more than two alternatives simultaneously. While there may be as many as ten important instruments which each can be given a wide range of values, policy makers will only talk about a few 'packages' that contain fixed quantities of some or all of the instruments.

Such a small number of packages span a space of a low dimension, for instance three, which is a sub-space of the instrument space. There is little point in selecting the alternatives from the full instrument space and finding afterwards that they could have been selected from a space of much lower dimension. A more efficient procedure is first to determine the sub-space and to choose the alternatives from it.

In practice, the reduction to three dimensions does not entail a great loss of efficiency in instrument use. Reduced forms of linear (or locally linearized) policy models usually come very close to a rank of at most three, even if the number of instruments is far greater. A given set of targets can thus be reached almost equally well by any of a large variety of instrument combinations selected from a three-dimensional sub-space.

2.2. *Credibility*

Policy makers do not like extreme alternatives, and may refuse to consider them, as being 'unrealistic' and a waste of time. Each alternative should thus look feasible and attractive to at least one influential member of the group of policy makers. This puts a constraint on the range of the alternatives that can be selected.

This credibility constraint is essential for the selection problem to have a finite solution. It may be relatively wide, if advisers believe that some policy makers will want to discuss certain alternatives that in the opinion of advisers have no chance of being accepted as final decisions. It may also be very narrow, if advisers feel that policy makers will from the very start refuse to discuss certain policies that nevertheless might very well have become the agreed outcome of a wider-ranging discussion.

2.3. *Diversity*

Policy makers should not waste time over discussing the distinctions between two alternatives that are very close together in every respect. Such 'fine-tuning' should be done later, if at all. Hence, the distance between any two alternatives should be kept above some limit.

2.4. *Number of alternatives*

If policy makers were given a large number of alternatives they would have to throw out most of them, until a manageable number remained. This initial cutting down would restrict the range of discussion in an unpredictable manner. It is better to submit fewer alternatives. In our example we suggest to submit three pairs of alternatives symmetrically disposed about what advisers believe to be the most likely outcome of the discussions. If symmetrical pairs are not used the number of alternatives may well have to be less than six.

3. THE OBJECTIVE OF THE SELECTION

3.1. *The expected loss*

In a three-dimensional space the alternatives selected will span a convex polyhedron. The outcome of the policy makers' discussions will be a convex combination of the alternatives, hence a point inside or on the polyhedron.

If the polyhedron is too small, the policy makers will end up on a face (using only three alternatives), on an edge (only two alternatives being used), or even in a vertex (one alternative used). In these cases the policy makers would have preferred a point outside the polyhedron. The alternatives have not enabled them to reach this 'ideal' compromise, and a loss has been incurred.

The objective of the advisers, in choosing alternatives, should be to minimize the expected value of this loss.

Minimizing such an expected loss implicitly assumes that policy makers if forced to reach a restricted compromise realize how much they have lost relative to the 'ideal' compromise they might have reached if given other alternatives. Policy makers, however, do not know the 'ideal' compromise for if they did they would choose it. As the minimization of expected losses is standard practice in the analysis of optimal decision making, and our application is only slightly more abstract than most, we have nevertheless stuck to it.

Instead of assuming that the dissatisfaction of policy makers forced to reach a restricted compromise can be measured, one may recall that sometimes policy makers are so dissatisfied that they order another set of alternatives, or ignore the alternatives and agree on some set of instrument values that looks least painful to them. Such cases harm both policy makers and advisers, and alternatives could be chosen so as to minimize the probability of their occurrence. Advisers need only minimize the probability of the occurrence of restricted compromises, which is much simpler computationally than integrating losses.

The minimization of expected losses as stated ignores 'recourse', i.e. the submission of a second set of alternatives. If recourse is admitted, at a cost, the resulting two-stage problem will be very complicated.

3.2. *The distribution of compromises*

To be able to compute the expected value of the losses one must have their probability distribution. This is a (subjective) probability distribution of an event happening only once. Every time it is assessed, circumstances, including the states of mind of the policy makers, must be appraised anew.

It may be defined as the probability distribution of the compromise that policy makers will reach if presented with a set of possible compromises containing it.

This definition assumes that the set of alternatives presented does not affect the compromise chosen. This assumption may not be very realistic. Often there will be a tendency for policy makers to move towards the mean of the alternatives submitted.

We have not tried to build a computable model taking such a centripetal tendency into account.

If the policy makers form an uneasy coalition of two opposing groups either group will be most interested in being seen to obtain a clear victory or, failing that, a clear defeat. There will then be a centrifugal tendency, optimum sets of alternatives will be extremely difficult to define, and the probability distribution of compromises, if it can be properly defined at all, will in any case no longer be unimodal.

If centripetal and centrifugal tendencies can be ignored the compromise distribution will normally be unimodal but not necessarily symmetrical in all or any directions. Advisers will, for instance, often feel that there is reasonable probability that they misread policy makers' intentions in one direction, but far less in the opposite direction. Asymmetrical distributions make the selection of optimum alternatives harder but not impossible. We have not tried to construct an example.

In order to obtain a probability distribution of compromises one may first set up a probability distribution of strictly convex social preference loss functions, and derive the distribution of optimal policies corresponding to those functions. The advantage of this roundabout procedure is that at present there is a certain amount of theory and practice of social preference function specification [cf. Johansen (2)]; it is easier to proceed from there. Some kind of social preference function will anyway be required to measure the loss, to policy makers, of a restricted compromise.

The mapping of a set of preference functions into the instrument space in order to obtain a set of 'efficient' policies is also practised by Deleau and Malgrange [1].

TABLE 1.

Reduced form of the policy model

| Targets | | Instruments | | | | | |
		autonomous investment i_{au}	government expenditure X_G	nominal wage rates l	indirect tax rates T_{Kau}	wage tax rates T_{Lau}	profit tax rates T_{Zau}
balance of payments surplus	$E-M$	—0.767	—0.549	—1.175	+0.580	+0.480	+0.226
investment	i	+1.107	+0.118	+0.018	—0.120	—0.100	—0.047
real wages	l_R	—	—	+0.560	—0.055	—0.070	—
consumer prices	p_c	—	—	+0.360	+0.055	—	—
employment	a	+0.570	+1.070	+1.540	—1.070	—0.880	—0.410
government surplus	S_G	+0.199	—0.715	—1.484	+0.779	+0.763	+0.888

PART II   A NUMERICAL EXAMPLE

4. THE POLICY MODEL

For our example we take the policy model used by Van Eijk and Sandee [4]. It has 6 targets and 6 instruments. Its linear reduced form is shown in Table 1. Most variables are measured in billions of guilders but l, l_R and p are in fractions and a is in percentages.

5. THE MODAL PREFERENCE FUNCTION

We shall derive the distribution of compromises from a distribution of social preference functions. The latter distribution will be centered around a 'modal' preference function which will also be used to measure the policy makers' losses through restricted compromises.

The modal preference function is related to the linear maximand used in the 1959 article [4]

$$\phi_1 = 1.0(E - M) + 0.2i + 5.0l_R - 7.5p_c + 0.2a + 0.5S_G + 0.25x_G$$

This was supposed valid in a 'facet' defined by certain intervals of the target variables, and the instruments could only be used within certain ranges; both kinds of interval are shown in Table 2. Outside the facet so defined, other linear maximands were supposed to hold on further facets.

To provide, after so many years, many more facets and a probability distribution of their parameters demanded too much of our imagination. Instead, we converted the optimisation problem into an unconstrained quadratic problem. Quadratic preference functions are, of course, more fashionable anyway, mostly because in combination with a linear model and additive disturbances they display certainty equivalence. It is also customary to have a minimand, or loss function, rather than a maximand. This function will then be convex and its matrix of second order coefficients will be positive definite.

The simplest matrix of quadratic coefficients is diagonal. Accordingly, we have provided the square of each of the 12 variables with a positive coefficient.

For the target variables, the linear and quadratic coefficients are chosen such that in the middle of each former interval the marginal disutility of the variable now equals the value give to it in the former linear objective function, while at the bounds of each interval, the marginal disutility equals 0.5 or

TABLE 2.

Preference coefficients and bounds in the linear case

Variables		Units	Pref. coeff.	Lower bound	Upper bound
Targets					
balance of payments surplus	$E-M$	10^9 gld	1.0	0.00	0.30
investment	i	10^9 gld	0.2	—0.50	0.50
real wages	l_R	1	5.0	—0.03	0.03
consumer prices	p_c	1	—7.5	—0.03	0.03
employment	a	%	0.2	—1.00	0.00
government surplus	S_G	10^9 gld	0.5	0.00	1.00
Instruments					
autonomous investment	i_{au}	10^9 gld	—	—0.10	0.50
government expenditure	x_G	10^9 gld	0.2	—0.30	0.00
nominal wage rates	l	1	—	—0.01	0.05
indirect tax rates	T_{Kau}	10^9 gld	—	—0.50	0.50
wage tax rates	T_{Lau}	10^9 gld	—	—0.10	0.10
profit tax rates	T_{Zau}	10^9 gld	—	—0.30	0.20

1.5 times the marginal disutility in the middle. By way of example consider $E-M$. Its quadratic coefficient will be 1.67 and its new linear coefficient 1.50. As a result, the marginal disutility in the middle of the interval, i.e. at 0.15 billion, is $-1.50+2\times1.67\times0.15=-1.0$ which equals the former linear disutility, as required. At the lower bound of 0.00 billion the marginal disutility is -1.50, that is 1.5 times as much. At the upper bound of 0.30 billion, the marginal disutility of the quadratic function equals -0.50, as desired.

For the instrument variables the interval bounds indicated where a further use of the instrument would be insupportable. We translated this fact into quadratic coefficients by making those inversely proportional to the squares of the widths of the intervals, with a coefficient of 0.314 to be explained below. Linear coefficients were added such that in the middle of each interval, the marginal disutility of the instrument would be zero. For $i_{au'}$ for instance, the quadratic coefficient is $0.314/0.6^2=0.87$ and the linear coefficient is -0.35 so that at 0.20 billion the marginal disutility is $-0.35+2\times0.87\times0.20=0$.

For government expenditure x_G which is both a target and an instrument, two quadratic coefficients were obtained as indicated. These were added up and the linear coefficient was chosen such that in the middle of the interval the marginal disutility equalled the former linear coefficient.

The proportionality coefficient 0.314 was obtained by adjusting it until the optimal solution just fitted within all bounds. The coefficients and the corresponding optimum are shown in Table 3.

TABLE 3.

Quadratic coefficients CQ, *linear coefficients* CL *and the optimum* XOPT *of the modal loss function*

Targets	Units	CQ	CL	XOPT	Instruments	Units	CQ	CL	XOPT
$E\text{-}M$	10^9 gld	1.67	—1.50	0.171	i_{au}	10^9 gld	0.87	—0.35	0.029
i	10^9 gld	0.10	—0.20	—0.012	x_G	10^9 gld	3.91	0.92	—0.208
l_R	1	41.67	—5.00	0.000	l	1	87.22	—3.49	0.009
p_c	1	62.50	7.50	0.007	T_{Kau}	10^9 gld	0.31	0	0.059
a	%	0.10	—0.10	—0.357	T_{Lau}	10^9 gld	7.85	0	0.023
S_G	10^9 gld	0.25	—0.75	0.381	T_{Zau}	10^9 gld	1.26	0.13	0.200

6. A SAMPLE OF PREFERENCE FUNCTIONS

In order to obtain a probability distribution of preference functions, each of the 24 coefficients was given an independent lognormal distribution, with an identical standard deviation in the logarithms. The magnitude of this standard deviation does not affect the results, as will be seen.

The lognormal distribution maintains the signs of the coefficients. The quadratic coefficients in particular remain positive and as no off-diagonal quadratic terms occur, any loss function in the distribution is strictly convex. Each loss function corresponds to a unique optimum policy, hence the probability distribution of loss functions corresponds to a probability distribution of optimal policies. Information about the latter distribution can be obtained by sampling.

A sample or grid of 528 points in the preference function distribution was chosen so that in the first half of the sample in each point two of the 12 quadratic coefficients were halved or doubled (all four combinations) while the other quadratic coefficients and all the linear coefficients were left at their modal values. An example of a grid point would be the quadratic coefficient of $E–M$ changed to 3.33 (or 0.83) and the quadratic coefficient of T_{Lau} put at 3.93 (or 15.70). As $\left[\begin{smallmatrix}12\\2\end{smallmatrix}\right]=66$ pairs of coefficients were considered, each giving rise to 4 grid points, 264 points were obtained. A similar operation on the linear coefficients provided the other half of the sample. Each point in the sample has the same probability.

This was the largest sample constructed. Other samples gave about the same results.

For each grid point the optimum policy was computed as deviation from the modal optimum policy shown in Table 3. These 528 deviation vectors were scaled by multiplication by the square roots of the quadratic coefficients in the modal loss function, to form the set S of vectors s_i, $i=1, \ldots, 528$.

In terms of these scaled vectors the modal loss function is spherical

$$\phi(s) = \phi(o) + s's \qquad (6.1)$$

The constant $\phi(o)$ can be set equal to zero. We can then say that in the space spanned by the s_i the loss of any policy, as measured by the modal loss function, equals the square of the Euclidean distance to the modal optimum in the origin. This is the main reason for using this particular scaling.

7. PROJECTION ONTO THREE DIMENSIONS

To simplify the construction of alternatives it is useful to reduce the variety of directions in the sample to three in such a way that as little as possible is lost of the information contained in the sample. This can best be effected by a projection of the sample in a three-dimensional subspace Γ chosen such that the projection remains as close as possible to the sample. Malinvaud (3, pages 40–43) calls a k – dimensional subspace closest to an m – dimensional set of points S an 'orthogonal regression' and proves that it is orthogonal to the $(m-k)$ last principal components of the $m \times m$ moment matrix SS'. It is therefore spanned by the first k principal components of SS', i.e. by the eigenvectors of SS' corresponding to the largest three eigenvalues of SS'.

In our sample, the 12×12 moment matrix SS' had 6 non-zero eigenvalues as follows:
0.368 0.254 0.207 0.095 0.070 0.007 adding up to 1. The other 6 eigen values were zero, as all 6 targets depend linearly on the 6 instruments.

The largest three eigen values add up to 83 per cent of the total, hence the sample can without great loss of accuracy be projected into a three-dimensional space.

The three main eigen vectors have been normalized to lengths of 1. Together they form the 12×3 matrix G. Table 4 lists these three principal components converted each into the units of Table 3 ('conventional units'). In these units, the lengths of the vectors are no longer 1.

TABLE 4.

Three eigen vectors of the optimum policy distribution

Targets	Units	Eigen value		
		0.368	0.254	0.207
E-M	10^9 gld	0.537	0.189	—0.220
i	10^9 gld	—0.245	—0.293	0.672
l_R	1	—0.029	—0.022	—0.025
P_c	1	0.025	0.020	0.025
a	%	—0.874	—0.083	—0.172
S_G	10^9 gld	0.642	—0.069	0.766
Instruments				
i_{au}	10^9 gld	—0.141	—0.271	0.663
x_g	10^9 gld	—0.184	0.447	0.085
l	1	—0.003	—0.001	0.002
T_{Kau}	10^9 gld	0.471	0.366	0.439
T_{Lau}	10^9 gld	0.019	0.010	0.019
T_{Zau}	10^9 gld	0.172	0.012	0.384

In principal component analysis it is often possible to give a verbal characterization of at least the first principal component. In this case, the first eigen vector describes the range between inflation and deflation. In the positive direction, taxes are increased, and expenditure and wages are decreased. By themselves, these instrument changes are valued negatively. As a result, the balance of payments surplus and the Government surplus increase, which in the modal loss function is positively valued. However, investment, real wages and consumption fall and prices rise, all negatively valued effects. The net marginal result is zero, as it should be with small variations around an optimum of a quadratic function.

8. THE DISTRIBUTION OF COMPROMISES

Our sample of 528 policies constitutes the 12×528 matrix S. Its projection on the subspace Γ is represented by a 3×528 matrix H obtained by

$$H = GS \qquad (8.1)$$

We shall now choose a model of the distribution of compromises and estimate its parameters from the sample projection H. It will be helpful to examine the second moment matrix of the sample projection first. We find

$$HH' = G'SS'G = G'GA = \Lambda \qquad (8.2)$$

where
$\Lambda = 3 \times 3$ diagonal matrix of main eigen values of SS'.

The first distribution model that now comes to mind is the multi-normal distribution.

$$f(h) = \exp(\alpha - \beta \, h' \Lambda^{-1} h) \qquad (8.3)$$

This, however, has infinite tails which do not occur in reality, and it cannot be integrated analytically which increases the burden of numerical integration.

We have therefore preferred the multi-parabolic distribution

$$f(h) = \begin{cases} \alpha(\psi - h'Mh) & \text{for } h'Mh \leqslant \psi \\ 0 & \text{elsewhere} \end{cases} \qquad (8.4)$$

where M is a positive definite diagonal matrix. Integration shows that the second moment matrix of this distribution is $\frac{1}{7} \psi M^{-1}$ hence Λ^{-1} is a suitable estimate for M.

The parameter ψ defines an ellipsoid Ψ beyond which policies are so extreme that it is unthinkable that the group of policy makers would ever compromise on them. It cannot be estimated from the sample. The assumed lognormal distribution of the preference function coefficients does not even correspond to such a constrained policy distribution. The determination of Ψ is therefore an arbitrary decision, additional to the choice of the modal preference function and the shape of the preference function distribution.

The parameter ψ should be chosen such that all imaginable combinations of the three principal components stay within Ψ. The first principal component, which could be verbally characterized, offers the best opportunity to gauge ψ. In 1957, advisers would probably have decided that *plus* or *minus* once this eigen vector was the furthest policy makers could ever be expected to go (the balance of payments shift of 537 million guilders would have been particularly illuminating), hence

$$\psi = 1/\lambda_1 = 2.717$$

where
λ_1 = largest eigen value.

The parameter α must ensure that the total mass of the distribution equals one. Integration shows that $\alpha = 0.353$.

9. THE ALTERNATIVES

We assume that the alternatives will be submitted as pairs of 'high' and 'low' values in three different directions, symmetrically chosen with respect to the modal optimum policy at the centre of the policy distribution. The three directions and the distances between 'high' and 'low' still have to be determined.

The alternatives must lie within a credibility constraint. We believe that in 1957, advisers would not have submitted alternatives containing more than half of the first principal component. For simplicity's sake we assume that in other directions the credibility constraint was encountered at policies with the same probability as that of half the first principal component. The credibility constraint thus assumes the form of an ellipsoid surface Δ concentric with the hull of Ψ, at half the distance from the centre.

As shown by (6.1), the loss of a policy, as measured by the modal loss function, equals the square of the Euclidean distance to the modal optimum. This also applies to the projections of such policies on the three-dimensional space Γ. It is therefore natural to assume that policy makers, if preferring a compromise C outside the octahedron will agree on a compromise C^* on the hull of the octahedron nearest to C, and that the loss they incur by having to choose C^* instead of C is measured by the square of the Euclidean distance between C and C^*.

As the probability of any C is given by the distribution of optimum policies (8.4), the expected loss can be found by integration of this squared distance over this distribution outside the octahedron. We have assumed that it is this expected loss that advisers try to minimize.

One or more pairs of alternatives may lie on coordinate axes ('axial pairs'). For reasons of symmetry there are only four possible configurations of the octahedron, viz. the one with three axial pairs:

$(a, 0, 0)$, $(-a, 0, 0)$, $(0, b, 0)$, $(0, -b, 0)$, $(0, 0, c)$, $(0, 0, -c)$

and three with only one axial pair, such as

$(a, b, 0)$, $(-a, b, 0)$, $(a, -b, 0)$, $(-a, -b, 0)$, $(0, 0, c)$, $(0, 0, -c)$

where a, b and c are positive numbers.

We want as large as possible an octahedron that fits within the credibility ellipsoid Δ. In the first configuration, the three axial pairs are immediately determined by Δ. In the second configuration, the single axial pair is also determined by Δ but the other two must be fitted together within an ellipse in such a way that the expected loss associated with the octahedron is minimized. This is a one-dimensional search along the ellipse, for which a Golden Section method is suitable.

Finally, the expected losses in each of the four octahedra can be compared and the octahedron with the smallest loss chosen. The result is shown in Table 5.

TABLE 5.

Optimum alternatives (weights of eigen vectors)

Alternatives	Eigen values		
	0.368	0.254	0.207
		weights	
1	—	0.415	—
2	—	—0.415	—
3	0.391	—	0.233
4	—0.391	—	—0.233
5	0.391	—	—0.233
6	—0.391	—	0.233

The first two alternatives stretch the second eigen vector as far as it will go inside Δ. The other alternatives do not use the second eigen vector at all and share the room within Δ between the first and the third eigen vector.

In conventional units the six alternatives look different enough (Table 6). Alternatives 1 and 2 are characterized by strong variations in Government expenditure x_G, compensated in their effect on the budget surplus by changes in indirect taxes T_{Kau}. Alternatives 3 and 4 vary autonomous investment i_{au}

while indirect taxes are used to keep the balance-of-payment surplus $E-M$ more or less stable. In alternatives 5 and 6, x_G, i_{au} and T_{Kau} are all varied together in an inflationary or a deflationary sense. As a result, the balance of payments surplus and employment vary strongly.

Little use is made of the possibility to vary the other instruments, viz. the nominal wage rate l, or the direct taxes T_{Lau} and T_{Zau}.

With these alternatives, the expected loss through restricted choice is 0.029. It may be compared to the expected loss of 0.321 if no alternatives would be presented and the modal policy would have to be accepted.

The importance of the expected losses mentioned may be assessed by means of the following reasoning. The expected losses are obtained from the modal loss function specified in Table 3. They can thus be related to changes in balance of payments surplus (or any other variable). In the modal optimum, $E-M$ equals 0.17 billion. To increase the loss by 0.321, $E-M$ would have to be reduced to -0.07 billion. In 1957, such a reduction in the prospective balance of payments surplus, which would have turned in into a deficit, would have been taken very seriously. Only alternative 6 goes just beyond it, but there improvements in investment and Government surplus largely

TABLE 6.

Optimum alternatives (conventional units)

	Modal Optimum	Alternatives					
		1	2	3	4	5	6
E-M	0.17	0.25	0.09	0.12	0.22	0.43	—0.09
i	—0.01	—0.13	0.11	0.15	—0.17	—0.26	0.24
l_R	0.00	—0.01	0.01	—0.01	0.01	—0.01	0.01
p_c	0.01	0.02	—0.00	0.01	0.00	0.01	0.00
a	—0.36	—0.39	—0.32	—0.40	—0.32	—0.66	—0.06
S_G	0.38	0.35	0.41	0.56	0.20	0.45	0.31
i_{au}	0.03	—0.08	0.14	0.18	—0.13	—0.18	0.24
x_G	—0.21	—0.02	—0.39	—0.19	—0.23	—0.30	0.12
l	0.01	0.01	0.01	0.01	0.01	0.01	—0.01
T_{Kau}	0.06	0.21	—0.09	0.16	—0.04	0.14	—0.02
T_{Lau}	0.02	0.03	0.02	0.03	0.02	0.03	0.02
T_{Zau}	0.20	0.21	0.20	0.29	0.11	0.18	0.22

compensate the disadvantage. We may conclude that a loss of 0.321 would have appeared quite large. The presentation of the six alternatives and the subsequent discussion by policy makers would thus certainly have been worthwhile.

LIST OF REFERENCES

1. Deleau, M., and P. Malgrange. *Stabilisation efficace des systèmes économiques.* Paper presented at the Séminaire d'Econométrie de M. Edmond Malinvaud, March 21, 1977.
2. Johansen, L. Establishing preference functions for macro-economic decision models. *European Economic Review* 5 (1974), 41–66.
3. Malinvaud, E. *Statistical Methods of Econometrics.* Amsterdam: North Holland. 1966.
4. Van Eijk, C. J. and J. Sandee. Quantitative Determination of an Optimum Economic Policy. *Econometrica* 27 (1959), 1–13.

Some Remarks on the Optimal Tax System

JAN TINBERGEN

1. OBJECTIVE AND LIMITATIONS OF THIS ESSAY

1.1. *Objective*

This essay constitutes an attempt to derive some features of an optimal tax system. For this purpose a simplified model of the economy has been used. The optimal tax system is considered to be part of an optimal order, defined as the state of the economy which maximizes a social welfare function Ω, to be specified later (see Subsection 1.2). The model used might be called semi-macro and concentrates on a number of features supposedly relevant to income distribution between groups of individuals characterized by different personality traits and working on jobs described by a number of job characteristics. The number of personality traits equals the number of job characteristics, and there is no restriction on this number. In this respect the model has a high degree of generality. The production function used is a function of capital used and of the quantities φ_a^b of employed persons where a is a vector of the intensities in which each personality trait is available in the group considered and b is a vector of the trait intensities usually required for a satisfactory execution of the job. The order of the components of the vectors a and b is the same, and components a_i and b_i therefore refer to the same trait or characteristic. In the language of job evaluation i is one of the aspects of a job and b_i the score of that aspect required for the job. It may or may not be equal to the value of a_i characterizing the person on the job. If all $a_i = b_i$ we write $a = b$. The quantity φ_a^b is the proportion of the labour force characterized by a and b, and the total of all φ therefore adds up to unity. In one version of the model the total number of people characterized by a given value of a has been considered given, that is

$$\sum_b \varphi_a^b = F_a \tag{1.11}$$

The total number of components of a and b is written A, and hence

$$i = 1, \ldots, A \text{ (number of aspects)}. \tag{1.12}$$

Assuming that each aspect can occur in grades $g = 1, ..., G$, the total of all possible values of a_i or b_k amounts to AG. In what follows we will omit indices i and k of the vector components. We will indicate the set of all values which a or b can assume as $a = 1, ..., AG$ and $b = 1, ..., AG$.

Personal welfare ω is supposed to be a function of $x_a^b - f(a, b)$, where x is income after redistribution and $f(a, b)$ a correction on x which represents the monetary compensation for all efforts made and inconveniences suffered in the execution of the job b. Satisfaction from work appears as a negative inconvenience. The mathematical shape of ω is such that $\partial \omega / \partial x$ is a (negatively) monotonous function of x.

The present essay constitutes a generalization of two earlier attempts to deal with the subject [cf. Tinbergen 1975 and 1977].

1.2. *Limitations*

Among the many limitations of the model chosen, four deserve special mention.

First, the economy considered is a closed economy. No balance of payments is considered.

Second, no breakdown into economic sectors has been made: the production function is supposed to apply to the economy's total output.

Third, to begin with, a social welfare function $\Omega = \Sigma \omega$ will be used, which in Sen's terminology is the 'welfarist approach' [Sen 1977]. This implies, among other things, that in the community considered no preference with regard to distribution is assumed to exist. It is interesting to observe that already without such a preference some rather egalitarian features of the optimum prevail. In Section 6 a simple example will be given of the direction in which the optimum is changed if a preference for less unequal incomes is assumed to prevail.

Fourth, we assume that each household supplies one member participating in production outside the household. It would not be difficult to introduce alternatives, but it would unnecessarily complicate the model.

2. COMPARATIVE STATIC APPROACH CHOSEN; SOME IMPLICATIONS

The analysis to be presented is static. Its results will apply also to a developing economy provided the development satisfies a number of conditions. No attempt will be made to set out the full list of these conditions. This also implies that no proof of the statement just made is provided. The only attempt made in this section is to remind the reader in a sketchy way of the type of assumptions presumably needed in order to prove that our results have a somewhat wider applicability than for a strictly stationary state. The main determinants of slow long-term development of an economy are the development of population, of total capital, of knowledge and its distribution over the most relevant groups of the population. We assume that these determinants are moving over time in a regular and slow way, comparable to a development without business cycles, catastrophes or sudden structural changes. Among the preconditions for such a development we mention the following, thought to be the most relevant.

The age composition of human population in total and the distribution of the school population must be such as to exclude sudden surpluses or deficits in the age group as well as the stocks of students of various levels of learning. Similarly the age composition of capital goods must be such as to let the total stock move regularly and in the proportion to the various parts of the active population required by the prevailing production functions, including the gradual changes occurring in technology. The use of scarce natural resources must switch gradually to the use of less scarce resources so as to avoid unexpected shortages.

In our model we do not consider the non-active part of the population, such as the student population or the pre-school and retired population. We do not identify the distribution of expenditures over consumption and investment, but assume that the investments necessary to let the capital stock grow regularly in the desired way do take place. We assume that those who leave school find jobs fitting their education and that the practical training on the job develops harmoniously. We do not specify the production function, which constitutes a wide applicability of our findings in respect to this aspect of development. Our assumption on individual welfare functions ω has already been specified. Although this constitutes a limitation on the validity of our findings, the arbitrary number of personality traits and job requirements offers the possibility of a compensation for this limitation. With our present very limited knowledge on welfare functions the procedure chosen seems permissible.

3. CENTRAL CASE CONSIDERED

3.1. *Individual Welfare Function*

The economy supposedly consists of a number of households, each of which belongs to a relatively homogeneous group characterized by the vector values a and b already mentioned in Section 1. All members of such a group supposedly have identical welfare functions, $\omega_{ab} = \omega\{x_a^b - f(a, b)\}$, also already mentioned. Although a and b refer mainly to personality traits and job characteristics relevant to production, we may also think of traits relevant to welfare rather than to production, such as family size; the inconvenience due to a large family must then be reflected in $f(a, b)$.

There are a few personality traits which depress ω to such an extent that for households of that kind – say those with a member having a serious physical or mental handicap – the level of welfare required by the optimum conditions cannot be attained. Some curves in the graphical representation of the nature of the optimum position may not have the point of intersection required. Only welfare lower than that for all others may be possible for such groups of handicapped persons and a rather arbitrary level will as a rule be chosen.

Another difficulty in defining personality traits is that some of them can very easily be changed, for instance, the speed with which a given job (task) can be performed. We will not deal with this difficulty in the present essay, but it is not difficult to build into the model speed incentives, such as piece rate payments.

3.2. *Social Welfare Function*

As already observed, in the 'central case' we will use a welfarist social welfare function $\Omega = \sum_j \omega_j$, where $j = 1, \ldots, J$ indicates a household. Even without adding distributive features into Ω we will arrive at rather egalitarian conclusions about the optimum order, as was also already observed. Apart from the introduction of distributive features, announced for Section 6, one or two words can be said about what could also be called an egalitarian feature of the welfarist choice made. That feature resides in the absence of weights given to the individual welfare functions ω_1 in our sum. Clearly various weight systems are conceivable as alternatives to our choice. Somewhat parallel to a method introduced by Cohen [1977], high weights could be used to reflect the social or political power of some groups, and variations in these weights will affect the optimum. Also Van Praag's idea [Van Praag, 1975] of making a distinction between the social welfare function, as perceived by various groups within society, is related to variable weights and in fact is a more sophisticated way of introducing social or political power. In this essay we leave it to the reader to make exercises with such alternatives.

3.3. *Restrictions Used to Define the Optimum*
The optimum order studied in this essay is defined as a set of variables' values satisfying a conditioned maximum of the social welfare function. The conditions are the usual restrictions the economy has to satisfy. One set of such restrictions expresses the availability of households with given personality traits of the active member. The total portion of the productive population with personality characteristics a will be indicated by F_a and the restriction consequently is

$$\sum_b \varphi_a^b = F_a \tag{3.31}$$

As one alternative, applicable only for longer-run policies and even then within limits, we will also use the assumption that personality characteristics can be changed by processes of learning and that accordingly only one restriction remains to be respected, namely

$$\sum_b \sum_a \varphi_a^b = 1 \tag{3.32}$$

3.4. *The Production Function*
The next restriction to be satisfied by the optimum is the economy's production function, stating that total product y depends on the quantities of various types of manpower and on the quantity of (physical) capital K used:

$$y = \text{prod} f (K, \varphi_a^b) \tag{3.41}$$

As already announced it will not be necessary in our model to specify the production function, which has the advantage of a high degree of generality. We do assume, however, that the production function is differentiable with respect to all φ.

3.5. *The Spending Pattern*
The last restriction we are going to introduce concerns one aspect of how national income is being spent. We assume two things only: (i) a given total net amount T of taxes minus subsidies has to be paid and (ii) there is no hoarding or overspending. This implies that disposable incomes x_a^b have to satisfy the equation

$$\sum \sum \varphi_a^b x_a^b + T = y \tag{3.51}$$

4.   INCOME DISTRIBUTION AND TAXATION IN THE CENTRAL CASE

4.1. *Formulation of the Optimum Problem*

From the preceding choices and assumptions made it is easily seen that our problem boils down to maximizing

$$\sum_{a=1}^{AG} \sum_{b=1}^{AG} \varphi_a^b \omega \{x_a^b - f(a, b)\} + \sum_{a=1}^{AG} \lambda_a \left(\sum_{b=1}^{AG} \varphi_a^b - F_a \right) +$$

$$+ \pi \{y - \text{prod} f(\varphi_a^b)\} + \rho \left(y - \sum_{a=1}^{AG} \sum_{b=1}^{AG} \varphi_a^b x_a^b - T \right) \equiv \Omega' \tag{4.1}$$

with regard to the variables φ, x and y and the Lagrangian multipliers λ_a $(a=1, ..., AG)$, π and ρ.

As a special case we will consider the choice $\lambda_a = \lambda$ $(a=1, ..., AG)$.

4.2. *Optimum Conditions; Solution I*

Assuming that all solutions satisfy the conditions that $x_a^b \geq 0$ and $\varphi_a^b \geq 0$ for all a and b the optimum will be described by the conditions $\partial\Omega'/\partial x = \partial\Omega'/\partial\varphi = \partial\Omega'/\partial y = 0$. We will consider three cases:

   I. all x and all $\varphi > 0$
  II. all $\varphi_a^b = 0$ if $a \neq b$
 III. all $\lambda_a = \lambda$

In the present subsection the optimum conditions are

$$\omega \{x_a^b - f(a, b)\} + \lambda_a - \pi \partial y/\partial \varphi_a^b - \rho x_a^b = 0 \tag{4.21}$$

$$\varphi_a^b \partial\omega/\partial x_a^b - \rho\varphi_a^b = 0 \tag{4.22}$$

$$\pi + \rho = 0, \text{ hence } \rho = -\pi \tag{4.23}$$

Since for Case I we assumed all $\varphi > 0$, it follows from (4.22) that:

$$\partial\omega/\partial x_a^b = \rho \tag{4.24}$$

Since we assumed $\partial\omega/\partial x_a^b$ to be a monotonous function of x_a^b it follows that

$$\omega_a^b = \rho_0 \tag{4.25}$$

Substituting (4.23) and (4.25) into (4.21) we get

$$\rho_0 + \lambda_a - \pi(y_a^b - x_a^b) = 0 \tag{4.26}$$

where y_a^b stands for income before tax of an individual or household (a, b).

Writing t_a^b for the optimal tax to be paid by such an individual it follows from (4.26) that

$$t_a^b = \frac{\rho_0 + \lambda_a}{\pi} \tag{4.27}$$

or the optimal tax only depends on the personality traits a and *has to be independent from the job – and hence the income y_a^b – chosen.*

4.3. *Optimum Conditions; Solution II*

Taking up Case II we find that all equations (4.22) where $a \neq b$ are automatically satisfied. Case II implies that only individuals (a, a) are present, meaning that everybody finds a job whose characteristics b coincide with her or his personal characteristics. This situation may be called one of *equilibrium between demand for and supply of* certain characteristics without implying an equality of prices (that is, incomes before tax). Writing φ_a for φ_a^a and x_a for x_a^a, we have

$$\varphi_a = F_a \tag{4.31}$$

and

$$\partial \omega / \partial x_a = \rho \text{ leading to } \omega_a = \rho_0 \tag{4.32}$$

Equation (4.22) becomes

$$\rho_0 + \lambda_a - \pi (y_a - x_a) = 0 \tag{4.33}$$

or

$$t_a = \frac{\rho_0 + \lambda_a}{\pi} \tag{4.33}$$

Again taxes depend only on a, but since $a = b$ we can interpret the tax system, if we so desire, as one in which taxes depend on the job. The relevance of this statement will be discussed in Section 7.

4.4. *Optimum Conditions. Solution III*

Considering Case III, where all λ_a are equal $(= \lambda)$, we find

$$y_a = \rho \tag{4.41}$$

and

$$t_a = \frac{\rho + \lambda}{\pi} \tag{4.42}$$

All individuals now pay the same tax $T / \Sigma \varphi = T$ $\tag{4.43}$

5. TAX REVENUE DEPENDS ON EDUCATION COSTS

So far total tax revenue T per active person was considered given. In Case III it is more realistic to assume that T depends on the costs of education which depend on the F_a. We will deal with an example only to show what changes have now to be introduced into our setup. The example chosen is one with three levels i of education as the characteristics of individuals and the same three levels as required for the execution of the job. As part of T we must now introduce costs of education. The latter will be assumed to consists of three items, namely:

1. Income foregone, which will be 0 for primary education, y_1 for secondary and y_2 for third-level education per person educated;
2. Costs of teachers which are, for the three levels, $n_1 \bar{y}_2$, $n_2 \bar{y}_3$ and $n_3 \bar{y}_3$ respectively, where n_i is the teacher-student ratio for education level i and $\bar{y}_i$ the teacher income at level i;
3. Costs of buildings and other fixed assets to be represented by g_i.
   A realistic choice for n_i is $n_1 = 0.03$, $n_2 = 0.04$ and $n_3 = 0.08$.

From Dutch sources we further estimate $g_1 = 0.018 \, y$, $g_2 = 0.015 \, y$ and $g_3 = 0.343 \, y$, where $y =$ average income per active person. Furthermore we estimate $y_1 = 0.9 \, y$, $y_2 = 1.6 \, y$ and $y_3 = 2.4 \, y$.

All cost figures quoted so far are, however, costs for one year of schooling of each type. Assuming an average active life of 40 years and schooling time of 6 years for each level, we have to multiply the figures mentioned by $6/40$, if we want to multiply them by the total active population φ_i of each type in order to arrive at the annual burden of education in the stationary state of the optimum.

Our example will be elaborated only for Case III, where $b = a$, that is, all jobs requiring an education level i are performed by people with that same education level. The spending restriction (3.51) will now have to be

$$y = \sum \varphi_i x_1 + T_0 + 0.010 \, \varphi_1 y + 0.17 \, \varphi_2 y + 0.080 \, \varphi_3 y +$$
$$+ 0.15 \, \varphi_2 y_1 + 0.15 \, \varphi_3 y_2 \tag{5.1}$$

As a consequence the optimum conditions for Case III are now changing. They become considerably more complicated. Not only are there 'interaction terms' such as those in $\varphi_i y$, but the last two terms in (5.1) should be written $0.15 \, \varphi_2 \, \partial \text{prod} \, f/\partial \varphi_1$ and $0.15 \, \varphi_3 \, \partial \text{prod} \, f/\partial \varphi_2$, respectively. The most important conclusions which can now be drawn without going into the specification of the utility and production functions are that the values of the utility or welfare functions for the three groups no longer have to be equal in the optimum position. At least for some specifications we now find that welfare for the lowest income group has to be higher than that for the two other groups. Also the types of tax equalities found before no longer apply.

6. INTRODUCTION OF INCOME DISTRIBUTION INTO SOCIAL WELFARE

We now propose to leave our welfarist social welfare function and, restricting ourselves to Case II, add to it a term expressing the fact that the more unequal incomes x_i are, the lower the social welfare function

$$\Omega = \sum_a \varphi_a \omega (x_a - f_a) - E \sum \varphi_a (x_a - y')^2 \tag{6.1}$$

where $y' = y - T$ constitutes the weighted average of x_a.

With this social welfare function the optimum conditions become

$$\omega(x_a - f_a) = E(x_a - y')^2 + \lambda_a + \rho(y_a - x_a) = 0 \quad a = 1, ..., AG \tag{6.2}$$

$$\varphi \partial_a \omega / \partial x_a - 2E\varphi_a(x_a - y') - \varphi_a \rho = 0 \quad a = 1, ..., AG \tag{6.3}$$

$$2E \sum \varphi_a(x_a - y') + \pi + \rho = 0 \tag{6.4}$$

Since $\sum \varphi_a(x_a - y') = 0$ we find again $\pi = -\rho$ $\qquad$ (6.5)

Since all $\varphi_a \neq 0$ we obtain from (6.3)

$$\partial \omega / \partial x_a = \rho + 2E (x_a - y') \tag{6.6}$$

This means that marginal utility (which is negatively monotonous) falls with increasing a. Hence utility will rise with increasing a. The distribution will change to the advantage of the lower and to the disadvantage of the higher incomes.

In order to interpret this result we should bear in mind that $\partial \omega / \partial x_a$ is a falling positive function of x_a. For $E = 0$ the optimum position requires that this function shows the same value for all a (cf. equation 4.32). For $E > 0$, that is, a positive value attached (in the social welfare function) to less inequality of incomes, equation (6.6) shows that $\partial \omega / \partial x_a$ must be lower for low x_a's than for high x_a's. A lower value of $\partial \omega / \partial \omega_a$ corresponds with a higher value of x_a, and the optimum is now characterized (as could be expected) by higher values for the x_a of the 'poor' than those of the 'rich'.

7. SUMMARY AND CONCLUDING REMARKS

Let us now interpret our findings.

To begin with, the important difference between Cases I and II on the one hand and Case III on the other which should be kept in mind is that in the former cases education costs are fixed because all F_a are supposed to be given. Only in Case III, where F_a may shift, should education costs be discussed, as was done explicitly in Section 5. Our treatment of Cases I and II does not need the introduction of education costs as a variable.

It is noteworthy that the optimum positions found in Cases I and II coincide with equitable distribution situations, as defined in Tinbergen 1975: all individual welfare levels are equal. This does not apply to Case III and to the alternative dealt with in Section 6, where a preference for less inequality was introduced into the social welfare function.

The optimal tax system found can be characterized as follows: In Case I we found (cf. 4.27) that taxes have to depend only on personality traits and not on job characteristics. This is the type of lump-sum tax dealt with in Tinbergen [1975a]. Its feasibility is doubtful, to say the least, and will depend on the development of psychotechnical tests.

In Case II we found the same result (cf. 4.33), but since job and personality characteristics are identical here, the tax can also be based on job characteristics and hence on income; it is inversely proportional to π, the marginal utility of product and linearly dependent on λ_a, the marginal utility of labour category a.

The result of equal taxes for all (cf. 4.43) for Case III is valid only if education costs are assumed to remain unaffected by the shifts in manpower quality found. As mentioned in Section 5, this result changes in favour of lower income groups at least in one specification investigated. A general treatment meets with considerable difficulties and has not been undertaken in this essay. For a much more general and sophisticated treatment the reader is referred to Ritzen [1977].

Finally the introduction of a preference for less unequal incomes into the social welfare function shows that the solution found for Case II changes again to the advantage of lower income groups, whose welfare should now be raised in comparison to that of higher income groups. This result may be interpreted to mean that the egalitarian result found for Case II in the 'welfarist' version is an understatement.

REFERENCES

Cohen, S. I. *Development Models with Different Decision-Makers*. A discussion note for a conference on 'Future research, planning and decision-making' held at the Conference House of the Polish Academy of Sciences, Jablonna, Poland, April 22–24, 1977. EUR, Centre for Development Planning.

Ritzen, J. M. M. R. *Education, economic growth and income distribution*. Amsterdam: North Holland, 1977.

Sen, A. K., On Weights and Measures: Informational Constraints in Social Welfare Analysis. Walras-Bowley Lecture, Econometric Society. Forthcoming in *Econometrica* (1977).

Tinbergen, J. *Income Distribution*: *Analysis and Policies*. Amsterdam: North Holland, 1975.

Tinbergen, J. *Income Differences*: *Recent Research*. Amsterdam: North Holland, 1975 [1975a]..

Tinbergen, J. *Die International Neuordnung und ihre Machbarkeit*. Verein für Sozialpolitik, 1977.

Van Praag, B. S. M. *De verdeling van inkomen en macht*. Leiden, 1975, (Dutch; The Distribution of Income and Power).

National Impulses and Their Impact on the World: an Example

JAN KOOYMAN, J. J. POST and ANTOINE N. R. SCHWARTZ*

1. INTRODUCTION

National models assume the rest of the world to be exogenous. World trade models generally focus on the development of trade – it's what they are constructed for – and neglect its effects on national developments. Consequently, feedback effects are not visible in either type. The need then is for an international model that allows for the simultaneous analysis of economic development of – ideally – all countries of the world. The tremendous amount of data gathering and analyses necessary to do this makes such a task almost impossible. For that reason models are being developed in various places that focus on smaller numbers of countries and if they incorporate the rest of the world divide it into the larger blocks of countries that are presumed to have sufficiently common characteristics to indeed allow for grouping them together, such as OPEC countries, centrally planned economies, etc. Two examples are LINK and COMET.

This article will briefly present in the second section a third effort, the METEOR model, which is being constructed at the Dutch Central Planning Bureau on behalf of the Secretariat of the European Communites.

In the third section the METEOR model will be used to see if, within the constraints of the model, it is possible to stimulate the world economy in general and the economy of the Common Market partners in particular, by giving impulses in the two larger E.C. countries, Germany and France.

A final section will present some conclusions and the limitations to which these conclusions are subject, as a consequence of the nature of the model.

* The authors are very much indebted to Messrs. P. Dullaart and R. A. M. Sorton, without whose help this paper could not have been written, but who, of course, are not responsible for the text.

2. THE METEOR MODEL, BRIEFLY

The METEOR model applies the approach to annual models developed by Verdoorn to a large number of countries, albeit simplified and modified in a number of ways.

Simplified since it is almost impossible to incorporate so much refined detail as Verdoorn does in his short-term model for the Netherlands, if one cannot make use of a number of specialized economists for each country that is included in the model; modified since, for linkage reasons, certain variables, exogenous in a national model, have to be endogenized in an international model.

The METEOR model, then, is an annual model able to analyse cyclical fluctuations. The variables are generally expressed as relative first differences (percentage changes). Extensive models were constructed for the United States, the Belgian-Luxembourg Economic Union, France, West-Germany, Italy, the United Kingdom and the Netherlands. The rest of the world was split up into Canada, Japan, Northern OECD and Southern OECD countries which were not individually represented in the model, OPEC countries, socialist countries and all other countries, for which very simple models were used not really doing much more than providing import multipliers for export demand, except for the socialist countries that remain exogenous. For the seven larger country models in METEOR an effort was made to have the models as similar in structure as data would allow for. This was done for the express purpose of maintaining understandability for the analist working with METEOR. Very different models for different countries would very much impede an understanding of how impulses would work through the model and overly increase its character as a black box. The same motive accounted for endeavours to keep behavioral equations relatively short.

The behavioral equations refer to:
- the value of *personal consumption* as a function of disposable income and the price of consumption goods
- the volume of *investment by enterprises* as a function of economic activity, prices of investment goods, excess capacity, liquidities and non-wage income
- the real level of *stock-piling* as a function of total expenditure, prices and excess capacity
- the volume of *exports of goods* as a function of world demand, relative export prices and excess capacity

- the volume of *imports of goods* as a function of total expenditure, stock-piling, relative prices and harvests
- *labour demand* as a function of economic activity, relative price and excess capacity
- the *wage rate* as a function of consumption price, labour productivity and labour market conditions
- the *consumption price* as a function of unit costs and demand pressure
- the *price of investment goods* as a function of unit costs and demand pressure
- the *export price* as a function of unit costs, competitors' prices, demand pressure and harvests
- the *import price* as a function of suppliers' prices and freight rates.

It holds for all behavioral equations that depending on goodness of fit various other variables might be introduced for some countries, and depending on the level of significance of coefficients some variables that are part of the ex-ante structure of the model might be eliminated.

All government controlled variables (revenues and expenditures) are exogenous, so as to allow for policy simulations. A number of other variables such as e.g. liquidities, investments in dwellings, labour supply and imports and exports of services are also exogenous. Capacity levels are derived from a peak line.

The bibliography annexed to this article allows the reader to inform himself in more detail than is feasible in this presentation; an extensive description giving statistical and economic characteristics of the final version will be forthcoming.

One problem has to be mentioned here as it has not yet been satisfactorily solved, and that is the formal closing of the model. On a world level imports of goods have to equal exports of goods, but since both imports and exports in the model are derived from estimated equations this equality will only exist by chance. This equality is achieved by solving the model without it and then distributing the difference between the world totals of imports and exports over all countries (and country groups) in the model by proportion-ally adjusting exports and iterating the model until the desired level of resolution is achieved (e.g. in the second decimal). This method functions admirably if only one year is solved. For dynamic runs, where for lagged endogenous variables, the model solutions of the preceding years are used rather than the observed data, the model tends to run down towards zero changes for total world trade, after three or four years. The dynamic multipliers of the adjustment mechanism seem to be very large. For dynamic runs, so far, we have therefore eliminated the formal consistency mechanism. The difference between total world imports and exports generally comes out at less than two percent and very often at less than one percent.

3. STIMULATING IMPULSES IN FRANCE AND WEST-GERMANY

Economic development of any nation greatly depends on developments in the rest of the world, apart from what happens at home. Certainly now in the middle seventies when growth rates are low and unemployment is high, the question can be asked whether it is true, as proposed by the OECD, that the stronger countries should, through stimulating measures, create a momentum in economic development that will help those countries where the economic situation is weak. It is also, for an economic union like the Common Market, interesting to see whether the impact of stimulae in the stronger countries does in fact help the weaker ones.

So what we did was start from two government controlled variables, i.e. net material government consumption and government investment and a third variable, investment in dwellings, where government can more or less easily influence development and simulate an impact of 10% of these expenditures in France and Germany. In 1967 weights this amounts to 1.3% of total expenditures for France and 1.4% of total expenditures for Germany. The expenditure incurred by the governments was covered by an increase in direct taxes. The impulse is maintained for three years. Even though METEOR is a short-term model, the time-lag structure is such, that first year effects of an impulse do not tell the full story. On the other hand, running the model for three years but not maintaining the impulse after the first year would mean reversing the impulse in the second year, almost completely eliminating the effects of the initial impulse, since the model is mostly linear.

The first year, simultaneous solution of the model gives an increase in GNP of 2.8% in France and 4.4% in Germany. Accumulated effects in the third year amount to respectively 1.2% and 2.0%. Increased production and final domestic demand stimulates import demand to the tune of, in the third year, 1.3% and 0.6%. This creates export stimulae in supplier countries where this in turn increases production and demand for imports and so the general level of activity is increased all over.

At the same time labour productivity increases, in particular in France and Germany, and excess capacity decreases. This leads to increased prices in France and Germany of respectively 3.0% and 0.7% for consumer goods in the third year.

One of the still disturbing features of the model now is apparent: the different effects of similar impulses in different countries. The platitude that no two countries have exactly the same economic structure and so it is not surprising that similar impulses have different effects will in our opinion not warrant these large differences. The only reason we can find is a purely statistical one: in the domestic price equations the constant term is negative in France and positive in Germany. Our interpretation is that the explanatory variables then overestimate effects in France and underestimate effects in Germany, since in impact multipliers analyses the effect of the constant term is eliminated. Its value is -1.6 in France and $+1.7$ in Germany in the consumption price equations and -1.3 and $+0.4$ in the investment price equations. The effects are seemingly strong enough to overrule the reverse signs in the wage rate equations ($+0.7$ and -1.6) and the export price equations ($+0.7$ and -3.1). The explanation is admittedly tentative and further analysis is certainly necessary before a firm conclusion can be drawn. The end result however, even if the numerical values involved still show disturbing differences between the two countries, is still in the direction which one would expect, and so the model certainly promises to be a useful starting point for future research.

The effects on other countries are as expected, once one realises how these effects come about. GNP increases by 0.5% in the United Kingdom and 0.4% in the United States resulting from increased foreign demand. Prices in countries with a large import content increase faster than in countries with a lower import content (0.9% in the United Kingdom and 0.3% in the United States for consumption goods). This also holds for export prices and consequently export stimulation in the United States is stronger (1.2% in volume) than in the United Kingdom (0.8%).

Balance of payments effects show similar results: deficits for France ($ 1000 mln.) and Germany ($ 3500 mln.), surpluses for most of the other countries such as the United States ($ 400 mln.) and the United Kingdom ($ 200 mln.). Tables giving more detailed results are to be found in the annex.

4. CONCLUSIONS

Research on METEOR has now progressed so far that impact multipliers can be calculated that are plausible in direction of effects, even though it is not always clear why effects are so different in magnitude in countries where impulses originate. It seems that the sign of the constant term in estimated equations does affect the magnitude of the multiplier, which is not unknown of course, but if it is true that the results are so diverging as they are for France and Germany, it seems clear that additional research has to be done to reduce the magnitude of the constant term.

It is also clear that international effects of stimulae are most favourable in those countries that have a low import content, resulting in a lower effect on their prices, which improves their international competitiveness, and so their export performance increases most with a better result for their balance of payments position. At the same time, for these countries the share of exports in total sales is also relatively small, so the effects on GNP are then also smaller than on countries with a larger export share.

These conclusions of course are conditional upon the nature of the model. METEOR is a cyclical model with a (peak-line) capacity trend. Impacts on investments do not affect capacity levels, hence no conclusions can be drawn about the long-run effects of increasing public expenditure and taxes. METEOR can only show how to fill in cyclical gaps in capacity utilization, but cannot show how to increase capacity.

BIBLIOGRAPHY

Hoogland, J. and Antoine Schwartz. *A Survey of Procedures Used at the Dutch Central Planning Bureau to Forecast Foreign Trade Data.* CPB reprint series No. 138, The Hague, 1972.
Kooyman, Jan. *The METEOR model.* Invited paper to the Third International Conference of Applied Econometrics, Brussels, February 4–6, 1976.
Kooyman, Jan and Antoine Schwartz. *Statistical Information and The International Linkage of Macro-Economic Models.* Invited paper to the 40th Session of the International Statistical Institute, CPB Occasional Paper No. 9, The Hague, 1975.
Schwartz, Antoine. *International Price Interdependence.* Internal Mimeograph of the Central Planning Bureau, The Hague, 1972.
Schwartz, Antoine. *The Effects of the Rise in Oil Prices on the Economy of Industrial Countries.* CPB Monograph No. 17, The Netherlands Government Publishing Office, The Hague, 1974.
Schwartz, Antoine and Wim Driehuis. Primary Commodities and the World Economy in: Wim Driehuis (ed.) *Primary commodity prices: Analysis and Forecasting.* Rotterdam: Rotterdam University Press, 1976.
Schwartz, Antoine and Jan Kooyman. Competition and the International Transmission of Inflation. *De Economist,* Vol. 123 No. 4, December 1975. pp. 723–748.

ANNEX: The effects on METEOR countries of a 10% increase in real public expenditure in net material consumption and public investment and investment in dwellings in France and Germany, with an unchanged government budget deficit by increasing direct taxes by an equal amount.

TABLE 1.

Balance of Payments mln. $.

Country	1st year	3rd year
United States	600	400
BLEU	0	100
France	—1100	—1000
West Germany	—1100	—3500
Italy	—100	—100
United Kingdom	—200	200
Netherlands	100	—100
Canada	100	—100
Japan	—200	—100
OECD North[a]	100	100
OECD South[a]	100	100
OPEC	100	100
Rest of the world	200	—700

[a] Excluding those countries for which separate models are used.

TABLE 2.

Export volume, percentage changes.

Country	1st year	3rd year
United States	1.9	1.2
BLEU	2.7	— 0.5
France	—3.2	—11.0
West Germany	—1.1	—11.1
Italy	2.5	0
United Kingdom	0.7	0.8
Netherlands	1.7	— 1.0
Canada	0.1	0.3
Japan	1.3	0.3
OECD North[a]	2.1	1.0
OECD South[a]	1.4	0.8
OPEC	1.1	0.3
Rest of the world	1.1	— 1.7

[a] Excluding those countries for which separate models are used.

TABLE 3.

Export prices, percentage changes.

Country	1st year	3rd year
United States	0	1.0
BLEU	0.8	1.7
France	3.5	6.9
West Germany	0.3	1.8
Italy	0.3	1.5
United Kingdom	0.3	1.1
Netherlands	1.0	0.9

TABLE 4.

GNP, percentage changes.

Country	1st year	3rd year
United States	0.4	0.4
BLEU	0.9	0.2
France	2.7	1.2
West Germany	3.7	2.0
Italy	0.2	0.3
United Kingdom	0.2	0.5
Netherlands	0.6	0

TABLE 5.

Price index of personal consumption, percentage changes.

Country	1st year	2nd year
United States	0	0.3
BLEU	0.2	0.8
France	0	3.0
West Germany	—0.1	0.7
Italy	0.2	0.7
United Kingdom	0	0.9
Netherlands	0.2	0.7

TABLE 6.

Employment, percentage changes.

Country	1st year	3rd year
United States	0.3	0.6
BLEU	0.6	0.7
France	1.2	1.6
West Germany	2.1	2.4
Italy	0	0.1
United Kingdom	0.2	0.2
Netherlands	0.2	0.2

Two-way Trade in a Verdoorn Type Model

C. A. VAN BOCHOVE and A. S. W. DE VRIES

1. INTRODUCTION

The international trade statistics often show simultaneous imports and exports of the same commodity, even on the highest level of disaggregation and for bilateral trade flows. This phenomenon is referred to as 'intra-industry trade' [Balassa, 1966] or 'two-way international trade' [Gray, 1973][1]; we prefer the latter, since two-way trade occurs not only on the industry level, but on all levels of aggregation.

1.1. *Significance of Two-way Trade*

The earliest reference to the existence of two-way trade possibly is Taussig [1915][2]: 'Here we find the perplexing phenomenon that commodities apparently of the same sort are both brought into the country and sent out from it'. The great empirical significance was first pointed out by Verdoorn [1960] in an[3] investigation of the effects of BENELUX: 'specialization ..., is to be found *within* rather than *between* these (121) categories of trade'.

Balassa [1966] extended Verdoorn's conclusion to the effects of the EEC. Studies by e.g. Kojima [1964], Grubel [1967], Rothschild [1970], Grubel and Lloyd [1971, 1975], Hesse [1974] and Blattner [1977] confirmed the existence (and substantial post-war increase) of two-way trade on a considerable scale.

Traditional theories of international trade do not readily explain the existence of two-way trade in the same commodity. One explanation, of course, would be that the phenomenon is due to aggregation. This was first suggested[4] by Taussig [1915]: '..., we may be certain that the commodities

---

1. Actually Kojima [1964] uses the term 'horizontal trade' while an older term [Taussig, 1915] is 'cross-shipments'; these terms are not widely used however.
2. p. 191, on American iron trade.
3. pp. 292–293.
4. pp. 500–501.

which cross each other are not in reality the same'. Two-way trade would then be simply the sum of the flows of two (or more) commodities for which the traditional theories hold true. Recently this idea was proposed by Finger [1975], who argues strongly that the literature on the subject is 'valueless' because available data show factor-proportions to vary more within than among industries – industries defined by 3-digit SITC groups as in most of the intra-industry literature. Three objections must be raised against these arguments:

1. Finger defines a product by its input-requirements. There is no reason for this: two identical products remain identical irrespective of their inputs. In Heckscher-Ohlin theory a product is *defined* to be homogeneous from the *buyer's* view, and *assumed* to be produced by one technology only; Finger's results argue against this H–O assumption rather than against intra-industry trade literature.
2. Grubel and Lloyd (1971) found that, though the intensity of two-way trade diminishes with the level of disaggregation, the phenomenon did certainly not vanish entirely even on the 7 digit SITC level; moreover: 'the patterns of intra-commodity trade are essentially preserved'.
3. It is often desirable to explain trade in commodity groups, which are not perfectly homogeneous directly rather than as aggregates of more narrowly defined products. Though it is true that the existence of two-way trade here would not refute traditional trade theories, the latter are nevertheless incapable of providing the desired kind of explanation.

1.2. *Explanations of Two-way Trade*
Following Grubel and Lloyd [1975][5] two groups of products may be distinguished in the explanation of two-way trade: functionally homogeneous and non-homogeneous products. Four reasons are mentioned in the literature concerned for the existence of two-way trade of the first type of products:

1. The trade may be *border trade* [Taussig, 1915][6]; the term derives from Grubel and Lloyd [1975]: a product for which transportation costs are high may be imported in a part of the country where the distance to foreign suppliers is less than to domestic, and exported in another part where the reverse is true.

5. pp. 71–84.
6. p. 191.

2. *Periodic trade* may occur [Haberler, 1933[7]; once again the term was introduced by Grubel and Lloyd, 1975]: trade based on periodic fluctuations in a nation's production of and demand for a commodity.
3. *Entrepôt and re-export trade* obviously show up as two-way trade, unless separately registrated [Haberler, 1933].
4. *Market imperfections* [Haberler, 1933]. One example [Grubel and Lloyd, 1975]: government regulations.

Non-homogeneousness of products may be caused by national and international differentiation as to style, model, kind, quality, etc.; furthermore advertising, distribution and selling effort in general cause products to be imperfect substitutes for all practical purposes. The degree and direction of differentiation is related to relatively static factors like natural resources, capital accumulation, human capital, company reputation; moreover, as emphasized by Grubel and Lloyd [1975] also to highly dynamic factors like the product cycle and technological gaps. Thus imperfect substitutability of internationally traded products is a structural rather than an incidental characteristic of the world economy. Consequently the same applies to two-way trade which is caused by non-homogeneousness, as argued by Grubel and Lloyd [1975] and Gray [1973]. This line of thought suggests[8] a number of hypotheses, put forward by Gray [1973] and tested by Pagoulatos and Sorensen [1975] in a cross-section analysis of 1965 and 1967 US trade: an inverse relation should exist between the intensity of two-way trade and:

1. the income differential of the trading-partners[9] (compare Linder's [1961] hypothesis);
2. mean shipping distance;
3. height of tariff and non-tariff barriers;
4. tariff and non-tariff barrier differential between partners.

Their results[10] confirm the validity of these hypotheses. This suggests that some degree of non-homogeneity of traded products is an important cause of two-way trade.

7. p. 32, note 3.
8. Also compare Davies [1977] and Gray [1977].
9. The same hypothesis was put forward and tested by Kojima [1970], p. 10.
10. Actually they also included the number of 4-digit SITC groups in each 3-digit category. This yielded, statistically significant, the expected positive sign; however, with a *t*-ratio that ranks only fifth in the equations, it seems by no means the most important determinant of the occurrence of two-way trade. This provides further argument against disaggregation as the sole approach of the phenomenon.

However, no formal model rigidly defining the degree of substitutability and deriving the existence of two-way trade has been developed yet. This is the purpose of the present paper, casting the analysis in terms of the *elasticities of substitution of demand*. Moreover, we demonstrate that imperfect adaptability of supply may also cause two-way trade, even in perfectly homogeneous products, formalizing this by the *elasticities of substitution of supply*. The last part of the paper is devoted to an empirical verification of a part of our model.

1.3. *Measurement of Two-way Trade*

A comprehensive description of the measures of two-way trade is found in[11] Grubel and Lloyd [1975]. Here it suffices to discuss the two most important.

A measure derived from Balassa [1966] is the most widely used; for the volume of total trade of some commodity his measure is

$$B = \left| \frac{x_{io} - x_{oi}}{x_{io} + x_{oi}} \right| \tag{1.1}$$

Here x_{io} represents the volume of exports from country i and x_{oi} imports into i. The measure varies between 0 (maximum two-way trade) and 1 (complete specialization) and is obviously inversely related to the intensity of two-way trade. To obtain direct proportionality Grubel and Lloyd [1971, 1975], Pagoulatos and Sorensen [1975], and Blattner [1977] prefer

$$B' = 1 - B, \tag{1.2}$$

The disadvantage of B and B' is their mathematical form: a combination of multiplicative and additive functions of the trade flows. This makes it troublesome to derive a direct estimator equation for B' and B from a model of the trade-flows. For this reason we prefer the measure used by Verdoorn [1960]

$$V = \frac{x_{io}}{x_{oi}} \tag{1.3}$$

Grubel and Lloyd [1975] regard as disadvantageous that the value of V depends on which of the flows is put in the numerator, while moreover, V is not even symmetric: the difference from unity (maximum two-way trade) too depends on which flow is in the numerator. These objections however are

11. pp. 20–28.

easily countered by consistently putting the largest [Grubel, 1967] or
smallest, [Kojima, 1964] flow in the numerator. Sometimes it is desirable to
retain the information which of the two flows is the larger; to obtain the
symmetry property in that case a logarithmic transformation may be applied.
This is actually done in the empirical section of this paper; in the theoretical
part V is used, because of its more immediate appeal.

2. A MODEL OF TWO-WAY TRADE

First a very simple two-country partial equilibrium model is presented to
demonstrate the existence of simultaneous *total* imports and exports of a
commodity. In Section 2.2 a more refined model is used to analyse *bilateral*
two-way trade.

2.1. *Total Two-way Trade Demand*

The elasticity of substitution of *demand* derives, of course, from Allen
and Hicks' theory of value [1934]. It was first applied on international trade
flows by Tinbergen, Derksen and Rombouts [CBS, 1938 and 1939]. Verdoorn
[1952] first expressed[12] the direct and cross-elasticities of import demand as
functions of the elasticity of substitution and the elasticity of total import
demand (apart from the import share of the flow concerned). Finally the
approach was formally linked up to the neoclassical model of international
trade by Armington [1968], who derived the substitution and demand
equations from a community indifference curve of the CES type; a stream-
lined version of his derivation is found in Verdoorn and Schwartz [1972].

Denoting by x_{ij} the volume of country j's demand for country i's products
and by p_{ij} and $\pi_{ij} - 1$ the corresponding seller's price and buyer-seller price
margin – including transport costs, import duty, etc. – measured as an ad
valorem decimal fraction, the substitution relation between demand for
imports and for domestic production of country 1 is

$$\frac{x_{21}}{x_{11}} = z_1 \left(\frac{p_{21}\,\pi_{21}}{p_{11}\,\pi_{11}} \right)^{\varepsilon} \quad \varepsilon < 0 \tag{2.1}$$

where ε denotes the (price-volume) elasticity of substitution. The commodity
is perfectly homogeneous if ε approaches infinity.

_____

12. Appendix A, p. 74. An English version is found in Verdoorn (1960), appendix A, p. 320.

Adopting ε internationally uniform[13], the corresponding relation for country 2 is

$$\frac{x_{12}}{x_{22}} = z_2 \left(\frac{p_{12}\,\pi_{12}}{p_{22}\,\pi_{22}}\right)^{\varepsilon} \tag{2.2}$$

The multiplicative constants z refer to the buyer's non-price preferences (i.e. the substitution ratio when prices are equal). For the time being total demand is assumed fixed (zero price elasticity); this assumption may be relaxed, but this alters only the magnitude of the effects, not the basic pattern.

Total demand for the commodity concerned of both countries, denoted by d_1 and d_2 is defined as

$$x_{11} + x_{21} = d_1 \tag{2.3}$$
$$x_{22} + x_{12} = d_2$$

Supply

The concept of a finite elasticity of substitution of *supply* was introduced explicitly in Verdoorn and Meyer zu Schlochtern [1964], but was already implicit in[14] Verdoorn [1960]. The present treatment is based to a considerable extent on a forthcoming paper by Verdoorn and Van Bochove, where the rationale for the concept is given, the implications spelled out and an empirical verification presented. Here it suffices to mention that a finite elasticity is caused by differences among the various markets in requirements regarding quality, promotional effort, etc.; furthermore, risk aversion tends to limit exporter's willingness to shift from one market to another. Denoting the internationally uniform elasticity of substitution by η, the relations of substitution between exports and the domestic market are[15]

$$\frac{x_{12}}{x_{11}} = g_1 \left(\frac{p_{12}}{p_{11}}\right)^{\eta} \qquad \eta > 0 \tag{2.4}$$

$$\frac{x_{21}}{x_{22}} = g_2 \left(\frac{p_{21}}{p_{22}}\right)^{\eta} \tag{2.5}$$

Analogous to z, g is the seller's non-price preference.

13. To simplify the analysis; the information thus lost is not very illuminating.
14. His supply equations are a special case, obtained if the elasticity of substitution between exports and domestic sales equals the elasticity of total supply: appendix B, eq. (13) and (14).
15. We do not specify a policy of quantity adaptation or of price setting (given the demand curve). As pointed out by Tinbergen [1951, p. 32] and in Verdoorn and Van Bochove (forthcoming), this is irrelevant to the mathematical formulation of the model.

Just as total demand, total supply in each country is fixed

$$x_{12} + x_{11} = s_1 \tag{2.6}$$
$$x_{21} + x_{22} = s_2$$

If equilibrium is to be obtained only three of the four market totals may be chosen freely, since $s_1 + s_2 = d_1 + d_2$.

Solution

The most elegant way to solve the model is to derive first a relation showing the relative average importance of international trade from the four substitution relations by elimination of prices

$$\frac{x_{12} x_{21}}{x_{11} x_{22}} = (g_1 g_2)^{\frac{-\varepsilon}{\eta - \varepsilon}} (z_1 z_2)^{\frac{\eta}{\eta - \varepsilon}} \left(\frac{\pi_{21} \pi_{12}}{\pi_{11} \pi_{22}} \right)^{\frac{\eta \varepsilon}{\eta - \varepsilon}}. \tag{2.7}$$

The expression on the right hand side of (2.7) is a constant, say ϕ, its value depending on non-price preferences and buyer-seller margins. The latter are generally higher in international than in national trade due to higher transportation costs and tariffs

$$\pi_{12} \pi_{21} > \pi_{11} \pi_{22} \tag{2.8}$$

The limiting values of ϕ w.r.t. η and ε being infinite are

$$\lim_{\varepsilon - \infty} \phi = g_1 g_2 \left(\frac{\pi_{21} \pi_{12}}{\pi_{11} \pi_{22}} \right)^{-\eta}$$

$$\lim_{\eta \to \infty} \phi = z_1 z_2 \left(\frac{\pi_{12} \pi_{21}}{\pi_{11} \pi_{22}} \right)^{\varepsilon} \tag{2.9}$$

$$\lim_{-\varepsilon, \, \eta \to \infty} \phi = 0$$

Thus ϕ approaches zero only if both η and $-\varepsilon$ are infinite.
Clearly the results (2.9) depend heavily on the condition (2.8) as the equality $\pi_{21} \pi_{12} = \pi_{11} \pi_{22}$ and $\eta = -\varepsilon$ yield

$$\phi = (g_1 g_2 z_1 z_2)^{\frac{1}{2}}, \tag{2.10}$$

irrespective the value of η, ε.

As long as the inequality (2.8) holds, the same value (2.10) of ϕ applies when $\varepsilon = \eta = 0$. If only one of the elasticities approaches zero, the limiting values are

$$\lim_{\varepsilon \to 0} \phi = z_1 z_2 \tag{2.11}$$

$$\lim_{\eta \to 0} \phi = g_1 g_2$$

The buyer-seller margins become irrelevant if one of the elasticities of substitution equals zero; moreover the limiting value is then invariant to the value of the second elasticity.

The solution of the model is completed by inserting the restrictions (2.3) and (2.6) into (2.7). This yields a quadratic equation in e.g. x_{12}

$$(1 - \phi) x_{12}^2 - \{(1 - \phi) s_1 - d_1 - \phi d_2\} x_{12} - \phi s_1 d_2 = 0 \qquad (2.12)$$

It can be proved that at all times one and only one solution for x_{12} suffices all obvious restrictions.[16]

Two-way Trade

Clearly $x_{12} = 0$ solves equation (2.11) if and only if $\phi = 0$, provided s_1 and d_2 are non-zero. Of course the same applies to x_{21}. Combining this result with (2.9) therefore, the conclusion is obtained: *two way trade is eliminated only if both the elasticities of substitution of demand and the elasticities of substitution of supply are infinite.*

Two remarks are in order:

1. The elasticity of substitution of demand formalizes the idea expressed in intra-industry literature, viz. imperfect homogeneity as a cause for two-way trade.
2. Here a new possible reason for two-way trade is added: *even if a commodity is perfectly homogeneous,* exporter's reluctance to shift from one market to another (e.g. η finite) may cause two-way trade.

If two-way trade is eliminated the direction of trade is of course determined by excess demand and supply conditions

$$
\begin{array}{llll}
x_{12} = s_1 - d_1 & \text{and} & x_{21} = 0 & \text{if} \quad s_1 > d_1 \\
x_{12} = 0 & \text{and} & x_{21} = d_1 - s_1 & \text{if} \quad s_1 < d_1
\end{array}
\qquad (2.13)
$$

A second value of ϕ is of special interest: unity. Clearly it is obtained if two conditions are fulfilled simultaneously:

1. No non-price preferences: g's and z's showing unit values.
2. Either ε or η is zero, or alternatively all buyer-seller margins are equal.

---

16. The solution should be non-negative and bounded by min $\{s_1, d_2\}$. For all non-negative values of φ, s_1, s_2, d_1, d_2 one and only one solution satisfies these conditions. The proof is elementary but rather laborious and therefore omitted.

In this case we have

$$x_{12} = \frac{s_1 d_2}{d_1 + d_2} \qquad x_{21} = \frac{s_2 d_1}{d_1 + d_2} \qquad\qquad (2.14)$$

The Verdoorn index takes the value

$$V = \frac{x_{12}}{x_{21}} = \frac{s_1}{s_2} \cdot \frac{d_2}{d_1} \qquad\qquad (2.15)$$

The intensity of two-way trade under conditions of full complementarity equals the ratio of exporter's total supply multiplied by the ratio of importer's total demand.

Numerical Examples

The results are illustrated in Table 1, which gives the trade matrix at different values of η and ε. Numerical values assigned to various parameters are

$$g_1 = g_2 = z_1 = z_2 = 1$$

$$\frac{\pi_{21}}{\pi_{11}} = \frac{\pi_{12}}{\pi_{22}} = 1.25$$

$$d_1 = 66.66 \qquad s_1 = 33.33 \qquad \text{(total production} = 100)$$

$$d_2 = 33.33 \qquad s_2 = 66.66$$

The table presents two extremes: near full complementarity ($\eta = -\varepsilon = 1$) and (near) perfect substitutability ($\eta = -\varepsilon = 100$) and two intermediate cases – the values 1 and 100 are selected to avoid problems of zero and infinite values.

TABLE 1.

The trade matrix at different values η and ε

importers exporters	$\eta = -\varepsilon = 1$		$\varepsilon = -1, \eta = 100$		$\varepsilon = -100, \eta = 1$		$\eta = -\varepsilon = 100$	
	1	2	1	2	1	2	1	2
1	23.3	10.0	24.3	9.0	24.3	9.0	33.33	0.0
2	43.3	23.3	42.3	24.3	42.3	24.3	33.33	33.33
V		.23		.21		.21		.00

Obviously two-way trade vanishes only if both η and ε are infinite. In Table 2 the gradual decrease of two-way trade as substitutability increases is demonstrated by x_{12} and the Verdoorn index.

TABLE 2.

Substitutability and two-way trade

$\eta=-\varepsilon$	x_{12}	$V=x_{12}/x_{21}$
0	11.1	.25
1	10.0	.23
2	8.8	.21
5	6.1	.16
10	2.8	.08
25	.2	.004
100,∞	.0	.000

2.2. *Bilateral Two-way Trade*

The existence of cross-shipments in a country's commerce with the world as a whole does not imply that the phenomenon occurs for each (or any) *bilateral* flow. In this section it is investigated when, if two-way trade exists where total trade is concerned, bilateral flows are of the two-way type. As above the analysis is of a partial equilibrium type, describing one commodity only.

Demand

Following Verdoorn and Schwartz [1972], three basic price elasticities can be distinguished

1. *The price elasticity of total demand, δ.*

Total demand for the commodity concerned in country j is determined by

$$d_j = \gamma_j y_j^{\beta_j} \left(\frac{p_{oj} \pi_{oj}}{p_{oj}^* \pi_{oj}^*} \right)^{\delta_j} \quad j = 1, ..., n \tag{2.16}$$

Here y_j represents income in country j, $p_{oj}\pi_{oj}$ is the commodity's average buyer's price; $p_{oj}^* \cdot \pi_{oj}^*$ is the general price-level of consumption. The number of countries is n, γ a constant, β the income elasticity.

2. *The elasticity of substitution*[17] *between foreign and domestic products,* ε.
The substitution relation total imports/domestic produce is

$$\frac{x_{rj}}{x_{jj}} = z_j \left(\frac{p_{rj}\, \pi_{rj}}{p_{jj}\, \pi_{jj}}\right)^{\varepsilon_j} \quad j = 1, ..., n \qquad (2.17)$$

Here r denotes the rest of the world; thus x_{rj} represents total imports.

3. *The elasticity of substitution between competing importers on a market,* E.
The substitution relation concerned

$$\frac{x_{ij}}{x_{hj}} = \frac{a_{ij}}{a_{hj}} \left(\frac{p_{ij}\, \pi_{ij}}{p_{hj}\, \pi_{hj}}\right)^{E_j} \quad \begin{array}{l} i = 1, ..., n \\ j = 1, ..., n \\ j \neq i,\ j \neq h \end{array} \qquad (2.18)$$

Note that a uniform elasticity is assumed between any pair of suppliers on
the market. This facilitates the analysis greatly, since no problems of consistency arise,[18] while

$$\sum_h \left\{ \sum_i \frac{x_{ij}}{x_{hj}} \right\}^{-1} = 1$$

The importance of the distinction between the two elasticities of substitution, E and ε should be emphasized. First, empirically they are found to have
distinctly different values; $\varepsilon = -.35$ for total Dutch imports, while $E \sim -2.8$
on the Dutch export market[19] and many estimates[20] are found around the
celebrated 'Tinbergen-two' and lower for individual products. Second the
difference is of theoretical importance; an example is the great significance[21]
of the value of E/ε to the effects of a customs union.

The demand side is completed by the definitions of the aggregates and
their prices ($j = 1, ..., n$)

$$x_{rj} = \sum_{i \neq j}^{n} x_{ij} \quad \text{(volume of total imports)} \qquad (2.19)$$

17. Not identical to the import elasticity, defined as: $d \ln x_{rj}/d \ln p_{rj}\, \pi_{rj}$; the relation
between both elasticities is in Verdoorn and Schwartz [1972]: $d \ln x_{rj}/d \ln p_{rj}\, \pi_{rj}$
$= \delta + (1-\mu)\ (\varepsilon - \delta)$; here μ is the import share.
18. The consistency problem is treated by Kooyman and Schwartz [1975].
19. The values found in the import and export equation of the Dutch 69C annual model
[Verdoorn, Post and Goslinga, 1971].
20. For example the early estimates by Tinbergen, Derksen and Rombouts [1938, 1939].
21. As pointed out in the illuminating paper by Petith [1977], who elaborates on the model
of Mundell [1964].

$$p_{rj}\pi_{rj} = \sum_{i \neq j} \frac{x_{ij}}{x_{rj}} p_{ij}\pi_{ij} \quad \text{(price of total imports)} \tag{2.20}$$

$$d_j = x_{rj} + x_{jj} \quad \text{(volume of total demand)} \tag{2.21}$$

$$p_{oj}\pi_{oj} = \frac{x_{rj}}{d_j} p_{rj}\pi_{rj} + \frac{x_{jj}}{d_j} p_{jj}\pi_{jj} \quad \text{(price of total demand)} \tag{2.22}$$

Supply

Total supply s_i $(i=1, \ldots, n)$ is assumed fixed. This is acceptable for short-term purposes under conditions of full employment; the assumption has the advantage of simplifying the analysis considerably, while the *distribution* of trade over the various markets is nevertheless adequately described[22].

On the analogy of the demand equations, we distinguish two types of elasticities of supply.

1. *The elasticity of substitution between the foreign and the domestic market, η.*
   The substitution exports/domestic sales is thus determined by:

$$\frac{x_{ir}}{x_{ii}} = g_i \left(\frac{p_{ir}}{p_{ii}} \right)^{\eta_i} \quad i = 1, \ldots, n \tag{2.23}$$

Here x_{ir} represents total exports, and p_{ir} the corresponding price.

2. *The elasticity of substitution between the various foreign markets, H.*
   The substitution equation concerned is:

$$\frac{x_{ij}}{x_{ik}} = \frac{w_{ij}}{w_{ik}} \left(\frac{p_{ij}}{p_{ik}} \right)^{H_i} \quad i, j = 1, \ldots, n \tag{2.24}$$
$$i \neq j \text{ and } i \neq k$$

The definitions of the supply aggregates are $(i=1, \ldots, n)$

$$x_{ir} = \sum_{j \neq i}^{n} x_{ij} \quad \text{(volume of total exports)} \tag{2.25}$$

22. For the purpose of the analysis of, for example the effects of a customs union, the assumption should be relaxed however, since the gains from a customs union arise not only out of a redistribution of total production, but also out of an expansion of total production as such.

$$p_{ir} = \sum_{j \neq i}^{n} \frac{x_{ij}}{x_{ir}} p_{ij} \qquad\qquad \text{(price of total exports)} \quad (2.26)$$

$$s_i = x_{ir} + x_{ii} \qquad\qquad \text{(volume of total supply)} \quad (2.27)$$

Equilibrium

The equilibrium condition of the n country system is

$$\sum_{i=1}^{n} s_i = \sum_{j=1}^{n} d_j \qquad\qquad\qquad (2.28)$$

The system thus obtained describes essentially all n^2 bilateral trade flows (national and international) and the corresponding prices as functions of:

1. Total supply by country.
2. Income and consumer-price level by country.
3. The buyer-seller margins finding reflection in π.

In the appendix the elimination of quantities is demonstrated; the resulting system of n^2 highly non-linear functions in the n^2 prices cannot be solved analytically. This leaves three options for the analysis of the model. First a linear approximation of the model is obtained by replacing the arithmetic definitions of the aggregates and their prices by geometric ones and applying a logarithmic transformation. The approach is acceptable as long as the flows concerned are of a comparable size; since however the purpose of our analysis is to find out when individual flows are or are not zero, this possibility is ruled out. A second approach is to differentiate the model and analyse the changes in the endogeneous variables. We are however primarily interested in whether or not two-way trade exists at all. Accordingly an iterative process, described in the appendix is used, to analyse the model numerically. The algorithm is fairly simple, but it has one limitation: convergence is obtained only for relatively low absolute values of η and ε (ca. 1.5). Thus the limiting cases for $\varepsilon \to -\infty$ and $\eta \to \infty$ cannot be analysed. This limitation is not very serious, since this analysis was effectively carried out for the two-country model in the previous section: here we are primarily concerned with the role of E and H.

One further remark on the model, concerning its title, is in order. We propose to call it a Verdoorn-type model of international trade, not only because many of its elements were first introduced by him[23], but also since he pioneered the actual application to practical economic problems, viz. the effects of customs unions.[24] It goes without saying that this is not *the* Verdoorn model: the fixation of total supply for example, is acceptable in the context of this paper, but evidently not generally realistic.

Numerical results.

The number of countries is limited to three, this being the minimum allowing analysis of the influence of E and H. The technique used is to apply variations around a central parameter set, shown in Table 3.

In this central set all countries are of equal size, all buyer-seller margins zero and non-price preferences absent; the elasticities have internationally

TABLE 3.

Central parameter set

Parameters	Values
Total production	
s	100
Income and general price	
$\gamma\, y$	100
$p_{oj}^{*}\ \pi_{oj}^{*}$	1.
Buyer-seller margins	
π	1.
Non price preferences	
z, g	1.
a, w	.5
Elasticities	
δ	—.5
$\eta = -\varepsilon$	.4
$H = -E$	2 and 100

23. The derivation of the direct and cross-elasticities of demand [1952], the clear distinction between the three basic elasticities of demand, E. ε and δ [1972], the finite elasticities of substitution of supply [1964 and forthcoming].

24. A pure demand *forecast* of the effects of a European customs union and the changes of exchange rates required to retain equilibrium balances of trade (1952), an analytical measurement of the effects of BENELUX, using a demand-supply model (1960), a residual imputation estimate based on a truncated reduced form of a demand-supply model of EEC and EFTA effects (1964, 1972); an analytic estimate of EEC and EFTA effect based on the demand equations (1972).

uniform values (experimentation with differentiated values yields roughly
the same results), the price elasticity of total demand being $-.5$, ε $-.4$ (i.e.
the value quoted above for total Dutch imports), while η is set equal to $-\varepsilon$.
The elasticities of substitution E and H assume two values: the Tinbergen-
two and 100 as a proxy for infinity.

The results are presented in Tables 4–7. Parameters different from the
central values are indicated; the trade matrices are presented in the usual
fashion: rows being exports, columns imports.

Table 4.1 corresponds to the central values, yielding a perfectly symmetric
matrix, diagonal elements being 50, off-diagonal 25; in Table 4.2 all non-
price preferences national-international trade are .5; the trade matrix shows
a similar distribution. In both cases all Verdoorn indices are unit valued and
identical matrices are obtained for both values of E and H. This holds no
longer true if, as in Tables 4.3 and 4.4, non-price preferences within country
1's imports exist.

Again the results are not surprising: some specialization occurs, the price
country 1 must pay for its preference is a slight decrease of total consumption, the main benefits being for the preferred country 3. If international
substitutability is (near) perfect, as in Table 4.4, this redistribution dis-
appears; the corresponding matrix of Verdoorn indices is quite regular and
shows that two-way trade remains substantial, notwithstanding the high
values of E and H. The same pattern emerges (not presented in the tables)
if similar supplier's preferences exist. Thus *if both E and H are infinite,
bilateral two-way trade is not necessarily eliminated even if (finite) non-price
preferences for different importers or exporters exist.* This inference is very
similar to the corresponding result obtained with regard to total two-way
trade in the previous section, viz. eq. (2.9).

In Table 5 one country (1) has substantial excess demand (60% of world
consumption if $\delta=0$; only 20% of production) and another (3) excess supply
(60% of world production, only 20% of consumption if $\delta=0$); thus a large
trade flow from 3 to 1 and a zero-flow in the other direction would be
predicted by traditional theories.

Table 5.1 shows spectacularly that *bilateral two-way trade persists, even
though substantial excess demand and supply exist*: excess supply in 3 is
$300-158.77=141.23$, excess demand in 1 is 118.78, but nevertheless 1's
exports to 3 are 22.69. Moreover, bilateral two-way trade even intensifies
somewhat as E and H approach infinity (5.2): V increases from .18 to .20.
If total consumption is fixed ($\delta=0$, Table 5.3) the incidence of two-way trade

TABLE 4.

Non price-preferences

Trade matrices x and Verdoorn indices V

4.1	Central values —$E=H=2$ and 100			4.2	$z_1=z_2=z_3=g_1=g_2=g_3=.5$ —$E=H=2$ and 100		

		x					x		
	1	2	3	0		1	2	3	0
1	50.0	25.0	25.0	100.0		66.7	16.7	16.7	100.0
2	25.0	50.0	25.0	100.0		16.7	66.7	16.7	100.0
3	25.0	25.0	50.0	100.0		16.7	16.7	66.7	100.0
0	100.0	100.0	100.0	300.0		100.0	100.0	100.0	300.0

		V					V		
1	—	1.0	1.0			—	1.0	1.0	
2	1.0	—	1.0			1.0	—	1.0	
3	1.0	1.0	—			1.0	1.0	—	

4.3	$a_{21}=.1$, $a_{31}=.9$ —$E=H=2$				4.4	$a_{21}=.1$ $a_{31}=.9$ —$E=H=100$			

		x					x		
	1	2	3	0		1	2	3	0
1	50.05	27.24	22.71	100.00		50.00	29.46	20.54	100.00
2	17.45	52.08	30.47	100.00		20.40	50.05	29.55	100.00
3	30.43	21.24	48.33	100.00		29.57	20.48	49.95	100.00
0	97.93	100.56	101.51	300.00		99.97	99.99	100.04	300.00

		V					V		
1	—	1.56	.75			—	1.44	.69	
2	.64	—	1.43			.69	—	1.44	
3	1.34	.70	—			1.44	.69	—	

TABLE 5.

Countries of different size, the rôle of δ and ε, η

Trade matrices x and Verdoorn indices V

	5.1 $s_3=300,\ \gamma_1 y_1^{\beta_1}=300$ $-E=H=2$				5.2 $s_3=300,\ \gamma_1 y_1^{\beta_1}=300$ $-E=H=100$			
	x				x			
	1	2	3	0	1	2	3	0
1	65.63	11.68	22.69	100.00	68.28	4.49	27.23	100.00
2	25.99	49.84	24.17	100.00	13.40	52.96	33.64	100.00
3	127.16	60.93	111.91	300.00	135.31	56.01	108.68	300.00
0	218.78	122.45	158.77	500.00	216.99	113.46	169.55	500.00
	V				V			
1	—	.45	.18		—	.34	.20	
2	2.22	—	.40		2.98	—	.60	
3	5.61	2.52	—		4.97	1.67	—	

	5.3 $s_3=300,\ \gamma_1 y_1^{\beta_1}=300$ and $\delta=0$ $-E=H=2$				5.4 $s_3=300,\ \gamma_1 y_1^{\beta_1}=300,$ $\eta=-\varepsilon=1.0$ $-E=H=2$			
	x				x			
	1	2	3	0	1	2	3	0
1	76.05	11.45	12.50	100.00	70.06	13.92	16.02	100.00
2	43.84	44.42	11.74	100.00	39.40	42.51	18.09	100.00
3	180.11	44.13	75.76	300.00	142.61	56.92	100.47	300.00
0	300.00	100.00	100.00	500.00	252.07	113.35	134.58	500.00
	V				V			
1	—	.26	.07		—	.35	.11	
2	3.83	—	.27		2.83	—	.32	
3	14.40	3.76	—		8.90	3.15	—	

TABLE 5.5.

Balance of trade and terms of trade country 2.

Table	Balance of trade (value)	Terms of trade (exp/imp)
5.1	23.81	2.62
5.2	7.68	1.04
5.3	67.70	3.07
5.4	36.54	2.25

decreases: all V's move away from unity. Again, however, bilateral two-way trade refuses to become extinct: even if E and H are 100 (not presented) the picture is essentially the same, changes being minor and comparable to those occurring when $\delta = -.5$. The same applies if the absolute value of η and ε is raised: two-way trade decreases somewhat, but, as shown in the previous section, even if they were to be infinite excess-demand and -supply alone would not remove total two-way trade entirely, neither apparently[25] bilateral two-way trade. Accordingly, *if both E and H are infinite, bilateral two-way trade is not necessarily eliminated between countries where substantial excess demand and supply exist, no matter which value δ and η, ε attain.*

In Table 5 another phenomenon is noteworthy as such: total consumption of the small country 2 diminishes if E and H are raised (113.46 vs originally 122.45) if η and ε are raised (113.35) and if δ is lowered 100.0). Thus the small country's volume of consumption benefits from considerable international trade between (partially) specialized countries if international substitutability is low and the price-elasticity of demand high. In Table 5.5 the corresponding balances and terms of trade are shown.

Clearly the loss in consumption occurred in moving δ from $-.5$ to 0 and $-\varepsilon = \eta$ from .5 to 1 is compensated by an improvement of the balance of trade and, in the case of δ, of the terms of trade. Most interesting however, is that if $-E$ and H are reduced from 100 to 2, not only the volume of consumption increases, but also the balance of trade surplus: country 2 happily takes advantage of the large international imbalances, as long as international

---

25. Since the algorithm used converges for low absolute values only, this inference slightly exceeds our direct evidence; circumstantial evidence (the direction of changes) however certainly warrants it.

TABLE 6.

The rôle of buyer-seller margins

Trade matrices x and Verdoorn indices V

6.1	$\pi_{13}=\pi_{31}=1.25$ $-E=H=2$				6.2	$\pi_{13}=\pi_{31}=1.25$ $-E=H=100$			
		x					x		
	1	2	3	0		1	2	3	0
1	50.69	25.92	23.39	100.00		50.81	26.42	22.77	100.00
2	25.15	49.70	25.15	100.00		25.28	49.44	25.28	100.00
3	23.39	25.92	50.69	100.00		22.77	26.42	50.81	100.00
0	99.23	101.54	99.23	300.00		98.86	102.28	98.86	300.00
		V					V		
1	—	1.03	1.00			—	1.05	1.00	
2	.97	—	.97			.96	—	.96	
3	1.00	1.03	—			1.00	1.05	—	

6.3	$\pi_{ij}=1.25$ for $i, j=1, \ldots, 3\ i \neq j$ $-E=H=2$ and 100			
		x		
	1	2	3	0
1	51.12	24.44	24.44	100.00
2	24.44	51.12	24.44	100.00
3	24.44	24.44	51.12	100.00
0	100.00	100.00	100.00	300.00
		V		
1	—	1.00	1.00	
2	1.00	—	1.00	
3	1.00	1.00	—	

preferences with respect to qualities etc. are substantial and suppliers' willingness to shift limited.

The rôle of the buyer-seller margins is demonstrated in Tables 6 and 7. In 6.1 and 6.2 the margins on the trade of 1 and 3 are 25% in both directions. Compared to Tables 4.1 and 4.2 this causes a slight change only: two-way trade between 1 and 3 remains considerable, even though E and H approach infinity. In 6.3 all off-diagonal ('international') buyer-seller margins are 25%. This causes a slight decrease of international trade, but, as seen in Section 2.2, international trade vanishes only if η and ε approach infinity.

More important are the results of Table 7: here the margin on trade from 1 to 3 is 25%, all other margins, including that of trade from 3 to 1, are zero. Reasons for these asymmetric values may be:

– differences in import duties between 1 and 3,
– differences in taxing etc. between 1 and 3,
– economies of scale in transportation.

The differential buyer-seller margins leave two-way trade largely intact as long as either H or E are finite: $V=.90$ if $-E$, $H=2$; $V=.83$ if only $H=100$ and $V=.84$ if only $E=-100$. However as soon as both H and E are near infinite (7.4) two-way bilateral trade vanishes: $V=.008$.

In summary the two main results achieved in this section are provided total production and consumption of the trading partners are non-zero and non-price preferences finite:

1. *In general simultaneous imports and exports of a commodity exist, except if, on the presence of differences in buyer-seller margins between national and international trade, both the (internationally uniform) elasticities of substitution (of national vs international trade) of supply η, and demand ε, are infinite.*

2. *As long as total two-way trade exists, bilateral two-way trade vanishes if and only if, given asymmetric buyer-seller margins between international trade flows, both the elasticities of substitution of supply H and of demand E are infinite.*

These results concur with some of the conclusions of Gray [1973] and Pagoulatos and Sorenson [1975] (Section 1.2): total two-way trade varies inversely with international transport costs (mean shipping distance) and height of tariff and non- tariff barriers, since these determine the difference between buyer-seller margins on national and international trade; tariff and non-tariff barrier *differentials* directly reduce bilateral two-way trade.

TABLE 7.

Differential-buyer-seller margins

Trade-matrices x and Verdoorn indices V

7.1	$\pi_{13}=1.25$				7.2	$\pi_{13}=1.25$			
	$-E=H=2$					$E=-2, H=100$			

		x					x		
	1	2	3	0		1	2	3	0
1	50.64	26.41	22.95	100.00		50.64	27.51	21.85	100.00
2	24.51	49.85	25.64	100.00		23.73	49.82	26.45	100.00
3	25.45	24.51	50.04	100.00		26.20	23.74	50.06	100.00
0	100.60	100.77	98.63	300.00		100.57	101.07	98.36	300.00

		V					V		
1	—	1.08	.90			—	1.16	.83	
2	.93	—	1.05			.86	—	1.11	
3	1.11	.96	—			1.20	.90	—	

7.3	$\pi_{13}=1.25$				7.4	$\pi_{13}=1.25$			
	$E=-100 \; H=2$					$-E=H=100$			

		x					x		
	1	2	3	0		1	2	3	0
1	50.65	27.35	22.00	100.00		50.43	49.21	.36	100.00
2	23.67	49.77	26.57	100.00		2.12	49.62	48.26	100.00
3	26.26	23.67	50.07	100.00		47.91	2.13	49.96	100.00
0	100.58	100.79	98.63	300.00		100.46	100.96	98.58	300.00

		V					V		
1	—	1.16	.84			—	23.23	.008	
2	.87	—	1.12			.04	—	22.65	
3	1.19	.89	—			133.16	.04	—	

3. EMPIRICAL ANALYSIS OF BILATERAL TWO-WAY TRADE

Proper empirical verification of the model of the previous section calls for simultaneous estimation of all elasticities of substitution, E, H, ε and η in a multi-country model. Theoretically this is possible by approximating the model by a linear system of first differences. This undertaking however is too ambitious for the present paper, since it would require, apart from international trade statistics, data on e.g. consumption, production and tariffs. Therefore verification is limited to the analysis of *bilateral* two-way trade, taking total imports, exports and the corresponding prices as exogenous.

3.1. *Price Effects.*

Estimator equations for the bilateral two-way trade indices V are derived from a system of *share* equations, similar to the substitution equations (2.18) and (2.24) between international trade flows.[26]

Estimator Equation

Consider countries 1 and 2, trading with each other and with the rest of the world; by μ a constant is denoted, by the subscript -1 the lagged variable and, as above, by x_{rj} total imports of j. The import share (demand) of the flow from 1 to 2 is

$$\frac{x_{12}}{x_{r2}} = \mu_{12} \left(\frac{p_{12}}{p_{r2}}\right)^{E_2} \left(\frac{p_{12}}{p_{r2}}\right)^{E_2^*}_{-1} \tag{3.1}$$

Three remarks are in order:

1. For notational convenience the share elasticity is denoted by E though it differs in general[26] from the elasticity of substitution.
2. The possibility of the existence of lags has to be investigated since time-series analysis is applied.[27]
3. The buyer-seller margins are assumed equal for all flows and thus drop out; alternatively, a constant difference is acceptable, since this only biases the estimate of the constant.

---

26. The approach is similar to the one in Verdoorn and Van Bochove (forthcoming). The reason for the use of *share* instead of *substitution* equations is the simplicity of the derivation. The relation between both types of equations is spelled out in Verdoorn and Van Bochove (forthcoming).
27. Tinbergen (1949) argues that elasticities are higher in the long run; accordingly some experiments were made with distributed lags, but these were unsuccessful.

The export share (supply) equation is

$$\frac{x_{12}}{x_{1r}} = \beta \left(\frac{p_{12}}{p_{1r}}\right)^{H_1} \left(\frac{p_{12}}{p_{1r}}\right)^{H_1^*}_{-1} \tag{3.2}$$

From (3.1) and (3.2) a reduced form for x_{12} is obtained by elimination of the bilateral price p_{12}. A similar reduced form holds for x_{21}; thus for the Verdoorn index a reduced form results, denoting by α a constant depending on $\mu_{12}, \mu_{21}, \beta_{12}$ and β_{21}

$$\frac{x_{12}}{x_{21}} = \alpha \left(\frac{p_{12}}{p_{r2}}\right)^{\frac{H_1 E_2^*}{H_1 - E_2}}_{-1} \left(\frac{p_{12}}{p_{1r}}\right)^{\frac{-H_1^* E_2}{H_1 - E_2}}_{-1} x_{1r}^{\frac{-E_2}{H_1 - E_2}} \cdot$$

$$\cdot x_{r2}^{\frac{H_1}{H_1 - E_2}} \left(\frac{p_{1r}}{p_{r2}}\right)^{\frac{H_1 E_2}{H_1 - E_2}} \cdot \left(\frac{p_{21}}{p_{r1}}\right)^{\frac{-H_2 E_1^*}{H_2 - E_1}}_{-1} \cdot \tag{3.3}$$

$$\cdot \left(\frac{p_{21}}{p_{2r}}\right)^{\frac{H_2^* E_1}{H_2 - E_1}}_{-1} \cdot x_{2r}^{\frac{E_1}{H_2 - E_1}} x_{r1}^{\frac{-H_2}{H_2 - E_1}} \left(\frac{p_{2r}}{p_{r1}}\right)^{\frac{-H_2 E_1}{H_2 - E_1}}$$

This equation can of course be estimated directly,[28] but practically, some problems arise. First, for reasons indicated below, the sample size is, after correction for lags and first-difference transformation, limited to 12, leaving only one degree of freedom. Second, some intercorrelation between the six price variables as well as between the 4 volume ratios must be expected to impede reliable estimation of the elasticities.

Accordingly some a priori restrictions are required. One approach is to assume internationally uniform values of the elasticities ($E_1 = E_2$, $E_1^* = E_2^*$, $H_1 = H_2$, $H_1^* = H_2^*$), as in Section 2. Some experiments along this line suggested however that the assumption is not very realistic, while multi-collinearity remains considerable. Therefore an alternative approach is adopted, i.e. to postulate, following Verdoorn and Meyer zu Schlochtern [1964], equal absolute values of the share elasticities of demand and supply flow by flow; moreover the elasticities' time lag structure is postulated to be identical

$$\begin{cases} E_1 = -H_2 & E_1^* = -H_2^* \\ E_2 = -H_1 & E_2^* = -H_1^* \end{cases} \tag{3.4}$$

---

28. Identification of the eight structural elasticities is however impossible, merely since (3.3) numbers eleven coefficients.

Thus for each flow one elasticity applies, but different flows have different elasticities.

Applying (3.4) to (3.3) some reshuffling yields a considerably simplified equation with only 5 parameters to be estimated:

$$\frac{x_{12}/x_{21}}{\sqrt{x_{1r}x_{r2}/x_{2r}x_{r1}}} = \alpha \left(\frac{p_{r2}}{p_{1r}}\right)^{\frac{H_1}{2}} \left(\frac{p_{r2}}{p_{1r}}\right)_{-1}^{\frac{H_1^*}{2}} \left(\frac{p_{2r}}{p_{r1}}\right)^{\frac{H_2}{2}} \left(\frac{p_{2r}}{p_{r1}}\right)_{-1}^{\frac{H_2^*}{2}} \tag{3.5}$$

The relation now obtained cannot, without the application of further a-priori restrictions, be used to obtain unique estimates of the elasticities, since a similar reduced form holds for bilateral prices, thus causing the system to be overidentified.[29] To the purpose of this section: the empirical analysis of bilateral two-way trade, it is however a highly suitable estimator equation.

The dependent variable is not the Verdoorn index proper, but a share-version: the two bilateral flows are measured as a geometric average of the export and import shares; e.g. for x_{12}: $\sqrt{x_{12}/x_{1r}} \cdot \sqrt{x_{12}/x_{r2}}$. The only independent variables are two relative aggregate prices, and their lagged versions; these are written so as to yield (theoretically) positive coefficients. As the lagged bilateral prices and all volumes have vanished from the right hand side the share-index depends on the constant only, i.e. on non-price influences, as soon as all aggregate prices are equal.

Sample Composition

In a cross-section analysis the non-price influences are different for each observation; thus if cross-section is adopted, all factors determining α should be included in the analysis. In a time-series analysis however, α and the H's are approximately constant, provided the composition of the bilateral flows is constant and bias of aggregation avoided. Time-series analysis on the highest possible level of disaggregation is therefore the easiest approach; if international publications are used, this implies an analysis on the 4 and 5 digit SITC level, which limits[30] the sample period to 1961–1974.

Above, the buyer-seller margins are assumed equal or at least constant for all flows into a country; if this holds true the difficult and laborious gathering of time-series on import duties can be avoided. In general all European countries have maintained differential tariffs, due to EEC, EFTA, BENELUX. Within the ori-

29. Simultaneous estimation of E and H is performed in Verdoorn and Van Bochove (forthcoming).
30. Previously only occasional flows were disaggregated in most statistics to the 4 or 5 digit level.

ginal six EEC countries however, the non-BENELUX countries Germany, France and Italy have applied only one tariff to members. Thus the products of which virtually all imports are from EEC countries are effectively subject to a uniform tariff. The sample consists therefore of 30 pairs of trade flows of 4 and 5 digit SITC groups of manufactured products between these countries. The 30 pairs are those with the highest average share of EEC in imports of the two countries in 1961 and 1970, with the restriction superimposed that in both years EEC's share in each of the country's imports should be at least 70%.

The sample thus obtained[31] is presented in Table 8. In column (1) the numbering of the pairs is indicated. Columns (2) and (3) show SITC code and heading; the sample consists of 20 different product groups, of which 6 are obviously finished manufactures; the others are mostly intermediate goods. Column (4) shows the countries concerned; the pair Germany – France occurs 17 times, Germany – Italy 5 times and France – Italy 8 times; the first country shown will be indicated as 1, the second as 2. Column (5) shows the selection-yardstick: the average share of EEC in the two countries' imports of the product ('61, '70), ranging from .786 to .954. Column (6) shows the Verdoorn-index for 1967: $V = x_{12}/x_{21}$. The indices attain a wide range of values: 9 are lower than .1 or higher than 10; 14 are between .1 and .5 or 2 and 10 and 7 are between .5 and 2.

Throughout the sample volumes are measured in metric tons; prices are unit values, measured in dollars. Finally it should be noted that in some cases the first or some of the first observations are zero (i.e. smaller than .5 tons); the choice of an arbitrary value to assign to these, necessitated by the use of logarithms, influences the coefficients substantially; therefore all zero observations are left out [32] or a dummy is applied.

Results

The actual specification of the estimator equation is not unambiguously determined: zero or first differences may be used, trends can occur, the correct time-lag should be determined. Thus in preparing the results, the following procedure is adopted:

---

31. Most data and all exchange rates are from OECD trade statistics; supplementary data from EEC trade statistics and from the national statistics (Statistisches Bundesamt, Ministère des Finances et des Affaires Economiques, Instituto Centrale di Statistica). An appendix with the data is available on request.
32. The first observation is omitted for pairs 7, 19 and 25; the first three for 6 and 29; a dummy is applied to the second observation of pair 24.

TABLE 8.

Sample composition and characteristics

Nr	SITC	Description	C'tries	EEC* share	ν
1	2	3	4	5	6
1	6421	Paper bags, paperboard boxes and other containers	GF	.827	.457
2	65122	Yarn combed sheeps lambs wools, not for retail	GF	.869	.001
3	65122	Yarn combed sheeps lambs wools, not for retail	GI	.809	.023
4	65122	Yarn combed sheeps lambs wools, not for retail	FI	.850	3.805
5	67311	Wire rod iron steel, not high carbon or alloy	GF	.929	.290
6	67311	Wire rod iron steel, not high carbon or alloy	GI	.843	1.012
7	67311	Wire rod iron steel, not high carbon or alloy	FI	.911	79.022
8	67321	Bars rods ex wire iron steel, n. h. c. o. a.	GF	.944	3.186
9	67341	Angles over 80 mm piling, n. h. c. o. a.	GF	.948	1.426
10	67341	Angles over 80 mm piling, n. h. c. o. a.	GI	.860	17.190
11	67341	Angles over 80 mm piling, n. h. c. o. a.	FI	.881	.644
12	67351	Angles under 80 mm, n.h.c.o.a.	GF	.889	2.435
13	67421	Med. plates 3–4.75 mm. ex. tinned, n.h.c.o.a.	GF	.898	.499
14	67431	Plates under 3 mm uncoated, n.h.c.o.a.	GF	.926	.352
15	6747	Tinned plates and sheets	GF	.954	.340
16	67481	Plates under 3 mm coated, n.h.c.o.a.	GF	.846	.535
17	67501	Hoop strip of other than high carbon or alloy steel	GF	.946	1.351
18	67501	Hoop strip of other than high carbon or alloy steel	GI	.865	5.779
19	67501	Hoop strip of other than high carbon or alloy steel	FI	.894	11.263
20	6783	Tubes and pipes of iron and steel, welded etc.	GF	.786	30.826
21	6971	Domestic stoves, boilers and cookers etc., NES	FI	.878	.113
22	71952	Machine tools for working wood, plastics etc.	FI	.816	.127
23	7241	Television broadcast receivers	GF	.899	120.111
24	7241	Television broadcast receivers	GI	.861	1.207
25	7241	Television broadcast receivers	FI	.927	.231
26	72501	Domestic refrigerators, electrical	GF	.893	77.098
27	7262	x-ray apparatus	FI	.809	.320
28	7321	Passenger motor cars other than buses	GF	.875	.983
29	73311	Bicycles and other cycles	GF	.856	.010
30	84144	Outer garments knitted, not elast. nor rubbered	GF	.817	.124

1. Estimation of equation (3.5) (after a logarithmic transformation) in zero and first differences, with and without a time trend.
2. Out of the four equations then obtained the one with the 'best' statistics-t-ratios, Von Neumann Ratio and, in doubtful cases R^2 – is retained; a trend is accepted only if its t-ratio is at least 1.0.
3. The lagged and non-lagged versions of a price variable, say P, are combined, yielding P' according to

$$P' = \frac{HP + H^*P_{-1}}{H + H^*}$$

Thus

$$P' = P_{-\tau} \text{ where } \tau = \frac{H^*}{H + H^*} \text{ if } H \cdot H^* > 0$$

$$P' = P + \Theta \Delta P \text{ where } \Theta = \frac{-H^*}{H + H^*} \text{ if } H \cdot H^* < 0$$

Two exceptions are made to this rule:

a. if either H or H^* is very insignificant compared to the other, and contributes little to the total explanation, it is neglected;
b. if, for $H \cdot H^* < 0$, the absolute difference between both coefficients is small ($\Theta > 3$) and insignificant, only the accelerator is retained. This approach is preferred to presenting the coefficients of P and P_{-1} separately, since the total value $\frac{1}{2}(H + H^*)$ of both (and its t-ratio) is essential rather than that of the separate coefficients.

4. The equation is reestimated with the thus obtained conditional specification.

The results are presented in Table 9. The first column shows the numbering of the pairs and the unit of measurement: zero (ZD) or first differences (FD). Column (2) shows the elasticity of the first price variable ($P_1 = \ln p_{r2}/p_{1r}$); below each coefficient the t-ratio is indicated. Column (3) shows the lag, (4) the accelerator; an asterisk denotes a conditional estimate of Θ, according to (3.6).

Columns (8) and (9) present the trend coefficient and the constant, (10) the Von Neuman Ratio and (11) the coefficient of determination.

TABLE 9.

Empirical results

Number Unit	P_1	Lag	ΔP_1	P_2	Lag	ΔP_2	trend	const.	VNR	R^2
1	2	3	4	5	6	7	8	9	10	11
1, ZD	1.27		.16*			2.35		.04	3.02	.807
	6.29					3.55		.75		
2, ZD			1.93	7.78	.66			—4.06	2.09	.165
			.79	1.40				—16.68		
3, ZD	3.99	.07		5.59	.59			—1.46	1.30	.459
	1.32			2.48				—3.48		
4, FD	5.56	.61		2.90	.67		.08	—.53	0.98	.306
	1.21			1.28			1.27	—1.15		
5, FD	.63	.52		3.25	.45			.00	1.92	.381
	.88			2.36				.06		
6, FD	13.15	.78		.42				.05	2.27	.201
	1.22			.15				.11		
7, ZD	3.85	1.00				2.18	—.10	2.95	2.27	.220
	.57					1.02	—1.01	3.46		
8, ZD	2.09	.44		—4.86	.50		.33	.29	2.15	.874
	2.61			—6.99			3.37	3.12		
9, FD	1.68	.82		—7.48	.63		.02	—.10	2.69	.703
	1.20			—3.78			1.03	—.96		
10, ZD	10.60		.25*	7.07	.21			1.60	2.25	.466
	1.96			2.55				2.55		
11, FD	10.33	.40		2.52		1.17*		.05	1.76	.471
	.93			2.16				.15		
12, ZD	1.03		.60*	—6.27	.77			.22	2.31	.752
	2.73			—5.51				2.68|		
13, FD	11.61	.06		3.01		.09*		—.02	3.14	.238
	1.57			.63				—.01		
14, ZD			2.39	2.87		.22*		—.81	1.29	.469
			2.97	1.85				—9.33		
15, ZD			—.45	2.01	.27		—.123	.12	1.42	.883
			—.37	1.20			—6.66	.90		
16, ZD	—2.31	.31		2.99	.34		.06	—.79	1.83	.592
	—2.23			1.76			3.14	—5.39		
17, ZD	19.26	.36		5.41	.28		—.11	5.07	3.21	.549
	2.68			1.15			—2.47	2.83		
18, FD	3.03		.40*	3.66	.56		.12	—.91	2.09	.538
	1.47			.75			1.59	—1.73		
19, FD	2.76	.57		—4.98	.47		.11	—.89	2.43	.405
	.80			—1.56			2.14	—2.59		
20, ZD	2.70	.71		—5.51		.11*		2.24	1.52	.357
	1.60			—2.21				8.78		
21, ZD	1.33	1.00		1.71	.28		—.21	.56	2.69	.973
	1.96			2.31			—9.86	3.41		
22, ZD	2.32	.66		1.93		2.50*	—.12	—.04	1.95	.887
	3.33			6.58			—6.43	—.31		

Number unit	P_1	Lag	ΔP_1	P_2	Lag	ΔP_2	trend	const.	VNR	R^2
1	2	3	4	5	6	7	8	9	10	11
23, ZD	13.66	.44		13.19	.33			.86	1.83	.785
	2.55			4.89				1.55		
24, ZD **			—3.68	7.14		.22*	—.25	1.92	1.48	.658
			—.86	2.72			—2.32	2.15		
25, FD	19.04	.58		.19				—.59	2.61	.683
	4.27			.08				—1.77		
26, ZD	—3.63		.37*	—.58		2.47*		1.97	2.07	.259
	4.81			—.71				4.85		
27, ZD	2.37	.59		—5.94	.61		—.01		2.31	.739
	3.07			—1.72			—1.55			
28, ZD	4.21	.56		—11.60	.47		—.05		1.86	.435
	2.34			—2.47			—1.82			
29, ZD	1.64	1.00		3.95	1.00		.54	—9.69	2.39	.615
	.91			.99			2.34	—3.83		
30, ZD	.94			2.09	1.00			—1.68	1.92	.866
	1.29			4.12				—19.51		

* Estimated conditionally, see text.
** Specification includes a dummy for the zero flow of the second year: —.543 (—.25).

The results are satisfactory: the vast majority of the price-elasticities has the correct, positive sign, as summarized in Table 10.

TABLE 10.

Number of price elasticities by t-ratio

	$t<1.0$	$1.0<t<2.0$	$t>2.0$	total
wrong sign	1	2	7	10
correct sign	10	16	18	44
accelerator only	3	1	2	6

Thus 44 of the 60 elasticities have the correct sign, of which 34 have a *t*-ratio higher than 1.

The degree of explanation is acceptable: R^2 ranges from .165 to .973, averaging .558. In 21 equations both price-elasticities are positive, they too average nearly the same R^2: .553. Of course this picture is somewhat flattered by the presence of trends, but the 15 equations in which no trend occurs, average .491 nevertheless.

3.2. *Non Price-effects*

Even on the 4 and 5 digit SITC level, shifts in the commodity composition can occur. These cause, if prices are measured as unit values, a bias of the price-elasticities. For 6 of the categories above additional data are available: volumes are measured not only in metric tons but also in numbers. Thus unit weight may serve as an index of commodity composition, or 'quality'.[33] If this is true, the share-relations of demand and supply can, following Verdoorn and Van Bochove (forthcoming)[34] be specified as

$$\frac{x_{12}}{x_{r2}} = \mu_{12} \left(\frac{p_{12}}{p_{r2}}\right)^{E_2} \left(\frac{p_{12}}{p_{r2}}\right)^{E_2^*}_{-1} \left(\frac{q_{12}}{q_{r2}}\right)^{\zeta_2} \left(\frac{q_{12}}{q_{r2}}\right)^{\zeta_2^*}_{-1} \tag{3.7}$$

$$\frac{x_{12}}{x_{1r}} = \beta_{12} \left(\frac{p_{12}}{p_{1r}}\right)^{H_1} \left(\frac{p_{12}}{p_{1r}}\right)^{H_1^*}_{-1} \left(\frac{q_{12}}{q_{1r}}\right)^{\xi_1} \left(\frac{q_{12}}{q_{1r}}\right)^{\xi_1^*}_{-1} \tag{3.8}$$

Here q_{ij} denotes unit weight of flow x_{ij} measured by metric ton; the expected value of $\zeta_2 + \zeta_2^*$ is positive, of $\xi_1 + \xi_1^*$ negative.

For similar reasons as above concerning H and E, the absolute values of the demand and supply parameters of the 'quality' indicators are postulated to be equal flow by flow

$$\begin{aligned} \xi_1 &= -\zeta_2 & \xi_1^* &= -\zeta_2^* \\ \xi_2 &= -\zeta_1 & \xi_2^* &= -\zeta_1^* \end{aligned} \tag{3.9}$$

The counterpart of (3.5) thus obtained is

$$\frac{x_{12}/x_{21}}{\sqrt{x_{1r}x_{r2}/x_{2r}x_{r1}}} = \alpha \left(\frac{p_{r2}}{p_{1r}}\right)^{\frac{H_1}{2}} \left(\frac{p_{r2}}{p_{1r}}\right)^{\frac{H_1^*}{2}}_{-1} \left(\frac{p_{2r}}{p_{r1}}\right)^{\frac{H_2}{2}} \left(\frac{p_{2r}}{p_{r1}}\right)^{\frac{H_2^*}{2}}_{-1} \cdot \tag{3.10}$$

$$\cdot \left(\frac{q_{1r}}{q_{r2}}\right)^{\frac{\zeta_1}{2}} \left(\frac{q_{1r}}{q_{r2}}\right)^{\frac{\zeta_1^*}{2}}_{-1} \left(\frac{q_{r1}}{q_{2r}}\right)^{\frac{\zeta_2}{2}} \left(\frac{q_{r1}}{q_{2r}}\right)^{\frac{\zeta_2^*}{2}}_{-1}$$

33. In each case a positive relation between weight and 'quality' is to be expected: pairs 23, 24 and 25 consist of TV receivers (color sets are heavier, portables lighter), 26 of domestic refrigerators where weight coincides with volume, 28 of motor cars and 29 of bicycles where childrens cycles are light and cheap.

Of course in some cases (TV sets and refrigerators) technical development lowers unit weight in the course of time, but this development are removed by the use of shares; thus only differences in composition between flows is retained.

34. Actually the analysis, based on a model disaggregated by weight per unit is somewhat more refined, but essentially the specification is the same.

TABLE 11.

Non-price influences

Number unit	P_1	Lag	ΔP_1	P_2	Lag	ΔP_2	Q_1	Lag	ΔQ_1	Q_2	Lag	ΔQ_2	Trend	Const.	VNR	R^2
23, ZD	6.04 (2.76)	.54		4.70 (3.31)		.25	11.31 (9.84)	.50		7.42 (4.09)		.42		.831 (1.55)	3.55	.981
24,** ZD			−1.41 (−.70)	11.30 (8.10)	.26		12.14 (7.86)	.78		1.90 (2.20)		.28		2.85 (7.39)	2.78	.943
25, FD	17.91 (4.15)	.40		−.70 (−.27)			.54 (1.75)		3.28	−.66 (−1.46)		.42		−.59 (−1.82)	2.12	.785
26, ZD	25.01 (3.05)	.29		4.07 (1.68)		.44	21.27 (3.41)	.69		1.48 (.42)		.83	1.01 (3.58)	−4.26 (−2.57)	2.57	.786
28, ZD	15.95 (3.70)	.93		−27.34 (−3.87)		.65	−13.47 (−3.16)	.43		−3.88 (−1.73)		.015	−.26 (−3.19)	−.42 (−1.53)	1.92	.738

Number unit	P_1+Q_1	Lag	P_2+Q_2	Lag	Trend	Const.	VNR	R^2
29, ZD	2.76 (2.19)	1.00	1.41 (.32)	1.00	.74 (3.61)	−8.03 (−4.93)	1.90	.717

Number unit	P_1+P_2	Lag	Q_1+Q_2	Lag	Trend	Const.	VNR	R^2
29, ZD	.97 (.73)	1.00	3.62 (2.11)	1.00	.58 (3.51)	−8.26 (−5.60)	2.58	.769

** 24 is inclusive of a dummy for the second year: −3.39 (−2.34).

Regression results for the 6 pairs concerned are presented in Table 11. The same procedure as above has been followed; Q_1 denotes $\ln q_{1r}/q_{r2}$.

For pair 29 two alternative conditional specifications are used: since the first three observations are zero-leaving, as lags are included, only one degree of freedom if unconditional regression is performed. The two alternatives are, resp: equal elasticities of price and non-price variables ($H_i = \zeta_i$ etc.) and uniform elasticities for all flows ($H_1 = H_2$, $\zeta_1 = \zeta_2$, etc.). In both cases the correct signs are found. This is generally the case: the weight variable has 8 times a positive sign, 3 times a negative. Only one equation is really bad: 28, being passenger motor cars (Germany-France); both weight coefficients are negative and one price variable (the one corresponding to French exports to Germany). In the case of pair 26 (refrigerators) however, the two price coefficients were negative above (cf. Table 10) but now obtain the correct, positive sign.

The weight variable generally contributes substantially to the total explanation: average R^2 for the six equations increases from .573 to .834.

SUMMARY

The results of the regression analysis are summarized in Table 12. All equations together yield 44 price elasticities of the correct, positive sign, and only 9 negative. The elasticities of substitution have on the average a t-ratio of 2.35 and a value of $H = -E = 5.98$. Thus the inference is justified that *the explanation of variations in the intensity of bilateral two-way trade based on finite elasticities of substitution of demand and supply, is compatible with the empirical evidence presented.*

The average value of the 8 positive elasticities of unit weights is 7.58, the average t-ratio being 3.46. Thus *the explicit introduction of unit weight as a correction for shifts in commodity composition may contribute substantially to total explanation.*

APPENDIX. THE N-COUNTRY MODEL: ELIMINATION OF QUANTITIES AND ALGORITHM FOR NUMERICAL ANALYSIS.

The model consists of a demand and a supply subsystem. In both subsystems either prices or quantities can be considered independent. Here the prices are chosen and quantities, demanded and supplied, are expressed in exoge-

TABLE 12.

Summary of empirical results

	Classification of coefficients by *t*-ratio							
	Number of price elasticities				Number of Non-price elasticities			
	t<1	1<*t*<2	*t*>2	Total	*t*<1	1<*t*<2	*t*>2	Total
Wrong sign	1	1	7	9	–	2	1	3
Correct sign	8	17	19	44	1	1	6	8
Accelerator only	3	1	2	6	–	–	–	–

	Average elasticities (and absolute *t*-ratios)	
Price elasticity	5.98	(2.35)*
Non-price elasticities	7.58	(3.46)

	Average coefficients of determination
Price variables only	.552
Incl. non price variables	.834

* Non zero elasticities only.

nous variables and prices. Market equilibrium then permits elimination of quantities and a system of n^2 equations in n^2 prices remains. The system can not be solved analytically, so only numerical solution is possible: to that purpose a simple algorithm is used. As the demand subsystem, if total demand in each country is fixed, is completely analogous to the supply subsystem, only an exhaustive treatment of the solution of the latter is given and just the final results for the former. Subsequently total demand is eliminated. It is noted that formulas preceded by A occur only in this appendix, while formulas without A refer to the same formulas in the main text.

Solution of the Supply Subsystem

A useful intermediate result is obtained by expressing the weights in the definition of the price of total exports p_{ir} in terms of bilateral prices. To that end (2.25) is substituted in these weights and in the resulting equation the substitution relation (2.24) is substituted

$$\frac{x_{ij}}{x_{ir}} = \frac{x_{ij}}{\sum_{k \neq i} x_{ik}} = \frac{w_{ij} p_{ij}^{H_i}}{\sum_{k \neq i} w_{ik} p_{ik}^{H_i}} \tag{A.1}$$

The price of total exports p_{ir} is expressed in the prices of all international trade flows out of country i upon substitution of (A.1) in (2.26)

$$p_{ir} = \sum_{j \neq i} \frac{w_{ij} p_{ij}^{H_i}}{\sum_{k \neq i} w_{ik} p_{ik}^{H_i}} p_{ij} \tag{A.2}$$

The solution for domestic sales x_{ii} is found upon elimination of x_{ir} out of (2.23) and (2.27); writing x_{ii} explicitly

$$x_{ii} = \frac{s_i}{1 + g_i \left(\dfrac{p_{ir}}{p_{ii}}\right)^{n_i}} \tag{A.3}$$

For convenience we retain p_{ir}, already expressed in bilateral prices only, in the equations.

The corresponding result for the international trade flows x_{ij} is obtained from

$$x_{ij} = \frac{x_{ij}}{\sum_{k \neq i} x_{ik}} \cdot \frac{x_{ir}}{x_{ii}} x_{ii} ,$$

where the identity (2.25) is used; substituting (A.1), (2.23) and (A.3):

$$x_{ij} = \frac{w_{ij} p_{ij}^{H_i}}{\sum_{k \neq i} w_{ik} p_{ik}^{H_i}} \cdot \frac{g_i \left(\dfrac{p_{ir}}{p_{ii}}\right)^{n_i}}{1 + g_i \left(\dfrac{p_{ir}}{p_{ii}}\right)^{n_i}} \cdot s_i \tag{A.4}$$

This completes the solution of the supply subsystem.

Solution of the Demand Subsystem

The *analogon* of (A.2) for the price of total imports is:

$$p_{rj} \pi_{rj} = \sum_{i \neq j} \frac{a_{ij} (p_{ij} \pi_{ij})^{E_j}}{\sum_{h \neq j} a_{hj} (p_{hj} \pi_{hj})^{E_j}} p_{ij} \pi_{ij} \tag{A.5}$$

Domestic sales

$$x_{jj} = \frac{d_j}{1 + z_j \left(\dfrac{p_{rj} \pi_{rj}}{p_{jj} \pi_{jj}} \right)^{E_j}} \qquad (A.6)$$

International trade flows

$$x_{ij} = \frac{a_{ij}(p_{ij}\pi_{ij})^{E_j}}{\sum\limits_{h \neq j} a_{ij}(p_{hj}\pi_{hj})^{E_j}} \cdot \frac{z_j \left(\dfrac{p_{rj}\pi_{rj}}{p_{jj}\pi_{jj}} \right)^{\varepsilon_j}}{1 + z_j \left(\dfrac{p_{rj}\pi_{rj}}{p_{jj}\pi_{jj}} \right)^{\varepsilon_j}} \cdot d_j \qquad (A.7)$$

In the equations (A.6) and (A.7) the only endogenous variable is d_j, which in turn depends on the price of total demand. The latter is easily expressed in all prices upon substituting (2.21) in the weights of (2.22); substitution of (2.17) then yields

$$p_{oj}\pi_{oj} = \frac{z_j \left(\dfrac{p_{rj}\pi_{rj}}{p_{jj}\pi_{jj}} \right)^{\varepsilon_j}}{1 + z_j \left(\dfrac{p_{rj}\pi_{rj}}{p_{jj}\pi_{jj}} \right)^{\varepsilon_j}} \, p_{rj}\pi_{rj} + \frac{1}{1 + z_j \left(\dfrac{p_{rj}\pi_{rj}}{p_{jj}\pi_{jj}} \right)^{\varepsilon_j}} \, p_{jj}\pi_{jj} \qquad (A.8)$$

The solution for domestic sales and international trade flows is now completed by substituting (A.8) in (2.16) and the resulting equation in (A.6) and (A.7) resp.

$$x_{jj} = \alpha_j \left\{ \frac{p_{jj}\pi_{jj} + z_j \left(\dfrac{p_{rj}\pi_{rj}}{p_{jj}\pi_{jj}} \right)^{\varepsilon_j} p_{rj}\pi_{rj}}{1 + z_j \left(\dfrac{p_{rj}\pi_{rj}}{p_{jj}\pi_{jj}} \right)^{\varepsilon_j}} \right\}^{\delta_j} \cdot \left\{ 1 + z_j \left(\dfrac{p_{rj}\pi_{rj}}{p_{jj}\pi_{jj}} \right)^{\varepsilon_j} \right\}^{-1} \qquad (A.9)$$

$$x_{ij} = \alpha_j \frac{a_{ij}(p_{ij}\pi_{ij})^{E_j}}{\sum\limits_{h \neq j} a_{hj}(p_{hj}\pi_{hj})^{E_j}} \left\{ \frac{p_{jj}\pi_{jj} + z_j \left(\dfrac{p_{rj}\pi_{rj}}{p_{jj}\pi_{jj}} \right)^{\varepsilon_j} p_{rj}\pi_{rj}}{1 + z_j \left(\dfrac{p_{rj}\pi_{rj}}{p_{jj}\pi_{jj}} \right)^{\varepsilon_j}} \right\}^{\delta_j} \cdot$$

$$\cdot \frac{z_j \left(\dfrac{p_{rj}\pi_{rj}}{p_{jj}\pi_{jj}} \right)^{\varepsilon_j}}{1 + z_j \left(\dfrac{p_{rj}\pi_{rj}}{p_{jj}\pi_{jj}} \right)^{\varepsilon_j}} \qquad (A.10)$$

where

$$\alpha_j = \gamma_j y_j^{\beta_j} (p_{oj}^* \pi_{oj}^*)^{-\delta_j}$$

Elimination of quantities

Elimination of the quantities by equating the relations concerned leaves a system of n^2 equations in n^2 prices. It is divided in two subsystems, viz. if $i=j$ and $i \neq j$.

Equating (A.3) and (A.9) yields n equations

$$p_{ii} = \frac{\alpha_i}{s_i} \cdot \left\{ \frac{p_{ii}\pi_{ii} + z_i \left(\dfrac{p_{ri}\pi_{ri}}{p_{ii}\pi_{ii}}\right)^{\varepsilon_i}}{1 + z_i \left(\dfrac{p_{ri}\pi_{ri}}{p_{ii}\pi_{ii}}\right)^{\varepsilon_i}} \right\}^{\delta_i} \cdot \frac{1 + g_i \left(\dfrac{p_{ir}}{p_{ii}}\right)^{\eta_i}}{1 + z_i \left(\dfrac{p_{ri}\pi_{ri}}{p_{ii}\pi_{ii}}\right)^{\varepsilon_i}} \cdot p_{ii} \qquad i = 1, ..., n \tag{A.11}$$

Equating (A.4) and (A.10) yields after rearrangement of terms the remaining $n(n-1)$ equations

$$p_{ij} = \left[\frac{\alpha_j}{s_i} \cdot \left\{ \frac{p_{jj}\pi_{jj} + z_j \left(\dfrac{p_{rj}\pi_{rj}}{p_{jj}\pi_{jj}}\right)^{\varepsilon_j}}{1 + z_j \left(\dfrac{p_{rj}\pi_{rj}}{p_{jj}\pi_{jj}}\right)^{\varepsilon_j}} \right\}^{\delta_j} \cdot \frac{1 + g_i \left(\dfrac{p_{ir}}{p_{ii}}\right)^{\eta_i}}{g_i \left(\dfrac{p_{ir}}{p_{ii}}\right)^{\eta_i}} \cdot \right.$$

$$\left. \cdot \frac{z_j \left(\dfrac{p_{rj}\pi_{rj}}{p_{jj}\pi_{jj}}\right)^{\varepsilon_j}}{1 + z_j \left(\dfrac{p_{rj}\pi_{rj}}{p_{jj}\pi_{jj}}\right)^{\varepsilon_j}} \cdot \frac{\displaystyle\sum_{k \neq i} w_{ik}p_{ik}^{H_i}}{w_{ij}} \cdot \frac{a_{ij}\pi_{ij}^{E_j}}{\displaystyle\sum_{h \neq j} a_{hj}(p_{hj}\pi_{hj})^{E_j}} \right]^{\frac{1}{H_i - E_j}} \tag{A.12}$$

$$i, j = 1, ..., n$$
$$i \neq j$$

The algorithm

The system described by (A.11) and (A.12) cannot be solved analytically. Numerical solution is possible by various methods; the algorithm used is not convergent for all parameter values, but preferred on account of its simplicity.

The procedure starts by inserting for each price in the right hand side of both subsystems a starting value p_{ij}^*; the prices of total exports and imports are obtained beforehand. An obvious choice for the initial values of bilateral prices is unity. Then new values are calculated by (A.11) and (A.12). The procedure is taken to have converged, when *all* calculated prices p_{ij} satisfy the acceptance criterion

$$\left| \frac{p_{ij} - p_{ij}^*}{\frac{1}{2}(p_{ij} + p_{ij}^*)} \right| < \varepsilon, \qquad i, j = 1, ..., n. \tag{A.13}$$

where ε is any small number, here chosen 10^{-6}. If (A.13) is violated for at least one p_{ij}, all p_{ij}'s calculated in that round are starting values in the following round.

Convergence is achieved fairly quickly for all values of the parameters, except for rather high values of ε and η. Clearly all numerators and denominators of the terms on the right hand side of (A.11) and (A.12) are of approximately the same order, the exceptions being the third terms. If for high values of η and ε the ratios p_{ir}/p_{ii} and p_{rj}/p_{jj} in some round are both much larger (smaller) than unity, the third term on the right hand side of (A.11) is skyrocketing (nearly zero), forcing p_{ii} near infinity (zero). As the reverse holds in the next round and so on, convergence cannot be achieved. Obviously for (A.12) the same applies. Therefore, the values assigned to η and $-\varepsilon$ have 1.5 as an upperbound.

REFERENCES

Armington, P. S. A theory of demand for products, distinguished by place of production. *I.M.F.Staff Papers*, 16, 1969, pp. 159–178.
Balassa, B. Tariff reductions and trade in manufactures among industrial countries. *American Economic Review*, LVI, 1966, pp. 466 sqq.
Blattner, N. Intraindustrieller Aussenhandel Empirische Beobachtungen im Falle der Schweiz und Theoretische Interpretationen. *Weltwirtschaftliches Archiv*, 113, 1977, pp. 88–103.
c.b.s. De invloed van het prijsniveau op den uitvoer, 1 & 2. *De Nederlandse conjunctuur*, 1938 pp. 117 sqq & 1939 pp. 19 sqq.
c.b.s. *De Nederlandse Conjunctuur, Speciale Onderzoekingen No. 1*. Albani, Den Haag, 1939 (Study carried out by J. B. D. Derksen and A. L. G. M. Rombouts under supervision of J. Tinbergen).
Davies, R. Two-way international trade: a comment. *Weltwirtschaftliches Archiv*, 113, 1977, pp. 179–181.
EEC, *Foreign trade statistics, analytical tables*.
Finger, J. M. Trade overlap and intra-industry trade. *Economic Inquiry*, 13, 1975, pp. 581–589.
Gray, H. P. Two-way international trade in manufactures: a theoretical underpinning. *Weltwirtschaftliches Archiv*, 109, 1973, pp. 19–38.
Gray, H. P. Two-way international trade: Reply. *Weltwirtschaftliches Archiv*, 113, 1977, pp. 182–184.
Grubel, H. G. Intra-industry specialization and the pattern of trade. *Canadian Journal of Economics and Political Science*, 33, 1967, pp. 374–388.

Grubel, H. G. and P. J. Lloyd. The empirical measurement of intra-industry trade, *Economic Record*, 47, 1971, pp. 494–517.

Grubel, H. G. and P. J. Lloyd. *Intra-industry trade*. Macmillan, London, 1975.

Haberler, G. *Der Internationale Handel*. Julius Springer, Berlin, 1933.

Hesse, H. Hypothesen zur Erklärung des Warenhandels zwischen Industrieländern. In: *Probleme der Weltwirtschaftlichen Arbeitsteilung*, Schriften des Vereins für Socialpolitik, N.F., Bd 78, Berlin 1974, pp. 41 sqq.

Hicks, J. R. and R. G. D. Allen. A reconsideration of the theory of value, *Economica*, (New series) 1.1–2, 1934, part I, pp. 52–76 and part II, pp. 196–219.

Instituto Centrale di Statistica. Republica Italiana, *Statistica Annuale del commercio con l'estero*.

Kojima, K. The pattern of international trade among advanced countries. *Hitotsubashi Journal of Economics*, 5, 1964, pp. 16–36.

Kojima, K., Structure of comparative advantage in industrial countries: a verification of the factor-proportions theorem. *Hitotsubashi Journal of Economics*, 11, 1970, pp. 1–29.

Kooyman, J. and A. N. R. Schwartz. *Statistical information and the international linkage of macro-economic models, Occasional Paper* C.P.B., The Hague, 1975.

Linder, S. B. *An essay on trade and transformation*. John Wiley and Sons, New York, 1961.

Ministère des Finances et des Affaires Economiques, Direction Générale des douanes et des droits indirects. *Statistique du commerce extérieur de la France*.

Mundell, R. A. Tariff preferences and the terms of trade, *Manchester School of Economic and Social Studies*, 32.1, 1964, pp. 1–13.

OECD, *Trade by Commodities, Series C*.

Pagoulatos, E. and R. Sorenson. Two-way international trade: an econometric analysis. *Weltwirtschaftliches Archiv*, 111, 1975, pp. 454–465.

Petith, H. C. European integration and the terms of trade. *Economic Journal*, 87, 1977, pp. 262–272.

Rothschild, K. W. Integration und Aussenhandelsstruktur. *Weltwirtschaftliches Archiv*, 106, 1970, pp. 36–56.

Statistisches Bundesamt (Wiesbaden). *Der Aussenhandel der Bundesrepublik Deutschland*, Reihe 2, *Spezial Handel nach Waren und Ländern*.

Taussig, F. W. *Some aspects of the tariff question*. Harvard University Press, Cambridge, 1915.

Tinbergen, J. Long term foreign trade elasticities. *Metroeconomica*, 1, 1949, pp. 174–185.

Tinbergen, J. *Econometrics*. George Allen & Unwin, London, 1951.

Verdoorn, P. J. Welke zijn de achtergronden en vooruitzichten van de economische integratie in Europa en welke gevolgen zou deze integratie hebben, met name voor de welvaart in Nederland? In: Vereniging voor de Staathuishoudkunde, *Praeadviezen* 1952, pp. 47–135.

Verdoorn, P. J. The intra-bloc trade of BENELUX, in: E. A. G. Robinson (ed.). *Economic consequences of the size of nations*. Macmillan, London, 1960, Chapter 19, pp. 291–329.

Verdoorn, P. J. and C. A. van Bochove. (forthcoming English version of) Het tarief-effect op internationale handelsstromen bij eindige aanbods-elasticiteiten. *Mimeo*.

Verdoorn, P. J. and F. J. M. Meyer zu Schlochtern. Trade creation and trade diversion in the common market, in: *Integration Européenne et realité économique*. De Tempel, Brugge, 1964.

Verdoorn, P. J., J. J. Post, S. S. Goslinga. Het jaarmodel 1969, Bijlage A in *Centraal Economisch Plan 1971*. C.P.B., The Hague, 1971.

Verdoorn, P. J. and A. N. R. Schwartz. Two alternative estimates of the effects of EEC and EFTA on the pattern of trade. *European Economic Review*, 3, 1972, pp. 291–335.

Accumulation of Durable Goods by Young Marrieds*

ROBERT FERBER AND LUCY CHAO LEE

1. INTRODUCTION

The purpose of this paper is to explore the rate at which young married couples accumulate durable goods and investigate to what extent socioeconomic and attitudinal variables differentiate between couples that tend to accumulate durable goods rapidly and those that do not. A particular focus is on the influence of the stock of durables on future stocks and durables purchases – do such stocks seem to depress or stimulate future purchases of stocks?

Paralleling these objectives, this paper is divided into four parts. Following a brief description of the data and the plan of analysis in this first part, information is provided in the second part on the rate of acquisition of different durable goods by the couples in the sample and of the extent to which different types of durable goods were purchased during the first five years of marriage. The extent to which couples differ in their ownership of stocks of durable goods at the end of these five years is also explored in this part. Factors that might influence the differential rates of acquisition of durable goods and different amounts of stock at the end of the five years are explored in the third part of the paper, where multivariate techniques are used to ascertain the extent to which such differences can be explained by socioeconomic and attitudinal variables. A final section of the paper summarizes the results obtained, discusses their implications and suggests avenues for future research.

1.1. *The Data*

The data used in this study come from a panel in Peoria and Decatur, Illinois, based on the cohort of couples married in the summer of 1968 in

* Revised version of a paper given at the 1975 annual meetings of the American Psychological Association. This work was performed as part of Grant SOC74–23458 of the National Science Foundation.

those two cities. The initial sample, selected in the fall of 1968, consisted of 313 couples. This panel had been interviewed nine times as of the date when this analysis was carried out. After nine waves, the size of the panel was down to 259, although the base for the analysis is less than this figure mainly because not all the couples were interviewed in each wave.

Various types of data have been collected during these interviews. The most relevant types for the purposes of this analysis are the following:

a. Purchases of durable goods.
b. Plans to purchase durable goods.
c. Socioeconomic characteristics of each member of the couple.
d. Information on various aspects of their personality and attitudes toward life.

A principal focus of these interviews was on the acquisition of major different durable goods, that is, those costing over $100.[1] More specifically, the durable goods covered in this study refer to 13 items, namely:

Automobiles
Televisions – black and white
Televisions – color
Stereos
Refrigerators
Freezers
Stoves
Washers
Dryers
Room air conditioners
Central air conditioning
Dishwashers
Disposals

Information on ownership of these durables was obtained on the first wave of interviews, as of the time of marriage (summer 1968), and similar information was obtained in the eighth wave, in the fall of 1973. In addition, purchase information on each of these durables was sought on each wave of interviews after Wave 1, so that purchases can be compared with ownership throughout this period.

1. Certain other durables are excluded from this analysis either because of their heterogeneous nature, e.g., furniture, or because of their low dollar value, e.g., irons.

1.3. *Plan of Analysis*

A central question explored in this study is the rate of purchase of these durable goods over the first five years of the marriage, and the relationship of these purchases to initial stocks and to socioeconomic and attitudinal characteristics of these couples. Thus, do couples in the early stage of their married life reduce their rate of purchases as they acquire more durable goods or do they keep acquiring durables more or less continuously? In other words, are these purchases better explained by the hypothesis of saturation or by the opposite hypothesis of rising aspirations? Also, are couples with relatively large stocks of durables at one time also likely to have relatively large stocks of durables at later times? To what extent do stocks at earlier times help explain later purchases and levels of stocks after socioeconomic and attitudinal variables are taken into account?

The analysis is carried out first by examining the relationships between purchases and ownership on the basis of cross-tabulations and then using two types of multivariate analysis to investigate the influence of possibly relevant variables in explaining durables ownership and purchases.

2. PURCHASE AND OWNERSHIP

A general idea of the relationship between durable goods purchases of particular products over the five year period and ownership of that product at the time of marriage is provided in Table 1 for each of the 13 durables covered in this study. One thing evident in this table is that an appreciable number of these durables were already owned by the couples at the time of marriage. Thus, approximately half or more of the couples owned at that time at least one automobile, a black and white television set, a stereo set, a refrigerator and a stove. Durables not owned at the time of marriage were primarily, as one might expect, durables that were in the growth phase of their product life cycle and hence were not widely owned by the population at large, such as color televisions, freezers, dishwashers and automatic garbage disposals.

In terms of purchase patterns, an examination of Table 1 suggests two distinct patterns. One pattern is for an equal percentage or more purchases of the durable to be made by the initial owners of that good. For example, of those couples owning a black and white television set at the time of marriage, 37 percent purchased additional sets in the following five years, whereas of those not owning a black and white television at the time of marriage, less than one-quarter bought these sets during the same period. Rather surprisingly, percentagewise more purchases by initial owners than initial nonowners were reported for central air conditioning, freezers, dishwashers and disposals. For each of these goods, however, the sample size is very small for the initial owners, and it appears that many of the purchases by this group were for replacement purposes.

TABLE 1.

Durables Ownership at Time of Marriage and
Number of Purchases in Subsequent Five Years

Durable good	Initial ownership (pct.)	Percent distribution by number of purchases of good			
		0	1	2 or more	Total
Automobile	Yes (96.5)	3.0%	18.5%	78.5%	100.0%
	No (3.5)	0	33.3	66.7	100.0
Television/	Yes (73.0)	63.0	33.9	3.1	100.0
black and white	No (27.0)	76.6	17.0	6.4	100.0
Television/	Yes (23.6)	61.0	26.8	12.2	100.0
color	No (76.4)	26.3	61.7	12.0	100.0
Stereo	Yes (60.9)	53.8	32.1	14.1	100.0
	No (39.1)	38.2	47.1	14.7	100.0
Refrigerator	Yes (51.7)	45.6	45.6	8.8	100.0
	No (48.3)	10.7	61.9	27.4	100.0
Freezer	Yes (1.7)	33.3	33.3	33.3	99.9
	No (98.3)	71.3	24.6	4.1	100.0
Stove	Yes (49.4)	45.3	50.0	4.7	100.0
	No (50.6)	13.6	56.8	29.6	100.0
Washer	Yes (20.1)	40.0	57.1	2.9	100.0
	No (79.9)	13.7	66.2	20.1	100.0
Dryer	Yes (13.8)	54.2	45.8	0	100.0
	No (86.2)	21.3	62.7	16.0	100.0
Room air conditioner	Yes (20.1)	65.7	25.7	8.6	100.0
	No (79.9)	44.6	40.3	15.1	100.0
Central air conditioner	Yes (3.4)	50.0	50.0	0	100.0
	No (96.6)	74.4	23.8	1.8	100.0
Dishwasher	Yes (1.7)	33.3	66.7	0	100.0
	No (98.3)	70.8	24.0	5.3	100.1
Disposal	Yes (2.9)	60.0	40.0	0	100.0
	No (97.1)	82.8	12.4	4.7	99.9

The second principal pattern, a pattern that would support the saturation hypothesis, is for more purchases to be made by initial nonowners than owners. As is evident in Table 1, this pattern is pronounced for color television sets, stereo sets, refrigerators, stoves, washers, dryers and room air conditioners. With the exception of the first two, all of these durables are household items, and all but dryers could probably be classified as necessities given the fact that most of these couples were purchasing homes during this period.

A broader picture of the overall relationship between purchases and initial ownership is provided by Table 2, which presents cross-tabulations of the number of durables purchased in the first five years after marriage by the number of durables owned at the time of marriage. Two sets of comparisons are presented, one including automobile purchases and the other excluding them, done to examine whether the inclusion of automobile purchases seems to alter the relationship between purchases and ownership for the other durables. To ensure enough observations in each category of durables owned, three such categories were constructed for the stock of durables in Wave 1 and also for the total purchases made in the five-year period.

Judging from Table 2, whether automobiles are included or excluded, the table indicates a pronounced tendency for those owning few durables at marriage to make more purchases later on. Thus, from Part A of Table 2, of those owning less than four durables, 36 percent bought 12 or more durables in the following five years as compared to only 21 percent of those owning six or more durables who made this many purchases. Also, note that the median number of purchases declines monotonically as the number of durables owned at marriage increases. The same relationships are apparent in Part B.

Clearly, the number of purchases made by these couples in the first five years of their marriage was substantial on any basis of comparison. It therefore seems relevant to ask what can be said of the pattern of these purchases. Thus, was this purchase rate rising over time, declining or something else?

Some information on this question is provided by Table 3. This table shows for the couples owning a particular number of durable goods as of one wave of interviews, what proportion purchased one or more durables to the time of the next wave.[2] To ensure enough observations in each category of durable

---

2. The definition of durables stock used here allows for only one durable of each good so that, for example, with 13 goods the maximum stock would be 13. An alternate definition allowing for more than one durable was also tried (assuming a purchase was reported as an addition to stock), and yielded no different results.

TABLE 2.

Durable Goods Ownership at Time of Marriage and Later Purchases

Number of durables purchased next five years	Number of durables owned at marriage			
	0–3	4–5	6–11	Total
A. Including automobiles				
2–7	23.0%	25.8%	39.5%	27.6%
8–11	40.5	38.7	39.5	39.6
12–20	36.5	35.5	21.0	32.8
Total	100.0%	100.0%	100.0%	100.0%
Median	10.0	9.0	8.0	9.0
Base (families)	74	62	38	174
B. Excluding automobiles				
2–5	23.0%	21.0%	42.1%	26.4%
6–8	35.1	48.4	36.8	40.2
9–17	41.9	30.6	21.0	33.3
Total	100.0%	100.0%	100.0%	99.9%
Median	7.5	7.0	6.0	7.0
Base (families)	74	62	38	174

goods owned, three such categories were formulated for every wave, namely, relatively few goods owned (at that time), an average number of goods owned, and many goods owned. The definitions for these three categories necessarily varied from one wave to another and it does not seem necessary to give them here; some idea of these definitions is provided on page 236 in connection with the multivariate analysis, where the definitions are given for Waves 1, 4 and 9. The main criterion in all cases was to have approximately equal numbers of families in the three groups in a particular wave.

As in the case of Table 2, these purchase percentages were computed both including and excluding automobiles. As an example of what Table 3 tells us, the first row of Part A indicates that of the couples owning few durables on Wave 1, 45 percent purchased one or more durables to the time of the second wave if automobiles are included, and 35 percent bought one or more durables during this period if automobiles are excluded. Also as of Wave 1,

TABLE 3.

Percent of Couples Purchasing Durables Between Waves t and t+1, by Durables Owned on Wave t

Period between Waves t and $t+1$	Percent of purchases by couples owning specified durables on Wave t			
	Few	Average	Many	Total sample
	A. Including automobiles			
1–2	45.1%	64.5%	60.5%	55.8%
2–3	69.5	57.1	55.9	60.9
3–4	43.5	56.9	51.9	50.6
4–5	65.2	56.7	55.9	58.6
5–6	83.6	82.5	83.1	83.3
6–7	83.0	84.8	66.7	79.9
7–8	72.7	52.9	72.6	64.4
8–9	68.0	62.7	77.1	69.0
	B. Excluding automobiles			
1–2	35.1%	51.6%	39.5%	42.0%
2–3	56.9	43.9	44.1	48.3
3–4	35.0	45.0	35.2	38.5
4–5	40.0	46.7	39.1	42.0
5–6	75.4	71.9	64.3	70.7
6–7	60.8	70.4	45.2	61.5
7–8	54.5	50.0	50.7	51.1
8–9	52.0	31.4	56.2	47.1

of the couples owning many durables, 60.5 percent bought at least one durable in the period to the second wave if automobiles are included, whereas this percentage is slightly under 40 percent if automobiles are excluded.

Now, what does this table tell us about purchase patterns? In both cases (including or excluding automobiles), the answer seems to vary with time after marriage. In the first six months couples owning many durables also purchased more durables than those owning only a few. In the next four years, however, couples owning a few durables purchased at least as many more durables as those with large inventories, though somewhat paradoxically often the highest frequencies of purchases are observed for the couples owning an average number of durables. By Wave 8, in the fifth year of marriage, a reversal seems to take place, with a higher frequency of purchases by couples owning many durables than by couples owning few durables.

In view of this rather mixed picture, it seems all the more necessary to turn to multivariate analysis to try to sort out the inventory effect on purchases from that of other factors that are undoubtedly affecting this relationship. This is the subject of the next section.

3. TESTS OF HYPOTHESES

At least two hypotheses would seem to evolve from the results of the preceding section. One hypothesis is that couples that start out at the time of marriage with a relatively large stock of durables tend to maintain relatively large stocks of durables as the marriage wears on. The presumption is that certain couples have an inherent preference for durables that manifests itself very early in the marriage and continues over time. Some evidence for this view is provided by those data in Table 1 that showed that, for some of the durables, the couples making the most purchases in the later years were those that owned these durables in the very beginning. However, the evidence on this point in Table 1 was rather mixed, plus the fact that those data referred to individual durables whereas we are now considering the aggregate of all durables covered in this study. In addition, we now seek to take into account other possibly relevant variables, both socioeconomic and attitudinal, to see if the couples that own more durables at one time of the marriage continue to own more durables at other times, at least within the relatively short span of time covered, after allowance for these other factors.

The second hypothesis stems from Tables 2 and 3 and focuses more directly on the phenomenon of saturation. Based on the foregoing results, it postulates that the stock of durables already owned exerts a negative influence on future purchases. In other words, couples with more durables on hand are less likely to add to their stock in the following years. While this hypothesis is suggested by the data in Tables 2 and 3, it remains to be determined whether the same relationships are obtained when other relevant variables are included in the analysis.

Both of these hypotheses are explored in a multivariate framework that includes attitudinal and purchase likelihood variables on the one hand and socioeconomic variables on the other hand. The fact that both of these types of variables had to be included in this analysis made possible the opportunity to explore their relative importance.

A wide range of attitudinal variables were available, principally relating to long-term goals and aspirations, shopping attitudes, satisfaction with life, and purchase likelihood;[3] the latter were the only variables specific to the durables under study. These variables were available separately for the husband and the wife, since this information had been collected from each member of the couple in self-administered, simultaneous interviews. Socioeconomic information was of the usual type, including income level, occupation of husband and of wife, education of each member of the couple, age of each, whether the wife was working at the time of the interview, and ownership of a home. A list of all the variables tested is included in the appendix.

The overall approach in this analysis was to investigate these two basic hypotheses using two different dependent variables, first, the stock of durables owned, and second, the increase in the stock over a period of time, both in net and gross terms. In each case, a 'best' set of socioeconomic and attitudinal variables was developed as described shortly, and to this set was added a variable for the stock of durables as of a preceding time. The exact procedure is best explained with regard to a particular dependent variable.

3.1. *Stock of Durables*

Since the stock of durables clearly varies with time, the influence of different variables on the amount of stock owned is best considered for different waves, to see whether the factors that are most effective in discriminating owners of many durables from owners of few durables are essentially the same over time.

For this purpose, the analysis was carried out at three different stages of the marriage – the time of marriage, Wave 4 (after two years of marriage), and the most recent wave, after five years of marriage. The reasons for the selection of the first and the third times are self-evident; the selection of Wave 4 is based on an examination of the dispersion of durables owned wave by wave and finding that this dispersion was a maximum at that time.

In each case, the sample was divided into three groups as a basis for multiple discriminant analysis. These groups are owners of relatively few durables, an average number, and relatively many durables. The exact

---

3. This variable was applicable only to Waves 4 and 9 and was constructed, for Wave 4, by summing for each couple all the likelihoods of .8 or more reported on the prior three waves; and for Wave 9 obtaining a similar sum over Waves 4–8 inclusive. Prior experimentation had shown that purchase likelihoods in this range were far more likely to be fulfilled than lower likelihoods.

breaking points obviously varied with time, and were set to have approximately equal numbers in each group. These breaking points are:

	Few	Average	Many
Wave 1	0–3	4–5	6–11
Wave 4	1–4	5–6	7–12
Wave 9	2–8	9	10–12

The independent variables in this analysis are the aforementioned socioeconomic and attitudinal variables. Three different models were tested, as follows:

1. To explore the contribution of all the socioeconomic variables, they were used in a discriminant analysis of the dependent variable of group membership as defined on the preceding page (Model 1).
2. At the same time, to test the importance of all the attitudinal variables, the entire set of such variables, including the purchase likelihood variable, was used in a separate discriminant model, using the same dependent variable (Model 2).
3. Based on the results of the previous two steps, those attitudinal and socioeconomic variables were selected that were clearly of major importance in terms of standardized coefficients, and a single multiple discriminant model estimated using this combined set of variables (Model 3). The number of durable goods owned as of the earlier stage was included as an independent variable for the Wave 4 and Wave 9 functions.

The results of these various computations are shown in Table 4. There are seven columns of figures in this table. The first column from the left is the value of Wilks' λ, a measure of 'poorness of fit' of these functions, higher values representing poorer fits. The following three columns indicate the significance of the two functions (since there were three categories of the dependent variable), both individually and in an overall sense, based on the F test. The last three columns present an 'accuracy classification matrix' for each model. In other words, each figure in these columns indicates what percent of the observations were classified in the correct category by the model. As an acid test of predictive ability and, also, to indicate whether influencing variables seem to change over time, the model was applied to the

TABLE 4.

Summary of Discriminant Model Results for Stock of Durables

Model	Wave	Wilks' λ	Overall	Fn. 1	Fn. 2	1	4	9
			Significance of functions[a]			Pct. correct on wave		
1. 14 socioeconomic	1	.66	.01	.01	no	61**	52*	39
	4	.64	.01	.01	no		63**	38
	9	.66	.01	.01	no			58**
2. 20 attitudinal	1	.63	no	no	no	59**	39	26
plus likelihood	4	.66	no	no	no		62**	31
variable	9	.57	no	.05	no			59**
3. 11 attitudinal,	1	.58	no	.05	no	64**	56**	37
10 socioeconomic,	4	.19	.01	.01	no		93**	41
a likelihood	9	.35	.01	.01	no			73**
variable, and number								
of durables owned								

a 'No' means that function is not significant at .05 level.   * A significant at 0.05 level.
** A significant at 0.01 level.

later waves as well. For this reason, there are accuracy percentages, for the Wave 1 model in each case, also for Wave 4 and Wave 9, and for the Wave 4 model in each case also for Wave 9.

As is evident from Table 4, differences among these first two models are not large. Model 1, containing the socioeconomic variables, yields slightly better goodness of fit and accuracy classification than Model 2, containing the attitudinal variables. However, when the stock of durables is added to the equations, sharp improvement is obtained for the Wave 4 and Wave 9 functions (Model 3). The goodness of fit increases markedly, as evidenced by the decrease in the value of Wilks' lambda, while at the same time the classification accuracy percentages increase sharply.

Also evident from Table 4 is that these models do not have a long 'life', at least in the case of the Wave 1 and the Wave 4 functions. In other words, a function fitted to data as of one time does not seem equally applicable to data for two or three years later. The only exception is Wave 1 of the models with the socioeconomic variables, which do appreciably better than naive forecasts for Wave 4 durable goods ownership. Even then, however, the accuracy of classification is appreciably less than that obtained for the period of observation.

Especially interesting is the fact that the same phenomenom exists for the models including stock of durables. Thus, whereas the Wave 4 function of Model 3 yields a much higher frequency of accurate classifications than the other models for Wave 4, little improvement is apparent when the same function is 'extrapolated' to classification of the observations for Wave 9.

TABLE 5.

Multiple Discriminant Estimates of Parameters of Model 3 for Stock of Durables

Variable	Wave 1		Wave 4		Wave 9	
	Fn. 1	Fn. 2	Fn. 1	Fn. 2	Fn. 1	Fn. 2
Economy minded (h)	a	a	a	1.42	1.15	a
Extravagant (h)	a	1.02	a	a	—1.23	a
Bargain seeking (h)	—1.28	a	—3.09	a	1.14	1.18
Price conscious (h)	1.25	a	a	a	—1.01	—1.25
Satisfied in life (h)	1.35	—1.43	a	1.08	a	1.37
Quality awareness (w)	a	—1.02	a	a	—1.41	a
Economy minded (w)	a	—1.04	—1.33	a	a	a
Experiment-prone (w)	a	1.98	a	a	a	a
Conservative (w)	a	a	—1.25	a	a	1.05
Timid (w)	a	1.17	a	a	a	a
Price conscious (w)	a	a	a	a	—1.12	a
Education (h)	1.40	—1.62	2.36	1.40	—1.50	a
Income level	a	a	—1.08	—1.51	a	a
Wife working	a	2.14	—1.20	—2.03	a	a
Home ownership	—2.57	a	—2.33	1.29	—1.66	a
Professional (h)	—1.40	2.05	a	a	—1.57	1.33
Managerial (h)	—1.47	a	a	a	a	1.79
Clerical (h)	a	a	a	2.07	a	1.17
Craftsmen (h)	a	—1.33	1.52	a	a	a
Semi-skilled (h)	a	—1.96	—1.23	a	—1.07	1.43
Unskilled (h)	1.04	a	a	1.03	—1.04	a
Likelihood of buying	—	—	—2.16	1.82	a	a
Number of durables owned last wave	—	—	—5.81	a	—1.04	a
Significance level	.05	no	0.01	no	0.01	no

a = Absolute value less than 1.00.

It would therefore seem that the effect even of this variable seems to be short-lived.

One implication of this result is that the factors influencing durable goods ownership at one time are not the same as the influencing factors at a later time. This is not unexpected because, especially at the times of Wave 1 and Wave 4, these couples were still in the initial stages of family formation (in a few cases also of family dissolution), so factors that may influence durable goods ownership at one time may not be the same as those influencing durables ownership at a later time. It should be noted, however, that an alternate explanation could be that these findings are a result of 'data searching', in view of the iterative process of selecting the best combinations of variables. With the relatively few observations, division of the sample into estimation and validation portions would not have been practicable in this instance. On the other hand, the uniformity of the results for all sets of variables would seem to suggest that they have significance beyond being just a statistical artifact.

To examine what types of variables are the most important in these models, and particularly to see what these models tell us on the validity of the satu-ration hypothesis, it is desirable to examine at least one of these models more carefully, and the logical choice would seem to be the best one, Model 3. The variables that were used in this model and the values of the standardized coefficients for each of the functions are shown in Table 5. Coefficients with an absolute value less than 1.00 are not shown in order to highlight the more important variables in the different component functions. The last line of this table indicates the significance level of each of the component functions.

The direction of the effects of these variables has to be determined with reference to the pattern of the means of the centroids of the different func-tions. These means are shown in the following tabulation, where Group 1 represents ownership of few durable goods and Group 3 represents owner-ship of many durable goods:

Group	Wave 1		Wave 4		Wave 9	
	Fn. 1*	Fn. 2	Fn. 1*	Fn. 2	Fn. 1*	Fn. 2
1	0.77	0.06	—1.35	0.12	—1.71	0.67
2	0.57	—0.31	—2.06	0.76	—2.14	0.41
3	0.28	0.08	—3.45	0.33	—2.48	0.70

Functions that are statistically significant at the .05 level or more are marked with an asterisk, only Function 1 in each case. For these functions, it is apparent lower values always indicate groups with more durable goods owned.

Keeping this in mind and turning back to Table 5, we see that in the case of the number of durables owned, both of its coefficients for the two significant functions (Wave 4 and Wave 9) have a negative sign, and the coefficient of this variable for Wave 4 is by far the largest in the entire set. This means that the net contribution of the inventory effect is to lead to still more stocks of durable goods, a finding that seemingly contradicts the saturation hypothesis. In other words, there was a clear tendency for couples owning many durable goods to own still more later on, a tendency which was especially strong in the third year of the marriage.

Indeed, most of the coefficients of these three significant functions are in the negative direction, especially home ownership and professional occupation. Home ownership has a clear negative effect, meaning in the present context that presence of this characteristic induces couples to own more durables, as one might expect. On the other hand, education of the husband seems to have a negative effect on the stock of durables, at least in the first couple of years of marriage, but acts to increase stocks later on. This may suggest that couples with higher education are more cautious in acquiring durables until their marriage, or their financial status, is on a firmer base.

Overall, the principal variables in these functions appear to be related to characteristics of the husband even though corresponding variables for the wives had been included initially. Rather surprisingly, in two of the three Function 1's, shopping attitudes of the husband appear to have more influence on durable goods purchases than shopping attitudes of the wife. From this point of view, however, it is relevant to note that these data include automobile purchases, a durable in which husbands are more likely to be interested.

A further test of these findings was made by subjecting these data to multiple regression analysis. This is possible in the present case since the dependent variable is essentially continuous, namely, number of durable goods. The results of this regression using the variables included in Model 3 are shown in Table 6, the coefficients being in standardized form. These results support the findings of the multiple discriminant analysis in the sense that they seem to contradict the saturation hypothesis, support the uniformly high significance of home ownership and highlight the generally greater influence of shopping attitude of the husband than of the wife. On the other hand, education of the husband is influential by the present analysis only in the Wave 9 function while wife working is statistically significant in the Wave 1 function, acting to depress purchases of durables.

TABLE 6.

Multiple Regression Estimates of Parameters of Model 3 for Stock of Durables

Variable	Wave 1	Wave 4	Wave 9
Economy minded (h)	a	a	—0.20*
Extravagant (h)	a	a	0.17*
Bargain seeking (h)	0.18	0.15*	—0.12
Price conscious (h)	—0.19	a	a
Satisfied in life (h)	a	a	a
Quality awareness (w)	0.12	a	0.16
Economy minded (w)	a	a	a
Experiment-prone (w)	a	a	0.10
Conservative (w)	0.12	a	a
Timid (w)	a	a	a
Price conscious (w)	a	a	a
Education (h)	a	a	0.28**
Income level	0.12	a	0.31**
Wife working	—0.24*	a	—0.14
Home ownership	0.37**	0.22**	0.23**
Professional (h)	0.19	a	0.11
Managerial (h)	0.20	a	a
Clerical (h)	a	a	—0.13
Craftsmen (h)	0.13	a	a
Semi-skilled (h)	a	a	0.12
Unskilled (h)	—0.13	a	0.11
Likelihood of buying	—	0.25**	a
Number of durables owned last stage	—	0.72**	0.17*
R^2 (adj.)	0.14*	0.73**	0.39**

a = Absolute value less than .10.
* Significant at .05 level.   ** Significant at .01 level.

3.2. *Durables Purchases*

The procedure used in the analysis of the purchase variables was essentially the same as that already described. Hence, it seems necessary only to present the results in this case. Moreover, since the earlier results were similar for the discriminant analysis and for the multiple regression, only the multiple regression approach was used in this case.

Two dependent variables were used to measure purchases. One was a measure of net change in the stock of durables, computed as the difference between the stock at one time and the stock at the earlier time. Two sets of differences were computed, one being the difference between the Wave 4 and Wave 1 stocks, and the other being the difference between the Wave 9 and the Wave 4 stocks. The other measure of durables purchases is a gross measure, obtained by aggregating all the purchases for both addition and replacement between two periods of time. Again, two such variables are involved, namely, all the purchases of these durables reported up to and including Wave 4, and all the purchases reported on Wave 5 to and including Wave 9.

The results obtained with the 'best' regression functions with each of these two variables on Wave 4 and on Wave 9 are shown in Table 7. An examination of this table reveals, among other things, that the use of the net purchase variable yields a much higher goodness of fit than gross purchases, especially for the Wave 9 function. This would seem to suggest that the net measure may be more meaningful for this type of analysis, possibly because gross purchases necessarily include purchases made for replacement purposes, and these are not usually of a discretionary nature.

Even more significant for the hypotheses being tested is that the variable for the stock of durables at the previous stage is now uniformly negative, and highly significantly so in three of the four functions. In other words, both on a net basis as well as on a gross basis, ownership of a relatively large stock of these durables at an earlier stage serves to depress the number of durables purchased later on. This depressing influence seems stronger for net purchases than for gross purchases, undoubtedly due to the important role of replacement purchases in the latter case.

Also noteworthy is that the purchase likelihood variable is highly significant on the Wave 4 function but not later on. This may be due to the fact that this variable by Wave 9 represented an accumulation of purchase likelihoods over five waves (nearly three years), which may be too long for such a variable to be relevant for this purpose.

In other respects, the results of Table 7 are very similar to those obtained

TABLE 7.

Multiple Regression Estimates of Parameters of Model 3 for Durables Purchases

Variable	Net purchases		Gross purchases	
	Wave 4	Wave 9	Wave 4	Wave 9
Economy minded (h)	—0.11	—0.14*	a	—0.16
Extravagant (h)	a	0.11*	a	0.12
Bargain seeking (h)	0.22*	a	0.26*	—0.11
Price conscious (h)	a	a	a	a
Satisfied in life (h)	a	a	a	a
Quality awareness (w)	a	0.11	a	a
Economy minded (w)	0.15	a	a	—0.15
Experiment-prone (w)	a	a	a	a
Conservative (w)	0.13	a	0.16	a
Timid (w)	a	a	—0.13	a
Price conscious (w)	a	a	—0.13	a
Education (h)	a	0.19**	a	0.17
Income level	0.14	0.21**	a	a
Wife working	a	a	a	—0.14
Home ownership	0.34**	0.16**	0.25*	a
Professional (h)	0.11	a	0.24	0.19
Managerial (h)	a	a	0.15	0.10
Clerical (h)	a	a	0.12	a
Craftsmen (h)	a	a	a	a
Semi-skilled (h)	0.17	a	0.33	0.24
Unskilled (h)	a	a	a	0.11
Likelihood of buying	0.38**	a	0.46**	0.17
Number of durables owned last stage	—0.38**	—0.83**	—0.13	—0.28**
R^2 (adj.)	0.37**	0.73**	0.26**	0.09

a = Absolute value less than .10.
 * Significant at .05 level.   ** Significant at .01 level.

using the stock of durables as dependent. Income and home ownership act to increase purchases, though not always significantly so, and the husband's shopping attitudes are usually more relevant than the wife's shopping attitudes in influencing durables purchases. Education of the husband also appears as a positive influence on purchases, at least for Wave 9, as it has in the prior functions using the stock of durables as dependent.

4. SUMMARY COMMENTS

The results of this study would seem to suggest that young couples that begin a marriage with a relatively large stock of durables tend to continue to maintain large stocks even though their net purchases tend to decline relative to couples owning smaller stocks at the beginning of the marriage. This tendency appears to be supported at least for the first six years of the marriage when both different analytical techniques and different definitions of the dependent variable are used. Thus, the definition of stock employed and the data presented here allowed for ownership of only one of each durable so that, for example, two television sets in a household would be counted as one for the purpose of this analysis. However, when this definition was changed to allow couples to own more than one of a particular durable, eliminating only those purchases that were reported as being for replacement, the results were unchanged.

In effect, these findings would seem to suggest both a habit effect and a saturation effect of the stock of durables at the same time. A habit effect may be said to be present in the sense that once they begin to accumulate the durables, couples continue to do so. Indeed, virtually no instances were recorded in these data of couples reducing their stocks, although this is only to be expected in view of the fact that these couples were in the early stages of family formation. At the same time, a saturation effect seems to exist in the sense that couples that have relatively large stocks of durables are likely to purchase fewer durables in the future than couples with relatively smaller stocks.

In evaluating these results, however, it should be stressed that the data relate to an aggregate collection of durable goods and to a sample of young married couples in two smaller cities of the country and, of course, to only the first few years of married life. Still, these are the years in which most durables are probably acquired, certainly for most couples at a greater rate than in later years, and in this sense these findings should serve as a basis for testing similar hypotheses on a broader scale.

APPENDIX: LIST OF VARIABLES

Quality awareness (h)
Economic minded (h)
Experiment prone (h)
Extravagant (h)
Conservative (h)

Bargain seeking (h)
Timid (h)
Price conscious (h)
Life is full of opportunities (h)
Satisfied in life (h)

Quality awareness (w)
Economic minded (w)
Experiment prone (w)
Extravagant (w)
Conservative (w)

Bargain seeking (w)
Timid (w)
Price conscious (w)
Life is full of opportunities (w)
Satisfied in life (w)

Likelihood of buying
Education (h)
Level of family income
Wife working
Home ownership

Husband's occupation
Number of children
Plan for expenditures
Family financial officer

Husband's occupation:
  professional
  managerial
  clerical
  craftsmen
  semi-skilled
  unskilled
  services and household

Note: (h) refers to husband's answers;   (w) refers to wife's answers.

A Comparison of Alternative Specifications of Market Share Models

P. S. H. LEEFLANG[1]

1. INTRODUCTION [2]

Since the early 1950's the scope of mathematical techniques in marketing has expanded far beyond 'classical statistics' and we have seen enormous productivity of model builders in marketing. Pioneering work in this area, among others, has been performed by Verdoorn [1956] and Ferber and Verdoorn [1962]. Yet the number of marketing models that are actually used in private industry or in the public sector remains rather low. Since the early 1970's the problem of implementation has been of concern to many practitioners and academicians. This means that we are now coming into an era of model building in marketing, where emphasis is on models that are good representations of reality but that are also easy to use: *implementable marketing models.*[3]

In this contribution to the 'liber amicorum' in honour of Professor P. J. Verdoorn we consider a subset of implementable models, namely market share models. These models are defined as models in which the fluctuations of the *relative* number of units of a particular brand purchased by the total population, that is, relative to the total number of units of the product class, are explained by the fluctuations in the relative values of marketing instruments and in the values of environmental variables. By relative values we mean the values of the marketing instruments of the brand under consideration divided by the values of the corresponding marketing instruments of the product class.

These models have received much attention in recent literature. Large-scale studies have been performed by Hör zu, Funk Uhr [1975] and Lambin

---

1. The author is indebted to Harry Broeksteeg for writing the computer programs and C. P. A. Bartels, R. R. v. d. Heuvel and Ph. A. Naert for their critical comment.
2. The text in the introduction and in Section 2 is partly based on Leeflang, Naert [1977] and Naert, Leeflang [1977, Ch. 1].
3. See Montgomery [1973].

[1976] using these kinds of models. These studies, however, do not give guidance to model builders with respect to the form of the structural relations to be used. Lambin [1976][4], for example, shows a number of alternative forms of these relations which can be used to explain the fluctuations in market shares, but, unfortunately, nothing is said about the *most preferable form*. In this study we shall compare a number of alternative specifications of market share models. In this respect our study can easily be compared with studies performed by Bultez [1977] and Bultez, Naert [1975]. They also evaluated a *subset* of the models that are considered in this paper indicating which specification is to be preferred.

We start to consider some criteria market share models should satisfy in order to call these models implementable. This is done in Section 2, where we also compare market share models with models in which brand sales[5] are used as a performance measure. In Section 3 we consider a couple of models which are linear in the parameters. In Section 4 we give a number of alternative specifications of multiplicative models. These models are non-linear in the parameters, but can be linearized. In these models we do not allow for differences in the response parameters across brands. Multiplicative models that allow for these differences are considered in Section 5. In this contribution we will pay much attention to logically consistent models, i.e. models that predict market shares that are between zero and one and sum to one.[6] In Section 2–5 we compare specifications that are logically consistent and some that are not. We evaluate the differences between these types of models using statistical criteria and also consider the difficulties which are met estimating and validating the models. All models are empirically tested on data of the dried soup market in the Netherlands and are extensions of models that are shown in Leeflang [1974]. Finally, Section 6 is devoted to an evaluation of all alternative specifications.

2. ON SOME PROPERTIES OF MARKET SHARE MODELS

In this section we will discuss why it is preferable to explain the demand of a particular brand by market share models instead of by models that explain brand sales. Subsequently we will carefully investigate which implementation

4. See Lambin [1976, exhibit 2.2].
5. Brand sales: total number of units of a particular brand, bought by the population of all spending units.
6. See Naert, Bultez [1973].

criteria related to model structure are satisfied by market share models and in what way these models could be modified in order to follow other implementation criteria related to model structure.

The structural relations of a marketing model quite often consist of a set of behavioral relations and definition relations possibly extended with technical relations and institutional relations. The behavioral relations usually refer to:

1. the demand for a *product class* (industry sales, primary demand);
2. the demand for a *particular brand*. The demand for a particular brand can be explained in two ways, namely:
   a. by models in which the fluctuations of the total number of units of a particular brand bought by the population of all spending units (*brand sales*) are explained;
   b. by models in which the fluctuations of the number of units of a particular brand, relative to the demand of a product class (*market shares*), are explained.

From these definitions of different levels of demand it follows that brand sales (S_{jt}) can be explained in the following ways:

1. relating the sales of brand j to
   a. instrument variables of brand j;
   b. instrument variables of competitive brands;
   c. environmental variables (set 1).
2. relating the sales of brand j to
   a. instrument variables of brand j;
   b. instrument variables of competitive brands;
   c. industry sales (V_t);
   d. another set of environmental variables (set 2); because a number of environmental variables of set 1 will only influence V_t, set 2 will be a subset of set 1.[7]
3. explaining industry sales (V_t) as well as market share of brand j (m_{jt}) and multiplying these response measures:

$$S_{jt} = m_{jt} \cdot V_t \tag{2.1}$$

It is often preferable to arrive at brand sales in the last-mentioned way because:

7. For an example we refer to Ferber, Verdoorn [1962, p. 519 – relation (11.20)].

1. it is possible to detect if changes in S_{jt} are caused either by changes in market size (V_t), by changes in the relative position of brand j (m_{jt}) or by both;
2. using market share as a dependent variable rather than brand sales avoids inclusion of some independent variables which are necessary with the latter type of demand model such as environmental variables and seasonal or cyclical factors causing expansion or contraction of the entire market. This only holds when these variables would be expected to influence demand for *all brands equally*;[8]
3. in this way a model concentrates attention on the competitive inter-actions among all brands in the market.

Other advantages which are inherent to the use of market share models are derived considering implementation criteria. A model must satisfy a number of criteria in order to be called an implementable model. Criteria of this kind have been formulated, for example, by Little [1970]. We could classify these criteria as belonging to two major model building dimensions, namely:

1. implementation criteria related to model structure or model specifi-cation;
2. implementation criteria related to the ease of use.[9]

In this contribution we concentrate on the first-mentioned criteria. Among the proposed criteria are the following:

A model should be:

1. simple;
2. complete on important issues;
3. adaptive;
4. robust.[10]

---

8. See: Beckwith [1972, p. 171], Leeflang [1977a, pp. 35–36], MacLachlan [1972, p. 378].
9. In addition to these criteria emphasis can be put on the total *process* of building models for decision makers, or *implementation* strategy/*process*. See, for example, Larréché [1975], Larréché, Montgomery [1975], Naert, Leeflang [1977, Ch. 13], Urban [1972, 1974].
10. To link the criteria 'simple' and 'complete' Urban and Karash [1971] introduced the notion of evolutionary model building. The criterion that a model should be built in an evolutionary way is not in fact a criterion related to structure, but to implementation process. For that reason this criterion will not be discussed here. Compare: Naert, Leef-lang [1977, Ch. 6.2] and Little [1975a, 1975b].

These criteria are briefly discussed below and related to properties that market share models have or should have.

1. Models should be *simple* because managers tend to reject models they do not understand. If we want managers to use models a natural prerequisite would be for models to be simple enough so that managers can understand them. On the other hand we know that the real world is not simple. For the model builder simplicity often implies keeping the number of variables down to a workable level. According to Aeyelts Averink [1972] this can be achieved in one or more of the following ways:

a. *clustering of variables*, which is typical for many econometric studies. For example, various competing brands are often aggregated into 'the competition'. Or the numerous marketing instruments are aggregated into a small number of classes, such as product, distribution, advertising, promotions and price.[11] That means, for example, advertising expenditures are not split up into television, radio, newspapers, magazines and billboards, but are treated as a total;

b. *introducing relative variables*. For example, the variable disposable income per capita replaces two variables, disposable income *and* number of people in the population. Similarly advertising share may be used instead of brand and product class advertising expenditures;

c. *dividing variables into segments*. A problem is segmented into sub-problems, each of which is analysed seperately, that is, considering only those variables related to each particular segment. When the subproblems have been analysed they can be combined in order to represent the total problem. Examples would be models of market segments, or models of individual products belonging to a wider assortment;

d. *phasing variables over different levels*. In demand models, for example, variables can be divided into classes according to the various levels of demand that can be distinguished. Fluctuations in product class sales can often be explained by fluctuations in environmental variables (such as disposable income per capita, a weather index, etc.) and fluctuations in aggregate values of marketing instruments (average price, product class advertising expenditures, total number of outlets where the product is available, etc.). Variations in market share can *largely* be explained by variations in relative or share values of the various classes of marketing instruments.[12]

11. On the notion of the concept 'classes of instruments', see Leeflang, Koerts [1973].
12. We have to keep in mind, however, that these are model builder oriented notions of simplicity which are not *always* acceptable to the user.

Explaining *market shares* by relative values of marketing instruments the number of variables can be kept down to a workable level. This means that in market share models *relative variables* are introduced. Explaining industry sales and market shares seperately in the way that has been indicated before, variables are also *phased* over different levels. In this way the number of environmental variables explaining the demand of a particular brand can be reduced. When marketing instruments are aggregated into a small number of classes of instruments, that means, when we *cluster* variables another reduction results. Thus, market share models can be constructed in such a way that they may be defined as being *simple*.

2. For a model to be a useful decision tool, it has to represent the relevant elements of the problem or, in other words, the model should be *complete on important issues*. Models may be incomplete because they do not account for:[13]

1. the effects of all relevant instrument variables and environmental variables;
2. the effects of competitive actions;
3. the effects of variables over time;
4. differences in the response parameters[14], etc.

With respect to the incorporation of the relevant *instrument variables* we have to remark that by clustering the marketing instruments information about the more detailed decisions which are made with respect to the 'lower-order' instruments[15] is lost. This problem, in principle, can be solved supplying the marketing mix market share model with a set of submodels, also called *modular models* or modules, such as a price, an advertising, a promotion model, etc.[16]

In market share models relatively little attention is given to the incorporation of *environmental variables*. Still these variables *may* influence market shares. As an example let us examine the following relations between the market share of a detergent brand j (m_{jt}) and the relative values of the marketing instruments, advertising ($a_{j, t-1}$) and effective distribution (d_{jt}),

13. See Leeflang [1974, pp. 115–117]; Leeflang, Koerts [1975]; Somermeyer [1967].
14. In addition to this, models may be called incomplete because they do no satisfy theoretical requirements which means that they are not based on theory in an adequate way. See Leeflang, Naert [1977].
15. See note 11.
16. An excellent example of modular model building is BRANDAID, a marketing mix model developed by Little [1975a, 1975b]. See also Leeflang [1977b, 1977c].

the market share in the preceding period $(m_{j,\,t-1})$ and the fraction of households with an automatic washing machine (HM_t)

$$m_{jt} = -7.25 - 1.10\,\frac{a_{j,t-1}}{\sum\limits_{r=1}^{n} a_{r,t-1}} + 10.60\frac{d_{jt}}{100} + 0.59m_{j,t-1} - 1.82HM_t$$

$$\text{(2.2)}$$

$$(-1.62)^{17}\ (-1.11)\qquad\qquad (2.12)\qquad\quad (4.21)\qquad (-2.04)$$

From this relation which is discussed in Leeflang [1977a] it can be deduced that there is a negative relation between the market share of brand j and the fraction of households with an automatic washing machine. This indicates that consumers substitute brand j by another, more appropriate brand, when they buy an automatic washing machine. From this example it may be clear that it is not always correct to assume that environmental variables equally influence demand for all brands.

Market share models, automatically, account for the *effects of competitive actions* because relative values of the variables are considered.

Modeling marketing *dynamics* by means of market share models would not cause particular difficulties as is shown by Bultez [1977] and Bultez, Naert [1977].

As is discussed in more detail in Section 3 it may also be necessary to allow for *differences* in some *response parameters* across brands in order to obtain a model which is complete on important issues. Thus, market share models, in principle, can be constructed in such a way that they are complete on a number of important issues.

3. Market behaviour is dynamic, which will cause parameters to change. If parameters have changed it should be easy to replace in a model previous estimates. More difficult, may be *adapting* a model to structural changes. An important facilitating factor will be again *modularity* of the model. The modular structure will prove particularly useful when a change involves one of a few of the modules but not all of them. Thus, supplying the marketing mix market share models with a set of submodels may lead to *complete* and *adaptive* models.

4. *Robust models* are models that have a structure that inherently constrains 'answers' to a meaningful range of values.[18] This means that constraints

---

17. *t*-values are in parentheses.
18. See Little [1970]. To avoid confusion, it should be made clear that robustness has a totally different meaning in statistics and econometrics. According to Theil [1971, p. 615], for example, a statistical test is called robust if it is insensitive to departures from the assumptions under which it is derived.

have to be put on the mathematical form of the relations. These forms should ensure that, when variables are in reality subject to sum or range constraints, their model counterparts should satisfy these same constraints. With respect to market share models robustness means that the model structure should constrain market shares to sum to one and to values between zero and one. Such models are logically consistent.

Although it has been pointed out that market share models can be constructed in such a way that they satisfy each of the implementation criteria, which have been discussed above, it will be difficult to construct market share models that satisfy all criteria *simultaneously*. Being *complete* on important issues is a criterion that conflicts with *simplicity*. We will also see that *completeness* may conflict with *robustness*. Particularly, this holds when we construct models that allow for differences in the response parameters. Finally *estimation and validation problems* arise in models that are constructed in such a way that they are *complete* and *robust*. These issues are discussed and illustrated in the following sections.

3. LINEAR MARKET SHARE MODELS (MODELS I, II)

In this context we define a linear model as a model that is linear in the parameters. In literature many examples of such models can be found.[19] We shall give a number of numerical specifications of linear market share models in this section in the relations (3.1) and (3.7). These relations are estimated using annual data on the dried soup market in the Netherlands. These data contain information on market shares and five classes of marketing instruments of five oligopolistic competitors in the market, namely: Royco, Maggi, Honig, Knorr and California.[20] The following variables are related to the market share of brand j in year t, m_{jt}; $j = 1, ..., 5$; $t = 1, ..., 10$.

$a_{j, t-1}$ = theme-advertising expenditures of brand j, $j = 1, ..., 5$ in year $t-1$;

19. See, for example, Beckwith [1972]; Houston, Weiss [1974], Lambin [1972a, 1972b, 1976]; Leeflang [1976, 1977a], MacLachlan [1972].
20. In order to compare the empirical results in this study with those in Leeflang [1974] the reader should be aware of the fact that in the last-mentioned study the performances and the marketing instruments of a small brand have been combined with the brand California. In this study we only consider the performances and instruments of the five competitors which have been mentioned.

s_{jt} = scheme-advertising expenditures (expenditures to promotions) of brand j, $j=1, \ldots, 5$ in year t;

p_{jt} = weighted average price of the varieties of brand j, $j=1, \ldots, 5$ in year t. These prices are weighted by the turnover share of the four most important varieties in the assortment, namely tomato, chicken, vegetable and 'other' soup varieties;

v_{jt} = number of varieties in the assortment of brand j, $j=1, \ldots, 5$ in year t, and

d_{jt} = effective store distribution of brand j, $j=1, \ldots, 5$ in year t.

It goes without saying that because lagged advertising expenditures are considered, theme-advertising expenditures in year, 0, 1, ..., 9 are used. Because we are primarily interested in alternative *structures* of market share models we shall not consider the effects of alternative combinations of these *variables* on m_{jt}, nor do we take the effects of market shares of brand j in preceding periods on m_{jt} into account.[21] The relations of model I are shown in (3.1). Model I is a linear model, with 'homogeneous reaction-parameters' which predicts market shares that sum to one.

3.1. *Model I – Linear – homogeneous reaction-parameters*

$$m_{jt} = \alpha_j + \beta_1 \frac{a_{j,t-1}}{\sum\limits_{r=1}^{5} a_{r,t-1}} + \beta_2 \frac{s_{jt}}{\sum\limits_{r=1}^{5} s_{rt}} + \beta_3 \frac{p_{jt}}{\sum\limits_{r=1}^{5} p_{rt}} + \beta_4 \frac{v_{jt}}{\sum\limits_{r=1}^{5} v_{rt}} +$$

$$+ \beta_5 \frac{d_{jt}}{\sum\limits_{r=1}^{5} d_{rt}} + \varepsilon_{jt} \qquad j = 1, \ldots, 5; \; t = 1, \ldots, 10. \tag{3.1}$$

where ε_{jt} = random disturbance terms which are normally-distributed with zero mean. The variances and covariances of the ε_{jt} are discussed in detail below. From (3.1) it can be seen that the reaction-parameters are the same for each brand. The relations only differ in the constant terms or *dummy variables* α_j. We shall prove that model I predicts market shares that sum to one for each period $t=1, \ldots, 10$. This proof is given because we believe that this proof is easier to follow than the proof given by McGuire, Farley, Lucas and Ring [1968]. When the unknown parameters of (3.1) have been estimated we get

21. For some examples of relations of this kind, we refer to Leeflang [1974, pp. 165–170].

$$\hat{m}_{jt} = \hat{\alpha}_j + \hat{\beta}_1 \frac{a_{j,t-1}}{\sum\limits_{r=1}^{5} a_{r,t-1}} + \hat{\beta}_2 \frac{s_{jt}}{\sum\limits_{r=1}^{5} s_{rt}} + \hat{\beta}_3 \frac{p_{jt}}{\sum\limits_{r=1}^{5} p_{rt}} + \hat{\beta}_4 \frac{v_{jt}}{\sum\limits_{r=1}^{5} v_{rt}} +$$

$$+ \hat{\beta}_5 \frac{d_{jt}}{\sum\limits_{r=1}^{5} d_{rt}} \qquad j = 1, ..., 5; \ t = 1, ..., 10 \tag{3.2}$$

where $\hat{m}_{jt}$ = the estimated market share of brand j at t.
Summing over all brands $j = 1, ..., 5$ and all periods $t = 1, ..., 10$ for this model, we get

$$\sum_{t=1}^{10} \sum_{r=1}^{5} \hat{m}_{rt} = 10 \left\{ \sum_{r=1}^{5} \hat{\alpha}_r + \sum_{l=1}^{5} \hat{\beta}_l \right\}. \tag{3.3}$$

As is shown in Appendix A it holds that

$$\sum_{t=1}^{10} \sum_{r=1}^{5} \hat{\varepsilon}_{rt} = 0 \quad \text{or} \quad \sum_{t=1}^{10} \sum_{r=1}^{5} m_{rt} = \sum_{t=1}^{10} \sum_{r=1}^{5} \hat{m}_{rt}. \tag{3.4}$$

Because the m_{jt} are the observed values of the market shares and the observed values sum to one for each period we get

$$\sum_{t=1}^{10} \sum_{r=1}^{5} m_{rt} = \sum_{t=1}^{10} \sum_{r=1}^{5} \hat{m}_{rt} = 10. \tag{3.5}$$

From (3.2), (3.3) and (3.5) we deduce that

$$1 = \sum_{r=1}^{5} \hat{\alpha}_r + \sum_{l=1}^{5} \hat{\beta}_l = \sum_{r=1}^{5} \hat{m}_{rt} \qquad t = 1, ..., 10. \tag{3.6}$$

Model I is an example of a model in which the *average* effects of the relative values of marketing instruments on market shares are estimated. In this model, we do not allow for differences in the response parameters across brands. It may be necessary to incorporate these differences into a model, the reason being that the corresponding instrument variables can be operated in so many different ways. The (theme-)advertising budget, for example, can be allocated in different directions in accordance with:

1. the media classes;
2. the media vehicle within the different media classes;
3. the media options;
4. the media insertions[22], and
5. the advertising message(s),

22. For a description of these concepts, the interested reader is referred to Little, Lodish [1969].

which are chosen. This means that budgets of equal size can be spent in different ways with corresponding different effects. It goes without saying that this does not hold for all marketing instruments and we should not allow for differences in the response parameters of all instruments. In model II (3.7) we allow the response parameter of the class of instruments theme-advertising to differ across brands. This parameter is called a heterogeneous (reaction-)parameter.

3.2. Model II – Linear-heterogeneous reaction-parameters

$$m_{jt} = \alpha_j + \beta_{1j} \frac{a_{j,t-1}}{\sum\limits_{r=1}^{5} a_{r,t-1}} + \beta_2 \frac{s_{jt}}{\sum\limits_{r=1}^{5} s_{rt}} + \beta_3 \frac{p_{jt}}{\sum\limits_{r=1}^{5} p_{rt}} + \beta_4 \frac{v_{jt}}{\sum\limits_{r=1}^{5} v_{rt}} +$$

$$+ \beta_5 \frac{d_{jt}}{\sum\limits_{r=1}^{5} d_{rt}} + \varepsilon_{jt} \qquad j = 1, \ldots, 5; \ t = 1, \ldots, 10. \qquad (3.7)$$

In contrast to the relations of model I it is not assured in this model that the predicted market shares sum to one for each period $t = 1, \ldots, 10$. As has been proved by Naert, Bultez [1973] for these kinds of relations[23] in general this is only assured when:

$$\beta_{1j} = \beta_1 \qquad j = 1, \ldots, 5. \qquad (3.8)$$

which is again model I. An important point to investigate is *how much it really matters* to have no guarantee that the predicted market shares do sum up to one.

Before we present the estimates of the parameter of the models I and II some remarks will be made concerning some features of these linear models. First, although it is assured in model I that the predicted market shares sum to one, it is not guaranteed that market shares are always greater than zero. This means that it is not guaranteed that model I is logically consistent.

Secondly, we have to discuss some features of the random disturbance terms, ε_{jt}. In this study we combine time-series data with cross-sectional data, because we consider simultaneously the effects of marketing instruments of different brands over time on market shares of different brands

---

23. Although Beckwith [1973] and McGuire, Weiss [1976] showed with counterexamples that the proof of Naert, Bultez [1973] could not be generalized because Naert, Bultez failed to consider so-called 'homogeneous *variables*' the proof holds for the relations and variables we consider. These relations satisfy some principles of dimensional analysis. See De Jong [1967], De Haan [1970].

over time. This implies that, probably, we have to account for such things as heteroscedasticity, mutual correlation and autocorrelation of the random disturbance terms. From the values of the Durbin-Watson statistic it will appear that there is no strong autocorrelation in the models we consider. We have to account, however, for heteroscedasticity and mutual correlation.

TABLE 1.

Parameter estimates of model I

Parameters	OLS	GLS
α_1)[a]	—0.3034	—0.3140
	(—4.0430)[b]	(—5.3198)
α_2	—0.4117	—0.4274
	(—5.4058)	(—6.9370)
α_3	—0.3306	—0.3500
	(—4.1777)	(—5.4705)
α_4	—0.3328	—0.3481
	(—4.3095)	(—5.7057)
α_5	—0.2955	—0.3051[d]
	(—4.5210)	
β_1	0.1094	0.1280
	(1.9912)	(2.9530)
β_2	0.2028	0.1422
	(2.6601)	(2.7674)
β_3	1.3522	1.4133
	(4.5073)	(5.2849)
β_4	0.0522	0.0166
	(0.5587)[c]	(0.2494)[c]
β_5	0.9573	1.0445
	(3.8880)	(4.5735)
R^2	0.9518	0.9633
$\bar{R}^2$	0.8929	0.9171
D.W.S.	1.6066	

a. $r=1=$Royco; $r=2=$Maggi; $r=3=$Honig; $r=4=$Knorr; $r=5=$California.
b. t-values are in parentheses in all tables.
c. Parameters which are non-significant at the 0.05 level.
d. Because GLS has been performed using $(n-1)T$ observations α_5 could be only determined using (3.6).

TABLE 2.

Parameter estimates of model II

Parameters	OLS	GLS
α_1	—0.2221	—0.2028
	(—2.7840)	(—4.8370)
α_2	—0.3677	—0.3286
	(—4.5853)	(—7.1767)
α_3	—0.3218	—0.2854
	(—3.9410)	(—6.1159)
α_4	—0.2677	—0.1980
	(—2.8261)	(—3.3834)
α_5	—0.2748	—0.2382
	(—3.9659)	(—6.8346)
β_{11}	—0.0034	0.0972
	(—0.0400)[a]	(1.3420)[a]
β_{12}	0.1120	0.1444
	(0.9327)[a]	(4.5787)
β_{13}	0.3326	0.3764
	(2.4572)	(6.9250)
β_{14}	0.0269	—0.1042
	(0.1844)[a]	(—0.7297)[a]
β_{15}	0.2357	0.2777
	(1.7297)[a]	(3.5057)
β_2	0.1818	0.1307
	(2.2990)	(3.6317)
β_3	1.1361	1.0306
	(3.5254)	(6.2721)
β_4	0.0407	0.0939
	(0.4250)[a]	(1.7747)[a]
β_5	0.9795	0.8632
	(3.6356)	(4.8126)
R^2	0.9597	0.9457
$\bar{R}^2$	0.9048	0.8719
D.W.S.	1.5399	
$D.$	1.663%	1.483%

a. Parameters which are non-significant at the 0.05 – level.

The variance-covariance matrix of the disturbances is discussed in Appendix B.

The ordinary least-squares (OLS) estimates and the (one-step) generalized least-squares (GLS) estimates of the parameters of the models I and II are shown in Table 1 and 2 respectively. In addition to the parameters the coefficient of determination (R^2), the adjusted coefficient of determination ($\bar{R}^2$) and the value of the Durbin-Watson statistic (D.W.S.)[24] are shown. In Table 2 the last row shows the 'D-statistic' which is defined as follows

$$\frac{\sum_{t=1}^{10} \left| \sum_{r=1}^{5} \hat{m}_{rt} - 1 \right|}{10} \cdot 100\% = D \qquad (3.9)$$

This statistic indicates the average absolute deviation of the sum of the predicted market shares and 1 in percentages per time period, where the average is taken over all time periods that are considered.

We shall conclude the discussion about the application of models I and II to the data on the dried soup market with the following remarks.

1. From the values of the coefficient of determination it can be inferred that the variance in the market shares can be explained in a satisfactory way by these models.

2. From (3.6) it can be deduced that:

$$\sum_{r=1}^{n} \hat{\varepsilon}_{rt} = \sum_{r=1}^{n} (m_{rt} - \hat{m}_{rt}) = 0 \qquad (3.10)$$

From (B.2), (B.3) and (3.10) we can conclude that the random disturbance terms are dependent. This means that in order to obtain a variance-covariance matrix with full rank the observations of one brand have to be deleted. As has been shown by McGuire, et. al. [1968] the variance-covariance matrix necessarily will have full rank, regardless of the choice of the observations to be deleted. They also proved that the GLS-estimates are invariant with respect to this choice. We deleted the observations of the n–th (5–th) brand California. The dummy variable α_5 could be found using (3.6) ($= -0.3051$). We also obtained GLS-estimates deleting the observations of brand 1. In this case $\hat{\alpha}_1 = -0.3171$ and $\hat{\alpha}_5 = -0.3049$, which supports the

---

24. The values of the Durbin-Watson statistic have been computed for each brand separately. Because these values do not differ significantly between brands average values are taken over all brands. These values are shown in the tables. For this reason it may be more appropriate to speak about a Durbin-Watson-like statistic.

proof of McGuire et. al. [1968], because the differences between these values and the values of α_1 and α_5 in Table 1 are due to rounding errors. Because (3.10) does not hold for model II, GLS-estimates are obtained using a variance-covariance matrix of the order $nT \times nT$.

3. In model I we have a large number of significant estimates of the dummy variables and the reaction-parameters. The only insignificant parameter estimate is the parameter β_4, which represents the effect of the relative value of the number of varieties in the assortment on market share. The sign of β_3 indicates that an increase in the average price of dried soups leads to an increase in market share, at least for the price range considered in this study. As has been pointed out by Leeflang [1974, p. 152] the variable price represents some 'quality'-aspects of the product.

In model II we have more insignificant parameters. Particularly most of the OLS-estimates of β_{1j} are insignificant. The parameters in the models I and II are about the same order of magnitude and, with the exception of (the insignificant value of) β_{14} in the GLS-estimation of model II, have the expected sign. Comparing some estimates of the parameters of model I with the corresponding parameter estimates in model II it is remarkable that $\hat{\alpha}_1$ and $\hat{\alpha}_4$ have become the largest dummy variables, whilst in model I $\hat{\alpha}_5$ has the largest value. The increases of the values of the dummy variables α_1 and α_4 are 'compensated' by the values of β_{11} and β_{14}. The parameters $\hat{\beta}_{11}$, $\hat{\beta}_{14}$ are low as compared with $\hat{\beta}_{15}$. From model II it can be concluded that brand 3 (Honig) has had the most effective use of the marketing instrument theme-advertising, averaged over the period under consideration.

4. From the value of the statistic D in Table 2 it can be deduced that the sum of the predicted market shares does not differ too much from 1. This implies that – in this case – it does *not* really matter to have a model in which the market shares do not sum up to one. We have to bear in mind that differences usually will be larger when we use these models to predict market shares for periods that are not considered in the 'analysis sample'. Particularly when we get a large number of significant heterogeneous (reaction-) parameters and the differences D are relatively small, linear models that allow for differences in the response parameters across brands (model II) should be preferred to linear models with homogeneous parameters in which the predicted market shares sum to one.

5. Discussing linear market share models we illustrated that *completeness* of a model may *conflict* with *robustness*. From the discussion in the prece-

ding paragraph we conclude that when D is small and a large number of the homogeneous and heterogeneous reaction-parameters is significant we prefer linear models with heterogeneous parameters to robust models which are not complete in this respect.

4. MULTIPLICATIVE MARKET SHARE MODELS – HOMOGENEOUS PARAMETERS (MODELS III, IV, V)

Multiplicative market share models have a number of desirable properties:

1. the estimated market shares are guaranteed to be greater than zero;
2. the interrelations between the marketing instruments are explicitly considered;
3. the interpretation of the parameters is easier than in linear market share models.

In the literature multiplicative market share models receive much attention.[25]

In this section we consider three multiplicative models with homogeneous reaction-parameters. The first model (model III) does not guarantee that market shares sum to one. In the second multiplicative model (model IV) we try to decrease the value of D ((3.9)) by constructing a quasi-duopoly model. Finally, model V is an example of a logically consistent multiplicative market share model with homogeneous reaction-parameters.

4.1. Model III – Multiplicative-homogeneous reaction-parameters

$$m_{jt} = e^{\alpha_j} \left[\frac{a_{j,t-1}}{\sum\limits_{r=1}^{5} a_{r,t-1}} \right]^{\beta_1} \left[\frac{s_{jt}}{\sum\limits_{r=1}^{5} s_{rt}} \right]^{\beta_2} \left[\frac{p_{jt}}{\sum\limits_{r=1}^{5} p_{rt}} \right]^{\beta_3} \left[\frac{v_{jt}}{\sum\limits_{r=1}^{5} v_{rt}} \right]^{\beta_4} \left[\frac{d_{jt}}{\sum\limits_{r=1}^{5} d_{rt}} \right]^{\beta_5} e^{\varepsilon_{jt}}$$

$$j = 1, ..., 5; \ t = 1, ..., 10.^{26} \tag{4.1}$$

25. See, for example: Aeyelts Averink [1972], Cowling, Cubbin [1971], Houston, Weiss [1974], Lambin [1970, 1972b, 1976], Leeflang [1974, 1976], Nakanishi, Cooper [1974], Verdoorn [1972], Wildt [1974]. For more detailed information, see: Bultez [1977].
26. When it is assumed that the ε_{jt} are normally-distributed this implies that the m_{jt} are lognormally-distributed which does not correspond to the assumption which has been made in the linear models. This contradiction can be eliminated when the ε_{jt} are embodied as additive terms in (4.1). This requires, however, non-linear estimation of (4.1) which we want to avoid. For this reason we chose for the assumption that the ε_{jt} are normally-distributed.

Taking (natural) logarithms the relations (4.1) are linearized. The parameters have been estimated by OLS and GLS.

Table 3 shows that the average difference between the sum of the predicted market shares and one per time period is equal to 1.186% and 1.124% when we estimate the parameters by OLS and GLS. In order to reduce the value of D a quasi-duopoly market share model has been developed. In this model we consider one brand j, $j=1, \ldots, 5$ and the combination of all brands r, $r=1, \ldots, 5$, $r \neq j$. This model is shown in the relations (4.2a).

4.2. Model IV – Multiplicative-homogeneous reaction-parameters – quasi-duopoly

$$m_{jt} = \frac{e^{\alpha_j} a_{j,t-1}^{\beta_1} s_{jt}^{\beta_2} p_{jt}^{\beta_3} v_{jt}^{\beta_4} d_{jt}^{\beta_5} e^{\varepsilon_{jt}}}{e^{\alpha_j} a_{j,t-1}^{\beta_1} s_{jt}^{\beta_2} p_{jt}^{\beta_3} v_{jt}^{\beta_4} d_{jt}^{\beta_5} e^{\varepsilon_{jt}} +}$$

$$+ e^{\alpha_{oj}} \left[\sum_{r \neq j}^{5} a_{r,t-1} \right]^{\beta_1} \left[\sum_{r \neq j}^{5} s_{rt} \right]^{\beta_2} \left[\sum_{r \neq j}^{5} p_{rt} \right]^{\beta_3} \left[\sum_{r \neq j}^{5} v_{rt} \right]^{\beta_4} \left[\sum_{r \neq j}^{5} d_{rt} \right]^{\beta_5} e^{\varepsilon_{ot}}$$

$$j = 1, \ldots, 5; \quad t = 1, \ldots, 10 \tag{4.2a}$$

$$def \quad \frac{I_j}{I_j + O(I_j)} \quad j = 1, \ldots, 5. \tag{4.2b}$$

where I_j refers to marketing efforts for brand j and $O(I_j)$ refers to marketing efforts of all competing brands of j.

Assuming that the oligopolistic market may be reduced to a quasi-duopoly a logically consistent model results. From (4.2b) it follows directly that

$$m_{ot} = \frac{O(I_j)}{I_j + O(I_j)} = 1 - m_{jt} \tag{4.3}$$

The parameters of this model can be estimated when m_{jt} is divided by m_{ot}

$$\frac{m_{jt}}{m_{ot}} = \frac{I_j}{O(I_j)} =$$

$$= e^{\alpha_j - \alpha_{oj}} \left[\frac{a_{j,t-1}}{\sum_{r \neq j}^{5} a_{r,t-1}} \right]^{\beta_1} \left[\frac{s_{jt}}{\sum_{r \neq j}^{5} s_{rt}} \right]^{\beta_2} \left[\frac{p_{jt}}{\sum_{r \neq j}^{5} p_{rt}} \right]^{\beta_3} \left[\frac{v_{jt}}{\sum_{r \neq j}^{5} v_{rt}} \right]^{\beta_4} \left[\frac{d_{jt}}{\sum_{r \neq j}^{5} d_{rt}} \right]^{\beta_5} e^{\varepsilon_{jt} - \varepsilon_{ot}} \tag{4.4}$$

Taking (natural) logarithms relation (4.4) is linearized and the parameters can be estimated except for the constant term. The term $e^{\alpha_j - \alpha_{oj}}$ has to be replaced by a new term $e^{\alpha_j^*} = e^{\alpha_j - \alpha_{oj}}$. The ratio of the number of observations

TABLE 3.

Parameter estimates of model III

Parameters	OLS	GLS
a_1	2.7084	2.5865
	(4.6777)	(7.6452)
a_2	2.1739	2.0325
	(3.8332)	(6.0211)
a_3	2.7928	2.6320
	(5.0053)	(7.8097)
a_4	2.6410	2.4956
	(4.6580)	(7.5434)
a_5	2.8837	2.7615
	(4.6382)	(7.5364)
β_1	0.1208	0.1400
	(2.3923)	(4.4185)
β_2	0.3006	0.2435
	(3.9401)	(4.6995)
β_3	1.2582	1.1710
	(3.9405)	(4.9752)
β_4	0.2533	0.2439
	(2.9712)	(4.9843)
β_5	0.7167	0.7669
	(3.5459)	(4.7349)
R^2	0.9611	0.9517
$\bar{R}^2$	0.9135	0.8924
D.W.S.	1.5457	
D	1.186%	1.124%

and the number of unknown parameters (10/6), however, is rather low, in order to obtain reliable estimates. In order to improve this ratio the parameters are estimated using the data of all brands over all time periods simultaneously.[27] [28] Then we have the same number of degrees of freedom $(50-10=40)$ as we had estimating the parameters in the models I, II and III.

27. A variant of model IV is shown in Bultez, Naert [1975]. They estimated relations such as (4.4) for *each* brand seperately.
28. For this model the variance-covariance matrix is of the order $nT \times nT$.

This gain in degrees of freedom is partly counterbalanced by the loss of market shares necessarily summing up to one, because

$$O(I_j) \neq \sum_{r \neq j}^{5} I_r \quad \text{for} \quad j = 1, ..., 5 \tag{4.5}$$

and so

$$\sum_{r=1}^{5} \frac{I_r}{I_r + O(I_r)} \neq 1. \tag{4.6}$$

From Tables 3 and 4 we see that this alternative specification has only slightly reduced the values of the D-statistic 1.023% and 1.049% as compared with 1.186% and 1.124% in model III. It is therefore questionable whether this specification leads to important improvements.

We conclude this section considering a logically consistent multiplicative model. The relations of model V are, however, somewhat more difficult to linearize than the preceding relations.

4.3. Model V – Multiplicative-homogeneous reaction-parameters – logically consistent

$$m_{jt} = \frac{e^{\alpha_j} a_{j,t-1}^{\beta_1} s_{jt}^{\beta_2} p_{jt}^{\beta_3} v_{jt}^{\beta_4} d_{jt}^{\beta_5} e^{\varepsilon_{jt}}}{\sum\limits_{r=1}^{5} e^{\alpha_r} a_{r,t-1}^{\beta_1} s_{rt}^{\beta_2} p_{rt}^{\beta_3} v_{rt}^{\beta_4} d_{rt}^{\beta_5} e^{\varepsilon_{rt}}} \quad j = 1, ..., 5; \; t = 1, ..., 10. \tag{4.7}$$

Using the ingenious transformation which has been developed by Nakanishi [1972] (4.7) can be linearized applying the following transformations.[29]
Let

$$\bar{m}_t = \left(\sum_{r=1}^{5} \ln m_{rt} \right) / 5;$$

$$\bar{\alpha} = \left(\sum_{r=1}^{5} \alpha_r \right) / 5;$$

$$\bar{a}_{t-1} = \left(\sum_{r=1}^{5} \ln a_{r,t-1} \right) / 5;$$

$$\bar{x}_t = \left(\sum_{r=1}^{5} \ln x_{rt} \right) / 5, \text{ where } x_{rt} = s_{rt}, \, p_{rt}, \, v_{rt}, \, d_{rt}.$$

$$\bar{\varepsilon}_t = \sum_{r=1}^{5} \varepsilon_{rt} / 5.$$

29. The parameters of (4.7) can also be estimated in a different way. By taking the ratios of m_{1t} and m_{jt} ($j = 2, ..., 5$) and taking logarithms (4.7) can also be linearized. As has been proved by Bultez [1977] the GLS estimates of the parameters which are obtained in this way are equal to the GLS estimates of the parameters which are estimated using (4.8).

TABLE 4.

Parameter estimates of model IV

Parameters	OLS	GLS
α^*_1	2.4286	2.3028
	(4.9232)[a]	(7.8138)
α^*_2	1.7561	1.6107
	(3.6624)	(5.4515)
α^*_3	2.4673	2.3050
	(5.2733)	(7.7914)
α^*_4	2.3184	2.1691
	(4.8476)	(7.5861)
α^*_5	2.6120	2.4772
	(4.7656)	(7.4417)
β_1	0.1165	0.1344
	(2.3006)	(4.3847)
β_2	0.2743	0.2309
	(3.6555)	(4.6387)
β_3	1.3030	1.2164
	(4.2148)	(5.2720)
β_4	0.2095	0.2008
	(2.3313)	(4.2915)
β_5	0.7803	0.7990
	(3.7466)	(4.8166)
R^2	0.9606	0.9512
$\bar{R}^2$	0.9124	0.8914
D.W.S.	1.5602	
D	1.023%	1.049%

a. The estimated dummy variables are the α_j^* 's $j=1,\ldots, 5$; where $\alpha_j^*=\alpha_j-\alpha_{oj}$.

The linearized form of (4.7) is then

$$\ln m_{jt} - \bar{m}_t = \alpha_j - \bar{\alpha} + \beta_1 (\ln a_{j, t-1} - \bar{a}_{t-1}) + \beta_2 (\ln s_{jt} - \bar{s}_t) +$$
$$+ \beta_3 (\ln p_{jt} - \bar{p}_t) + \beta_4 (\ln v_{jt} - \bar{v}_t) +$$
$$+ \beta_5 (\ln d_{jt} - \bar{d}_t) + \varepsilon_{jt} - \bar{\varepsilon}_t$$
$$j = 1, \ldots, 5; \quad t = 1, \ldots, 10. \tag{4.8}$$

The parameters of this linearized form are estimated by OLS and GLS. As has been pointed out by Bultez and Naert [1975] there is contemporaneous correlation of the disturbances in (4.8) because

$$\sum_{r=1}^{5} \{\varepsilon_{rt} - \bar{\varepsilon}_t\} = \sum_{r=1}^{5} \varepsilon_{rt} - 5 \sum_{r=1}^{5} \varepsilon_{rt}/5 = 0 \qquad t = 1, ..., 10. \tag{4.9}$$

This implies that observations of a certain brand should be deleted again in order to obtain a non-singular variance-covariance matrix of the residuals.[30]

In this model the dummy variables α_j can only be determined when we give one of these variables an arbitrary value. Therefore we set $\bar{\alpha} = 0$.[31] From (4.7) it can easily be deduced that this operation does not have any effect on m_{jt}. In Table 5 the parameter estimates of model V are shown.

From Tables 3, 4 and 5 the following conclusions can be drawn:

1. In all models the fluctuations in the market shares are explained in a satisfactory way.
2. The number of significant parameters in all models is large. Unlike in model I and model II β_4 is significant in all models.
3. The value of D in model III and model IV is again very low.
4. The values of the reaction-parameters are of the same order of magnitude.
5. When we do not allow for differences in response parameters it is recommended to specify market share models in accordance with model V. The estimation procedure will not give specific problems.

5. MULTIPLICATIVE MARKET SHARE MODELS – HETEROGENEOUS PARAMETERS (MODEL VI, VII)

In Section 3 it has been shown that implementation criteria related to *robustness* come into conflict with criteria related to *completeness* of a model when we construct linear market share models. We showed that *linear* models which predict market shares that sum to one do not allow for differences in the response parameters across brands. In this context completeness refers to the necessity of incorporating these differences into a model.

---

30. Thus, the variance-covariance matrix is of the order $(n—1)T \times (n—1)T$.
31. This implies that we do not use the definition of dummy variables which is used by Bultez, Naert [1975]. Because we take deviations of the means of all variables in (4.8), it automatically holds that: $\sum_{r=1}^{n} \alpha_r - \bar{\alpha} = 0$. This can be verified from Table 5.

TABLE 5.

Parameter estimates of model V

Parameters	OLS	GLS
α_1	0.0678 (1.7240)[a]	0.0843 (2.8289)
α_2	—0.4666 (—13.9696)	—0.4735 (—24.7569)
α_3	0.1451 (2.9277)	0.1181 (2.8595)
α_4	—0.0026 (—0.0681)[a]	—0.0332 (—1.2384)[a]
α_5	0.2563 (3.8966)	0.3043[b]
β_1	0.1302 (2.6827)	0.1481 (5.4731)
β_2	0.2844 (3.8267)	0.1906 (4.3596)
β_3	1.2806 (4.2071)	1.6264 (5.7748)
β_4	0.2462 (2.8398)	0.2563 (5.7220)
β_5	0.7647 (3.9159)	0.7969 (4.7283)
R^2	0.9648	0.9733
$\bar{R}^2$	0.9216	0.9397
D.W.S.	1.5413	

a. Parameters which are non-significant at the 0.05 – level.
b. Because GLS has been performed using $(n-1)T$ observations α_5 has been determined in an indirect way using $\bar{\alpha}=0$.

In this section we give an example of a model that allows for differences in the response parameters over various brands and is logically consistent: model VII. Before we present model VII we consider a multiplicative model with heterogeneous response parameters for the variable theme-advertising which is not logically consistent: model VI.

5.1. *Model VI – Multiplicative-heterogeneous reaction-parameters*

$$m_{jt} = e^{\alpha_j} \left[\frac{a_{j,t-1}}{5 \atop \sum\limits_{r=1} a_{r,t-1}} \right]^{\beta_{1j}} \left[\frac{s_{jt}}{5 \atop \sum\limits_{r=1} s_{r,t-1}} \right]^{\beta_2} \left[\frac{p_{jt}}{5 \atop \sum\limits_{r=1} p_{rt}} \right]^{\beta_3} \left[\frac{v_{jt}}{5 \atop \sum\limits_{r=1} v_{rt}} \right]^{\beta_4} \left[\frac{d_{jt}}{5 \atop \sum\limits_{r=1} d_{rt}} \right]^{\beta_5} e^{\varepsilon_{jt}}$$

$$j = 1, \ldots, 5; \; t = 1, \ldots, 10. \tag{5.1}$$

The parameter estimates of model VI are shown in Table 6.[32]

Model VII is shown in the relations (5.2). Suggestions to develop this kind of model are found in McGuire, Weiss [1976] and Weverbergh, Naert, Bultez [1977].

5.2. *Model VII – Multiplicative-heterogeneous reaction-parameters – logically consistent*

$$m_{jt} = \frac{e^{\alpha_j} a_{j,t-1}^{\beta_{1j}} s_{jt}^{\beta_2} p_{jt}^{\beta_3} v_{jt}^{\beta_4} d_{jt}^{\beta_5} e^{\varepsilon_{jt}}}{\sum\limits_{r=1}^{5} e^{\alpha_r} a_{r,t-1}^{\beta_{1r}} s_{rt}^{\beta_2} p_{rt}^{\beta_3} v_{rt}^{\beta_4} d_{rt}^{\beta_5} e^{\varepsilon_{rt}}} \quad j = 1, \ldots, 5; \; t = 1, \ldots, 10. \tag{5.2}$$

This model can be estimated and linearized similarly to (4.8)

$$\ln m_{jt} - \bar{m}_t = \alpha_j - \bar{\alpha} + \tfrac{4}{5}\beta_{1j} \ln a_{j,t-1} - \tfrac{1}{5} \sum_{r \neq j}^{5} \beta_{1r} \ln a_{r,t-1}$$

$$+ \beta_2 (\ln s_{jt} - \bar{s}_t) + \beta_3 (\ln p_{jt} - \bar{p}_t) + \beta_4 (\ln v_{jt} - \bar{v}_t) +$$

$$+ \beta_5 (\ln d_{jt} - \bar{d}_t) + \varepsilon_{jt} - \bar{\varepsilon}_t$$

$$\text{for each } j = 1, \ldots, 5; \; t = 1, \ldots, 10. \text{ [33]} \tag{5.3}$$

where $\bar{m}_t$, $\bar{\alpha}$, $\bar{s}_t$, $\bar{p}_t$, $\bar{v}_t$, $\bar{d}_t$ and $\bar{\varepsilon}_t$ are defined in the same way as in Section 4.

Bultez and Naert [1975] estimated parameters of a variant of model VII, which accounts for heterogeneous reaction-parameters of *all* marketing instruments. We do not estimate the parameters of this model because:

---

32. GLS estimates are obtained using a variance-covariance matrix which is of the order $nT \times nT$.

33. Relation (5.3) can also be written as

$$\ln m_{jt} - \bar{m}_t = \alpha_j - \bar{\alpha} + \beta_{1j} \ln a_{j,t-1} - \tfrac{1}{5} \sum_{r=1}^{5} \beta_{rj} \ln a_{r,t-1} + \cdots,$$

which leads to

$$\ln m_{jt} - \bar{m}_t = \alpha_j - \bar{\alpha} + \{\beta_{1j} - \tfrac{1}{5}\beta_{1j}\} \ln a_{j,t-1} - \tfrac{1}{5} \sum_{r \neq j}^{5} \beta_{rj} \ln a_{r,t-1} + \cdots$$

from which (5.3) follows.

1. the number of unknown parameters (30) is too large, particularly if we compare this number with the number of observations (50 observations OLS; 40 observations GLS);
2. it is not necessary to allow reaction-parameters to differ over brands for *all* instruments. Particularly this is less relevant for variables such as price and distribution.

Estimating the parameters of this model Bultez and Naert found high degrees of multicollinearity between the variables. They proved that transformations such as (5.3) induce a high degree of multicollinearity even if the raw varia-bles are uncorrelated. This can also be seen from the structure of the matrix of observations of the independent variables which is shown for model VII in Appendix C. The estimated values of the parameters of model VII are shown in Table 7.[34]

From Table 6 and 7 the following conclusions can be drawn.

1. The estimated values of the parameters in model VI can be compared with the 'corresponding' estimates in the models II and III. The estimated values of $\hat{\beta}_2$, $\hat{\beta}_3$, $\hat{\beta}_4$ and $\hat{\beta}_5$ in model VI are '*about*' the same order of magni-tude as the corresponding estimates of model III. The same holds for the values of the heterogeneous reaction-parameters. In model II and in model VI $\hat{\beta}_{13}$ has the largest value, followed by $\hat{\beta}_{12}$ and $\hat{\beta}_{15}$ while the values of $\hat{\beta}_{11}$ and $\hat{\beta}_{14}$ are always small, insignificant and even negative. We see, however, that the value of the D-statistic is large as compared with the models II, III and IV. In order to decrease D we estimated a variant of model IV, a quasi-duopoly model, which in this case accounts for heterogeneous para-meters. The value of D decreased only slightly from 2.278% to 2.179% (OLS) and from 2.262% tot 2.168% (GLS).

2. Many parameters of model VII are *insignificant* and the *order of magnitude* of the insignificant parameters does not correspond with the values of the estimated parameters in a model with about the same structure: model V. This means that even in models in which we account for heterogeneous reaction-parameters of only one marketing instrument transformations such as (5.3) induce a *relative high degree* of *multicollinearity*.

The mutual order of magnitude of the dummy variables α_j differs re-

---

34. GLS estimates are obtained using a variance-covariance matrix of the order $(n—1)T \times (n—1)T$.

TABLE 6.

Parameter estimates of Model VI

Parameters	OLS	GLS
α_1	2.2024 (3.4183)	1.9993 (4.5952)
α_2	1.8915 (2.8849)	1.5954 (3.6707)
α_3	2.7634 (4.5893)	2.5147 (6.7729)
α_4	1.9670 (2.5955)	1.5603 (2.9717)
α_5	2.3960 (3.5880)	2.2261 (5.5228)
β_{11}	0.0003 (0.0026)[a]	0.0826 (1.0178)[a]
β_{12}	0.1484 (1.8298)[a]	0.1686 (2.8274)
β_{13}	0.2795 (2.6681)	0.3247 (6.6347)
β_{14}	—0.1100 (—0.6278)[a]	—0.1520 (—1.0690)[a]
β_{15}	0.0442 (0.3441)[a]	0.1516 (1.5338)[a]
β_2	0.3391 (4.2703)	0.2985 (5.5913)
β_3	0.9654 (2.7375)	0.9438 (4.6503)
β_4	0.2529 (2.6776)	0.2770 (4.7530)
β_5	0.7570 (3.1229)	0.5889 (2.9133)
R^2	0.9659	0.9551
$\bar{R}^2$	0.9196	0.8940
D.W.S.	1.4253	
D	2.278%	2.262%

a. Parameters which are non-significant at the 0.05 -level.

TABLE 7.

Parameter estimates of model VII

Parameters	OLS	GLS
α_1	0.1418 (0.1558)[a]	—0.2931 (—0.2889)[a]
α_2	—0.2078 (—0.4561)[a]	—0.0265 (—0.0599)[a]
α_3	—1.0950 (—1.6084)[a]	—0.8962 (—1.4235)[a]
α_4	1.4809 (2.2369)	1.1440 (1.9009)[a]
α_5	—0.3199 (—0.4172)[a]	—0.0718 [b]
β_{11}	0.1192 (0.7430)[a]	0.2407 (1.3698)[a]
β_{12}	0.0839 (1.1846)[a]	0.1110 (2.1208)
β_{13}	0.3284 (3.1791)	0.3481 (3.5518)
β_{14}	—0.0981 (—0.8946)[a]	0.0062 (0.0604)[a]
β_{15}	0.2085 (1.4772)[a]	0.2121 (1.2476)[a]
β_2	0.2830 (3.6815)	0.1883 (2.9658)
β_3	0.3991 (0.8774)[a]	0.6822 (1.6131)[a]
β_4	0.2866 (3.2439)	0.2620 (3.1845)
β_5	0.6431 (2.3233)	0.7697 (2.4659)
R^2	0.9712	0.9749
$\bar{R}^2$	0.9319	0.9387
D.W.S.	1.3517	

a. Parameters which are non-significant at the 0.05 -level.
b. Because GLS has been performed using $(n-1)T$ observations. α_5 has been determined in an indirect way using $\bar{\alpha}=0$.

markably from those of model V or model II. The same holds for the reaction-parameter $\hat{\beta}_3$. The standard deviations of the GLS-estimates of $\hat{\beta}_{12}$ and $\hat{\beta}_{14}$ of model VII (0.0523; 0.1018), however, are smaller than the corresponding standard deviations of the corresponding estimates of model VI.

With respect to the multicollinearity problems we finally have to remark that a 'source' for multicollinearity in model VII is that in model VII absolute (high) values of marketing instruments and relative (small) values of marketing instruments are considered in combination. This can be seen from (C.2). Experiments with models in which the absolute values of marketing instruments are substituted by relative values show that the multicollinearity can be decreased.[35]

3. Comparing model VI and model VII we believe that the advantages of model VII are *somewhat smaller* than the advantages of model VI; the main disadvantage being the relative high degree of multicollinearity which occurs in model VII. When as has been indicated in the preceding paragraph multicollinearity can be decreased model VII will become more promising.

6. EVALUATION

In this contribution we compared a number of alternative specifications of market share models by testing these models empirically on data in which the performances of different brands over different time-periods are considered simultaneously. Desirable characteristics of market share models are that:

1. these models are *complete* on important issues, where we paid specific attention to heterogeneity of the reaction-parameters;
2. these models are *robust*, where we concentrated on logical consistency;
3. the parameters can be *estimated* without much difficulty, where we especially dealt with multicollinearity of the independent variables in linearized forms. These forms have to be constructed in order to estimate the parameters.

Considering models that are *linear* in the parameters we found that the property that predicted market shares sum up to one comes into conflict with the property that a model allows parameters to vary over brands. In

35. See Leeflang [1977d].

cases where relative good fits and significant values of the parameter estimates are obtained and the average absolute deviation of the sum of the
market shares from 1 is small, we prefer models that are *not logically consistent* but that account for *heterogeneity* of the *reaction-parameters*.

For reasons pointed out in Section 3, we prefer *multiplicative* models to
linear models. In multiplicative models which *do not account for differences*
in some *reaction-parameters* over different brands we prefer a *logically
consistent model which can be linearized* after an ingenious transformation,
with parameters that can be estimated without difficulty (model V). We want
to point out that these models with homogeneous parameters are not so
attractive to develop from a firm's decision-making point of view. These
models may, however, be relevant from a more theoretical point of view,
for example, in order to build a theory about the effectiveness of the different marketing instruments during product-life cycles.

In multiplicative models which *do account for differences* in some *reaction-
parameters* across brands we have to make a choice between:

1. models that are logically consistent but cannot be transformed for
   estimation in a way as to avoid multicollinearity problems;
2. models that can be estimated without difficulty but that are not logically
   consistent.

From the models we investigated with relative good fits and many significant reaction-parameters we prefer multiplicative models with *heterogeneous
reaction-parameters* that are, however, *not logically consistent*.

Finally, it may be concluded from this contribution that although it is
useful to formulate implementation criteria in order to obtain implementable
models all these criteria cannot be satisfied simultaneously. This is particularly true when we also want to avoid estimation problems. This illustrates
that by building implementable marketing models we will often be faced
with the choice between approximating reality more closely and avoiding
estimation problems. [36]

36. Bultez, Naert [1975, pp. 532–533].

APPENDIX A. A PROOF THAT THE SUM OF THE ESTIMATED VALUES OF THE RAN-
DOM DISTURBANCE TERMS IS ZERO

Consider the following linear model:

$$y = X\beta + \varepsilon \qquad\qquad (A.1)$$

where

y = a column vector of n values taken by the dependent variable;

X = a matrix of order $n \times \Lambda$ of values taken by the Λ independent variables
  $x_1, .., x_\Lambda$ and $x_1 = 1$ for all n;

β = a column vector of Λ unknown parameters, and

ε = a column vector of n non-observable random disturbance terms.

A well-known OLS-estimate of ε is[37]

$$\hat{\varepsilon} = My = M\varepsilon \qquad\qquad (A.2)$$

where

$M = [I - X(X'X)^{-1}X']$, and

 I = a unity-matrix.

From the definition of M it can easily be deduced that:

$$X'M = 0. \qquad\qquad (A.3)$$

Premultiplying (A.2) by X' we get

$$X'\hat{\varepsilon} = X'M\varepsilon = 0. \qquad\qquad (A.4)$$

Because the first column vector of X is a $n \times 1$ vector ι

$$\iota' = [1, ..., 1], \qquad\qquad (A.5)$$

We deduce from (A.4) that

$$\iota'\hat{\varepsilon} = 0. \qquad\qquad (A.6)$$

37. See, for example, Theil [1971, p. 193].

APPENDIX B. THE STRUCTURE OF THE VARIANCE-COVARIANCE MATRIX OF THE RANDOM DISTURBANCE TERMS

Pooling cross-section and time-series data the variances and covariances of the random disturbance terms may have a specific structure. The general structure has been discussed in detail, for example, by Kmenta [1971, pp. 512–514].

We consider the case in which we do *not* have to account for *autocorrelation* but just for heteroscedasticity and mutual correlation of the random disturbance terms

$$E(\varepsilon_{jt}^2) = \sigma_{jj} \qquad j = 1, ..., n,$$

$$E(\varepsilon_{it}, \varepsilon_{jt}) = \sigma_{ij} \qquad i, j = 1, ..., n, \ i \neq j. \tag{B.1}$$

The variance-covariance matrix of the disturbances Ω, has the following structure

$$\Omega = E \begin{bmatrix} \varepsilon_{11} \\ \varepsilon_{12} \\ \vdots \\ \varepsilon_{1T} \\ \varepsilon_{21} \\ \vdots \\ \varepsilon_{nT} \end{bmatrix} \begin{bmatrix} \varepsilon_{11} \varepsilon_{12} \cdots \varepsilon_{1T} \varepsilon_{21} \cdots \varepsilon_{nT} \end{bmatrix} =$$

$$= \begin{bmatrix} E(\varepsilon_{11}^2) & E(\varepsilon_{11}\varepsilon_{12}) \ldots E(\varepsilon_{11}\varepsilon_{1T}) & E(\varepsilon_{11}\varepsilon_{21}) \ldots E(\varepsilon_{11}\varepsilon_{nT}) \\ E(\varepsilon_{11}\varepsilon_{12}) & E(\varepsilon_{12}^2) & \ldots E(\varepsilon_{12}\varepsilon_{1T}) & E(\varepsilon_{12}\varepsilon_{21}) \ldots E(\varepsilon_{12}\varepsilon_{nT}) \\ \vdots & \vdots & \vdots & \vdots & \vdots \\ E(\varepsilon_{11}\varepsilon_{1T}) E(\varepsilon_{12}\varepsilon_{1T}) \ldots & E(\varepsilon_{1T}^2) & E(\varepsilon_{1T}\varepsilon_{21}) \ldots E(\varepsilon_{1T}\varepsilon_{nT}) \\ E(\varepsilon_{11}\varepsilon_{21}) E(\varepsilon_{12}\varepsilon_{21}) \ldots E(\varepsilon_{1T}\varepsilon_{21}) & E(\varepsilon_{21}^2) & \ldots E(\varepsilon_{21}\varepsilon_{nT}) \\ \vdots & \vdots & \vdots & \vdots & \vdots \\ E(\varepsilon_{11}\varepsilon_{nT}) E(\varepsilon_{12}\varepsilon_{nT}) \ldots E(\varepsilon_{1T}\varepsilon_{nT}) & E(\varepsilon_{21}\varepsilon_{nT}) \ldots & E(\varepsilon_{nT}^2) \end{bmatrix} =$$

$$= \begin{bmatrix} \sigma_{11}I \ \sigma_{12}I \ldots \sigma_{1n}I \\ \vdots & \vdots & \vdots \\ \sigma_{n1}I \ \sigma_{n2}I \ldots \sigma_{nn}I \end{bmatrix} \tag{B.2}$$

where I = a unity matrix of the order $T \times T$.
This means that Ω is of the order $nT \times nT$.
The σ_{ij} are estimated by

$$\hat{\sigma}_{ij} = \frac{1}{T - k - 1} \sum_{t=2}^{T} \hat{\varepsilon}_{it} \hat{\varepsilon}_{jt}, \tag{B.3}$$

where

T = number of time periods that are considered (in our case $T=10$);
k = the number of parameters estimated in each relation (in our case $k=6$);
$\hat{\varepsilon}_{jt}$ = the estimated values of the residuals. These values have been obtained by the ordinary least-squares method (OLS) (compare (A.2)).

Substituting (B.3) in (B.2) we obtain a numerical specification of the variance-covariance matrix of the random-disturbance terms. This matrix can be used to apply the generalized least-squares method (GLS).

When the disturbances are dependent we have to delete observations of one brand, for example, the $n-$th brand, in order to obtain a variance-covariance matrix with full rank. In these cases the matrix Ω is of the order $(n-1)T \times (n-1)T$.

APPENDIX C. THE STRUCTURE OF THE MATRIX OF OBSERVATIONS OF THE IN-
DEPENDENT VARIABLES OF THE MULTIPLICATIVE LOGICALLY CONSISTENT MARKET
SHARE MODEL WITH HETEROGENEOUS REACTION-PARAMETERS

After model VII has been linearized in accordance with (5.3) the relations of this model can be written in matrix notation as

$$m^* = X^*\beta + \varepsilon^* \tag{C.1}$$

where,

$m^{*\prime}$ = $(1 \times nT)$-vector of market shares;
$m^{*\prime}$ = $(m^*_{11}, m^*_{12}, ..., m^*_{1T}, m^*_{21}, ..., m^*_{nT})$;
m^*_{jt} = $\ln m_{jt} - \overline{m}_t$;
$\overline{m}_t$ = $\sum\limits_{r=1}^{n} \ln m_{rt}/n$;
β' = $[1 \times (n+L)]$-vector of unknown parameters;
n = number of brands and so the number of unknown dummy-variables $\alpha_j, j = 1, ..., n$;
L = number of reaction parameters;
$\varepsilon^{*\prime}$ = $(1 \times nT)$-vector of random-disturbance terms;
$\varepsilon^{*\prime}$ = $[\varepsilon^*_{11}, \varepsilon^*_{12}, ..., \varepsilon^*_{1T}, \varepsilon^*_{21}, ..., \varepsilon^*_{nT}]$;
ε^*_{jt} = $\varepsilon_{jt} - \bar{\varepsilon}_t$;
$\bar{\varepsilon}_t$ = $\sum\limits_{r=1}^{n} \bar{\varepsilon}_{rt}/n$.

The structure of the matrix of observations X^* is shown in (C.2). The matrix X^* is of the order $nT \times (n+L)$:

$$
\begin{bmatrix}
\vdots\, 0 & \cdots\, 0 & \frac{4}{5}\ln a_{1,0} - \frac{1}{5}\ln a_{2,0} \cdots - \frac{1}{5}\ln a_{5,0} & s_{1,1}^* & p_{1,1}^* & v_{1,1}^* & d_{1,1}^* \\
\iota_T \vdots & \vdots & \vdots & \vdots & & & \vdots \\
\vdots\, 0 & \cdots\, 0 & \frac{4}{5}\ln a_{1,9} - \frac{1}{5}\ln a_{2,9} \cdots - \frac{1}{5}\ln a_{5,9} & s_{1,10}^* & p_{1,10}^* & v_{1,10}^* & d_{1,10}^* \\
& & & & & & \\
0 \;\vdots\; \vdots 0..0 - \frac{1}{5}\ln a_{1,0} & \frac{4}{5}\ln a_{2,0} \cdots - \frac{1}{5}\ln a_{5,0} & s_{2,1}^* & p_{2,1}^* & v_{2,1}^* & d_{2,1}^* \\
\vdots\, \vdots\, \iota_T \vdots\, \vdots & \vdots & \vdots & & & & \vdots \\
0 \;\vdots\; \vdots 0..0 - \frac{1}{5}\ln a_{1,9} & \frac{4}{5}\ln a_{2,9} \cdots - \frac{1}{5}\ln a_{5,9} & s_{2,10}^* & p_{2,10}^* & v_{2,10}^* & d_{2,10}^* \\
& & \vdots & & & & \\
0 \;\cdots\, 0 \vdots \;\vdots\; - \frac{1}{5}\ln a_{1,0} - \frac{1}{5}\ln a_{2,0} \cdots & \frac{4}{5}\ln a_{5,0} & s_{5,1}^* & p_{5,1}^* & v_{5,1}^* & d_{5,1}^* \\
\vdots & \vdots\, \vdots\, \iota_T \vdots & \vdots & & & & \vdots \\
0 \;\cdots\, 0 \vdots \;\vdots\; - \frac{1}{5}\ln a_{1,9} - \frac{1}{5}\ln a_{2,9} \cdots & \frac{4}{5}\ln a_{5,9} & s_{5,10}^* & p_{5,10}^* & v_{5,10}^* & d_{5,10}^*
\end{bmatrix}
$$

$$(C.2)$$

where

$$\iota_T' = (1 \times T)\text{-vector} = (1, \ldots, 1);$$
$$x_{jt}^* = \ln x_{jt} - \bar{x}_t ;$$
$$\bar{x}_t = \sum_{r=1}^{n} \ln x_{rt}/n ; \quad \text{and}$$
$$x_{jt} = s_{jt}, p_{jt}, v_{jt}, d_{jt} .$$

Studying the structure of this matrix and particularly the structure of the columns 6–10 it is not surprising that transformation (5.3) induces a high degree of multicollinearity.

BIBLIOGRAPHY

Aeyelts Averink, G. J. Micro Economische Modellen voor het Marketing Beleid. *Maandblad voor Accountancy en Bedrijfshuishoudkunde.* Vol. 46, 1972, pp. 125–135.
Beckwith, N. W. Multivariate Analysis of Sales Responses of Competing Brands to Advertising. *Journal of Marketing Research*, Vol. 9, 1972, pp. 168–176.
Beckwith, N. W. Concerning the Logical Consistency of Multivariate Market Share Models. *Journal of Marketing Research*, Vol. 10, 1973, pp. 341–344.
Bultez, A. V. Econometric Specification and Estimation of Market Share

Models: The State of the Art. *Zeitschrift für Betriebswirtschaftliche Forschung*, (forthcoming), 1977.

Bultez, A. V., Naert, Ph. A. Consistent Sum-Constrained Models. *Journal of the American Statistical Association*, Vol. 70, 1975, pp. 529–535.

Bultez, A. V., Naert, Ph. A. *Does Lag Structure Really Matter in Optimizing Advertising Spending*. Working Paper 77–13, European Institute for Advanced Studies in Management, Brussels 1977.

Cowling, K., Cubbin, J. Price, Quality and Advertising Competition: An Econometric Investigation of the United Kingdom Car Market. *Economica*, Vol. 38, 1971, pp. 378–394.

De Haan, H. *De Toepassing van de Dimensieanalyse op de Econometrie*. Reeks van de Faculteit der Economische en Sociale Wetenschappen, Katholieke Universiteit, Leuven 1970.

De Jong, F. J. *Dimensional Analysis for Economists*. North-Holland Publishing Company, Amsterdam 1967.

Ferber, R., Verdoorn, P. J. *Research Methods in Economics and Business*. Macmillan, New York 1962.

Hör zu, Funk Uhr. *Marktmechanik 1*. Axel Springer Verlag, Hamburg 1975.

Houston, F. S., Weiss, D. L. An Analysis of Competitive Market Behavior. *Journal of Marketing Research*, Vol. 11, 1974, pp. 151–155.

Kmenta, J. *Elements of Econometrics*. The MacMillan Company, New York 1971.

Lambin, J. J. *Modèles et Programmes de Marketing*. Presses Universitaires de France, Paris 1970.

Lambin, J. J. Is Gasoline Advertising Justified? *Journal of Business*, Vol. 45, 1972a, pp. 585–619.

Lambin, J. J. A Computer On-Line Marketing Mix Model. *Journal of Marketing Research*, Vol. 9, 1972b, pp. 119–126.

Lambin, J. J. *Advertising Competition and Market Conduct in Oligopoly over Time*. North-Holland Publishing Company, Amsterdam 1976.

Larréché, J. C. *Marketing Managers and Models: A Search for a Better Match*. Research Papers Series, No. 157, INSEAD, Fontainebleau 1975.

Larréché, J. C., Montgomery, D. B. *A Framework for the Evaluation of Marketing Models*. 1975 mimeographed.

Leeflang, P. S. H. *Mathematical Models in Marketing, A Survey, the Stage of Development, Some Extensions and Applications*. H. E. Stenfert Kroese B.V., Leiden 1974.

Leeflang, P. S. H. Marktonderzoek en Marketingmodellen. *Jaarboek van de Nederlandse Vereniging van Marktonderzoekers*, Vol. 2, 1976, pp. 217–252.

Leeflang, P. S. H. Organising Market Data for Decision Making through the Development of Mathematical Marketing Models. *Proceedings of the ESOMAR Seminar on Marketing Management Information Systems: Organising Market Data for Decision Making*, Brussels, 1977a, pp. 29–54.

Leeflang, P. S. H. De Marketing Mix I, Samenhang der Marktinstrumenten. *Economisch Statistische Berichten*, Jrg. 62, 1977b, pp. 143–149.

Leeflang, P. S. H. De Marketing Mix III, Bepaling van de Effectiviteit der Marktinstrumenten. *Economisch Statistische Berichten*, Jrg. 62, 1977c, pp. 549–555.

Leeflang, P. S. H. *More on the Logical Consistency of Market Share Models.* Memorandum van het Instituut voor Economisch Onderzoek, Faculteit der Economische Wetenschappen, Rijksuniversiteit te Groningen, 1977d, (forthcoming).

Leeflang, P. S. H., Koerts, J. Modelling and Marketing: Two Important Concepts and the Connection between Them. *European Journal of Marketing*, Vol. 7, 1973, pp. 203–217.

Leeflang, P. S. H., Koerts, J. A Concise Survey of Mathematical Models in Marketing, in Elliot, K., (ed.), *Management Bibliographics & Reviews*. Vol. 1, Bradford, B.C.D. Books, 1975, pp. 101–124.

Leeflang, P. S. H., Naert, Ph. A. *Models in Marketing: The State of the Art.* Working Paper, European Institute for Advanced Studies in Management, Brussels 1977.

Little, J. D. C. Models and Managers: The Concept of a Decision Calculus. *Management Science*, Vol. 16, 1970, pp. B–466–485.

Little, J. D. C. BRANDAID: A Marketing-Mix Model Part I: Structure. *Operations Research*, Vol. 23, 1975a, pp. 628–655.

Little, J. D. C. BRANDAID: A Marketing-Mix Model Part II: Implementation, Calibration and Case Study. *Operations Research*, Vol. 23, 1975b, pp. 656–673.

Little, J. D. C. Lodish, L. M. A Media Planning Calculus. *Operations Research*, Vol. 17, 1969, pp. 1–35.

McGuire, T. W., Farley, J. U., Lucas, R. E., Jr., Ring, W. L. Estimation and Inference for Linear Models in which Subsets of the Dependent Variable are Constrained. *Journal of the American Statistical Association*, Vol. 63, 1968, pp. 1201–1213.

McGuire, T. W., Weiss, D. L. Logically Consistent Market Share Models II. *Journal of Marketing Research*, Vol. 13, 1976, pp. 296–302.

MacLachlan, D. L. A Model of Intermediate Market Response. *Journal of Marketing Research*, Vol. 9, 1972, pp. 378–384.

Montgomery, D. B. The Outlook for MIS. *Journal of Advertising Research*, Vol. 13, June 1973, pp. 5–11.

Naert, Ph. A., Bultez, A. V. Logically Consistent Market Share Models. *Journal of Marketing Research*, Vol. 10, 1973, pp. 334–340.

Naert, Ph. A., Leeflang, P. S. H. *Building Implementable Marketing Models*. Martinus Nijhoff Social Sciences Division, Leiden 1977.

Nakanishi, M. Measurement of Sales Promotion Effect at the Retail Level – A New Approach. *Marketing Education and the Real World – Dynamic Marketing in a Changing World*, Combined A.M.A. Proceedings of the Spring and Fall Conferences, 1972, pp. 338–343.

Nakanishi, M., Cooper, L. G. Parameter Estimation for a Multiplicative Competitive Interaction Model – Least Squares Approach. *Journal of Marketing Research*, Vol. 11, 1974, pp. 303–311.

Somermeyer, W. H. Specificatie van Economische Relaties. *De Economist*, Vol. 115, 1967, pp. 1–26.

Theil, H. *Principles of Econometrics*. North-Holland Publishing Company, Amsterdam 1971.

Urban, G. L. *An Emerging Process of Building Models for Management Decision Makers*. Working Paper, No. 591–72, Alfred P. Sloan School of Management, M.I.T., 1972.

Urban, G. L. Building Models for Decision Makers. *Interfaces*, Vol. 4, 1974, pp. 1–11.

Urban, G. L., Karash, R. Evolutionary Model Building. *Journal of Marketing Research*, Vol. 8, 1971, pp. 62–66.

Verdoorn, P. J. Marketing from the Producer's Point of View. *Journal of Marketing*, Vol. 20, 1956, pp. 221–235.

Verdoorn, P. J. Marktonderzoek en Marktbeleid. *Maandblad voor Accountancy en Bedrijfshuishoudkunde*, Vol. 46, 1972, pp. 100–114.

Weverbergh, M., Naert, Ph. A., Bultez, A. V. *Logically Consistent Market Share Models: A Further Clarification*. Working Paper 77–28, European Institute for Advanced Studies in Management, Brussels 1977.

Wildt, A. R. Multifirm Analysis of Competitive Decision Variables. *Journal of Marketing Research*, Vol. 11, 1974, pp. 50–62.

The Marketing Mix and Brand Quality

KRISTIAN S. PALDA*

> 'The quality that counts is what sells'.
> B. Stein, *Wall Street Journal*, 27/2/1976.

1. THE MARKETING MIX AND ITS OPTIMIZATION

The concept of the marketing mix is central to both the positive micro-economic analysis of the typical modern industrial or service firm, the oligopolistic seller, and to the normative managerial analysis of the marketing function. The firm is seen as influencing the demand for its brand (which is one of several being sold in a product market) by any one of the four instruments of marketing policy: price, product quality, promotion (communication with customers either by advertising or personal selling or both), and the choice of distribution channels. The fundamental question is: how do, or should, sellers optimize the input levels of the instruments to attain maximum profits?

In 1956 Professor Verdoorn proposed a geometric optimality rule for the choice of marketing mix input levels [15.] It constitutes one of the two basic approaches to mix optimization whose influence is still present in modern marketing managerial thought. Its basic premise is that the marketing decision variables are *discrete* rather than continuous. It is useful to summarize briefly the Verdoorn contribution as well as the other important one, that of Dorfman and Steiner, in order to give a better appreciation of the optimization issue and to introduce the topic of brand quality.

1.1. *The Verdoorn Scheme*

Consider four instruments (inputs) of marketing policy: price, brand quality, promotion and distribution channels. None of these variables is continuous. Assume that production cost is both a function of quantity sold and a function of the brand quality. Assume also that beyond a certain point all the marketing inputs are subject to diminishing returns as far as their sales

---

* The mathematical formulations in Section 3 have been developed in cooperation with André Boyer, IAE, Université de Nice. See also [13].

influence is concerned. Draw a diagram (Figure 1), with quantities to be sold plotted on the abscissa, and total revenue and total cost on the ordinate.

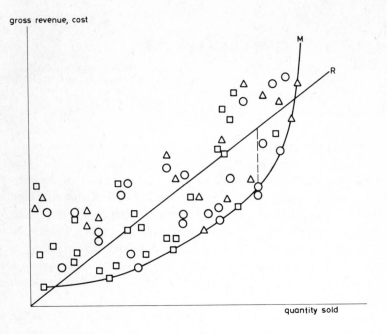

Figure 1

For a particular price contemplated, draw in a straight line (*R*) through the origin. Price being given, total revenue varies proportionately to total sales.

Consider now three possible qualities of the brand and designate these symbolically as triangle, square and circle. For each of the contemplated brand qualities, evaluate the effect of a number of combinations of promotional outlays and distributive channels arrangements, upon sales and costs. Thus for instance, at the specified price it is expected that *x* units of triangle quality will be sold at the total cost (production *and* marketing) of *y*, when a certain combination of trade channels and promotional efforts is resorted to.

Such a diagram is filled out for all technically and economically plausible configurations of marketing mixes, that could be applied with a given price and three different brand qualities.

The dots representing the minimum cost of each combination for each volume of sales at the given price, are then joined by the dashed minimum-cost piece-wise linear curve. (Going from west to east, none of the dots must be below the curve; the successive combinations on the curve must show increasing cost). The most profitable combination of inputs is then found at the dot at which the vertical distance between the total revenue and minimum cost curves is greatest.

Similar diagrams can be drawn up for different prices envisaged, and each time a minimum cost curve can be drawn. (This is not done here because of space limitations). The various price lines with their corresponding cost curves can be superimposed in what Verdoorn calls a recapitulation diagram and the *maximum maximorum* profit combination read off from it.

Naturally a similar analysis can be performed using numbers arranged in tables rather than diagrams, and this appears nowadays the more popular version in marketing texts [8].

1.2. *The Dorfman-Steiner Scheme*

The other major approach to mix optimization differs from Verdoorn's only in one premise: the decision variables are considered to be *continuous* variables. Its foundations were laid down in the so-called Dorfman-Steiner theorem [5].

Leaving out, for simplicity's sake, the distribution channel variable, the following demand and cost functions are postulated

$$q = q\,(p, s, x) \tag{1}$$
$$c = c\,(q, x) \tag{2}$$

where

$q =$ units sold per period
$c =$ average cost
$p =$ unit price
$s =$ promotional outlays
$x =$ index of quality

The resulting profit function is then

$$\pi = pq\,(p, s, x) - qc\,(q, x) - s \tag{3}$$

Dorfman and Steiner have shown that the standard calculus profit maximization results can be converted into the following, econometrically verifiable optimality conditions

$$- e_{q, p} = p \frac{\partial q}{\partial s} = e_{q, x} \frac{p}{x(\partial c/\partial x)} \tag{4}$$

where the e's are demand elasticities.

This theorem has since been progressively generalized to derive classical elasticities *after* competitive reaction has worked itself out, that is, to take account of the typical oligopoly situation [9]. It has become a centerpiece of current econometric work concerned with the marketing mix.

1.3. *The Quality Issue*

Nonetheless, no matter whether the marketing instruments are taken to be discrete variables (the Verdoorn assumption) or continuous ones (the Dorfman-Steiner premise) the problem of defining and measuring brand quality in relevant and operational terms remains largely unsolved to date. *Relevance* in this context means definition and measurement in market response terms, be they of a perceptual or behavioral variety. *Operationality* has a double meaning. First, the quality index should be expressed in economic terms comparable to those of the other mix variables. Second, research and production people must be given a translation of the economic quality index into technical terms.

2. DEFINING AND MEASURING BRAND QUALITY

Preoccupation with the concept of product-brand quality has been evident in marketing and economic literature for at least a dozen years. (Note that throughout our discussion the word *brand* rather than product quality is employed to stress that all quality comparisons are made *within* a product class, between brands). Such concern has not, however, had as its ultimate purpose the marketing mix issue.

Steaming along but unaware of each other on two amazingly parallel paths, applied social psychologists in marketing and microeconomists have defined a product brand as a particular constellation of product attribute levels. Marketing scholars proposed a positioning of brands along a quality dimension in terms of *perceptual* measures. Economists suggested that a *revealed preference* measure, defined in terms of market price, would best serve as an index of brand quality.

2.1. *The Fishbein Perceptual Measure*

The Fishbein multi-attribute linear compensatory model of attitudes is the most representative example of perceptual measures of brand quality currently used in marketing. (The word 'quality' is, however, rarely used – brand positioning or other expressions are preferred). In its simplest version it is represented as

$$A_{jk} = \sum_{i=1}^{n} W_{ik} \cdot B_{ijk} \tag{5}$$

where

i = attribute i; j = brand j; k = consumer k
B_{ijk} = consumer k's belief about the level of attribute i present in brand j
W_{ik} = importance weight attached by consumer k to attribute i

The Fishbein approach is based on the premise that a correct measure of attitude will yield a good prediction, first of preference and then of choice as postulated by the hierarchy of effects hypothesis [12]. This is the presumed link between an attitudinal evaluation of global brand quality and actual buying behavior. It also has diagnostic potential: if we know, for all product brands, the relative importance of quality attributes and, for *our* brand, the evaluation beliefs of perceptors on each attribute, we recognize the strong and weak points as far as the perceived individual quality aspects of our brand are concerned.

Yet the Fishbein model has important weaknesses which prevent its direct utilization in the definition and measurement of brand quality for mix optimization purposes:

a. attitude scores are not good predictors of choice behavior [1];
b. the model is strictly a single-consumer model and generalizations to market segments or the total market are fraught with all the statistical pitfalls of aggregation which have not so far been successfully overcome [11];
c. there is strong evidence that not only do evaluation beliefs affect attitudes, but that attitudes also influence beliefs (simultaneous bias, called in this instance 'halo effect') [2];
d. operationality: for mix optimization purposes attitude scores are not economically meaningful entities; for production and research personnel perceptual measures (a beer's 'fullbodiedness') are not valid guides to product modification [6].

2.2. *The Hedonic Revealed Preference Measure*

The hedonic price index approach, pioneered by Griliches [7] and supported by Lancaster's theoretical writings [10] can be called a *revealed preference* brand quality measure, because it is based on overt market behavior. The premise is that the many brands or models of a particular product are nothing else but bundles of a reasonably small number of characteristics or attributes common to them all, but present in differing levels (including zero levels) in each. The method relies on fitting by regression the prices of various brands of a product to identifiable *physical* product attributes in a cross-section (or pooled time-series cross-sections) of brands such as

$$\log p_i = a + \sum_{k=1}^{n} b_k z_{ki} + e_i \tag{6}$$

where

p_i = the list or transactions price of the i-th brand

z_{ki} = the quantity of attribute k present in the i-th brand. (This need not be a continuous variable, but a dummy indicating the presence or absence of a discrete attribute).

The error term e is taken to represent the effect of left-out variables.

The analogy to the Fishbein model is striking, but the hedonic model has the following advantages:

a. unlike the attitude score the dependent variable here, the quality-related price, is a revealed preference or market behavior-derived measure; moreover, since it is the result of the choices of the whole market, no aggregation difficulties are present;

b. the regression method allows logarithmic rather than linear relationships;

c. the dozens of empirical applications gave unvariably good statistical results;

d. the regression coefficients yield an implicit price of each product attribute.

Its one major drawback concerns its application to consumer non-durables characterized by product attributes carrying a high psychological charge.

Indeed, the method has so far been applied only to industrial and consumer durable goods with easily identified physical characteristics. Yet work going on in marketing on 'psychophysical transforms' [6], aimed at operationalizing perceptual concepts for the benefit of product designers and production engineers, should remedy this weakness. It appears possible to translate such perceptual adjectives as effervescent, medicinal and strong-tasting, into such chemical or physical counterparts as CO_2 content, traces of licorice or dilution level. Once the product attribute levels for a class of brands are spelled out in quantitative terms the hedonic regression method can be applied.

The second major drawback of the hedonic method was, until recently, the underspecification of the regression relationship between the list price of a brand in a market cross-section, and the various quality attributes: such a price is obviously not only a function of product characteristics but also of oligopolistic powers at the disposal of sellers.

Using computer rentals (prices) and three types of computer performance characteristics (speed, capacity and age) as their basic observations, Ratchford and Ford [14] added manufacturer dummies to their cross-sectional regressions to 'sponge up' the oligopolistic elements. In this manner they obtained a 'pure', quality-related price'

$$\log \hat{p}_i = a + \hat{B}z - d_n \tag{7}$$

from the price regression

$$\log p_{ij} = a + Bz + \sum_{j=1}^{n-1} D_j M_j + e_{ij} \tag{8}$$

where

i = subscript designating a brand
j = subscript designating a manufacturer
z = a vector of product attributes
M = a dummy variable (0,1) for the presence of j in the observation

and where

$d_n = -(1/n)(D_1 + ... + D_{n-1})$ measures the impact of the suppressed D_n

This '"pure", quality-related price' of brand i represents an unbiased, market sanctioned evaluation of the brand's quality.

3. OPTIMAL BRAND QUALITY IN THE OPTIMAL MIX

It follows from the preceding argument that the pure, quality-related price $\hat{p}_i$ is a straightforward candidate for use as an economically meaningful unidimensional index of brand i's quality along with the other unidimensional variables of the marketing mix. Let us call this $\hat{p}$ hedonic quality. Such use, does however, require a re-definition of the accepted notion of classical price.

We shall rarely, if ever, observe an actual or list price of a brand i of manufacturer j, p_{ij}, which would be identical to the estimated pure quality-related price, $\hat{p}_i$, of that brand. Let us define a *quality-adjusted price* of brand i as [4]

$$u_i = p_{ij}/\hat{p}_i = \exp(\log p_{ij} - \log \hat{p}_i) \tag{9}$$

The u_i represents the price of brand i after the effect of quality-attribute differences had been removed. Since we defined quality in terms of price, we must use for the price variable a 'residual', larger of smaller than one, as the case may be $u_i \gtrless 1.00$.

This quality-adjusted price can be then employed to estimate the price elasticity of brands as if the brands were physically homogeneous goods.

The presence of oligopolistic elements was mentioned as being the reason for a possible 'contamination' of the quality-related price and thus the necessity of a fuller specification. But what else are such oligopolistic elements but the deployment of the marketing mix strategies? Thus the difference between (or better, the ratio of) list price and quality-related price represents the deliberate setting of the mix levels on the part of the firm. (It is actually a cousin to Lerner's monopoly index when the demand function contains a quality variable).

The managerially relevant question is, of course, whether u_i is optimal and it rejoins the question of prime interest here: is the (hedonic) quality $\hat{p}_i$ of the brand optimal in the context of the overall marketing mix? (In addition, the market-evaluated implicit prices of each individual product attribute (whether defined straightforwardly *ab initio* in technical terms or *via* the psychophysical transform) serve as inputs into possible brand quality level modification by the research and production departments).

With these definitions it is now possible to derive the equilibrium conditions for the profit-maximizing marketing mix, using econometrically estimable relationships [13]. In the spirit of the Dorfman-Steiner theorem, as modified by Lambin [9], the previously nebulous brand quality is replaced with the hedonic quality $\hat{p}$ in the demand and cost functions, and price with the quality-adjusted price, u. Since, however, quality modifications typically require research and development outlays, r, a third equation, specifying the quality-research relationship, must be added.

In analogy to eqs. (1) to (4) we write

$$q = q\,(\hat{p},\,u,\,s) \tag{1'}$$

$$c = c\,(q,\,\hat{p}) \quad (2'') \; r = r\,(\hat{p}). \tag{2'}$$

$$\pi = \hat{p}\,u\,q\,(\hat{p},\,u,\,s) - q(\hat{p},\,u,\,s)\,\{c\,[q(\hat{p},\,u,\,s),\,\hat{p}]\} - r\,(\hat{p}) - s \tag{3'}$$

and derive the equilibrium marketing mix conditions as

$$- e_{q,\,u} = \hat{p}u\,\frac{\partial q}{\partial s} = e_{q\hat{p}}/(-1 + \gamma_{c\hat{p}} + \gamma_{r\hat{p}}) \tag{4'}$$

where

$$\gamma_{c\hat{p}} = \frac{\partial c}{\partial \hat{p}}\frac{\hat{p}}{c},\; \gamma_{r\hat{p}} = \frac{dr}{d\hat{p}}\frac{\hat{p}}{r}$$

are the internal cost elasticities.

It must, of course, be assumed, that the internal cost relationships can be estimated, in particular the function $r = r\,(\hat{p})$, relating development expense to product quality. (The demand relationships have a long history of successful measurement). Implicitly, this is done every time a budget is allocated to product development activities. And, as a bonus of the preceding analysis, the optimal development budget can also be derived and tied closely to market conditions [3].

4. CONCLUSIONS

The hedonic way to the specification of brand quality and the optimization of such quality within the context of the marketing mix has been presented with reference to physical goods. There is, of course, nothing to prevent its application to services. The method does, however, break down in the absence of price competition. Where governmental monopoly (such as railways), or a government sponsored cartel (such as the banking system) occupies the market, an unbiased assessment of buyers' revealed preferences is not possible. Put differently, the hedonic method (as well as the perceptual method) can only be applied when inter-brand, intra-product class comparisons are possible.

The scope of application of the proposed method does, nevertheless, remain wide. The next step is the indispensable econometric verification of its feasibility.

REFERENCES

[1] Bass, F. M., E. A. Pessemier, D. R. Lehmann. An experimental study of relationships between attitudes, brand preferences and choice. *Behavioral Science*, Nov. 1972, 532–41.

[2] Beckwith, N. E., D. R. Lehmann. The importance of halo effects in multi-attribute attitude models. *Journal of Marketing Research*, Aug. 1975, 265–75.

[3] Boyer, A., K. S. Palda. Optimal development budgets tied to the marketing mix. *R & D Management*, Oct. 1975, 1–13.

[4] Cowling, K., J. Cubbin. Price, quality and advertising competition, *Economica*, Nov. 1971, 378–94.

[5] Dorfman, R., P. O. Steiner. Optimal advertising and optimal quality, *American Economic Review*, Dec. 1954, 826–36.

[6] Green, P. E. Marketing applications of MDS, *Journal of Marketing*, Jan. 1975, 24–31.

[7] Griliches, Z. Hedonic price indexes for automobiles, in *The price statistics of the federal government*, National Bureau of Economic Research: New York, 1961.

[8] Kotler, P. *Marketing management*. Prentice-Hall: Englewood Cliffs, 1976.

[9] Lambin, J. J., P. A. Naert, A. Bultez. Optimal marketing behavior in oligopoly. *European Economic Review*, 6, 1975, 105–28.

[10] Lancaster, K. *Consumer demand: a new approach*. Columbia University Press: New York, 1971.

[11] McCann, J. M., D. J. Reibstein, D. R. Wittink. *Market segmentation via derived importance weights*. Krannert School – Purdue University working paper No. 518, June 1975.

[12] Palda, K. S. The hypothesis of a hierarchy of effects. *Journal of Marketing Research*, Feb. 1966, 13–24.

[13] Palda, K. S., A. Boyer. *A unidimensional product quality index for marketing mix and R & D budget optimization*. Paper presented at the 1977 Saarbrücken meetings of the European Academy of Marketing.

[14] Ratchford, B. T., G. T. Ford. A study of prices and market shares in the computer main frame industry. *Journal of Business*, Apr. 1976, 194–218.

[15] Verdoorn, P. J. Marketing from the producer's point of view, *Journal of Marketing*, Jan. 1956, 221–35.

On Average and Variance of Demand Components in a Purchase Event-Purchase Quantity Model

J. VERHULP

1. INTRODUCTION

In this contribution we analyse demand and fluctuations in demand for certain types of consumer goods. We do this within the framework of a model where the total quantity purchased is defined as the multiplication of a number of components.[1] The starting point of our analysis is the quantity of standard units of (branded) consumer goods purchased by household i in time period t, its average and its variance.

To do this we take a stochastic approach. This is stochastic not in the first place in terms of sampling properties of certain estimators but in terms of variability on population level, i.e. the idea that the quantity purchased at a given purchase occasion can be considered a draw from a probability distribution governed by a set of parameters. From the work of Ehrenberg [2], Morrison [7] and Benishay [1], to mention some contributors to the field of study, we know that for a market researcher it makes sense to take this stochastic viewpoint, because it offers an explanation for empirically observed demand variability.

In the Sections 2, 3, 4 and 5, we develop a general framework for analysing average and variance of the various model components and of the demand total, on the individual level. In the Sections 6 and 7 we aggregate over N households respectively over a longer time period T.

In Section 8 we discuss an even more general case. In section 9 we propose some well-known probability distributions and their relevant properties, which could be used to model the individual behavior. Finally we give some results about population heterogeneity.

---

1. For other multiplicative models in the field of Marketing Research, compare Ferber and Verdoorn [1962, pp. 154–155] on income elasticities, and Verdoorn [1972, pp. 100–114] on 'Marktonderzoek en Marktbeleid').

2. THE BASIC MODEL

We postulate the following model

$$V_{it} = X_{it} \, Y_{it} \, Z_{it} \tag{1}$$

where

$V_{it} = 0, 1, 2, \ldots, m$; the physical number of standard units purchased by household i in period t.

$X_{it} = 0,1$; a dummy-variable which equals zero when in period t, household i does not make *any* purchase at all and unity otherwise.

$Y_{it} = 1, 2, 3, \ldots, l$; the number of purchase events [2, p. 56] for i in t, *conditional* upon $X_{it} = 1$.

$Z_{it} = 1, 2, 3, \ldots, f$; the number of standard units purchased on average per purchase event; for practical purposes we prefer Z_{it} to be a discrete stochastic variable, although we are aware of the basically continuous character of a variable which has been defined an average. Like Y_{it} this variable is conditional upon $X_{it} = 1$.

We prefer to define this model as a purchase event-purchase quantity model, because we explicitly take into consideration the amount purchased at any purchase occasion. In notes to Sections 4 and 5 we complete relation (1) with a value component (price) so that we can study average and variance of both quantities and values.

3. UNSPECIFIED CASE: MEAN AND VARIANCE OF V_{it}

When working with conditional variables like Y_{it} and Z_{it} it proves to be rewarding to make a distinction with respect to two cases. The first case is when $X_{it} = 1$, the second when $X_{it} = 0$. Let us introduce probability π_{it}, that $X_{it} = 1$ will be realized, and probability $(1 - \pi_{it})$, that it will be $X_{it} = 0$. In fact most of the time we consider the outcome X_{it} to be governed by a Bernouilli distribution with mean π_{it} and variance $\pi_{it} (1 - \pi_{it})$.[2]

So when π_{it} is the probability that household i will purchase at least one time in period t, when $\overline{V}_{it}(1)$ is the average number of standard purchased conditional upon $X_{it} = 1$, when $S^2_{V_{it}}(1)$ is the conditional variance, when it is

---

2. It will be clear that in this way we introduce independence between X and Y, Z. In Section 8 we analyse the case of dependence.

obvious that for the case $X_{it} = 0$ we can put $\overline{V}_{it}(0) = 0$ and $S^2_{V_{it}}(0) = 0$, we can verify with help of simple statistics

$$\overline{V}_{it} = \pi_{it} \, \overline{V}_{it}(1) + (1 - \pi_{it}) \, \overline{V}_{it}(0) \tag{2}$$
$$= \pi_{it} \, \overline{V}_{it}(1)$$

and

$$S^2_{V_{it}} = \pi_{it} S^2_{V_{it}}(1) + (1 - \pi_{it}) S^2_{V_{it}}(0) + \pi_{it}(\overline{V}_{it} - \overline{V}_{it}(1))^2 +$$
$$+ (1 - \pi_{it})(\overline{V}_{it} - \overline{V}_{it}(0))^2 =$$
$$= \pi_{it} S^2_{V_{it}}(1) + \pi_{it}(\overline{V}_{it} - \overline{V}_{it}(1))^2 + (1 - \pi_{it}) \overline{V}^2_{it}, \tag{3}$$

which with help of (2) can be rewritten as

$$S^2_{V_{it}} = \pi_{it} S_{V_{it}}(1) + \pi_{it}(1 - \pi_{it}) \overline{V}^2_{it}(1) \tag{4}$$

So the overall variance on the individual level can be expressed as a function of the conditional varince and conditional squared average, and the purchase probability (all for i in t).

Interesting for the explanation of variability in this respect, is the role played by π_{it} at given levels of the conditional variance and squared average: when $0 < \pi_{it} < .50$ increases of π_{it} result in increasing overall variance. What happens when $.50 < \pi_{it} < 1.00$ depends on the ratio between the conditional variance and the squared average.

4. UNSPECIFIED CASE; AVERAGE AND VARIANCE WHEN Y AND Z ARE INDEPENDENT

The expressions for the average and variance in case of independent variables Y and Z, i.e. no covariance between number of purchase events and purchased quantity, are rather simple to assemble, again by making a distinction for the 'no-purchase' and 'purchase' case. Knowing that $V_{it}(0) = 0$ when $X = 0$, $V_{it}(1) = Y_{it} Z_{it}$ when $X = 1$, it will be clear that

$$\overline{V}_{it}(1) = \overline{Y}_{it} \overline{Z}_{it} \tag{5}$$

in case of independent variables. From Goodman [4, p. 55] we know that the conditional variance can be expressed as

$$S^2_{V_{it}}(1) = \overline{Y}^2_{it} S^2_{Z_{it}} + \overline{Z}^2_{it} S^2_{Y_{it}} + S^2_{Y_{it}} S^2_{Z_{it}} \tag{6}$$

With help of the results (2) and (4) we can establish

$$\bar{V}_{it} = \pi_{it}\, \bar{V}_{it}(1) = \pi_{it}\, \bar{Y}_{it}\, \bar{Z}_{it} \tag{7}$$

and

$$S^2_{V_{it}} = \pi_{it}\, S^2_{V_{it}}(1) + \pi_{it}(1 - \pi_{it})\, \bar{V}^2_{it}(1)$$

$$= \pi_{it}\big[\bar{Y}^2_{it}\, S^2_{Z_{it}} + \bar{Z}^2_{it}\, S^2_{Y_{it}} + S^2_{Y_{it}}\, S^2_{Z_{it}}\big] + \pi_{it}(1 - \pi_{it})\, \bar{Y}^2_{it}\, \bar{Z}^2_{it} \tag{8}$$

so the average and variance of the quantity purchased are explicitly expressed in the first and second moments of the component stochastic variables.

Note: Sometimes we are confronted with multiplication of three or more independent components. For the general case of the variance of M components we refer to Goodman [4].

An interesting extension of our model can be achieved by taking into consideration the monetary dimension. For just this case, omitting lower indices

a. $V' = X\, Y\, Z\, P,$

where

P = average price paid
V' = value of purchased quantity

b. $\bar{V}'(1) = \bar{Y}\, \bar{Z}\, \bar{P}$

With help of the general definition by Goodman:

c. $$S^2(1) = \bar{Y}^2\, \bar{Z}^2\, \bar{P}^2 \left[\left(\frac{S^2_Y}{\bar{Y}^2} + 1\right)\left(\frac{S^2_Z}{\bar{Z}^2} + 1\right)\left(\frac{S^2_P}{\bar{P}^2} + 1\right) - 1 \right]$$

$$= \bar{Z}^2\, \bar{P}^2\, S^2_Y + \bar{Y}^2\, \bar{P}^2\, S^2_Z + \bar{Y}^2\, \bar{Z}^2\, S^2_P + \bar{P}^2\, S^2_Y\, S^2_Z +$$

$$+ \bar{Z}^2\, S^2_Y\, S^2_P + \bar{Y}^2\, S^2_Z\, S^2_P + S^2_Y\, S^2_Z\, S^2_P$$

Again with help of (2) and (4):

d. $\bar{V}' = \pi\, \bar{Y}\, \bar{Z}\, \bar{P}$

e. $$S^2 = \pi\big[\bar{Z}^2\, \bar{P}^2\, S^2_Y + \bar{Y}^2\, \bar{P}^2\, S^2_Z + \bar{Y}^2\, \bar{Z}^2\, S^2_P + \bar{P}^2\, S^2_Y\, S^2_Z + \bar{Z}^2\, S^2_Y\, S^2_P +$$

$$+ \bar{Y}^2\, S^2_Z\, S^2_P + S^2_Y\, S^2_Z\, S^2_P\big] + \pi(1 - \pi)\, \bar{Y}^2\, \bar{Z}^2\, \bar{P}^2$$

5. UNSPECIFIED CASE; AVERAGE AND VARIANCE WHEN Y AND Z ARE DEPENDENT

We can imagine that for the case of a number of consumer goods – e.g. food items – independence of number of purchase events and quantity purchased will be more the exception than the rule. Modern 'wheeled consumers' often purchase infrequently but in large quantities, while other types of consumers (older people for example) purchase at high frequency (nearly every day) but in rather small quantities.

For this case we develop as in Section 5; it can be easily demonstrated that $V_{it}(1)$ will be

$$\bar{V}_{it}(1) = \bar{Y}_{it}\,\bar{Z}_{it} + \text{Cov}\,[Y_{it},\,Z_{it}] \tag{9}$$
$$= \bar{Y}_{it}\,\bar{Z}_{it} + E[y_{it}\,z_{it}]$$

where $y_{it} = Y_{it} - \bar{Y}$, etc.

From Goodman [4. p. 58] we borrow the result with respect to the conditional variance

$$S^2_{V_{it}}(1) = \bar{Y}^2\,\bar{Z}^2 \left\{ E\left[\left(\frac{Y_{it}}{\bar{Y}_{it}}\right)^2 \left(\frac{Z_{it}}{\bar{Z}_{it}}\right)^2 \right] - \left[\frac{E(Y_{it}Z_{it})}{\bar{Y}_{it}\bar{Z}_{it}}\right]^2 \right\} \tag{10}$$

So again with help of (2) and (4)

$$\bar{V}_{it} = \pi_{it}\,\bar{V}_{it}(1) = \pi_{it}\,[\bar{Y}_{it}\,\bar{Z}_{it} + E(y_{it}\,z_{it})] \tag{11}$$

and

$$S^2_{V_{it}} = \pi_{it}\,\bar{Y}^2_{it}\,\bar{Z}^2_{it} \left\{ E\left[\left(\frac{Y_{it}}{\bar{Y}_{it}}\right)^2 \left(\frac{Z_{it}}{\bar{Z}_{it}}\right)^2 \right] - \left[\frac{E(Y_{it}Z_{it})}{\bar{Y}_{it}\bar{Z}_{it}}\right]^2 \right\} +$$
$$+ \pi_{it}(1 - \pi_{it})\,\{\bar{Y}_{it}\bar{Z}_{it} + E(y_{it}\,z_{it})\}^2 \tag{12}$$

NOTE: As before we may wonder about the situation with more than two dependent variables. When again we introduce a third depending variable P for average price, the result for the conditional average and variance will be as follows.

It can be easily verified (again without lower indices) that

a. $\bar{V}(1) = \bar{X}\,\bar{Z}\,\bar{P} + \bar{Y}\,E(z\,p) + \bar{Z}\,E(y\,p) + \bar{P}\,E(y\,z) + E(y\,z\,p)$

where $y = Y - \bar{Y}$, etc.

Using Goodman's formula again:

b. $S^2_V(1) = \bar{Y}^2\,\bar{Z}^2\,\bar{P}^2 \left\{ E\left[\left(\frac{Y}{\bar{Y}}\right)^2 \left(\frac{Z}{\bar{Z}}\right)^2 \left(\frac{P}{\bar{P}}\right)^2 \right] - \left[\frac{E(Y\,Z\,P)}{\bar{Y}\,\bar{Z}\,\bar{P}}\right]^2 \right\}$

For V and S^2_V, compare the derivations c) and d) in Section 4 above.

6. AGGREGATION OVER N HOUSEHOLDS, TIME PERIOD t

In this section we pay attention to the average and variance of variables on the level of the total market, i.e. when we aggregate the individual values over N households. From the point of view of the user of market research output, at least four outcomes are important:

1. How many households have been effective buyers in period t (purchased at least one time or one standard unit): N_e? Alternatively as proportion: N_e/N?
2. How many purchase events took place in period t?
3. How much was the overall average quantity purchased?
4. How much was the total quantity purchased in t?

With respect to these how many/much questions, we are again interested in average level and variance, which are dealt with in the next 4 subsections.

6.1. *The Number or Proportion of Effective Buyers (Households)*
The number of purchasing households can be defined as

$$N_t(e) = \sum_{i=1}^{N} X_{it} \tag{13}$$

On average this number will be

$$\bar{N}_t(e) = E[N_t(e)] = E\left[\sum_{i=1}^{N} X_{it}\right] = \sum_{i=1}^{N} E[X_{it}] = \sum_{i=1}^{N} \bar{X}_{it} = \sum_{i=1}^{N} \pi_{it} \tag{14}$$

The variance will be

$$S_{N_t(e)}^2 = \sum_{i=1}^{N} S_{X_{it}}^2 = \sum_{i=1}^{N} \pi_{it}(1 - \pi_{it}) \tag{15}$$

in case of independent Bernouilli-trials.
  More commonly expressed in terms of proportions

$$\frac{N_t(e)}{N} = \frac{1}{N}\sum_{i=1}^{N} X_{it} \tag{16}$$

with average

$$\frac{\bar{N}_t(e)}{N} = \frac{\sum_{i=1}^{N} \bar{X}_{it}}{N} = \frac{\sum_{i=1}^{N} \pi_{it}}{N}, \tag{17}$$

and variance

$$S^2_{N_t(e)} = \frac{1}{N^2} S^2_{N_t(e)} = \frac{1}{N^2} \sum_{i=1}^{N} S^2_{X_{it}} = \frac{1}{N^2} \sum_{i=1}^{N} \pi_{it}(1 - \pi_{it}) \qquad (18)$$

6.2. The Number of Purchase Events in t
We define the total number of purchase events in t

$$Y_t = \sum_{i=1}^{N_t(e)} Y_{it} \qquad (19)$$

The long run expectation of this variable will be

$$\bar{Y}_t = E\left[\sum_{i=1}^{N_t(e)} Y_{it}\right] = \sum_{i=1}^{N_t(e)} \bar{Y}_{it} \qquad (20)$$

The general expression for the variance of Y_t can be developed with help of pooling as in section 3. The result is (ignoring covariances):

$$S^2_{Y_t} = \sum_{i=1}^{N} \pi_{it} S^2_{Y_{it}} + \pi_{it}(1 - \pi_{it}) \bar{Y}^2_{it}, \qquad (21)$$

In case of homogeneity with respect to Y:

$$S^2_{Y_t} = S^2_{Y(t)} \bar{N}_t(e) + \bar{Y}^2_{(t)} S^2_{N_t(e)}, \qquad (22)$$

where $S^2_{Y(t)}$ and $\bar{Y}^2_{(t)}$ are constant over the population.[3]

6.3. The overall average quantity purchased in t
We defined the stochastic variable Z_{it} as the number of standard units per purchase event. Again omitting the lower index i to indicate the overall character:

$$\bar{Z}_t(e) = \frac{1}{N_t(e)} \sum_{i=1}^{N_t(e)} \bar{Z}_{it}, \qquad 22^*$$

over the population of effective buyers; in this subsection we assume $N(e)$ to be fixed,

$$\bar{Z}_t = \frac{1}{N} \sum_{i=1}^{N_t(e)} \bar{Z}_{it}, \qquad (22^{**})$$

over the total population.

3 The result (22) is given by Benishay [1], p. 298.

With respective variances:

$$S^2_{Z_t(e)} = \frac{1}{N_t(e)^2} \left[\sum_{i=1}^{N_t(e)} S^2_{Z_{it}} + \sum_i \sum_j \text{Covar}(Z_{it}, Z_{jt}) \right] i, j = 1 \dots N_t(e)$$

$$(22^{***})$$

$$S^2_{Z_t} = \frac{1}{N^2} \left[\sum_{i=1}^{N_t(e)} S^2_{Z_{it}} + \sum_i \sum_j \text{Covar}(Z_{it}, Z_{ji}) \right] i, j = 1 \dots N \tag{23}$$

6.4. *The total quantity purchased in t.*

The long range expected total quantity purchased can be denoted as $\bar{V}_t$, when we define

$$V_t = \sum_{i=1}^{N} V_{it},$$

it can be verified that:

$$\bar{V}_t = \sum_{i=1}^{N} \bar{V}_{it} \tag{24}$$

which with help of (11) can be rewritten for the most general case

$$\bar{V}_t = \sum_{i=1}^{N} \pi_{it} \left[\bar{Y}_{it} \bar{Z}_{it} + E(y_{it} z_{it}) \right] \tag{25}$$

The variance can be expressed as

$$S^2_{V_t} = \sum_{i=1}^{N} S^2_{V_{it}} + 2 \sum_i^N \sum_j^N \text{Covar}(V_{it}, V_{jt}) \, i, j = 1, \dots, N \tag{26}$$

With help of (12) for the most general case

$$S^2_{V_t} = \sum_{i=1}^{N} (\pi_{it} \, \bar{Y}^2_{it} \, \bar{Z}^2_{it}) \left\{ E \left[\left(\frac{Y_{it}}{\bar{Y}_{it}} \right)^2 \left(\frac{Z_{it}}{\bar{Z}_{it}} \right)^2 \right] - \left[\frac{E(Y_{it} Z_{it})}{\bar{Y}_{it} \bar{Z}_{it}} \right]^2 \right\} +$$

$$+ \pi_{it}(1 - \pi_{it}) \left\{ \bar{Y}_{it} \bar{Z}_{it} + E(y_{it} z_{it}) \right\}^2 + 2 \sum_i^N \sum_j^N \text{Covar}(V_{it}, V_{jt})$$

$$(27)$$

The formulae (25) and (27) clearly indicate the potential sources of variation with respect to total period-demand. The reader may verify the effect of certain simplifications as total or partial independence, non-stochastic components, etc.

7. AGGREGATION OVER N HOUSEHOLDS, TIME PERIOD T

The behaviour of components and total can be studies over time. When T is a period of time of length Kt, when $K > 1$, it will be interesting to know the additional sources of variation introduced by aggregating over time. For this case we focus on the behaviour of the total quantity purchased in a time period T, under conditions of stationarity with respect to the parameters of the individual distributions of X, Y and Z. We define:

$$V_T = \sum_{t=1}^{K} \sum_{i=1}^{N} V_{it} \tag{28}$$

$$\bar{V}_T = E[V_T] = \sum_{t=1}^{K} \sum_{i=1}^{N} \bar{V}_{it} = \sum_{t=1}^{K} \bar{V}_t = K \bar{V}_t \tag{29}$$

With help of (11) again

$$\bar{V}_T = K \sum_{i=1}^{N} \pi_{it} [\bar{Y}_{it} \bar{Z}_{it} + E(y_{it} z_{it})] \tag{30}$$

The development of the variance causes some trouble, i.e. it is rather difficult to find an elegant shorthand notation. We chose the following solution.

From the general formula* for the variance of sums of variables, it is clear that together with a number of individual variances (equal to the number of variables in the total sum), we need a number of covariance terms, which equals the number of combinations which can be permuted from the number of variables in the sum. With N households and K periods, there result (KN) individual variances and $\binom{KN}{2}$ combinations with respect to covariances. A number of these terms will be constant because of the assumption of stationarity. When the individual observations V_{it} are arranged in matrix form, so that in the rows we find the N values for a given t, and in the columns the K individual values for a given household, than we can number the elements of that matrix from left to right as 1, 2, ..., (NK). The variance can be written as

$$S_{V_T}^2 = \sum_{i=1}^{N} \sum_{t=1}^{K} S_{V_{it}}^2 + \sum_{g=1}^{(KN-1)} \sum_{h=g+1}^{KN} \text{Covar}(V_g, V_h) \tag{31}$$

In case of stationarity $S_{V_{it}}^2$ is constant over time so that the first term on the right can be expressed as

*. [6, p. 178].

$$\sum_{i=1}^{N} \sum_{t=1}^{K} S_{V_{it}}^2 = K \sum_{i=1}^{N} S_{V_{it}}^2$$

It seems reasonable to assume that only a small number of covariance terms will have an important effect on the variance, i.e. a number of $N \times \binom{K}{2}$ co-variances which describe the dependence between V_{it_1} and V_{it_2}, etc.

Because of stationarity it will be true that

$$\text{Covar }(V_{i,_1}, V_{it_2}) = \text{Covar }(V_{it_2}, V_{it_3}), \text{ etc.}$$

So per household i about $\binom{K}{2}$ times the 'same' covariance

$$\binom{K}{2} \text{Covar }(V_{it_1}, V_{it_2})$$

Under these conditions the second term on the right of (31) can be written as

$$\sum_{i=1}^{N} \binom{K}{2} \text{Covar }(V_{it_1}, V_{it_2}) = \binom{K}{2} \sum_{i=1}^{N} \text{Covar }(V_{it_1}, V_{it_2})$$

The whole expression (31) rewritten

$$S_{V_T}^2 = K \sum_{i=1}^{N} S_{V_{it}}^2 + \binom{K}{2} \sum_{i=1}^{N} \text{Covar }(V_{it_1}, V_{it_2}) \qquad (32)$$

for the case of negligible cross-covariances.

8. DEPENDENCE BETWEEN X AND Y (AND Z)

The outcomes in the above sections were based on the assumption of independence between X and the other variables. We think this will be an important case in the empirical world. Moreover it will not always be possible to find probability distributions for Y and Z which with respect to the probabilities $Pr(Y) = 0$ and $Pr(Y) > 0$ (and so for Z) will show satisfactory fit to empirical distributions.

Nevertheless the case of dependence is an interesting one, so with the help of the definitions given before, we will pay some attention to it. In this section we define:

$V_{it} = 0, 1, 2, \ldots, m$
$X_{it} = 0, 1$

$Y_{it} = 0, 1, 2, ..., 1;$ $Y_{it} = 0$ if $X_{it} = 0$
$$Y_{it} > 1 \text{ if } X_{it} = 1$$
$Z_{it} = 0, 1, 2, ..., f;$ $Z_{it} = 0$ if $X_{it} = 0$
$$Z_{it} > 1 \text{ if } X_{it} = 1$$

Applying a and b from the note to section 5 we find

$$\overline{V}_{it} = \overline{X}_{it} \, \overline{Y}_{it} \, \overline{Z}_{it} + \overline{X}_{it} \, E\,(y_{it}\, z_{it}) + \overline{Y}_{it} \, E\,(x_{it}\, z_{it}) + \tag{33}$$
$$\overline{Z}_{it} \, E\,(x_{it}\, y_{it}) + E(x_{it}\, y_{it}\, z_{it})$$

and

$$S^2_{V_{it}} = (\overline{X}_{it} \, \overline{Y}_{it} \, \overline{Z}_{it})^2 \left\{ E\left[\left(\frac{X_{it}}{\overline{X}_{it}}\right)^2 \left(\frac{Y_{it}}{\overline{Y}_{it}}\right)^2 \left(\frac{Z_{it}}{\overline{Z}_{it}}\right)^2 \right] - \left[\frac{E\,(X_{it}\, Y_{it}\, Z_{it})}{\overline{X}_{it} \, \overline{Y}_{it} \, \overline{Z}_{it}} \right]^2 \right\}$$
$$\tag{34}$$

Interpreting these results we have to hold in mind the fact that in this section $\overline{Y}_{it}$ and $\overline{Z}_{it}$ are the averages over the variables Y_{it} and Z_{it} as defined above, i.e. variables which can take zero values.

As before $\overline{V}_t$, $S^2_{V_t}$, $\overline{V}_T$, $S^2_{V_T}$ can be derived by substitution of (33) and (34) in the relevant expressions (24), (26), (28) and (31).

The dependence between X and Y (and Z) in this section is of a special kind: Whenever $X=0$, the $Y=0$ and $Z=0$. Whenever $X=1$, then $Y>1$ and $Z>1$, a case for which it will be very difficult to find an appropriate multivariate distribution.

Ehrenberg introduces dependence between X and Y in a very elegant, but at the same time restrictive way, by postulating a Poisson distribution over the variable $V=(XY)$.

The parameter λ of the distribution (the average number of purchase events) determines the purchase probability π, that is the cumulative probability of $V>1$. But the relationship between λ and π is very specific, so that for a number of empirical situations it would be more convenient to proceed under the assumption of independence.

9. SOME PROBABILITY DISTRIBUTIONS, THEIR AVERAGE AND VARIANCE

From an analytical point of view it is interesting to reflect about probability distributions describing behaviour on the individual level. We can substitute their averages and variances in the general formulae to get a more specific picture of average and variance, say with respect to the individual level, the aggregated level in t and that in T.

For X_{it} we can think of the Bernouilli distribution as being adequate; for the sake of simplicity we omit lower indices

$$f(X) = \pi^X (1 - \pi)^{1-X}, \quad X = 0,1 \tag{35}$$

$$\overline{X} = \pi \tag{36}$$

$$S_X^2 = \pi (1 - \pi) \tag{37}$$

For Y_{it} we need discrete distributions, which for the conditional case are truncated, so that Y will be restricted to the domain $Y = 1, 2, 3, \ldots$ Two potential candidates are the Poisson distribution and the Geometric distribution. For the truncated Poisson distribution

$$f(Y) = \frac{\lambda^Y e^{-\lambda}}{Y! \, (1 - e^{-\lambda})} \quad Y = 1, 2, 3 \ \ldots \tag{38}$$

It can be shown that the average will be

$$\overline{Y} = \frac{\lambda}{1 - e^{-\lambda}} \tag{39}$$

and the variance

$$S_Y^2 = \overline{Y} \frac{1 - e^{-\lambda} - \lambda e^{-\lambda}}{1 - e^{-\lambda}} \tag{40}$$

So for the truncated Poisson distribution, mean and variance are not exactly equal. However in case of relatively high values of λ (which can be realized by proper choice of the time period t) we may approximate the term within brackets by unity, so that mean and variance will be about equal to each other.

Just like the non-truncated Poisson distribution the truncated distribution has only one parameter.

The truncated Geometric distribution will possibly show good fit to purchase behaviour, when just one purchase event in t is the modal case with probability P.

$$f(Y) = P(1 - P)^{Y-1} \tag{41}$$

with average

$$Y = \frac{1}{P} \tag{42}$$

and variance

$$S_Y^2 = \frac{1 - P}{P^2} \tag{43}$$

For the average quantity purchased, Z_{it}, again the Geometric and the Poisson distribution may be used. For higher values of the Poisson-parameter λ, the Normal distribution with parameters μ_z and σ_z^2 can be used as an approximation.

Dependence between components can be modelled by a Poisson distribution for the configuration of X and Y, and approximately, by a Bivariate Normal distribution for the dependence between Y and Z, in case of relatively high values for λ_x and λ_z. The covariance between Y and Z can be expressed as

$$\text{Covar } (Y, Z) = \rho \sigma_Y \sigma_Z$$

where ρ stands for the coefficient of correlation between Y and Z, and σ_Y and σ_Z are standard deviations.

Substitution of the averages and variances of relevant distributions in the general formulae V_{it} provides us with a specific insight into the contribution of the various parameters to $\overline{V}_{it}$ and $S_{V_{it}}^2$.

When certain assumptions are made regarding population heterogeneity, i.e. the distribution of parameters over the population of N households, it will be possible to find specific expressions for $\overline{V}_t$, $S_{V_t}^2$, $\overline{V}_t$ and $S_{V_T}^2$ (results for the aggregated level).

Heterogeneity among households with respect to the parameter π_{it} of the Bernouilli distribution or the parameter P of the Geometric distribution can be described with help of a Beta distribution with parameters α and β[4].

As an example for P

$$f(P) = \frac{\Gamma(\alpha + \beta)}{\Gamma(\alpha)\, \Gamma(\beta)}\, P^{\alpha-1} (1 - P)^{\beta-1} \qquad 0 < P < 1 \qquad (44)$$

$$\alpha > 0$$

$$\beta > 0$$

with average

$$\overline{P} = \frac{\alpha}{\alpha + \beta} \tag{45}$$

and variance

$$S_p^2 = \frac{\alpha \beta}{(\alpha + \beta)^2 (\alpha + \beta + 1)} \tag{46}$$

---

4. [5, p. 60], the authors speak of a Compound Beta Bernouilli model.

Heterogeneity with respect to the Poisson parameter λ can be described by a Gamma distribution with parameters γ and ϕ

$$f(\lambda) = \frac{1}{\Gamma(\gamma)\,\phi^\gamma}\,\lambda^{\gamma-1}\,e^{-\lambda/\phi}, \qquad 0 < \lambda < +\infty \tag{47}$$

$$\gamma > 0$$

$$\phi > 0$$

with average

$$\bar{\lambda} = \gamma\phi \tag{48}$$

and variance

$$S_\lambda^2 = \gamma\phi^2 \tag{49}$$

This is the case of a 'Gamma mixture of Poissons' or a 'Compound Poisson Model'*. Ehrenberg postulated a Poisson distribution for Y_{it}', the number of purchase events (unconditional: $Y_{it}' = 0, 1, 2, \ldots$), and a gamma distribution of $\lambda(Y_{it}')$ over the population of N households. He showed that for that case the distribution of the number of purchase events in t over N households, will be a Negative Binomial one with average equal to the average of the Gamma distribution.

We now illustrate the case of X, Y and Z independent, where X has the Bernouilli distribution and Y and Z (conditional upon $X = 1$) have truncated Poisson distributions. For simplicity we omit lower indices;

We know

$$V = X\,Y\,Z \tag{1}$$

$$\bar{V} = \pi\,\bar{Y}\,\bar{Z} \tag{7}$$

with help of (39)

$$\bar{V} = \pi\,\frac{\lambda(Y)}{1 - e^{-\lambda(Y)}} \cdot \frac{\lambda(Z)}{1 - e^{-\lambda(Z)}} \tag{50}$$

Considering:

$$S_V^2 = \pi\left[\bar{Y}S_Z^2 + \bar{Z}S_Y^2 + S_Y^2 S_Z^2\right] + \pi(1 - \pi)\,\bar{Y}^2\bar{Z}^2, \tag{8}$$

* [6, p.123].

Substituting for variances,

$$S_V^2 = \pi \left[\overline{Y}^2 \overline{Z} \left(\frac{1 - e^{-\lambda(Z)} - \lambda(Z) e^{-\lambda(Z)}}{1 - e^{-\lambda(Z)}} \right) + \right.$$

$$+ \overline{Y} Z^2 \left(\frac{1 - e^{-\lambda(Y)} - \lambda(Y) e^{-\lambda(Y)}}{1 - e^{-\lambda(Y)}} \right) +$$

$$+ \overline{Y} \overline{Z} \left(\frac{1 - e^{-\lambda(Z)} - \lambda(Z) e^{-\lambda(Z)}}{1 - e^{-\lambda(Z)}} \right)$$

$$\left. \left(\frac{1 - e^{-\lambda(Y)} - \lambda(Y) e^{-\lambda(Y)}}{1 - e^{-\lambda(Y)}} \right) \right] + \pi (1 - \pi) \overline{Y}^2 \overline{Z}^2 \tag{51}$$

Terms like $\lambda(\cdot) e^{-\lambda(\cdot)}$ will be small positive numbers approaching zero when $\lambda(.)$ increases. So we may write:

$$S_V^2 \approx \pi \left[\overline{Y}^2 \overline{Z} + \overline{Y} \overline{Z}^2 + \overline{Y} \overline{Z} \right] + \pi (1 - \pi) \left[\overline{Y}^2 \overline{Z}^2 \right], \tag{52}$$

which for purchase probabilities close to unity may be approximated

$$S_V^2 \approx \overline{Y}^2 \overline{Z} + \overline{Y} \overline{Z}^2 + \overline{Y} \overline{Z} = \overline{Y} \overline{Z} (\overline{Y} + \overline{Z} + 1) \tag{53}$$

10. SOME APPROXIMATIONS IN CASE OF KNOWN HETEROGENEITY; X, Y AND Z INDEPENDENT

Within the framework of this contribution it is not possible to fully analyse all modes of aggregation dealt with in Section 6. Just for the purpose of illustration we aggregate over N households in period t, under the assumptions of Section 9.

Definition:

$$V_t = \sum_{i=1}^N V_{it}$$

under our assumptions

$$E(V_t) = \overline{V}_t = \sum_{i=1}^N \pi_{it} \overline{Y}_{it} \overline{Z}_{it} \tag{25}$$

Parameters are defined as averages on the *individual* level. When we denote $\pi_{.t}$, $\overline{Y}_{.t}$ and $\overline{Z}_{.t}$ as averages over N households, it will be clear that – under our assumption of independence – we may write alternatively

$$\overline{V}_t = N \pi_{.t} \overline{Y}_{.t} \overline{Z}_{.t} \tag{54}$$

For the case of a Beta distribution of π_{it}, Gamma distributions of $\lambda(Y)_{it}$ and $\lambda(Z)_{it}$, we find

$$\pi_{.t} = \frac{\alpha}{\alpha + \beta} \tag{55}$$

$$\overline{Y}_{.t} = \frac{\lambda_{Y_{.t}}}{1 - \exp(-\lambda_{Y_{.t}})} = \frac{\gamma_Y \phi_Y}{1 - \exp(-\gamma_Y \phi_Y)} \tag{56}$$

$$\overline{Z}_{.t} = \frac{\lambda_{Z_{.t}}}{1 - \exp(-\lambda_{Z_{.t}})} = \frac{\gamma_Z \phi_Z}{1 - \exp(-\gamma_Z \phi_Z)} \tag{57}$$

and so

$$\overline{V}_t = \frac{N\alpha}{\alpha + \beta} \cdot \frac{\gamma_Y \phi_Y \gamma_Z \phi_Z}{(1 - \exp[-\gamma_Y \phi_Y])(1 - \exp[-\gamma_Z \phi_Z])} \tag{58}$$

which for the case of $\lambda_{Y_{it}}$ and $\lambda_{Z_{it}}$ not too small may be approximated by

$$\overline{V}_t \approx \frac{N\alpha}{\alpha + \beta} \gamma_Y \phi_Y \gamma_Z \phi_Z \tag{59}$$

With respect to variance we know for this case of independence

$$S_{V_t}^2 = \sum_{i=1}^{N} S_{V_{it}}^2 ; \tag{26}$$

substitution of (8)

$$S_{V_t}^2 = \sum_{i=1}^{N} \left[\pi_{it} \{ \overline{Y}_{it}^2 S_{Z_{it}}^2 + \overline{Z}_{it}^2 S_{Y_{it}}^2 + S_{Y_{it}}^2 S_{Z_{it}}^2 \} + \pi_{it}(1 - \pi_{it}) \overline{Y}_{it}^2 \overline{Z}_{it}^2 \right] \tag{60}$$

In case of relatively large values for the Poisson parameters we may substitute $S_{Z_{it}}^2 \approx \overline{Z}_{it}$ and $S_{Y_{it}}^2 \approx \overline{Y}_{it}$

$$S_{V_t}^2 = \sum_{i=1}^{N} \left[\pi_{it} \{ \overline{Y}_{it}^2 \overline{Z}_{it} + \overline{Z}_{it}^2 \overline{Y}_{it} + \overline{Y}_{it} \overline{Z}_{it} \} + \pi_{it}(1 - \pi_{it}) \overline{Y}_{it}^2 \overline{Z}_{it}^2 \right] \tag{61}$$

Terms like

$$\sum_{i=1}^{N} \pi_{it} \overline{Y}_{it}^2 \overline{Z}_{it}$$

may for independent components be approximated by

$N . E(\pi_{it}) E(\overline{Y}_{it}^2) E(\overline{Z}_{it})$, where the expectation is defined over N households.

Again when the Poisson parameters are relatively large we may approximate:

$$E[\bar{Y}_{it}^2] \approx E[\lambda(Y)_{it}^2] = Var\,\lambda(Y)_{it} + E[\lambda(Y)_{it}]^2$$

In case of a Gamma distribution for $\lambda(Y)_{it}$, with help of (48) and (49):

$$Var\,\lambda(Y)_{it} = \gamma_Y\,\phi_Y^2\,; \tag{62}$$

$$[E\,\lambda(Y)_{it}]^2 = \gamma_Y^2\,\phi_Y^2 \tag{63}$$

so that we may approximate:

$$\sum_{i=1}^{N} \pi_{it}\,\bar{Y}_{it}^2\,\bar{Z}_{it} \sim N\cdot\frac{\alpha}{\alpha+\beta+1}\cdot(\gamma_Y\,\phi_Y^2 + \gamma_Y^2\,\phi_Y^2)\cdot\gamma_Z\,\phi_Z$$

The variance $S_{V_t}^2$ may, under our assumptions, be approximated by:

$$S_{V_t}^2 \approx \frac{N\alpha}{\alpha+\beta}\left[(\gamma_Y\,\phi_Y^2 + \gamma_Y^2\,\phi_Y^2)\,(\gamma_Z\,\phi_Z) + \right.$$

$$+ (\gamma_Z\,\phi_Z^2 + \gamma_Z^2\,\phi_Z^2)\,(\gamma_Y\,\phi_Y) + (\gamma_Y\,\phi_Y\,\gamma_Z\,\phi_Z)] +$$

$$\left.+ \frac{N\alpha\beta}{\alpha+\beta}\left[(\gamma_Y\,\phi_Y^2 + \gamma_Y^2\,\phi_Y^2)\,(\gamma_Z\,\phi_Z^2 + \gamma_Z^2\,\phi_Z^2)\right]. \tag{63}$$

Again, a rather simple expression in terms of parameter of the Beta and Gamma distributions, which describe population heterogeneity.

11. SOME CONCLUSIONS

We defined a purchase event-purchase quantity model on the level of the individual household, and showed the behaviour of average and variance of purchased quantities under various assumptions.

From the most general formulae it is clear that a great number of factors affect average and variance of total demand, results only becoming manageable by ignoring covariances and cross-covariances.

In the last sections we proposed some well-known probability distributions, to describe individual behaviour and the behaviour of individual parameters over the population.

As an illustration, we roughly approximated mean and average of total demand, in a period t for the case of known individual Bernouilli and truncated Poisson distributions, and known heterogeneity as described by Beta and Gamma distributions.

REFERENCES

[1] Haskel Benishay. Random Sums of Random Variables as Economic Processes: Sales. *Journal of Marketing Research*, August, 1967, pp. 296–302.
[2] A. S. C. Ehrenberg. *Repeat-Buying, Theory and Applicatoins*. Amsterdam-London, 1972.
[3] Robert Ferber and P. J. Verdoorn. *Research Methods in Economics and Business*. New-York, 1962.
[4] Leo A. Goodman. The Variance of the Product of K Random Variables. *American Statistical Association Journal*, March 1962, pp. 54–60.
[5] W. F. Massey, D. B. Montgomery and D. G. Morrison. *Stochastic Models of Buying Behavior*. Cambridge, Mass., 1970.
[6] A. M. Mood, F. A. Graybill, D. C. Boes. *Introduction to the Theory of Statistics*. Third Ed., Tokyo, 1974.
[7] Donald G. Morrison. A Stochastic Interpretation of the Heavy Half. *Journal of Marketing Research*, May, 1968, pp. 194–198.
[8] P. J. Verdoorn. Marktonderzoek en Marktbeleid. *Maandblad voor Accountancy en Bedrijfshuishoudkunde*, Vol. 46, 1972, pp. 100–114.

Advertising, Market Structure and Performance: A Re-interpretation of Emperical Findings on the Compatibility of Advertising and Competition*

A. VAN DER ZWAN*

1. INTRODUCTION

The distinction between 'selling costs' and 'production costs' occupies an important place in economic thinking in catering for the market by the sellers. The first systematic treatment of selling costs in economic theory is often considered to be that of Chamberlin [1933]. Braithwaite's contribution [1928] is thereby neglected, though her treatment of the problem of selling costs was formulated in reference terms that to a great extent coincide with the conceptions put forward by Chamberlin.

In both of these studies, the costs of adapting the product to demand are regarded as true costs of production, including those of packing, sorting and grading, holding, transport and that of bringing buyer and seller together, because these are considered payments for services indispensable to the marketing of commodities. They, however, regard selling costs as different in nature, because they are thought to represent 'expenditure by the seller, not in putting the goods on the market, but in inducing the buyer to accept them'.[1]

Kaldor [1950–51][2] has stressed the arbitrariness in this distinction between selling costs aimed at adapting demand to the product as opposed to costs of production aimed at adapting the product to demand. The setting of the demarcation line between adaptation of product and demand involves the judgement of the investigator, since no sensible distinction can be drawn between the manufacturer's expenditures on styling the commodity and on its subsequent promotion on the market. Knight [1921] had already raised this question of the causal distinction of a utility inherent in the commodity itself from the utility added in the process of creating the demand for a

---

* Part of the material presented here was included in a paper for the Nijenrode Conference on Industrial Organization, 9–14 August 1976.
1. Braithwaite [1928], p. 17.
2. Kaldor [1950–51], pp. 22–23.

commodity.[3] This contradictory view does not merely stem from the difference in Knight's outlook, namely the point of view of the entrepreneur who has to cope with risk and uncertainty in questions of marketing policy and who will, apart from its effectiveness, be indifferent in regard to the choice of his instruments – either product quality and variety or selling and promotional effort – as long as these contribute to the reduction of his risks.

Chamberlin and Braithwaite did not give full credit to the fact that the functions to be performed by the market in the case of industrial products not only comprise the bringing of buyer and seller together and the fixing of the conditions of sale, but also the specification of the products to be manufactured. In farming, as compared with manufacturing, there is limited opportunity for choice regarding variations in characteristics of products, while the manufacturer's problem essentially consists of making an independent choice in regard to the great range of feasible variations in the finished product. In this connection, Phelps [1937] launched the concept of anticipation[4]: 'Unless a manufacturer has orders in advance, he must *anticipate* what consumer wants and choices will be. Thus in many cases, production is directed, not by consumers' choices in the first instance, but by *anticipation* on the part of producers of what consumers' choices will be. The tool which the business man must then use is *observation* of the market'.

Kaldor[5] also underlined this point of the complexity and the greater range of variation of industrial products of which only a small fraction can, economically speaking, actually be made available on the market. He proposed the term *initiation* for the notion for which Phelps phrased his anticipation. Here lies the origin of the imperfections of the markets for industrial goods. Because the necessary degree of standardization across the market cannot be achieved and thereby goodwill not eliminated, hence the unity of the market cannot be assured as is the case with staple commodities.

Selling costs can arise at all stages in the process of manufacture and distribution, in so far as the commodity produced embodies special features, and/or is sold jointly with complementary services in the form of advertising and promotion. Two contradictory visions can be developed in regard to the incurrence of selling costs in particular commodities. Consistent with her

---

3. Knight [1921], p. 339. Cf. Preface to the re-issue, pp. XIII–XIV (Series of Reprints of Scarce Tracts in Economic and Political Science, The London School of Economics and Political Science, 1933). See also Triffin [1940], p. 169 n.
4. Phelps [1937], p. 74.
5. Kaldor [1950–51], p. 16.

treatment of selling costs, Braithwaite argued that with 'advertised' commodities it cannot be said that the price tends to equal the cost of production: 'For the price does not tend to be equal to the 'true' cost of production of the commodity, but to that amount plus what the producer thinks it worthwhile to add in the way of advertisement costs'.[6] This reference to the work of Braithwaite cannot go without explicitly mentioning that she recognised the important possibility that advertisement may affect the cost of manufacture (including the indispensable marketing costs) and that, therefore, the final price of the commodity may be lowered although it includes the cost of advertisement. She objected to the idea about advertisement costs as payments for services which bear fruit in the new valuation of the commodity arrived at by the consumer.

Telser [1964], in his well-known article, took the opposite view, and by means of a straightforward extension of the classical theory he took into account the product variety offered to consumers within a commodity class. Thus he argued that consumers face a price schedule such that 'price differentials among the various models reflect the marginal costs of the different specifications'.[7] He extended this argumentation by treating advertising as an input supplied jointly with the physical product. Telser could have referred to one of his predecessors at the University of Chicago, who made the following evaluation nearly 45 years before: 'The outstanding fact is that the ubiquitous presence of uncertainty permeating every relation of life has brought it about that information is one of the principal commodities that economic organization is engaged in supplying. From this point of view it is not material whether the 'information' is false or true, or whether it is merely hypnotic suggestion. As in all other spheres of competitive economic activity, the consumer is the final judge. ... If a certain name on a fountain pen or safety razor enables it to sell at a fifty per cent higher price than the same article would otherwise fetch, then the name represents one third of the economic utility in the article, and is economically no different from its colour or design or the quality of the point or cutting edge, or any quality which makes it useful or appealing'.[8]

Illustrative of the problematic character of the issue is the circumstance that Knight, who is the author of this quotation, in a preface to the re-issue of his essay in 1933 retracted his standpoint, which has had and still has a great impact on economic thinking.

6. Braithwaite [1928], p. 19.
7. Telser [1964], p. 539.
8. Knight [1921], pp. 261–262.

In any case, in his retrospective reflections on economic theory and his own contribution to it, Knight criticized the classical tradition in two respects that have a bearing on the matter at hand. He declared himself in sympathy with the reaction against classical price-theory economics.[9] Specifically, he reacted against the way in which price-economics deals with a social system in which every individual treats all others and society merely as instrumentalities and conditions to his own optimization, ignoring that resource allocation and the system of market relations themselves are culture-history facts and products. To this he added as his overall judgement that economics like any social science implies recognition of and dealing with social values, and consequently cannot be economic without being both political and ethical. He also criticized the classical thinkers for their neglecting to see economic power as a possible consequence of economic liberty and the cumulative tendency to inequality caused by the freedom to use power and to get more of it.[10]

Thus, while one can essentially agree with the young Knight in his objections to the distinction between 'real' and 'nominal' utilities, it does not follow from these – as the older Knight fully recognised – that the problem of catering for the market can be designated as merely an economic problem in the sense that no social and cultural values are involved. Telser's reasoning behind his extension of advertising as an input supplied jointly with the physical product comes to the very assertion about the costs of advertisement and its impact on the valuations by consumers that Braithwaite so fiercely rejected and that was disclaimed by Knight in retrospect.

This contradiction in vision once again elucidates that, in this debate, the proposition of values on the part of the investigators themselves is involved. When the investigator feels that he has engaged in speculation, he will be inclined to turn to 'empirical evidence'. And many authors on the subject of the compatibility of advertising and competition have asserted that no generalisations can be made on theoretical grounds as to the questions of how far the selling price of the product can be raised by the expenditure of selling costs, and, respectively, how much of the margin between the selling price and the 'true' production costs tends to be taken up by these outlays. To overcome this complication, they have tried to sustain their findings by empirical evidence. Braithwaite did so by taking into account the profound changes in market organization in the field of manufactured goods – the rise

9. Ibid., p. XII.
10. Ibid., p. XVIII.

of manufacturer's brand control – that she had witnessed, and she tried to trace the meaning of her experience. Kaldor and Silverman [1948] went as far as to make a formal statistical analysis of advertising expenditure in the United Kingdom during the thirties. From their extensive fieldwork they derived, as their most prominent analytical result, a cross tabulation of the advertising intensity (advertising-to-sales ratio) against the degree of concentration across 118 different commodities[11], which has won fame for its clear and, at the same time, plausible implications: 'It may be concluded therefore that large-scale advertising is a pecularity of the system of distribution known as 'manufacturers' brand control', where the commodities are sold to final consumers under the manufacturer's trade mark, and usually at prices fixed by the manufacturers themselves. It also shows that, in most trades, the manufacturers' advertising is concentrated among a small number of firms, while the percentage of advertising in manufacturer's sales was largest in those trades where between four and nine firms accounted for the bulk of advertising. It appears, therefore, that large-scale advertising is peculiar to industrial situations which are neither monopolistic nor competitive, but which, in the language of economic theory, are called 'oligopolies' – the market being divided between a few competing producers'.[12]

Basing himself on postwar data covering 42 consumer goods industries in the United States, Telser contested these findings, though he tested only for a monotonic relationship between concentration and advertising intensity, while Kaldor and Silverman's result suggested a curvilinear relationship. Telser has been justly criticized for his omission,[13] but his critics cannot alter the fact that a test for curvilinearity put to the same data and employed in the way that Telser tested for a linear relationship would still fail to produce statistically significant results. Comanor and Wilson [1967] and Guth [1971] in following their track have enriched Telser's theoretical starting-point and data base by taking more variables into consideration and by putting different relationships to test. Their findings have been broadly accepted, though Porter's results [1974] have shed another light on the conclusions that were drawn by Comanor and Wilson.

11. Kaldor and Silverman [1948], Table 13, p. 35.
12. Ibid., pp. 36–37.
13. See for instance Cable [1972], p. 107.

2. REVIEW OF THE PROPOSED MECHANISMS FOR ADVERTISING TO AFFECT CONCENTRATION AND PERFORMANCE

Four aspects (or mechanisms) can be distinguished with regard to the effect of advertising on selective demand (i.e. the demand for the products of a particular firm), that have relevance for the relation between advertising, economic concentration and market performance.

1. In the first place, there is the problem of the pulling power of advertising in different trades and industries. The sales response of advertising must at least be adequate to compensate for the outlay. Under highly competitive conditions with a large number of nearly equal-sized firms, the benefits of the advertising by individual firms spill over to competitors. This phenomenon was referred to as 'substitution evil' among businessmen in the United States during the twenties.[14] That a certain degree of concentration can be regarded as a precondition for large-scale advertising must be considered.

In connection with this condition, there is the function of anticipation or initiation and the question of the agent who is actually fulfilling this function in the market. Kaldor did pay a good deal of attention to this aspect of market organization and distinguished between markets dominated by manufacturers and those dominated by distributors, either wholesalers or retailers.[15] The essential implication of domination refers to the control of product characteristics, and therefore product differentiation and selling effort. If the influence on the purchase decision by the consumer is exerted mainly by the distributor – through the control of product specification and/or the provision of indispensable information and other attendant services –, his bargaining power *vis-a-vis* the manufacturer is totally different from that in markets dominated by manufacturers. Porter [1974] has rightly stressed this aspect of market organization and arrived at the following conclusion.[16] 'Thus the relative power of the retail and manufacturing stages determines the distribution of rents between stages. However the retailers' selling efforts enhance product differentiation and hence the total rents available. Therefore, the *level* of rents to the manufacturing and retail stages depends simultaneously on the structure of the manufacturing stage, the structure of the retail stage and the interaction between them'.

We drew a similar conclusion after a study of the antagonism of manu-

14. Braithwaite [1928], p. 31.
15. Kaldor [1950–51], pp. 17–21.
16. Porter [1974], p. 421.

facturers and retailers with regard to the 'functional position' within certain channels of trade and industry.[17] For the rest, it can be properly observed that the notion of functional domination has a long tradition and can, for instance, be found in an exposition by R. G. Hawtrey: 'The share of each dealer in the business of the market depends partly on the amount of his capital, but still more on the people accustomed to deal with them'.[18]

So functional domination affects the distribution of both selling effort and rents between the stages of production. There is no broadly accepted view on the *origins* of retailers' and manufacturers' domination in a particular trade or industry.

Porter[19] ascribes the origins to the nature of the consumer's choice and relates them to the convenience or nonconvenience character of commodities that can be derived from consumers' buying characteristics. Since the distribution of rents is also involved in this matter, the causal flow of events can be the other way round: once manufacturing in a particular industry is dominated by the distribution channels, it can hardly free itself from that dependent position, due to a lack of funds to enlarge the scale of production and engage in product development and large-scale selling effort, so that consumers' buying characteristics merely reflect the prevailing supply conditions. Technical and/or organizational characteristics of production, which were particularly stressed by Kaldor [1950–51],[20] cannot be precluded as alternative causes for this phenomenon.

In any case it can be established – and we will provide ample evidence for this point – that the structure of the manufacturing stage in distributors' dominated industries differs most significantly from that in manufacturers' dominated industries.

These differences can be assessed in terms of concentration, minimum efficient plant size, absolute capital requirements and advertising intensity. The particular industries in all the Western economies that can be regarded as distributor dominated comprise (ready made) clothing, leather, footwear, carpets and furniture.

---

17. A. van der Zwan [1971], p. 24.
18. R. G. Hawtrey. *The Economic Problem*. p. 39; cited by Kaldor [1950–51], p. 17. Another valuable source in this respect is: George Burton Hotchkiss. *Milestones of Marketing*. New York, 1938, pp. 152–153 and 179–180.
19. Porter [1974], pp. 420–421 and footnote 14 on p. 423.
20. Kaldor [1950–51], p. 19, mentioned among other things the economies of internal standardization of product and production.
21. Vernon [1971], p. 250.

2. The second problem relates to the returns to scale in advertising. In the first place, there is the possibility of increasing returns to advertising owing to the responsiveness of sales; this was referred to by Vernon [1971] as the 'direct mechanism' for advertising to affect concentration.[21] Economies of scale in advertising in this sense form a highly disputed issue in economic science. Kaldor [1950–51] believed strongly in economies of scale that favor the leading firms.[22] It is rare to find empirical evidence to sustain this believe and, although an instance can be found in Alderson [1958][23], the functional relationship that was envisaged by Kaldor and others, namely a sigmoid shaped curve with threshold effects and gradually decreasing sales responsiveness to advertising, cannot be found. Simon [1970] is the author who, after a series of empirical studies, has been the most outspoken in rejecting the conclusion that there are economies of scale in advertising – apart from effects that can result from the media rate structure – over the relevant ranges of operation. Lambin [1976][24], in a recent volume on an econometric investigation in Western European countries, claims that his results present strong evidence for decreasing returns to advertising as the general rule. But even where economies of scale do not exist as a general rule in the employment of advertising to induce sales, increasing returns may prevail in production. Advertising, by increasing the scale of output, may foster concentration in an indirect way. Comanor and Wilson paid ample attention to this phenomenon; among other things by introducing minimum efficient plant scale as a variable in whose presence the relation between advertising, concentration and performance should be examined.

3. The third problem concerns advertising as a source and symptom of product differentiation. In agreement with Comanor and Wilson[25] and Porter,[26] product differentiation can be defined formally as the degree of cross price inelasticity of final consumer demand for a given brand relative to competing brands. In fact, this definition goes back to Triffin [1940], who dealt with 'heterogeneous competition' in a similar manner.[27] But the operational significance of this formal definition rests largely upon the (underlying) supposition of the *stability* of the individual brand's demand

22. Kaldor [1950–51], p. 13.
23. Alderson, p. 97.
24. Lambin, Ch. 6.
25. Comanor and Wilson [1967], pp. 424–425.
26. Porter [1974], p. 420.
27. Triffin [1940], p. 103–108.

schedule (selective demand curve) to enable its empirical assessment over a reasonable range of operation.

Cable, who forms a notable exception with regard to paying attention to the theory underlying the relation between seller concentration and advertising intensity, re-examined in his paper the theoretical hypotheses about advertising and concentration with the aid of the rules for optimal advertising behaviour of the firm. But though he stressed the importance of incorporating an interaction term (cross elasticity) to extend the conditions to oligopoly situations, he did not actually try to estimate these terms in his empirical analysis.[28]

Both on considerations of practicality (the availability of detailed data in sufficient numbers of observations to allow the statistical estimation of the large number of parameters involved) and theoretical reasoning (the required stability of the selective demand curves), the operational significance of cross price elasticity as a measure for product differentiation can be seriously questioned. And so the difficulties that surround the concept of product differentiation, with all its complexity of idea and reference, cannot be adequately suppressed by putting forward this formal definition.

Kaldor[29] refers to the contribution of advertising in making the public brand-conscious. Porter[30] also stresses advertising as a prime strategy for the manufacturer in differentiating his product and developing a strong brand image, not merely to influence the public, but, as far as the convenience distribution channel is concerned, to overcome barriers which obstruct entry into these outlets and to gain access to distribution. The practical importance of this last element is not to be underestimated, but its origins lie in the brand consciousness of the public. Comanor and Wilson[31], citing Bain, also found advertising to be the most important source of product differentiation in the consumer goods industries. Generally the view is held that physical product characteristics in many consumer goods industries are or, at least, have become less important in differentiating the product, because the development of really superior product characteristics is difficult and their pay off limited because they can be overcome by competitors, through advertising claims. By differentiating their products through advertising, manufacturers try to shift the basis of choice away from price and objective product characteristics, because competition along these lines can

28. Cable [1972], p. 108.
29. Kaldor [1950–51], p. 18.
30. Porter [1974], p. 423.
31. Comanor and Wilson [1967], p. 425.

easily impair their market position and thereby their profit. Succcessful differentiation of the market would thus lead to high penetration costs and absolute cost disadvantages for new entrants and thereby stimulate and maintain industrial concentration.

There is an antinomy in this picture of market behaviour, regarding both the demand and the supply side of this problem. Brand conciousness rests upon the desire for a settled routine, according to Kaldor[32], who – in a very interesting footnote – placed this motive of human conduct opposite to the desire for change and novelty. He recognised that too much routine may become oppressive, because it becomes monotonous and will provoke departure from routine for its own sake. The so-called psychology of simplification and complication comprises more recently developed concepts, put forward by Howard and Sheth [1969][33] in their learning theory of consumer behaviour. They used these concepts in quite the same context as Kaldor used his desire for settled routine versus change and novelty. If we accept this view of consumer behaviour, then every routine that is being developed in the market has a built-in self-defeating tendency: brand loyalty and brand switching form a pair of related phenomena, looked upon in the context of consumer behaviour.

The view of brand consciousness through advertising as the base for product differentiation also implies that the degree of market imperfection can be measured by advertising expenditure and by the price premium (shift of the selective demand curve) that is realised through advertising. Advertising is believed not only to compensate for its outlay, but the advertised product as a 'composite commodity' is also expected to be sold at a price that exceeds the sum of the separate costs. But why should the 'price premium' be retained in the form of profit by the advertising firms? A considerable part or even the whole of it might be taken up by the expenses incurred in order to enlarge and defend market shares.

When, in fact, the price premium is retained in the form of profit, competitors will be attracted. To what extent will they be discouraged by the barriers they face in the form of the existing brand loyalty? Their strategy need not be to penetrate the same market segments that apparently have been created – this is implied in the hypotheses of penetration cost, incurred at new entrance as a consequence of product differentiation – but rather could be to push product differentiation further by creating new segments,

32. Kaldor [1950–51], p. 18.
33. Howard and Sheth [1969], p. 27–28.

either through the development of alternative – not necessarily superior – product formulas, or through the design of different – not necessarily better – advertising claims. The technical limitations in this field (observing the relevant range of operation) cannot constitute an obstacle of principal nature, due to the fact that with industrial products only a small fraction of the feasible range of the product is actually made available. Thus, technically speaking, there is always room for modification with regard to styling and particular use characteristics, like format, appliance features, and the like.

These modifications in themselves may create selective demand, and, even when they can be considered as marginal compared to existing products and their meaning is mainly situated in the advertising claims, they may appeal to the market because of the latent desire on the side of the customer to depart from routine.

The exposition so far is fairly general, though not to a greater extent than the hypothesis of product differentiation leading to concentration, but what is more serious: it has no clue.

We will try to provide this missing element. Consistent with the exposition given, we will situate the missing element on both sides of the market. Products are not inherently differentiable: they are or can become so because of values held by consumers.

Through product differentiation, psychological and use values are connected to products and competing brands. The scope for making such links, respectively, for appealing alternately to the desires for settled routine and change and novelty, will not be the same for every product-class. Generally speaking, we can expect a greater scope for these in the case of commodities that have a high relevance for the consumers' personal lives and in which they take a special interest. In psychological literature this is referred to as 'ego-involvement' of commodities. In an *economic* context we can only cope with this phenomenon in terms of budget analysis and the income elasticity of separate commodity groups. We assert that personal involvement particularly applies to groups of commodities and services with the highest income elasticities. A notable reference in this respect is Phelps.[34]

As to the supply side, we can observe that the tendency to split up the market into several market segments with different product characteristics and advertising appeals forces the competitors to operate with an extended range of products or even separate brands (multi-brand strategy!) which frustrates the advantages of internal standardization in production and

---

34. Phelps [1937], p. 87.

distribution. So economically speaking there are limits to the operation of extended product and brand lines. Therefore we expect this phenomenon to be more significant in more rapidly, growing markets. And in several studies this factor has been taken into account: Vernon [1971] and Cable [1972] are relevant sources in this matter.

Considered from both sides of the market, we come to the same somewhat paradoxical conclusion, namely that we expect multi-brand policy to play a more prominent role in particular commodity groups that show expansion and high income elasticities and where, at the same time, advertising intensity is high and concentration moderate. These markets, as competitive fields, may show *gravitational instability*.[35]

We have the opinion that this aspect makes itself persistently felt in the empirical findings that have been reported in the literature: notably in those studies, or parts of studies, that do not refer to industries or trades as units of analysis, but to economically meaningful markets, that is to say that rival firms regard these as their field of direct competition. We want to point to the work of Telser [1964], Vernon [1971] and Cable [1972], particularly.

Of these authors, Telser is most explicit on this point. From his analysis of the share stability in 3 different commodity groups, Foods, Soaps/waxes/ polishes and Toiletries/cosmetics, he concluded that they differed sharply both in advertising intensity and in share stability. The more heavily advertised categories did show more instability than the much less advertised category.[36]

From supplementary sources, it can be established that the heavily advertised commodities belong to the category of consumer goods that have the highest income elasticities. Telser explained his findings on the grounds that there is more frequent introduction of new products and brands in the more heavily advertised category, and existing brands are apparently unable to maintain continued consumer acceptance: 'According to this interpretation the relatively intensive advertising of certain goods is associated with high turnover of brands within the product class. ... Contrary to popular belief, there may well be more entry and competition among the firms that produce heavily advertised goods'.[37]

It seems to us that at this point Telser extended his findings a little too far, but they fit in with our hypothesis of *particular* commodity groups that have high advertising intensity and moderate concentration.

35. An expression quoted from Kaldor [1950–51], p. 13.
36. Telser [1964], p. 550.
37. Ibid.

Vernon, in his study of 18 therapeutic markets within the pharmaceutical industry, produced regression results[38] that are of direct relevance to our proposition. His results indicate that market share *instability* is positively related to the promotional intensity, as well as to the growth rate of sales of a market, while promotional intensity and concentration turn out to be negatively related. Concentration also seems to be lower in markets with more frequent introduction of new products and brands.

Cable composed a 26-market sample comprising Food items, Other household nondurable products (polishes etc.) and Toiletries/cosmetics. His sample, drawn from U.K. sources, can therefore be compared with the sample Telser used for the testing of his statement on market share stability. Unfortunately Cable did not test for share stability, and the interpretation of his findings within the proposed framework cannot be that straightforward as in the case of Telser's and Vernon's results. From his regression equations with advertising or goodwill intensity as dependent variable, in connection with the simple correlation matrix for the included explanatory variables, it can however be concluded that for Cable's sample:

- Advertising/goodwill intensity is firmly related in a positive sense to concentration, measured either by a curvilinear relation with the Herfindahl index, or by a linear relation with the concentration ratio.
- Advertising/goodwill intensity is most significantly related in a positive sense with a dummy variable that measures 'sensitive product areas' (that is to say products like Toiletries/cosmetics with high income elasticities) and with the number of brands in the market.
- The 'sensitive product areas' dummy variable and the number of brands are both negatively related to concentration.

These findings, in combination, suggest that in Cable's sample of markets a sub-sample can be allocated with high advertising/goodwill intensity, moderate concentration and high turnover of brands. The markets in this sub-sample are to be found in the category of commodities with high income elasticity.

4. A last subject that should be dealt with in this section refers to an interesting hypothesis put forward by Sherman and Tollison [1971, 1972]. According to their hypothesis, both advertising and profitability should be

---

38. Vernon [1971]. We refer here to his regression equation (3a) on p. 257 and to equation (1b), (1c) on p. 252–253 respectively. Vernon's results are, statistically speaking, only indicative significance.

regarded as contingent upon technological factors that give rise to inter-industry differences in 'Cost Variability'. From a methodological point of view, Sherman and Tollison take a position in this matter that is similar to the one we will take, i.e. to take into consideration nonspecified influences and to test the relationships between advertising and performance against these influences and observe whether the already established relationships hold or vanish.

Cost variability is defined by Sherman and Tollison as the variability of total cost with short-run output and approximated for their empirical investigation by the ratio of labour and material costs to the value of shipments in *Census of Manufacturers* data.[39]

Total cost varies more as marginal cost becomes higher, and, at profit maximizing equilibrium for the firm according to the Dorfman-Steiner Theorem, such cost variability can be linked to both the marginal value product of advertising and the price elasticity of demand. If some additional conditions hold, advertising and cost variability can subsequently be related across industries. Since cost variability depends largely on technological factors, it seems more apt to be the determinant of advertising than vice versa. Cost variability, Sherman and Tollison argue, is also related to profit when uncertainty is present, through the effect it has on the variance of profit. If cost variability can be related in this way to profitability as well, it can be labeled as the omitted variable, leading in the same instances to high advertising and high profitability.

The hypothesis put forward by Sherman and Tollison and tested by them against empirical evidence is highly interesting, but we must also establish that their elaboration of the thesis is open to criticism. In the first place, there is the additional condition which should hold before advertising and cost variability can be related across industries. A relation between advertising and cost variability may hold for firms within an industry, but it will only hold across industries as long as the industries face similar advertising response functions. In the light of our earlier exposition on distributor versus manufacturer dominated industries, it will be clear that we are sceptical about the supposition of inter-industry similarity of the advertising response functions.

In the second place, an objection should be made against their deduction of a (formal) relation between advertising outlays and cost structure in the

---

39. Adjustments have been made in this measure to remove possibly spurious associations between cost fixity and advertising. A similar adjustment for profit could not be made because the relevant information was lacking.

context of (Dorfman-Steiner) profit maximization of the firm. In our view it is not correct to deduce from a parity relation between the marginal value product of advertising, μ, the (negative of) price elasticity of demand, η, and the cost ratio, $p/p - MC$, that we can expect μ to be lower when short-run marginal cost is relatively small.[40] While this expectation forms a necessary condition for the statement that advertising outlays will be higher as total costs are less variable with short-run output, the crucial advertising appropriation rule comes to the following condition:

$$(p - MC)\frac{\partial f}{\partial s} > 1$$

which says that advertising outlays are increased as long as the pulling power of advertising is adequate to compensate at least for the outlay. Since, according to the Dorfman-Steiner Theorem, the optimal price is set in a fixed proportion to MC, given the price elasticity, the magnitude of the price-cost margin in absolute terms $p - MC$ is bound to increase with MC. And so, in the case of high MC, the advertising appropriation, given similar advertising response curves, can and will be prolonged till lower values of responsiveness have been reached, which implies that higher outlays result. From the Dorfman-Steiner Theorem, we can only infer that advertising outlays will be higher as total costs are *more* variable with short-run output. Of course this last statement is fully contingent upon the magnitude of the price elasticity of demand. Within a Dorfman-Steiner world, demand refers to *selective* (or *particular*) demand, i.e. demand faced by an individual firm. And so the magnitude of the elasticity of this demand schedule is mainly determined by the *substitution* component.

In fact, according to the Dorfman-Steiner Theorem the (relative) price-cost margin $p - MC/p$ is exclusively determined by the elasticity of demand, in other words by the competitive conditions of the market. Thus we come to the conclusion that the hypothesis put forward by Sherman and Tollison, which implies that advertising outlays will be higher as total costs are less variable with short-run output, can only be maintained when an over-compensating relation can be supposed between advertising and the price elasticity of selective demand; a relation that should be contingent upon technological factors which determine cost variability.

One should realise, however, that this supposition comes to the very thesis of product differentiation by means of advertising. But with one

40. Sherman and Tollison [1971], p. 398.

additional element of great importance, i.e. that such a policy of product differentiation would then be conditioned by technological factors which determine cost variability. If this proposition were correct, it would hardly be possible to discriminate between the risk and the effect it has on the variance of profit, on the one hand, and product differentiation, on the other hand, as determinants of profitability.

Conclusion

We conclude from our review of mechanisms that have been proposed in the literature for advertising to affect concentration and performance that the testing of relations between advertising, concentration and market performance cannot be based on results from simple regression or correlation analysis. There are many extraneous influences – from institutional and other sources – that should be dealt with, while the impact of concentration, etc. should be examined in the presence of other variables.

More specifically we have called attention to three major sources of extraneous influence, viz.:

– Market organization; particularly the aspect of functional domination. Since in empirical studies advertising intensity is being assessed as advertising or promotional expenditure by manufacturers with a breakdown to industry, consideration should be given to the circumstance that a stratum of industries is being dominated by the distribution channels and therefore cannot be regarded as drawn from the same universe as the other industries.
– Product differentiation as a source of market imperfection can play a dual role in connection with the relation between advertising and concentration. High advertising intensity can be concurrent to gravitational instability of the market, manifesting itself at the market level in a high turnover of brands. We have to state here explicitly that the empirical evidence that we have cited to sustain this statement is restricted to the turnover of brands within a product class. This does not imply a correspondingly high turnover of firms at the industry level. But it is reasonable to expect an association between the two phenomena. At the industry level we expect to find a certain subgroup with high advertising intensity and only moderate concentration, notwithstanding the barriers to entry that high advertising outlays are supposed to represent.
– Technological factors that give rise to inter-industry differences in Cost Variability, and by the consequences this variability has in terms of

product differentiation, might affect advertising. Either via the resulting market power, or via the variance of profit, cost variability might in the same instances lead to higher profits and higher advertising outlays.

There are alternative research strategies to cope with these sources of extraneous influence: control by excluding these influences from the sample, control by stratification (grouping within the sample) with regard to major extraneous factors, or control by specifying the influences as multiple explanatory variables in a regression model. The specification in regression models by means of dummy variables and grouping within the sample can be regarded as close substitutes. They differ however in regard to the statistical conditions involved. For our empirical investigation we have chosen for the alternative of grouping to incorporate the theoretical notions that have been obtained above. We have worked out this device in several ways, depending on the number of observations available. Apparently to the extent that observations are available, more different groups can be distinguished in a statistically useful way. Worked out one way or the other, the basis is always the notion of forming more homogeneous groups within the sample of data to test for the effect that the sources of extraneous influence may have had on the particular outcome of a study in which the sample was – wrongly – conceived of as drawn from one universe.

3.   EMPIRICAL INVESTIGATION

3.1. *Empirical Data Used*
The data for this investigation have been derived from the empirical studies reported in the literature, and they comprise:

a. Kaldor and Silverman [1948]-data for the U.K. during the thirties with regard to advertising intensity (measured as the advertising to sales ratio in 1935) and degree of concentration (measured as the smallest number of firms spending more than 80 percent of total advertising expenditure for the year 1938). The unit of analysis used in this study is the individual commodity or commodity group. In their publication the authors have reported a cross-tabulation of the two separate variables across 118 different commodities in Table 13, which gives average advertising to sales ratios for thirteen concentration classes. This table of aggregated results formed our starting point.

To be able to put the data to statistical testing, variances are needed in addition to averages, and, therefore, the individual (commodity) data underlying Table 13 had to be recollected. Fortunately this can be done by collating Kaldor and Silverman's Table 12, reporting on 135 different commodities and Table 75, reporting on 117 different items. As is often the case with collating two data files, some information gets lost, due to irretraceable combinations and the like. We have been able to recollect the data for 104 different items. The (unweighted) averages of ad to sales ratios per concentration class show, however, quite the same pattern as Kaldor and Silverman's Table 13 (Table 1).

TABLE 1.

Advertising intensity as an average
Advertising to sales ratio per concentration class

Smallest number of firms spending 80% or more	Number of commodities included	Ad to sales ratio %	
		Average (unweighted)	Standard deviation
1,2	16	7.3	6.5
3,4	26	13.0	11.1
5,6	20	9.6	12.3
7–9	16	16.3	14.0
10–12	9	11.2	11.9
13+	17	5.4	8.9
total	104	10.6	11.3

In addition every commodity or commodity group has been characterised by the broad budget category to which it can be accounted, so that a breakdown of the data by budget category can be made.

b. U.S. *consumer goods industry data* (Three Digit Industries). We have combined the data files reported by:

1. Telser [1964] in this Table 1: concentration ratios for the years 1947, 1954, 1958 and advertising to sales ratios for the years 1948, 1954, 1957 in 44 industries;
2. Comanor and Wilson [1967] in their Table A2: profit rates and advertising to sales ratios in 41 industries averaged over the period 1954–1957;

3. Guth [1971] in his Table I and II: concentration ratios, Lorenz concentration coefficients, minimum efficient size ratios, absolute capital requirements ($) and advertising to sales ratios in 35 industries for the years 1958 and 1963;
4. Sherman and Tollison [1971] in their Table A2: average profit rates (1954–1957), advertising to sales ratios (1954–1957), cost fixity (1954) and rate of growth in demand (1947–1957) in 38 industries.[41]

Collating of these files (notably in the case of the data given by Comanor/Wilson and Guth) leads to some loss of observations, because the industries covered by these authors differ. This leads to sets of data that change by number of observations according to the variables and years involved. In Table 2 we give a summary of the different data sets that actually will be used.

TABLE 2.

Summary of the data sets regarding U.S. consumer goods industry used in the statistical testing

Variables/years involved	Number of 3-digit industries
b.1 CR 47 × AS 48	42
CR 54 × AS 54	42
CR 58 × AS 57	40
b.2 PR 54–57 × AS 54–57	39
PR 54–57 × CR 54–57	39
PR 54–57 × ACR 58	31
b.3 CR 58 × MES 58	34
CR 63 × MES 63	34
Log Lorenz 58 × ACR 58	34
Log Lorenz 63 × ACR 63	34
b.4 PR 54–57 × AS 54–57	38
PR 54–57 × CF 54	38
PR 54–57 × GR 47–57	38

41. In the subsequent analysis the number of industries entered in the estimation may differ slightly from 38 due to compatibility with other results reported in this article, or to extreme observations that have been omitted.

In this table the variables have been denoted as follows:

ACR	Absolute Capital Requirements
AS	Advertising to Sales ratio
CF	Cost Fixity
CR	Concentration Ratio (4 firm)
GR	Growth of demand (rate of)
(Log) Lorenz	(Log of) Lorenz Coefficient
MES	Minimum Efficient Size
PR	Profit Rate

3.2. *Hypotheses Tested and Statistical Techniques Used*
Following the same classification that we used in the preceding section, we give an overview of the hypotheses that have been put to test.

Ad a. The conclusion drawn by Kaldor and Silverman from their empirical findings has been cited above. They suggested a curvilinear relationship between advertising intensity and degree of concentration. We will test this hypothesis on the individual commodity data and check for the influence of extraneous influences that could have produced the particular outcome. Due to the fact that the number of observations is relatively large, a classification in 5 broad categories is feasible. We will use a classification that corresponds to those frequently used in budget analysis:

1. Food
2. Beverages, tobacco, etc.
3. Durables
4. Clothing, footwear, furniture, etc.
5. Other goods (toiletries, cosmetics, household products)

In this breakdown the category (4) corresponds to the above mentioned *distributor dominated markets*, while category (5) contains the products with highest income elasticities. The categories Durables (3) and Other goods (5) have been tested for heterogeneity. The subdivisions that have been made and the calculations of averages and variances within these subgroups seem to warrant their summarizing within one category.

Ad b1. Telser contested Kaldor's findings by testing for a monotonic relationship between concentration and advertising across 42 U.S. consumer goods industries. In the first place, we will test for curvilinearity against linearity on the same sample, but reversing the regression equation that Telser employed. This reverse has no particular significance, except that it makes more sense to have concentration as an explanatory variable in the curvilinear case. This test obviously involves the employment of the regression technique. But we will also test, by means of the analysis of variance and grouping of the industries in the sample, for the possible *suppression* of a relationship as a result of extraneous influence. It is noteworthy to point to it here, for one may equally be misled in assuming that an absence of relationship is real, whereas the absence may be due to the intrusion of an extraneous variable.[42]

*Ad b*2. Comanor and Wilson extended and modified Telser's design to incorporate essential elements that were lacking: the effect of advertising on the minimum efficient scale of firms and the absolute capital requirements (over and above those needed for physical plant and equipment) that may be involved in the running of successful advertising campaigns.

These two factors were incorporated as explanatory variables next to advertising intensity and concentration, in a relation with profit rate as a dependent variable. Minimum efficient scale, absolute capital requirements, concentration and advertising intensity are supposed to represent barriers obstructing entry in this context and hence constitute sources of market power that would manifest themselves primarily in profit rates. Comanor and Wilson reported findings that consistently show that profit rates across industries can – within their design – most successfully be explained by the advertising intensity (advertising to sales ratio) and absolute capital requirements, while concentration plays a secondary role. We will investigate to what extent their relationships may have been produced by extraneous influences.

*Ad b*3. Guth returned to the starting point of the advertising-concentration controversy insofar as he related concentration as a dependent variable to advertising intensity. He added minimum efficient scale and absolute capital requirements as explanatory variables to this relation. Besides that, he tried different measures for concentration, such as the Lorenz coefficient, and tested for log linear as well as linear relationships. His linear and log linear relations produced equally good results in regressions with the con-

---

42. Morris Rosenberg. *Logic of Survey Analysis.* New York 1968, Ch. 4, is a valuable source of information on this subject.

centration ratios. With the Lorenz coefficients the log linear relations did markedly better, with surprisingly significant results for the (inverse of the) advertising to sales ratio.

*Ad b*4. Sherman and Tollison tested the already established relationship between advertising and performance against the influence of cost fixity and concluded that it could indeed be ascribed to the dependence of both advertising and performance on a common factor. Besides that, they showed that growth of demand can be employed as an additional factor in the explanation of performance. We will verify whether respective to what extent these findings can be placed under a more general principle of a grouping of industries.

With one exception that we mentioned above – the employment *ad b*1 of the regression technique in a test for curvilinearity in the advertising-concentration relation – we will make use of the analysis of variance as statistical technique for the testing of the hypotheses.

We will combine the analysis of variance with the grouping in the sample of u.s. industries, like we did for the u.k. sample of commodities. But in the case of the u.s. sample of industries, our possibilities are more restricted because of the limited number of observations.

We will employ two alternative classifications:

HB1, classification in two groups: clothing, leather, footwear, carpets and furniture, etc. as *distribution dominated industries* versus the other industries.

HB2, classification in three groups: clothing, etc. versus soaps, drugs, perfumes/cosmetics, books and periodicals as high income elasticity industries versus the other industries.

These classifications incorporate the extraneous influences on which we have commented in detail above.

The employment of the analysis of variance is, in our opinion, preferable to the regression analysis that has generally been practised in this field of investigation. The advantages of the regression technique in this context are somewhat doubtful, since its employment is mainly directed towards the testing for significance of the individual regression coefficients on the basis of T-values in multiple relationships – but without bringing in prior knowledge regarding the functional relationships and/or the most likely value of coefficients.

Thus the advantage that lies in the incorporation of (moderately) interrelated explanatory variables is self-defeating, because T-values of individual coefficients are highly sensitive to multi-collinearity. The employment of the analysis of variance is obviously no matter of principle, because it belongs to the same class of methods as the regression technique. Its advantages in our case are to be sought mainly in its straightforwardness in application to the testing of hypotheses.

The employment of the one-way analysis of variance does not need further comment here. In the case of more than one independent variable, the complication of intercorrelation also arises in the context of the analysis of variance. The presence of unequal and disproportionate cell frequencies in the design-matrix results in correlation of the classification variables and complicates the prime task: to discriminate between the individual influence of multiple causes. To solve this problem we have chosen the so-called *step-down analysis* which involves an *initial ordering* of the effects and then an estimating of each effect adjusted for those preceding it in the ordering and ignoring of those following it.

Overall and Spiegel [1969] give an excellent and nontechnical exposition of the characteristics of this variant compared to others (among which is the conventional analysis of variance). We want to stress here that the distinct variants differ in what they show as main effects, not in the interaction effects that are given. The application of the step-down method is advocated by Overall and Spiegel[43] in the case of testing a logical hierarchy of hypotheses. Our case is similar to theirs: the feeling that much previous research had failed to distinguish adequately between market organization and factors such as the absolute capital requirements, etc. It seems likely that capital requirements should be primarily and substantially affected by market organization. Accordingly, the step-down method was utilized to test a logically ordered hierarchy of hypotheses. The impact of market organization as incorporated in the described grouping of commodities and industries was tested disregarding other factors. The influence of capital requirements was tested after the adjustment for market organization. The utilization of the step-down analysis seems to be appropriate in this case.

3.3. *Empirical Findings**

Ad a. First we give a table (Table 3) in which we summarize some of the raw data on the distinct commodity categories.

---

43. Overall and Spiegel [1969], p. 321.
* We are indebted to Drs. W. J. de Wreede and Mr. C. Ouwerkerk, who gave valuable assistance in producing the statistical results.

TABLE 3.

Advertising intensity and degree of concentration
for the distinct commodity categories

Category	Number of commodities included	Median number of firms spending 80% or more	Ad to sales ratio	
			Average (unweighted)	Standard deviation
1. Food	27	4	9.9	11.8
2. Beverages, tobacco etc.	15	7	6.5	5.2
3. Durables	24	6	7.8	5.7
4. Clothing etc.	13	10–12	2.8	3.3
5. Other goods	25	6	20.6	13.9
Total	104	5	10.6	11.3

Out of a Multiple Range Test on advertising intensity (Least Significant Difference Procedure) for homogeneous subsets, three nonoverlapping subsets came to the fore, namely the categories 1–3, 4 and 5 respectively. This indicates that the total sample is composed of totally different sub-samples.

In the formal testing we proceeded as follows: first we have tested in a one-way analysis of variance for differences in advertising intensity among the concentration classes that were given in Table 1 above. This testing produced the following results:

One-way analysis of variance:
advertising intensity on concentration classes[44]

Number of DF	
total	103
between groups	5
F-ratio	2.209
F-prob.	0.059
Cochran's C test for equal variances	0.266
C-prob.	0.214
Polynomial fit for curvilinearity Prob. quadratic term	0.010

So the test produced nonsignificant results, but suggested a substantial improvement in testing with a curvilinear relationship. In order to incorporate this curvilinearity, we made a new grouping of the concentration classes. We experimented with several groupings and chose the one that produced the greatest differences in average advertising intensity between the groups (Table 4).

TABLE 4.

Advertising intensity and degree of concentration
(Testing for curvilinear relationship)

Smallest number of firms spending 80% or more	Number of commodities included	Ad to sales ratio	
		Average (unweighted)	Standard deviation
7–9	16	16.35	14.0
3–6/10–12	55	11.5	11.6
1,2/13+	33	6.3	7.7
Total	104	10.6	11.3

One-way analysis of variance: advertising intensity on concentration classes (curvilinear relation).

Number of DF	
total	103
between groups	2
F-ratio	4.924
F-prob.	0.009
Cochran's C	0.502
C-prob.	0.015

44. The test for equal variances within the 'treatment groups' is essential because the statistical testing with the aid of the analysis of variance is based on this assumption. Test results can be sensitive to deviations from this assumption. This is to a lesser extent, the case with deviations in the distribution of the criterion variable from normality. From a series of investigations in which F tests were applied to data derived from deliberately created nonnormal distributions, Cochran [1947] showed only minor deviations from the true probability limits. Some of our 'treatment groups' do show moderate skewness. But estimated on Cochran's results, this skewness is not serious enough to have an impact on the conclusions drawn from the tables.

With the curvilinear relation incorporated, the test results show statistical significance at the 99% level – which seems to substantiate the suggestion by Kaldor and Silverman.

As the next step in the formal procedure, we tested for a curvilinear relation between advertising intensity and degree of concentration *within* the distinct commodity categories, in a similar way as for the total sample. The results are given in Table 5.

TABLE 5.

Testing for curvilinear relation between advertising intensity and concentration within the distinct commodity categories

Commodity category	Number of DF (total)	F-ratio	F-prob.
1. Food	26	0.019	0.195
2. Beverages, tobacco etc.	14	1.182	0.341
1/2. Food and Beverages etc.	41	0.486	0.615
3. Durables	23	0.737	0.495
4. Clothing etc.	12	1.182	0.341
5. Other goods	24	1.537	0.236
Total	103	4.924	0.009

The results show beyond doubt that, through the effect of extraneous influences, the particular composition of the Kaldor and Silverman sample is responsible for the curvilinear relation that the aggregated set of commodities seemed to suggest so convincingly. The statistical insignificance showed here is by no means due to the smaller number of observations within the separate groups. The combined group 1/2, with no less than 42 observations, does behave in quite the same way as the smaller groups. An additional advantage of the pooling of groups 1/2 was that the skewness of the distribution of the ad-to-sales ratios was lessened as compared to the distribution within the separate groups.

A step-down analysis on the original classification according to concentration (Table 1) confirms the finding that the relation between advertising intensity and degree of concentration vanishes once the grouping of commodities in introduced (Table 6).

TABLE 6.

One-way analysis of variance as compared to step-down analysis of advertising intensity on concentration after commodity grouping in three nonoverlapping subsets

One-way (advertising intensity on concentration)

	Sum of squares between groups	DF	F-ratio	F-prob.
Between	1,341	5	2.209	0.059
Within	11,897	98		
Total	13,238			

Step-down (advertising intensity on concentration after commodity grouping)

	Sum of squares between classes	DF	F-ratio	F-prob.
Main effects	4,126	7	6.896	0.001
Commodity grouping	3,604	2	21.079	0.001
Concentration	522	5	1.222	0.305
Interaction	1,675	9	2.177	0.031
Residual	7,436	87		
Total	13,237	103		

After adjustment for commodity grouping has been made – the grouping in 3 nonoverlapping subsets suggested itself as most appropriate here and is similar to HB2 for the U.S. sample of industries – additional explanatory power of concentration is nearly negligible and, in any case, nonsignificant. The interaction term, on the other hand, puts itself in the front. The total of explained variance (main effects and interaction term) can be read from the R^2, which amounts to 0.312.

Our preliminary conclusion is that the empirical evidence for Kaldor's assertion on the advertising-concentration issue turns out to be nonconvincing. The observed curvilinear relationship can be ascribed to the influence of noncontrolled and nonspecified factors.

Ad b. By way of a general view of the U.S. sample of industries, we produce in Table 7 some of our test results with regard to the variables concerned and to a breakdown of the sample in groups of industries according to HB1 and HB2.

TABLE 7.

One-way analysis of variance of the respective industry characteristics on HB1 or HB2.

Characteristic		Data set concerned	DF	Grouping	F-ratio	F-prob.
Concentration-ratio	'58	GUTH	33	HB1	10.8	0.003
	'58	TELSER	39	HB1	13.1	0.001
	'63	GUTH	33	HB1	21.1	0.000
Lorenz coefficient	'58	GUTH	33	HB1	24.3	0.000
	'63	GUTH	33	HB1	24.7	0.000
Ad/Sales ratio*	'58	GUTH	33	HB2	9.8	0.001
	'58	TELSER	41	HB2	11.3	0.000
	'63	GUTH	33	HB2	14.7	0.000
Profit rate	'54–'57	C/W	38	HB2	10.8	0.000
MES*	'58	GUTH	33	HB1	4.7	0.036
	'63	GUTH	33	HB1	8.1	0.008
ACR*	'58	GUTH	33	HB2	7.2	0.003
	'63	GUTH	33	HB2	9.2	0.001
Cost Fixity	'54	S/T	37	HB2	15.5	0.000
Growth	'47–'57	S/T	36	HB2	7.1	0.003

All *F*-ratios turn out to be significant at the 95% level, while nearly all of them are significant at the 99% level. To amplify this picture we give average values for the variables with a breakdown of the sample according to HB2 (Table 8).

* On basis of the employed tests, the assumption of equal variances must be rejected and the analysis of variance be regarded as indecisive. The additional tests for homogeneous subsets show, however, that the distinct groups (according to HB1 respectively HB2) can still be regarded as homogeneous with respect to the concerned industry characteristics.

TABLE 8.

Average values for industry characteristics with a breakdown according to HB2

	Average values		
	Clothing etc.	Income elastic goods	Others
Ad/sales ratio (%)			
Guth '58	1.37	7.19	2.96
Guth '63	1.05	7.68	3.16
Profit rate (%)			
C/W '54–'57	4.50	12.22	8.36
Abs. Capital requirements ($)			
Guth '58	1,925	20,131	15,253
Guth '63	2,290	37,724	19,749
Concentration ratio (%)			
Guth '58	22.9	33.9	46.2
Guth '63	19.4	34.5	46.2
Minimum efficient scale (%)			
Guth '58	1.21	1.93	4.44
Guth '63	0.98	2.35	3.96
Growth (ratio)			
S/T '47–'57	1.22	2.12	1.47
Cost fixity (%)			
S/T '54	18.2	37.2	20.0

It cannot be doubted that the grouping of industries according to HB1 and HB2 differentiate significantly with regard to every industry characteristic involved in this investigation. This phenomenon of sharply contrasting sectors within the consumer goods industry can, by itself, produce relationships between variables across the industries.

We want to point to some other interesting conclusions that can be derived from these general findings. The results amply substantiate our assertion on the structure of the manufacturing stage in distributors dominated industries. The differences in structure manifest themselves in every characteristic.

Another interesting phenomenon is reflected in the changes over time of ACR within the distinct groups of industries. The income elastic goods sector nearly doubled its value, while the increases in the other sectors are only moderate. The shifts in ACR may be partly ascribed to shifts in the minimum efficient size among the groups, while the other factors show more stability over time. For another part, the increase in the ACR must be due to the expansion of these industries as such. These results confirm the hypothesis of an expanding sector within the consumer goods industry that produces highly differentiated products and shows moderate concentration and equally moderate minimum efficient size of the firm. Although this sector is characterized by very high absolute capital requirements – which may be partly due to the requirements with regard to advertising – this factor does not seem to prohibit entry, nor can the high advertising intensity be designated as an effective barrier to entry in this sector.

Ad b1 The test results on the curvilinearity in the relation between advertising intensity and concentration can be read from Table 9.

TABLE 9.

Test for curvilinearity in the relation between
advertising intensity and concentration
(*Telser data set; N = 42*)

	Regression coefficients (*T*-values between brackets)			Multiple correlation coefficient	*F*-ratio
	Constant	*CR*	$(CR)^2$	(*R*)	
Ad/sales ratio linearly on					
Concentration ratio '47	1.51	.021(1.05)		.16	1.10
'54	1.83	.023(1.06)		.16	1.11
'57	1.97	.025(1.09)		.17	1.18
Ad/sales ratio curvilinearly on					
Concentration ratio '47	.76	.065(.85)	—.0005(—.60)	.19	.72
'54	1.01	.070(.88)	—.0005(—.61)	.19	.73
'57	.97	.085(.96)	—.0007(—.70)	.20	.83

The results hardly need comment, there is not the faintest support to be found in them for a curvilinear relationship across the industries within the total sample.

The one-way analyses of variance of concentration ratio on ad/sales ratio obviously confirm the regression results in Table 9 and repeat the Telser findings in this matter. The suppression of underlying relationships is suggested by the results of the step-down analysis reported below (Table 10).

TABLE 10

Analysis of the relation between concentration ratio (%) and ad/sales ratio after adjustment for grouping

(*Step-down according to HB1*)

		Sum of squares between classes	DF	F-ratio	F-prob.	R^2
1947	Main effects	3,796	3	4.598	0.008	
	HB1	3,730	1	13.554	0.001	
	AS	66	2	0.120	0.999	
	Interaction	2,954	1	10.736	0.003	
	Total	16,931	41			0.224
1954	Main effects	4,621	3	5.403	0.004	
	HB1	4,584	1	16.080	0.001	
	AS	37	2	0.064	0.999	
	Interaction	2,645	1	9.277	0.004	
	Total	17,814	41			0.259
1958	Main effects	4,279	3	5.007	0.006	
	HB1	3,853	1	13.527	0.001	
	AS	426	2	0.748	0.999	
	Interaction	776	1	2.723	0.104	
	Total	15,025	39			0.285

We will try to refrain from attaching too much weight to the results in Table 10. They do confirm, in the first place, the well established fact that grouping differentiates according to concentration and advertising intensity, while the direct relation between these two variables across the industries fail to produce significance before and after adjustment has been made for grouping. But in two of the years investigated and in a similar test for the prewar U.K. sample of commodities, the interaction term contributes significantly to the explanation of the variance.

These results at least indicate that, with proper control on the unspecified factors that do play a role in this question of industrial organization and market behaviour, a relation between advertising and concentration might be demonstrated.

Ad b2. Comanor and Wilson produced regressions with profit rate as a dependent, and concentration, ad/sales ratio and absolute capital requirements as explanatory variables.

In the first place, we have tested, in a one-way analysis of variance, for the separate and simple relations between the dependent and independent variables involved. In the case of the ad/sales ratio and the concentration ratio, we failed to produce very significant results.

This outcome, which contradicts the results reported by Comanor and Wilson, may well be due to the fact that the independent variable in an analysis of variance is introduced by way of classification. Of course some loss of information can result from classification on a variable as compared to its full variation in the case of regression analysis.

Below we report on the effect of the independent variables in the one-way case as compared to the step-down analysis, that is after adjustment has been made for grouping (Table 11).

TABLE 11.

Profit rates ('54–'57) explained by ad/sales ratio ('54–'57), concentration ratio ('54–'57) and absolute capital requirements ('58); one-way versus step-down analysis

	Sum of squares between classes	DF	F-ratio	F-prob.
Ad/sales ratio				
One-way	55	2	1.937	0.157
Step-down (HB2)	9	2	0.409	0.999
Concentration ratio				
One-way	73	2	2.658	0.082
Step-down (HB1)	12	2	0.504	0.999
Absolute Capital requirements				
One-way	140	2	6.208	0.006
Step-down (HB2)	28.5	2	1.531	0.236

With the restrictions kept in mind that we mentioned earlier and considering the fact that the interaction does not play a role in any of the three cases, we may state that the results in this table prove that the relations between profit rates and the explanatory variables tend to be caused by underlying differences in structure. These structural differences among the groups of industries make them act as *clusters* in the multi-variate 'industry-space'. This clustering determines, to a large extent, any representation that is derived from the industry configuration in this space.

Ad b3. Guth tested for relations with concentration ratio (Lorenz coefficient) as dependent and ad/sales ratio, minimum efficient size and absolute capital requirements as explanatory variables. We shall put his findings to the test and report the results in the table given below (Table 12).

We have chosen for Guth's most significant findings in terms of T-ratios, with the notable exception of the relation between the Lorenz coefficient taken linearly and the ad/sales ratio taken reciprocally. This is due to the fact that testing by means of the analysis of variance does not lend itself to the discrimination between the ad/sales ratio and its reciprocal.

TABLE 12.

Concentration explained by minimum efficient size and absolute capital requirements (1958 and 1963); one-way versus step-down analysis

	Sum of squares between groups	DF	F-ratio	F-prob.
Concentration ratio (%) on:				
MES '58				
One-way	5,434	2	11.015	0.000
Step-down (HB2)	1,885	2	3.580	0.041
MES '63				
One-way	6,789	2	22.618	0.000
Step-down (HB2)	2,465	2	8.139	0.002
Log Lorenz coefficient on:				
ACR '58				
One-way	0.226	2	13.120	0.000
Step-down (HB1)	0.039	2	2.271	0.120
ACR '63				
One-way	0.113	2	3.933	0.029
Step-down (HB1)	0.002	2	0.081	0.999

Interaction did not manifest itself in either of the two cases reported here. The results seem plain and clear in their interpretation. The strong relationships between concentration, on the one hand, and minimum efficient size and absolute capital requirements, on the other hand, have been caused by nonspecified influence.

Ad b4. Sherman and Tollison tested for regression relationships with profit rate as a dependent and six other industry characteristics as explanatory variables. One of their more specific aims was to show that, once cost fixity is adopted as an explanatory variable, the contribution of ad/sales ratio becomes negligible. There is no doubt that they succeeded in showing this. Only because the step-down analysis of variance is particularly apt to demonstrate such effects, can we give the outcome on this point (Table 13).

From the relations with ad/sales ratio, respectively, cost fixity, presented also in this table, it becomes clear that the influence of these variables is, practically speaking, incorporated in the grouping according to HB2. Surprisingly enough, some of the empirical findings of Sherman and Tollison themselves already indicated such a result: the strong interrelationship between advertising and cost variability could only be established by them for the C/W-sample of industries, which contains a distributor dominated cluster of industries, while this relationship turned out to be much weaker and hardly significant for the Mann-sample, which the authors have also employed and which does not contain such a cluster.

Though ad/sales ratio and cost fixity as industry characteristics share a common element, their interrelation is far from indicating a complete overlap, as the findings show; cost fixity has a much greater explanatory power with regard to profitability of industries than ad/sales ratio.

Growth of demand turns out to have an impact on profitability that clearly goes beyond the grouping of industries. This can mean two different, not necessarily mutually exclusive, things: growth has such a penetrative impact on profitability that it can be related to inter-industry differences at the *individual*, as well as at the *group* level, or our grouping is less efficient than it could be. There are indications in support of the view that growth has indeed a very strong effect on profitability. Norman Toy and others [1974], for example, provide ample evidence for this claim, even at the individual *firm* level. Their samples of firms on which the correlations were estimated are quite large.

In this context it is noteworthy to mention that their estimation also points to a strong *negative* relation between profitability and the variation of the earnings rate over time (!) as an indicator of the risk effect.[45] This empirical outcome can only be explained by the dominance of monotone decreases of earnings rates in cases of high variation. In any case, this finding is contrary to those reported by Sherman and Tollison [1972], which are less convincing anyway, because they are based on intra-class variation of earnings rates.

TABLE 13.

Profit rates (54'–'57) explained by ad/sales ratio ('54–'57), cost fixity (1954) and rate of growth of demand ('47–'57); one-way versus step-down analysis

	Sum of squares between groups	DF	*F-ratio*	*F*-prob.
Ad/sales ratio ('54–'57)				
One-way	51	2	1.740	.189
Step-down (CF)	18	2	.848	.999
Step-down (HB2)	7	2	.341	.999
Cost fixity (1954)				
One-way	157	2	6.724	.003
Step-down (HB2)	34	2	1.664	.204
Growth of demand ('47–'57)				
One-way	256	2	14.504	.000
Step-down (HB2)	113	2	7.427	.002

4. CONCLUSIONS

When recapitulating our findings, we concentrate on three issues.

1. Distributor domination of some of the consumer goods industries, on the one hand, which is concurrent to deconcentration in manufacturing, small-sized manufacturing firms stripped of market power, and, on the other hand, the presence of an expanding sector that produces high income elastic (and therefore highly differentiable) goods and pairs high advertising intensity with moderate concentration both at the market- and industry-level have serious implications for the investigation of industrial organization.

45. Toy [1974], p. 878.

These two phenomena make themselves felt as structural differences among groups of industries, while these groups act as clusters in a multivariate 'industry-space'. Any representation derived from the configuration of industries within this space reflects its particular traits. To reinforce this conclusion, we have calculated the inter-industry distances across the seven industry-characteristics, given by Sherman and Tollison, for the 38 industries that we have taken into our investigation (see Appendix). Comparison of the within-group with the between-group distances supports our claim.

Thus the slopes of the regression lines that have been reported turn out to be determined, to a great extent, by the location of the clusters of industries. These slopes should, therefore, not be interpreted as reflecting 'inter-industry', but 'inter-industry group' differences. Since too little attention has been given to these factors, the empirical findings reported in the literature on the compatibility of advertising and concentration are, to a certain extent, deficient. The important question, of course, is to what extent they are and whether the deficiencies are prohibitive.

2. We have demonstrated that most of the statistical relations between what are considered as key-variables in the issue of advertising and industrial concentration have been caused by extraneous influences. But does it follow from this fact that the observed relations can be nullified and the correlations be designated as 'spurious'? Not necessarily so. The answer to this question largely depends on the interpretation of the findings in terms of policy-recommendations.

These recommendations do not interest us, per se, in the context of this contribution, but they are important with regard to a full appreciation of the consequences that have been connected with the findings. Comanor and Wilson, for instance, point to the fact that cross-sectional studies tend to emphasize the long run differences between industries and interpret these differences as *structural* rather than behavioural.

So far, so good. But their policy recommendations[46] testify that they see a direct connection between their reported statistical relations and policy-making: 'Current policies which tend to emphasize the role played by concentration may need to be supplemented by those concerned directly with the nature and extent of product differentiation'. Since they repeatedly pointed to advertising as a '*source and symptom*' of product differentiation, this can only mean that they advocate a form of control of advertising to supplement

46. Comanor and Wilson [1967], pp. 437–438.

anti-trust policy in order to reduce market power and excess profit. In the same manner, Kaldor suggested that the advertising-concentration relation that he observed implied deconcentration as a likely effect of a reduction in advertising imposed on the industry.[47]

Apart from the merits that these policy-measures may have, we question them, in this context, as being supported by the findings only in a very specific sense. Reducing market power, either by deconcentration or public control of advertising, does, *within the range of observation that the* U.K. *sample of commodities and the* U.S. *sample of industries provide*, actually mean the institution of distributor domination of the market instead of the domination by manufacturers through control of product specification and/or selling effort. This puts the manufacturing stage into a dependent position, which, at the same time, will bring about small-scale manufacturing units and the like.

We think that these consequences, apart from questions of feasibility and desirability, have not been anticipated by those who defend the policy measures in the light of the observed statistical relationships. The concept of countervailing powers, with regard to the manufacturing and distributing stages within a trade channel, seems to offer a point of reference for policy making which is more compatible with the empirical findings.

Cross-sectional studies tend to emphasize long run differences between industries. If this observation is summarized in the word *structural*, it should be used in the sense of '*constellational*'. The constellation that industrial organization exibits has resulted from historical developments and patterns.

Viewed within this frame of reference, it is unlikely that adequate conclusions can be drawn from models that represent this constellation as being reversible, let alone as being reversible in its essential characteristics by the manipulation of symptoms.

3. We have tried to demonstrate that the statistical relationships between advertising, concentration and performance, reported in the economic literature, cannot be interpreted in terms of 'Stimulus-Response' schemes and that these relationships also lack a basic character because they can be derived from a structural grouping of industries; this provokes the following question: what are the fundamental characteristics of this grouping which give it antecedence *vis-à-vis* other factors?

We have based our grouping on functional domination within (vertical)

47. Kaldor [1950–51], p. 13.

channels of trade and industry, respectively, on priority patterns of consumers and other consumption characteristics. Admitted that there is no
unique way to decide on the ranking of factors according to their antecedence,
it seems plausible enough that functional dependence ranks before such
factors as advertising outlays. But does the same hold for our grouping
vis-à-vis cost fixity, the more so since cost fixity is related to technology and
seems to influence performance in combination with growth of demand. At
this point, a parallel can be drawn to the enlightening study of productivity
and technical change by Salter, who – after an empirical analysis of variation
between industries – came to the conclusion that the extent of increases in
labour productivity could be explained primarily by the impact of three
influences: (i) improvements in technical knowledge, (ii) potential economies
of scale, and (iii) factor substitution. These three influences were regarded
by Salter as highly interrelated, even complementary and dependent upon
the increases in output: '... realisation of economies of scale depends upon
increases in output which are in part induced by technical advances; while
factor substitution is prompted by changes in relative factor prices which to
some extent originate in technical change itself'.[48]

Technical advances, economies of scale and factor substitution were
thought of by Salter as largely confining their impact to 'best-practice' costs,
while being reflected in industry wide costs and productivity through the
(forced) abandonment of high-cost obsolete methods and voluntary replacement, which achieves the same result. As a general rule this process is
expected to lead to an expansion of output and a fall in price as a result of
an increase in productivity. Most remarkable in this context, however, are
the variations between industries. Salter's sample of 28 industries also contains some industries that belong to the cluster of what we have defined as
distributor dominated consumer goods industries. These particular industries obviously show the typical characteristics of low cost fixity, low
increase of output and low labour productivity over time and high increase
of price.[49] In other words, these industries lag behind the general trend in
the economy. These findings remarkably fit the cross-sectional results of the
U.S. sample of industries and emphasize once more that within the range
of observation that the U.K. sample of commodities and the U.S. sample of
industries provide, low advertising intensity may not be associated with
'competitive conduct' over time.

---

48. Salter [1969], p. 143.
49. Ibid., Tables 14 and 18.

Apparently the opportunities for the realization of technical advance, economies of scale and factor substitution differ between industries. We fully agree with Salter, who observed that the whole pattern of causation in this context is far too complex to admit of any simple interpretation with the available data; the observed developments can only be thought of as the result of a complicated interplay between new methods of production, costs, prices and productivity.[50]

It is our view that this complicated interplay of technical and economic factors does not fail to put its stamp on the organization and structure of the market. The resulting inter-market differences find their expression in the proposed grouping of industries that incorporates many different aspects of this interrelated complex.

APPENDIX   INTER-INDUSTRY DISTANCES FOR 36 INDUSTRIES ACROSS SEVEN INDUSTRY-CHARACTERISTICS WITH A GROUPING ACCORDING TO HB2. *(Average values for within- and between-group distances).*

	Clothing etc.	Income elastic goods	Others
Clothing	2.02	4.12	2.82
Income elastic goods	4.12	3.04	3.55
Others	2.82	3.55	2.65

N.B. The euclidean distance measure has been employed after standardization of the data-matrix on variables (zero-mean and unit variance). The data-matrix has been obtained from Sherman and Tollison [1971, Table A2].

Euclidean measures technically assume an orthogonal space (i.c. industry-space). In case of correlation, which is apparently the case here, an implicit weighting is effected by the variance of the components that underly the associated variables.

Two industries have been excluded from the calculation of inter-industry distances, because each of them has an extreme value on one of the variables, which would have completely distorted the overall picture. Both industries belong to the group of 'Others'.

50. Ibid., p. 144.

REFERENCES

Alderson, W. [1958]. Measuring the Sales Effectiveness of Advertising. A Progress Report. *Proceedings of the 4th Annual Conference of the Advertising Research Foundation.* New York, 1958.

Braithwaite, Dorothea [1928]. The Economic Effects of Advertisements. *The Economic Journal,* Vol. 38, March, pp. 16–37.

Cable, John [1972]. Market Structure, Advertising Policy and Intermarket Differences in Advertising Intensity. In: Keith Cowling (ed.). *Market Structure and Corporate Behaviour: Theory and Empirical Analysis of the Firm.* London: Gray-Mill Publs.

Chamberlin, E. H. [1933]. *The Theory of Monopolistic Competition.* Cambridge, Mass.: Harvard University Press.

Cochran, W. G. [1947]. Some Consequences when the Assumptions for the Analysis of Variance are not Satisfied. *Biometrics,* Vol. 3, March, pp. 22–38.

Comanor, William S. and Thomas A. Wilson [1967]. Advertising, Market Structure and Performance. *The Review of Economics and Statistics,* Vol. XLIX, November, pp. 423–440.

Guth, Louis A. [1971]. Advertising and Market Structure Revisited. *Journal of Industrial Economics,* Vol. XIX, April, pp. 179–198.

Howard, John A. and Jagdish N. Sheth [1969]. *The Theory of Buyer Behavior.* New York: Wiley & Sons.

Kaldor, Nicholas [1950–51]. The Economic Aspects of Advertising. *The Review of Economic Studies,* Vol. XVIII, pp. 1–27.

Kaldor, Nicholas and Rodney Silverman [1948]. *A Statistical Analysis of Advertising Expenditure and of the Revenue of the Press.* Cambridge: The National Institute of Economic and Social Research of Economic and Social Studies, vol. 8.

Knight, Frank H. [1921]. *Risk, Uncertainty and Profit.* Boston: Houghton Mifflin Company. Reprinted in 1933 as no. 16 in the Series of Reprints by the London School of Economics and Political Science, London.

Lambin, J. J. [1976]. *Advertising, Competition and Market Conduct in Oligopoly Over Time.* Amsterdam: North-Holland Publishing Company.

Overall, John E. and Douglas K. Spiegel [1969]. Concerning Least Squares Analysis of Experimental Data. *Psychological Bulletin,* Vol. 72, No. 5, pp. 311–322.

Phelps, D. M. [1937]. Marketing Research; Its Function, Scope and Method. *Michigan Business Studies,* Vol. VIII, Number 2, pp. 69–149.

Porter, Michael E. [1974]. Consumer Behavior, Retailer Power and Market Performance in Consumer Goods Industries. *The Review of Economics and Statistics*, Vol. LVI, November, pp. 419–436.

Salter, W. E. G. [1969]. *Productivity and Technical Change*. Cambridge: Cambridge University Press, 2nd edition.

Sherman, Roger and Robert Tollison [1971]. Advertising and Profitability. *The Review of Economics and Statistics*, Vol. LIII, No. 4, pp. 397–407.

Sherman, Roger and Robert Tollison [1972]. Technology, Profit Risk, and Assessments of Market Performance. *Quarterly Journal of Economics*, Vol. LXXXVI, No. 3, pp. 448–462.

Simon, Julian L. [1970]. *Issues in the Economics of Advertising*. Urbana: University of Illinois Press.

Telser, Lester G. [1964]. Advertising and Competition. *The Journal of Political Economy*, Vol. LXXII, December, pp. 537–562.

Toy, Norman and others [1974]. A comparative international study of growth, profitability, and risk as determinants of corporate debt ratios in the manufacturing sector. *Journal of Financial and Quantitative Analysis*, 1974 Proceedings, November, pp. 875–886.

Triffin, R. [1940]. *Monopolistic Competition and General Equilibrium Theory*. Cambridge, Mass.: Harvard University Press.

Vernon, John M. [1971]. Concentration, Promotion, and Market Share Stability in the Pharmaceutical Industry. *Journal of Industrial Economics*, Vol. XIX, pp. 246–266.

Zwan, A. van der [1971]. Marketing: Aanduiding en Plaatsbepaling. In: J. A. A. van Doorn (ed.). *Marketing Maatschappelijk*. Rotterdam: Rotterdam University Press, pp. 3–24.

Selected Bibliography
of Professor Dr. P. J. Verdoorn

A. *Quantitative Structural Analysis, Business Cycles, and Growth:*

1. *De verstarring der produktiekosten.* Haarlem: De Erven F. Bohn N.V., 1943; Ph. D. Thesis, pp. 164.
2. Problematiek van het verstarringsverschijnsel. *De Economist,* 93 (1944/5) pp. 282–295 en pp. 363–372.
3. Het onbevredigend niveau onzer arbeidsproduktiviteit. *Economisch-Statistische Berichten,* 31, 1526, 7 augustus 1946, pp. 503–506.
4. Vereischten voor herstel der arbeidsproductiviteit. *De Ingenieur,* 59, 10, 1947 pp. A97–A102.
5. Loonshoogte en Werkgelegenheid. *De Economist* 95 (1947) pp. 513–539.
6. *Arbeidsduur en welvaartspeil.* Leiden: H. E. Stenfert Kroese, N.V. 1947, pp. 275.
7. Fattori che regolano lo sviluppo della produttivita del lavoro. *L'Industria,* Milano, 1949, pp. 3–11.
8. With F. Th. van der Maden. *Enige gegevens betreffende de toekomstige behoefte aan medici.* Amsterdam: Koninklijke Nederlandse Maatschappij tot Bevordering der Geneeskunst, 1952, pp. 48.
9. Complementary and long-range projections. *Econometrica,* 24, 4, October 1956, pp. 429–450.
10. With C. J. van Eijk: *Experimental short-term forecasting models,* The Hague: Central Planning Bureau, 1958, pp. 103.
    Paper presented to the 20th European Meeting of the Econometric Society, Bilbao, September 1958.
11. The role of capital in long-term projection models. *Cahiers Economiques de Bruxelles,* 5, October 1959, pp. 49–69.
12. De grensproductiviteit van het kapitaal. *Economisch-Statistische Berichten,* 2217, 13 jan. 1960, pp. 24–27.
13. With J. J. Post. Capacity and short-term multipliers, in Hart P. E., G. Mills & J. K. Whitaker (Eds.). *Econometric Analysis for National*

Economic Planning (Colston Papers No. 16). London: Butterworth, 1964, pp. 179–198.

14. With J. J. Post. Short and long term extrapolations with the Dutch forecasting model 1963-D, in Wold, H. O. A. (Ed.). *Modelbuilding in the human sciences*. Monaco: Union Européene d'Editions, 1964, pp. 89–123.

15. Government-Industry Planning Interrelationships. *California Management Review* Vol. VIII, no. 2, 1965, pp. 51–58.

16. The short-term model of the Central Planning Bureau and its forecasting performance (1953–1963), in *Macro economic models for planning and policy making*, Geneva: United Nations, 1967, pp. 35–51.

17. With J. J. Post. Comparisson of the prewar and postwar business cycles in the Netherlands, in Bronfenbrenner, M. (Ed.): *Is the business cycle obsolete?*, New York: Wiley, 1969, pp. 436–466.

18. With J. J. Post and S. S. Goslinga. Het jaarmodel 1969, in *Centraal Economisch Plan 1971*, Den Haag: Staatsuitgeverij, 1971, pp. 181–201.

19. Some Long Run Dynamic Elements of Factor Price Inflation, in Bos, H. C., H. Linnemann, P. de Wolff (Eds.). *Economic Structure and Development, Essays in Honour of Jan Tinbergen*. Amsterdam: North Holland Publ. Co., 1973, pp. 111–137.

B. *International Trade and Integration:*

20. Welke zijn de achtergronden en vooruitzichten van de economische integratie in Europa en welke gevolgen zou deze integratie hebben, met name voor de welvaart in Nederland? *Preadvies voor de Vereniging voor de Staathuishoudkunde*, 1952, pp. 47–135.

21. A Customs Union for Western Europe: Advantages and Feasibility. *World Politics* vol. 6, 1954, pp. 481–500.

22. The intra-bloc trade of Benelux, in Robinson, E. A. G. (Ed.). *The economic consequences of the size of the nation*, London: Macmillan, 1960, pp. 291–329.

23. With F. J. M. Meyer zu Schlochtern. Trade creation and trade diversion in the Common Market, in *Intégration Européenne et réalité économique* (Collège d'Europe: Cahiers de Bruges). Brugge: De Tempel, 1964, pp. 95–138.

24. With A. N. R. Schwartz. Two Alternative Estimates of the Effects of E.E.C. and E.F.T.A. on the Pattern of Trade. *European Economic Review*, 3,3, Nov. 1973, pp. 291–335.

25. With C. A. van Bochove. Measuring Integration Effects. *European Economic Review* 3,3, Nov. 1972, pp. 337–349.
26. Economische Gevolgen der Handelspolitieke Integratie binnen de E.E.C., 1956–1970. Bijlage III bij het *Rapport Advies Commissie Europese Unie*, Kamerstuk 13426, 1974–'75, pp. 120–127.

c. *Market Research, Marketing and Purchasing:*

27. *Grondslagen en techniek der marktanalyse.* Leiden: H. E. Stenfert Kroese N.V., 1950, pp. 667.
28. *De eigen markt der onderneming* (Inaugurele Rede). Leiden: H. E. Stenfert Kroese N.V., 1952, pp. 28.
29. *De doelmatigheid van het budget.* Preadvies voor het 172e Reclamecongres van het Genootschap voor Reclame, 1954.
30. Waarom een 'marketing audit'? *Doelmatig Bedrijfsbeheer* 7, 2, (Februari 1955), pp. 22–25.
31. Elementen ener theorie van de verkoop. *Maandblad voor Accountancy en Bedrijfshuishoudkunde* 29, 3, 1955, pp. 99–115.
32. Marketing from the producer's point of view. *Journal of Marketing* 20,3, Jan. 1956, pp. 221–235.
33. With Robert Ferber. *Research Methods in Economics and Business*, New York: Macmillan, 1962, pp. 573.
34. *Het commercieel beleid bij verkoop en inkoop.* Leiden: H. E. Stenfert Kroese N.V., 1964, pp. 565.
35. Marktonderzoek en Marktbeleid. *Maandblad voor Accountancy en Bedrijfshuishoudkunde* 46, 3/5 Maart/Mei, 1972, pp. 100–114.